The Doctrines of Men
A Terrible Truth

By
Patrick Cooke

Oracle Research Publishing
2342 Shattuck Avenue Suite 834
Berkeley, California 94704

Library of Congress Control Number: Pending

ISBN 0972434720

Printed in the United States of America

All Inquiries:
Oracle Research Publishing
2342 Shattuck Avenue Suite 834
Berkeley, California 94704

To Contact by Email:
admin@oraclepublish.com

Acknowledgement

I would like to thank Billie Brinkley for her dedication and research to this work.

The Doctrines of Men

From that point in history a concerted effort was undertaken to erase all traces of the doctrines, practices, and beliefs of the first church established by Jesus, the Christ. Sadly, that effort was successful and the result is a church founded completely on the doctrines laid out by the early founders of the church.

With complete ignorance of this reality, the church proudly stands in the shadow of the pagan cross Constantine mandated as its symbol, claiming to be the true church of Jesus while teaching the doctrines of men. They occupy buildings, preaching from pulpits to people in pews, none of which have scriptural basis, and all paid for with money given by those people under the mistaken belief they are following a scriptural mandate that does not exist. They threaten a condemnation in hell or a reward in heaven, neither which are found in the Bible, if they do or do not follow laws also not found in the Bible. They worship on a day when no such day of worship is found in scripture, and celebrate holidays with pagan origins which replaced the actual Holy Days that are found in scripture, but were outlawed by the Emperor Constantine. They pray loudly and publicly when Jesus says to pray privately, and they let all the world know of their meager charitable efforts, also mandated to be done without such openness. They ignore the reality of the God they claim to worship, misrepresent the character of the man that God became, and hide the true destiny of the people they claim to lead. This work reveals the truth about all these hypocrisies, contradictions, and the manmade doctrines and practices, and presents the real concepts they replaced. It is also presented with the epitome of scriptural caveats: "Prove all things; hold fast that which is good." (I Thessalonians 5:21).

Neither this work, nor any serious quest for the truth in any area of life, should ever be approached without absolute dedication to this very solid principle. All the concepts researched in this writing were carefully vetted scripturally for proper context and accuracy with the goal of enlightenment and edification only. It is not intended to change the way the religious matters of this world are conducted, as that would be impossible with the power the church wields. It is intended to present a clear view of how that power was gained, expose the contradictions of its authority, and reveal the amazing truths it hides from its followers.

Every concept presented here has been thoroughly researched. The context of every scripture presented as evidence has been carefully considered. The source of all scripture used in this work is from the Authorized King James Version of the Bible, the version most commonly used in the Protestant Church. All translation is based on Strong's Exhaustive Concordance. No commentaries or other theological treatise was used. This will simplify any objective research into the context and integrity of the concepts introduced in this writing.

2

An Introduction

Where possible, the scriptures relating to a concept are presented within the main body of the book. However, in the interest of convenience to the reader, where a higher volume of verses are present, and needed, they are contained in the Appendices. The Appendices are a wealth of verses collected and categorized on the true gospel of Jesus, eternal life, love, wisdom, freedom, faith, power, plus many other topics, and are a most valuable treasure. They contain the most revealing and complete collection of the grossly overlooked roles, importance, and value of Women in the Bible, and the Lost Books List is unique in its value, being perhaps the most extensive ever presented. The Appendices are more than reference; they are a collection of biblical truths containing some of the highest knowledge ever given to humanity.

The charge of heresy is certain to be leveled at this work, and justifiably so. The Merriam-Webster Dictionary defines heresy as: 1 a : adherence to a religious opinion contrary to church dogma b : denial of a revealed truth by a baptized member of the Roman Catholic Church c : an opinion or doctrine contrary to church dogma 2 a : dissent or deviation from a dominant theory, opinion, or practice b : an opinion, doctrine, or practice contrary to the truth or to generally accepted beliefs or standards.

Every aspect of this work is "contrary to church dogma", a "denial of a revealed truth", and a "dissent or deviation from a dominant theory" as presented by that church, and contradictory to "generally accepted beliefs or standards" held by those loyal to all Bible-based religions. It is only by questioning the unquestionable authority of the church that these truths were revealed. What you are about to read will change your understanding of virtually everything biblical. It is only by following the principle to "prove all things" that those truths will be validated.

The Doctrines of Men

The Reality of God

- Is the God of the pulpit the God of the Bible, or a god of manmade doctrine?

- Are the religious leaders the creation and tool of God or is God the creation and tool of religious leaders?

The Church View:

There is one being, creator, unseen, all wise, all-powerful, vengeful, and intolerant. And most importantly, if they *don't* tell you, *don't* ask.

The Bible View:

The God of the Bible is a family of supreme spiritual beings named the Elohiym, which is headed by the omnipotent and Supreme Being in the universe named El and called the Father in the Bible. All power, love, and substance in the universe is created and controlled by this family and all the power possessed by that family originates with El. The God, who created life on this planet, and known as the God of Israel, is named Yhovah. He is the most powerful and senior family member of the Elohiym under El, and became the man called Jesus.

The concept of God is a matter of each individual's belief and there are probably no two alike, not much unlike any individual's opinions about any given subject. Therefore, this is not an attempt to form opinions, rather to present what the Bible says about the God of the Bible, not the God of any religious belief.

How Many gods?

The first thing that must be considered is the number of Gods spoken of in the Bible. That would be somewhere between two and an infinite number. The very first time the actual word 'God' appears in the Bible, it is translated from the word elohiym, the plural form of the word elowahh, in the first verse of the first book. In this verse it speaks of the Elohiym creating the known world. And, this is the word that is most often translated into God in the Old Testament, a word that appears almost 4000 times.

The word that appears over 31,000 times to describe the mightiest of the Elohiym is Yhovah, pronounced yeh-ho-vaw'. This is the Elohiym that first made contact with Moses, appeared to and spoke with the prophets, and became the first human incarnation of the Elohiym, Jesus the Christ. (See JESUS) Yhovah, though not specifically named, is probably the God of record in the Garden of Eden. Jesus referred to a higher being than himself called the Father from the word "pater", which literally means father. This distinct relationship is outlined here:

♦ **1 Corinthians 8: 5** For though there be that are called gods, whether in heaven or in earth, (as there be gods many, and lords many,) 6 But to us there is but one God, the Father, of whom are all things, and we in him; and one Lord Jesus Christ, by whom are all things, and we by him.

The power is from the Father God and the action is from Jesus, AKA, Yhovah. Therefore, there are at least two distinct entities. There is one verse in particular that indicates other Elohiym:

♦ **Psalms 89:6** For who in the heaven can be compared unto the Lord? who among the sons of the mighty can be likened unto the Lord?

And what could be clearer than the following?

♦ **Psalms 82:1** God stands in the congregation of the mighty; He judges among the gods.

This verse, more than any, shows that, indeed, there are many Gods ruled by a Supreme God. The words God and gods in this verse are both taken from Elohiym, which means the mighty ones. The word mighty is taken from El, which means The Almighty, the Father. The verse is saying this:

The Mighty Ones stand in a family with The Almighty who is in the center and He guides the Mighty Ones.

• Everywhere the word God is taken from the word Elohiym it is a plural word and should be properly rendered as "Gods". However, in some instances, the translators were *forced* to use the plural gods, other than the instances referring to false gods. They are presented here:

♦ **Genesis 3:5** For God doth know that in the day ye eat thereof, then your eyes shall be opened, and ye shall be as gods, knowing good and evil.

♦ **Exodus 15:11** Who is like unto thee, O LORD, among the gods? who is like thee, glorious in holiness, fearful in praises, doing wonders?

♦ **Exodus 18:11** Now I know that the LORD is greater than all gods: for in the thing wherein they dealt proudly he was above them.

♦ **Exodus 22:28** Thou shalt not revile the gods, nor curse the ruler of thy people.

23:32 Thou shalt make no covenant with them, nor with their gods.

♦ **Deuteronomy 4:28** And there ye shall serve gods, the work of men's hands, wood and stone, which neither see, nor hear, nor eat, nor smell.

♦ **Deuteronomy 10:17** For the LORD your God is God of gods, and Lord of lords, a great God, a mighty, and a terrible, which regardeth not persons, nor taketh reward:

♦ **Joshua 22:22** The LORD God of gods, the LORD God of gods, he knoweth, and Israel he shall know; if it be in rebellion, or if in transgression against the LORD, (save us not this day,)

The Reality of God

♦ **1 Samuel 4:8** Woe unto us! who shall deliver us out of the hand of these mighty Gods? these are the Gods that smote the Egyptians with all the plagues in the wilderness.

♦ **1 Samuel 28:13** And the king said unto her, Be not afraid: for what sawest thou? And the woman said unto Saul, I saw gods ascending out of the earth.

♦ **1 Kings 19:2** Then Jezebel sent a messenger unto Elijah, saying, So let the gods do to me, and more also, if I make not thy life as the life of one of them by to morrow about this time.

♦ **1 Kings 20:23** And the servants of the king of Syria said unto him, Their gods are gods of the hills; therefore they were stronger than we; but let us fight against them in the plain, and surely we shall be stronger than they.

♦ **1 Chronicles 16:25** For great is the LORD, and greatly to be praised: he also is to be feared above all gods.

♦ **2 Chronicles 2:5** And the house which I build is great: for great is our God above all gods.

♦ **Psalms 82:6** I have said, Ye are gods; and all of you are children of the most High.

♦ **Psalms 86:8** Among the gods there is none like unto thee, O Lord; neither are there any works like unto thy works.

♦ **Psalms 95:3** For the LORD is a great God, and a great King above all gods.

♦ **Psalms 96:4** For the LORD is great, and greatly to be praised: he is to be feared above all gods.

♦ **Psalms 97:9** For thou, LORD, art high above all the earth: thou art exalted far above all gods.

♦ **Psalms 135:5** For I know that the LORD is great, and that our Lord is above all gods.

♦ **Psalms 136:2** O give thanks unto the God of gods: for his mercy endureth for ever.

♦ **Psalms 138:1** I will praise thee with my whole heart: before the gods will I sing praise unto thee.

♦ **Daniel 2:11** And it is a rare thing that the king requireth, and there is none other that can shew it before the king, except the gods, whose dwelling is not with flesh

♦ **Daniel 2:47** The king answered unto Daniel, and said, Of a truth it is, that your God is a God of gods, and a Lord of kings, and a revealer of secrets, seeing thou couldest reveal this secret.

♦ **Daniel 4:8** But at the last Daniel came in before me, whose name was Belteshazzar, according to the name of my God, and in whom is the spirit of the holy gods: and before him I told the dream, saying,

♦ **Daniel 4:9** O Belteshazzar, master of the magicians, because I know that the spirit of the holy gods is in thee, and no secret troubleth thee, tell me the visions of my dream that I have seen, and the interpretation thereof.

◆ **Daniel 4:18** This dream I king Nebuchadnezzar have seen. Now thou, O Belteshazzar, declare the interpretation thereof, forasmuch as all the wise men of my kingdom are not able to make known unto me the interpretation: but thou art able; for the spirit of the holy gods is in thee.

◆ **Daniel 5:11** There is a man in thy kingdom, in whom is the spirit of the holy gods; and in the days of thy father light and understanding and wisdom, like the wisdom of the gods, was found in him; whom the king Nebuchadnezzar thy father, the king, I say, thy father, made master of the magicians, astrologers, Chaldeans, and soothsayers;

◆ **Daniel 5:14** I have even heard of thee, that the spirit of the gods is in thee, and that light and understanding and excellent wisdom is found in thee.

◆ **Daniel 11:36** And the king shall do according to his will; and he shall exalt himself, and magnify himself above every god, and shall speak marvellous things against the God of gods, and shall prosper till the indignation be accomplished: for that that is determined shall be done.

The Names of God

These are not all the names of God, just the prominent and important ones. It should be noted that the word "Yahweh", commonly pronounced 'yah-way', is not presented here. This is a traditional pronunciation not found in the Hebrew or the Greek. The definitions presented here are taken from Strong's Exhaustive Concordance.

Old Testament

• Elohiym - Pronounced el-o-heem', plural of Elowahh; gods in the ordinary sense; but specifically used (in the plural thus, especially with the article) of the supreme God; occasionally applied by way of deference to magistrates; and sometimes as a superlative:

• Yhovah (Also Lord) - Pronounced yeh-ho-vaw', (the) self-Existent or Eternal; Jehovah, Jewish national name of God:

** *Mistakenly or purposefully mistranslated to angels in; Psalms 8:5: Psalms 8:4. What is man, that thou art mindful of him? and the son of man, that thou visitest him? 5. For thou hast made him a little lower than the angels, and hast crowned him with glory and honour.*

• Elyown (Most High) - Pronounced el-yone'; an elevation, i.e. lofty; as title, the Supreme:

• El - Pronounced ale, shortened from 'ayi (352 below); strength; as adjective, mighty; especially the Almighty (but used also of any deity):

• Yhovih - Pronounced yeh-ho-vee', a variation of Yhovah, in order to prevent the repetition of the same sound

• Adonay (Also Lord) - Pronounced ad-o-noy'; the Lord (used as a proper name of God only):

- Adown (Lord) - Pronounced aw-done' , or adon ; sovereign, i.e. controller (human or divine):
- Shadday (The Almighty) - Pronounced shad-dah'-ee; the Almighty
- Elowahh - Pronounced el-o'-ah; a deity or the Deity:
- Elahh - Pronounced el-aw', (Aramaic) corresponding to HSN0433; God
- Yahh - Pronounced yaw, contraction for Yhovah, and meaning the same; Jah, the sacred name:
- Tsuwr - Pronounced tsoor, or tsur; properly, a cliff (or sharp rock, as compressed); generally, a rock or boulder; figuratively, a refuge; also an edge (as precipitous)
- Mare (Lord) - Pronounced maw-ray', (Chaldee), in the sense of domineering; a master:
- Eliyhuw - Pronounced el-ee-hoo'; God of him;

New Testament
- Theos - Pronounced theh'-os; a deity, especially (with the) the supreme Divinity
- Kurios - Pronounced koo'-ree-os; supreme in authority
- Philotheos - Pronounced fil-oth'-eh-os; fond of God, i.e. pious:
- Pater - Pronounced pat-ayr'; a "father" (literally or figuratively, near or more remote):

How Real is God?

Defining God, as presented from the pulpit, can be a very confusing issue. The supremacy, eternity, and omnipotence of God are all recognized, as well as God's role as creator of all life. Vague generalities, void of meaningful specifics, permeate most doctrinal approaches to the nature of God, which effectively places the concept of God in a more mythical dimension than a solid presence in the real world. "Knowing God" is presented in an equally ethereal manner, often relegated to a matter of "personal understanding". Any concept that God may have a physical presence is rejected as heresy. It is this insistence by orthodox Christian dogma that God has no physical presence, or practical relevance, outside of a building with pews and collection plates, that is perhaps the saddest of all doctrinal realities.

The pulpit will agree that the existence of God is something that must be accepted as a matter of "faith", and certainly nothing could be more important in scripture than the reality of the main character. How this relates to the biblical edict to "Prove all things", as found in 1 Thessalonians 5:21 and Romans 12:2, is in direct relationship to the biblical definition of faith. As with the existence of God, the concept of faith is presented by the pulpit as some mysterious thing beyond the understanding of mere mortals in spite of the Bible's clear definition of faith.

♦ "Now faith is the substance of things hoped for, the evidence of things not seen." (Hebrews 11:1) is not some vague, mysterious concept. The two defining words, "substance" and "evidence", do not contradict the edict to "prove all things", they reinforce it. The meaning of the word in the original Greek , pistis, pronounced pis'-tis, is persuasion, brings the "prove" in "prove all things" into sharp focus. The "substance" and the "evidence" of the presence of God is clearly presented in the Bible. You are persuaded by the substance and evidence you perceive, and there is a wealth of both in scripture.

God's Association with the Physical

One of the greatest travesties in biblical interpretation was the bizarre attempt by the King James translation group to completely alter a single verse, not that this was the only instance, just one of the strangest and most relevant. By changing the actual meaning of this verse, a master key to the true nature of God will not fit the lock hiding an amazing truth from humanity. Here is this obscure verse in the translated form:

♦ And the Lord said unto Moses, Lo, I come unto thee in a thick cloud, that the people may hear when I speak with thee, and believe thee for ever. And Moses told the words of the people unto the Lord. (**Exodus 19:9**)

In this form the focus of the statement is on Moses and seems to indicate that God is coming to the people in this way to give legitimacy to the words of Moses. What the translators are implying God is saying is "I come to you in this thick cloud so that the people will hear when I speak to you and believe you forever." This makes the whole concept all about Moses.

However, in this verse the words 'unto thee', in the phrase "*I come unto thee*", 'with thee', in the phrase "*speak with thee*", 'thee', in the phrase "*believe thee forever*", and the words "that" and "may", in the phrase "*that the people may hear*", were all added by the translators. This completely alters the meaning of the verse as can be seen with the added words removed:

• *And the Lord said unto Moses, Lo, I come in a thick cloud, the people hear when I speak, and believe for ever. And Moses told the words of the people unto the Lord.*

This changes the whole concept, from giving Moses credibility, to a clear statement about the reality of God's presence. He is saying that the thick cloud is associated with making the people listen to and believe him, not *listen to and believe* Moses. A simple view of this verse in a concordance will attest to these additions. This is verified by other biblical statements and gives a new meaning to the word 'glory', the relationship of glory of the "clouds" God appears with, and God's actual physical presence:

The Glory of God

The "glory" of God is not just something perceived in the mind; it is very real and refers to the sights, sounds, and actions "seen" and "heard" when God makes his presence known. Throughout the Bible certain aspects of God's presence are consistent. His appearances are big, they are bright, and they are loud. It is almost obvious that Yhovah is purposely presenting a light and sound extravaganza to impress the people. And that is what he says he is doing and why he explained this to Moses in Exodus 19:9, (Page 15)

♦ And it came to pass, as Aaron spake unto the whole congregation of the children of Israel, that they looked toward the wilderness, and, behold, the glory of the Lord appeared in the cloud. (**Exodus 16:10**)

♦ And ye said, Behold, the Lord our God hath shewed us his glory and his greatness, and we have heard his voice out of the midst of the fire: we have seen this day that God doth talk with man, and he liveth. Now therefore why should we die? for this great fire will consume us: if we hear the voice of the Lord our God any more, then we shall die. (**Deuteronomy 5:24-25**)

This verse does not specifically refer to clouds, but the fire from which the voice of God is speaking is clearly associated with clouds Deuteronomy 1.

♦ "Who went in the way before you, to search you out a place to pitch your tents in, in fire by night, to shew you by what way ye should go, and in a cloud by day"(**Deuteronomy 1:33**)

♦ And it came to pass, when the priests were come out of the holy place, that the cloud filled the house of the Lord, So that the priests could not stand to minister because of the cloud: for the glory of the Lord had filled the house of the Lord. (**1 Kings 8:10-11**)

♦ And the Lord will create upon every dwelling place of mount Zion, and upon her assemblies, a cloud and smoke by day, and the shining of a flaming fire by night: for upon all the glory shall be a defence. (**Isaiah 4:5**)

♦ As the appearance of the bow that is in the cloud in the day of rain, so was the appearance of the brightness round about. This was the appearance of the likeness of the glory of the Lord. And when I saw it, I fell upon my face, and I heard a voice of one that spake. (**Ezekiel 1:28**)

♦ And then shall appear the sign of the Son of man in heaven: and then shall all the tribes of the earth mourn, and they shall see the Son of man coming in the clouds of heaven with power and great glory. (**Matthew 24:30**)

♦ And then shall they see the Son of man coming in the clouds with great power and glory. And then shall he send his angels, and shall gather together his elect from the four winds, from the uttermost part of the earth to the uttermost part of heaven. (**Mark 13:26 - 27**)

♦ And then shall they see the Son of man coming in a cloud with power and great glory. (**Luke 21:27**)

From just these few verses it can be seen that God exhibits a dynamic, very real presence that is described as glory, and that he uses the "clouds" for a specific purpose, transportation, at least while on Earth, being the most logical need we can assume.

Eyewitnesses to God's Physical Presence

The actual physical body of Yhovah is described by eyewitness testimony in scripture. Though such a concept is condemned in orthodox religion and is regarded as heresy, the words of Moses, Daniel, and the Apostle John make such a charge a moot point

The Eyewitnesses

Moses Sees God

A little understood and effectively ignored experience by Moses strongly reinforces the very physical presence of God. Moses actually asked to see God and was granted that request. From the scenario scripted in the Bible we find a very simple, yet incredible thought-provoking event. God places Moses in a fissure of a large rock and walks past the rock. As he passes by, he holds his hand up preventing Moses from seeing his face, but allows him to view God from behind as he has passed. Here is the biblical rendering of this event:

♦ And he said, I beseech thee, shew me thy glory. And he said, I will make all my goodness pass before thee, and I will proclaim the name of the Lord before thee; and will be gracious to whom I will be gracious, and will shew mercy on whom I will shew mercy. And he said, Thou canst not see my face: for there shall no man see me, and live. And the Lord said, Behold, there is a place by me, and thou shalt stand upon a rock: And it shall come to pass, while my glory passeth by, that I will put thee in a Clift of the rock, and will cover thee with my hand while I pass by: And I will take away mine hand, and thou shalt see my back parts: but my face shall not be seen. (**Exodus 33:18-23**)

There can be no doubt that three very specific things are represented in this scriptural account of an actual eyewitness to the physical presence of God.
• He can be detected with human vision.
• He has a body form with parts similar to humans. A face, which presumes a head, a hand, which one assumes is attached to an arm, and a torso.
• His physical presence, especially his face, can either cause harm to a human, or for some other reason, must not be seen by humans.

The Reality of God

Daniel Sees God

♦ I beheld till the thrones were cast down, and the ancient of days did sit, whose garment was white as snow, and the hair of his head like the pure wool: his throne was like the fiery flame, and his wheels as burning fire. (**Daniel 7:9**)

John Sees God

John, the Apostle, the author of Book of Revelation, also was an eyewitness to the physical body of the God Yhovah, and more descriptive than Daniel's account. It is not a great leap to consider that Daniel is describing the same God, before he became Jesus, and John is describing him after his resurrection and return to a "godly" state.

♦ I was in the Spirit on the Lord's day, and heard behind me a great voice, as of a trumpet, Saying, I am Alpha and Omega, the first and the last: and, What thou seest, write in a book, and send it unto the seven churches which are in Asia; unto Ephesus, and unto Smyrna, and unto Pergamos, and unto Thyatira, and unto Sardis, and unto Philadelphia, and unto Laodicea. And I turned to see the voice that spake with me. And being turned, I saw seven golden candlesticks; And in the midst of the seven candlesticks one like unto the Son of man, clothed with a garment down to the foot, and girt about the paps with a golden girdle. His head and his hairs were white like wool, as white as snow; and his eyes were as a flame of fire; And his feet like unto fine brass, as if they burned in a furnace; and his voice as the sound of many waters. And he had in his right hand seven stars: and out of his mouth went a sharp twoedged sword: and his countenance was as the sun shineth in his strength. And when I saw him, I fell at his feet as dead. And he laid his right hand upon me, saying unto me, Fear not; I am the first and the last: (*Revelation 1:10-17*)

Here Yhovah, an Elohiym, a God, is described as having feet, a chest, a head, hair, hands, eyes, and a mouth.

The Physical Sounds of God

The emanation of loud sound and the broadcasting of amplified voices booming from the vehicles of God are another strong indication of the advanced technological nature of the Elohiym. Sounds like thunder, trumpets, and great, thunderous voices that all can hear, but where no individual can be seen speaking, are the norm when the vehicles are present. The following verse actually verifies that, indeed, somebody is heard speaking whom the listeners cannot see. With the advancement of modern communications and recordings, this is a recently discovered phenomenon.

13

- **God Speaks:**

♦ **Deuteronomy 4:12** And the Lord spake unto you out of the midst of the fire: ye heard the voice of the words, but saw no similitude; only ye heard a voice but saw no similitude; only ye heard a voice.

Similitude means a visible likeness, or embodiment: Clearly they are as amazed by hearing a person speak remotely as the first telephone caller or radio listeners were.

- **And the voice of God is physically "heard" many times in scripture:**

♦ **Exodus 20:22** And the Lord said unto Moses, Thus thou shalt say unto the children of Israel, Ye have seen that I have talked with you from heaven.

God emphasizes the importance of the act of speaking from the sky.

♦ **Deuteronomy 4:12** And the Lord spake unto you out of the midst of the fire: ye heard the voice of the words, but saw no similitude; only ye heard a voice but saw no similitude; only ye heard a voice

Moses emphasizes that Yhovah actually broadcast his voice, but did not actually appear.

♦ **Deuteronomy 4:36** Out of heaven he made thee to hear his voice, that he might instruct thee: and upon earth he shewed thee his great fire; and thou heardest his words out of the midst of the fire.

♦ **Deuteronomy 5:4** The Lord talked with you face to face in the mount out of the midst of the fire,

♦ **Deuteronomy 5:22** These words the Lord spake unto all your assembly in the mount out of the midst of the fire, of the cloud, and of the thick darkness, with a great voice: and he added no more. And he wrote them in two tables of stone, and delivered them unto me.

♦ **Deuteronomy 5:**23 And it came to pass, when ye heard the voice out of the midst of the darkness, (for the mountain did burn with fire,) that ye came near unto me, even all the heads of your tribes, and your elders;

♦ **Deuteronomy 5:24** And ye said, Behold, the Lord our God hath shewed us his glory and his greatness, and we have heard his voice out of the midst of the fire: we have seen this day that God doth talk with man, and he liveth. 25 Now therefore why should we die? for this great fire will consume us: if we hear the voice of the Lord our God any more, then we shall die.

♦ **Deuteronomy 31:15** The Lord talked with you face to face in the mount out of the midst of the fire,

♦ **Daniel 4:31** While the word was in the king's mouth, there fell a voice from heaven, saying, O king Nebuchadnezzar, to thee it is spoken; The kingdom is departed from thee.

♦ **Matthew 3:16** And Jesus, when he was baptized, went up straightway out of the water: and, lo, the heavens were opened unto him, and he saw the Spirit of God descending like a dove, and lighting upon him: 17 And lo a voice from heaven, saying, This is my beloved Son, in whom I am well pleased.

14

♦ **Matthew 24:31** And he shall send his angels with a great sound of a trumpet, and they shall gather together his elect from the four winds, from one end of heaven to the other.

♦ **Mark 1:10** And straightway coming up out of the water, he saw the heavens opened, and the Spirit like a dove descending upon him: 11 And there came a voice from heaven, saying, Thou art my beloved Son, in whom I am well pleased. 12 And immediately the Spirit driveth him into the wilderness.

♦ **Luke 3:21** Now when all the people were baptized, it came to pass, that Jesus also being baptized, and praying, the heaven was opened, 22 And the Holy Ghost descended in a bodily shape like a dove upon him, and a voice came from heaven, which said, Thou art my beloved Son; in thee I am well pleased.

♦ **Luke 9:34** While he thus spake, there came a cloud, and overshadowed them: and they feared as they entered into the cloud. 35 And there came a voice out of the cloud, saying, This is my beloved Son: hear him. 36 And when the voice was past, Jesus was found alone. And they kept it close, and told no man in those days any of those things which they had seen.

♦ **John 12:28** Father, glorify thy name. Then came there a voice from heaven, saying, I have both glorified it, and will glorify it again. 29 The people therefore, that stood by, and heard it, said that it thundered: others said, An angel spake to him.

♦ **Acts 9:7** And the men which journeyed with him stood speechless, hearing a voice, but seeing no man.

♦ **Acts 11:9** But the voice answered me again from heaven, What God hath cleansed, that call not thou common.

♦ **Acts 22:6** And it came to pass, that, as I made my journey, and was come nigh unto Damascus about noon, suddenly there shone from heaven a great light round about me. 7 And I fell unto the ground, and heard a voice saying unto me, Saul, Saul, why persecutest thou me? 8 And I answered, Who art thou, Lord? And he said unto me, I am Jesus of Nazareth whom thou persecutest. 9 And they that were with me saw indeed the light, and were afraid; but they heard not the voice of him that spake to me. 10 And I said, What shall I do, Lord? And the Lord said unto me, Arise, and go into Damascus; and there it shall be told thee of all things which are appointed for thee to do.

Jesus speaks from the sky.

♦ **Hebrews 12:25** See that ye refuse not him that speaketh. For if they escaped not who refused him that spake on earth, much more shall not we escape, if we turn away from him that speaketh from heaven:

♦ **2 Peter 1:17** For he received from God the Father honour and glory, when there came such a voice to him from the excellent glory, This is my beloved Son, in whom I am well pleased.

This is referring to the encounter at the baptism of Jesus.

♦ **2 Peter 1:18** And this voice which came from heaven we heard, when we were with him in the holy mount.

This is a reference to the voice they heard at the Transfiguration.

The Obvious Presence of God

♦ **Exodus 20:18** And all the people saw the thunderings, and the lightnings, and the noise of the trumpet and the mountain smoking: and when the people saw it, they removed, and stood afar of.

♦ **Exodus 19:16** And it came to pass on the third day in the morning, that there were thunders and lightnings, and a thick cloud upon the mount, and the voice of the trumpet exceeding loud; so that all the people that was in the camp trembled.

♦ **Psalms 18:13** The Lord also thundered in the heavens, and the Highest gave his voice; hail stones and coals of fire. 14 Yea, he sent out his arrows, and scattered them; and he shot out lightnings, and discomfited them.

♦ **Acts 9:3** And as he journeyed, he came near Damascus: and suddenly there shined round about him a light from heaven: 4 And he fell to the earth, and heard a voice saying unto him, Saul, Saul, why persecutest thou me?
Jesus, who uses bright, flashing lights from the sky to get his attention, confronts Paul.

♦ **1 Corinthians 15:52** In a moment, in the twinkling of an eye, at the last trump: for the trumpet shall sound, and the dead shall be raised incorruptible, and we shall be changed.

The Image and Likeness of God

The Appearance of God

The general appearance of the Elohiym can be found in the Old Testament. The appearance of Yhovah, in more detail, can be found in the New Testament. A clear indication of the actual body of God is found in how he chose to form mankind.

♦ **Genesis 1:26.** And God said, Let us make man in our image, after our likeness: and let them have dominion over the fish of the sea, and over the fowl of the air, and over the cattle, and over all the earth, and over every creeping thing that creepeth upon the earth.

If the Elohiym made man in their image and their likeness, then an Elohiym must have a body, a head, arms, legs, and other similar parts to men. How close that similarity is can not be determined here, but is made more clear in these descriptions of the of mankind:

♦ **Genesis 5 1** This is the book of the generations of Adam. In the day that God created man, in the likeness of God made he him;

♦ **Genesis 9 6**. Whoso sheddeth man's blood, by man shall his blood be shed: for in the image of God made he man.

♦ **1 Corinthians 11 7** For a man indeed ought not to cover his head, forasmuch as he is the image and glory of God: but the woman is the glory of the man.

♦ **2 Corinthians 3 17** Now the Lord is that Spirit: and where the Spirit of the Lord is, there is liberty. 18. But we all, with open face beholding as in a glass the glory of the Lord, are changed into the same image from glory to glory, even as by the Spirit of the Lord.

♦ **James 3 9** Therewith bless we God, even the Father; and therewith curse we men, which are made after the similitude of God.

God and Physical Devices

God uses very physical devices in his dealings with mankind:

The Ark of the Covenant

♦ **Leviticus 16:2** And the Lord said unto Moses, Speak unto Aaron thy brother, that he come not at all times into the holy place within the vail before the mercy seat, which is upon the ark; that he die not: for I will appear in the cloud upon the mercy seat.

♦ **Numbers 7:89** And when Moses was gone into the tabernacle of the congregation to speak with him, then he heard the voice of one speaking unto him from off the mercy seat that was upon the ark of testimony, from between the two cherubims: and he spake unto him.

♦ **Psalms 80:1** Give ear, O Shepherd of Israel, thou that leadest Joseph like a flock; thou that dwellest between the cherubims, shine forth.

♦ **Joshua 3:15** And as they that bare the ark were come unto Jordan, and the feet of the priests that bare the ark were dipped in the brim of the water, (for Jordan overfloweth all his banks all the time of harvest,) 16 That the waters which came down from above stood and rose up upon an heap very far from the city Adam, that is beside Zaretan: and those that came down toward the sea of the plain, even the salt sea, failed, and were cut off: and the people passed over right against Jericho. 17 And the priests that bare the ark of the covenant of the Lord stood firm on dry ground in the midst of Jordan, and all the Israelites passed over on dry ground, until all the people were passed clean over Jordan.

♦ **1 Samuel 5:11** So they sent and gathered together all the lords of the Philistines, and said, Send away the ark of the God of Israel, and let it go again to his own place, that it slay us not, and our people: for there was a deadly destruction throughout all the city; the hand of God was very heavy there.

♦ **1 Samuel 6:6** And when they came to Nachon's threshingfloor, Uzzah put forth his hand to the ark of God, and took hold of it; for the oxen shook it. 7 And the anger of the LORD was kindled against Uzzah; and God smote him there for his error; and there he died by the ark of God.

The Rod Of Moses

♦ **Exodus 4:17** And thou shalt take this rod in thine hand, wherewith thou shalt do signs.

♦ **Exodus 7:20** And Moses and Aaron did so, as the LORD commanded; and he lifted up the rod, and smote the waters that were in the river, in the sight of Pharaoh, and in the sight of his servants; and all the waters that were in the river were turned to blood.

♦ **Exodus 8:15** And the LORD spake unto Moses, Say unto Aaron, Stretch forth thine hand with thy rod over the streams, over the rivers, and over the ponds, and cause frogs to come up upon the land of Egypt.

♦ **Exodus 8:16** And the LORD said unto Moses, Say unto Aaron, Stretch out thy rod, and smite the dust of the land, that it may become lice throughout all the land of Egypt. And they did so; for Aaron stretched out his hand with his rod, and smote the dust of the earth, and it became lice in man, and in beast; all the dust of the land became lice throughout all the land of Egypt.

♦ **Exodus 9:23** And Moses stretched forth his rod toward heaven: and the Lord sent thunder and hail, and the fire ran along upon the ground; and the Lord rained hail upon the land of Egypt. 24 So there was hail, and fire mingled with the hail, very grievous, such as there was none like it in all the land of Egypt since it became a nation.

♦ **Exodus 10:13** And Moses stretched forth his rod over the land of Egypt, and the LORD brought an east wind upon the land all that day, and all that night; and when it was morning, the east wind brought the locusts

♦ **Exodus 14:16** But lift thou up thy rod, and stretch out thine hand over the sea, and divide it: and the children of Israel shall go on dry ground through the midst of the sea.

♦ **Numbers 20:8** Take the rod, and gather thou the assembly together, thou, and Aaron thy brother, and speak ye unto the rock before their eyes; and it shall give forth his water, and thou shalt bring forth to them water out of the rock: so thou shalt give the congregation and their beasts drink

♦ **Numbers 20:**11 And Moses lifted up his hand, and with his rod he smote the rock twice: and the water came out abundantly, and the congregation drank, and their beasts also.

God Uses Physical Devices to Communicate

Exodus 28:30 states that the Urim and Thummim were placed in a breastplate which was worn by Aaron, the high priest, and that this breastplate was able to reveal God's JUDGMENT. In Numbers 27:21 is an account of the Urim being used to give judgment; it showed what God wanted Israel to do.

Josephus, a well-known Jewish historian, wrote about the Urim and Thummim in Book Three, Section Eight of his book "Antiquities of the Jews." He describes the Urim as being two sardonyx stones which were placed on the shoulders of the high priest; and the Thummim, he says, were twelve stones which were set in three rows of four stones in a breastplate which the high priest also wore. When God wished to guide the Israelites, He often did so by means of these stones. Josephus states, "God declared beforehand by these twelve stones which the high priest bear on his breast, and which were inserted into his breastplate, when they should be victorious in battle; for so great a splendor shone forth from them that the army began to march, that all the people were sensible [aware] of God being present for their assistance."

A Transporter Beam?

♦ **Judges 13:20** For it came to pass, when the flame went up toward heaven from off the altar, that the angel of the Lord ascended in the flame of the altar.

A Cloaking Device?

♦ **Job 26:9** He holdeth back the face of his throne, and spreadeth his cloud upon it.

The Reality

Presented here in the above verses are but a few of the specific references to the very real presence of the Elohiym known as Yhovah. Not included is the temple, a physical structure he designed and commissioned the nation of Israel to construct, the physical sacrifices he demanded, nor the commands to use physical objects to perform certain tasks. God is very real.

● God said he uses "dark clouds" so the people will hear and believe in him.
● God has a physically detectable body evidenced by prominent eyewitness testimony.
● God has a voice and he speaks directly to humans.
● The "glory" of God is represented by physically detectable sights and sounds.
● God said he created mankind to look like him.
● God uses very real, very destructive, and very deadly weapons.

To deny that God has physical presence, "substance", and that there is clear "evidence" in scripture of this presence is to deny the existence of that scriptural proof.

The Doctrines of Men

Having been in the forefront of alternative theology for several years the response received to this concept from the Christian mainstream is consistent:
"God is not physical!"
"God does not need to have a physical presence!"
"You are demeaning God!"
"Your words are blasphemous!"
"You twist and alter the words of God!"
"Heretic!"
And the ever popular condemnation:
"You will rot in a fiery Hell for eternity!"

To this we have very simple responses:
• We did not say God was physical in appearance, Moses, Daniel, and John said that.
• We did not say God needed a physical presence, God told Moses that.
• We are not demeaning God, and if you think that, speak to the one who inspired the scriptures we refer to.
• We are not blaspheming, we are quoting scripture to back up every word, again talk to the one who inspired those scriptures.
• We do not twist or alter the word of God; we started this writing by untwisting a very prominent verse that the translators obviously altered themselves.
• We are heretics by the concise explanation of the word as defined by the Merriam-Webster Collegiate Dictionary:1 a : adherence to a religious opinion contrary to church dogma b : denial of a revealed truth by a baptized member of the Roman Catholic Church c : an opinion or doctrine contrary to church dogma 2 a : dissent or deviation from a dominant theory, opinion, or practice b : an opinion, doctrine, or practice contrary to the truth or to generally accepted beliefs or standards.
• We are not fazed by the threat of an everlasting torture in a place created by the minds of men, any more than we are of any other fictional place designed to scare people into submission and financial extortion. Please read our chapter on Hell for a better understanding of this belief.

The god of the pulpit is vague and mysterious for a very good reason. Their vengeful and oppressive god does not exist, except in the well-conditioned minds of those who are subjected to a steady diet of a pre-masticated and pre-digested concept, regurgitated, in pabulum form by the church, after all the value and any reality has been removed. The church has created its god in its own image and after its likeness. The pulpit god is no more scriptural than the many other false doctrines of the church discussed in this work.

Jesus, the Christ

The Church View:

Jesus was a man created by God in the womb of Mary, who was a poor social outcast ,who healed the sick, did other miracles, and died for our sins.

The Bible View:

Jesus was the God of the Old Testament who took human form, was a well-known and highly respected figure in the society in which he lived, who conquered death to save the human race from certain destruction and allow all mankind to achieve eternal life.

Jesus Is and Was God

The God that gave Moses the commandments also turned water into wine as the human, Jesus. The Bible provides ample evidence that the God of the Old Testament and the nation of Israel was born to a human mother in what appears to be a form of advanced bioengineering. The Lord of Hosts, Yhovah, the highest ranking Elohiym, became the human, Jesus, lived an exemplary life, was killed, was resurrected from the dead, and then returned to his natural form as an Elohiym. It is as Yhovah that he will return. He led Israel out of Egypt and landed at the Chebar River in front of Ezekiel. And, Jesus was beamed up after he conquered death as the Christ. The nature of Jesus as God is why he possessed the power to heal and perform any number of miracles. Jesus was resurrected from the dead because he was a spiritual being in human form. It was a beam of light from the sky that Jesus was using, which blinded Paul and it he that disclosed the Revelation to John. The dual nature of Jesus is clearly stated several times, but none more clearly than that which was stated by the apostle John:

♦ **John 1:1** In the beginning was the Word, and the Word was with God, and the Word was God. 2 The same was in the beginning with God. 3 All things were made by him; and without him was not any thing made that was made. 4 In him was life; and the life was the light of men. 5 And the light shineth in darkness; and the darkness comprehended it not. 6 There was a man sent from God, whose name was John. 7 The same came for a witness, to bear witness of the Light, that all men through him might believe. 8 He was not that Light, but was sent to bear witness of that Light. 9 That was the true Light, which lighteth every man that cometh into the world. 10 He was in the world, and the world was made by him, and the world knew him not. 11 He came unto his own, and his own received him not. 12 But as many as received him, to them gave he power to become the sons of God, even to them that believe on his name: 13 Which were born, not of blood, nor of the will of the flesh, nor of the will of man, but of God. 14 And the Word was made flesh, and dwelt among us, (and we beheld his glory, the glory as of the only begotten of the Father,) full of grace and truth. 15 John bare witness of him, and cried, saying, This was he of whom I spake, He that cometh after me is preferred before me: for he was before me. 16 And of his fulness have all we received, and grace for grace. 17 For the law was given by Moses, but grace and truth came by Jesus Christ. 18 No man hath seen God at any time; the only begotten Son, which is in the bosom of the Father, he hath declared him.

John Further Declared His Divine Origin

♦ **John 3:31** He that cometh from above is above all: he that is of the earth is earthly, and speaketh of the earth: he that cometh from heaven is above all.

♦ **John 6:38** For I came down from heaven, not to do mine own will, but the will of him that sent me.

♦ **John 8:23** And he said unto them, Ye are from beneath; I am from above: ye are of this world; I am not of this world.

♦ **John 10:30** I and my Father are one. 31 Then the Jews took up stones again to stone him. 32 Jesus answered them, Many good works have I shewed you from my Father; for which of those works do ye stone me? 33 The Jews answered him, saying, For a good work we stone thee not; but for blasphemy; and because that thou, being a man, makest thyself God. 34 Jesus answered them, Is it not written in your law, I said, Ye are gods? 35 If he called them gods, unto whom the word of God came, and the scripture cannot be broken; 36 Say ye of him, whom the Father hath sanctified, and sent into the world, Thou blasphemest; because I said, I am the Son of God?   37 If I do not the works of my Father, believe me not. 38 But if I do, though ye believe not me, believe the works: that ye may know, and believe, that the Father is in me, and I in him.

♦ **John 16:28** I came forth from the Father, and am come into the world: again, I leave the world, and go to the Father.

In his testimony from the Revelation, we find more from John:

♦ **Revelation 1:7** Behold, he cometh with clouds; and every eye shall see him, and they also which pierced him: and all kindreds of the earth shall wail because of him. Even so, Amen. 8 I am Alpha and Omega, the beginning and the ending, saith the Lord, which is, and which was, and which is to come, the Almighty.

♦ **Revelation 1:10** I was in the Spirit on the Lord's day, and heard behind me a great voice, as of a trumpet, 11 Saying, I am Alpha and Omega, the first and the last: and, What thou seest, write in a book, and send it unto the seven churches which are in Asia; unto Ephesus, and unto Smyrna, and unto Pergamos, and unto Thyatira, and unto Sardis, and unto Philadelphia, and unto Laodicea.

♦ **Revelation 21:6** And he said unto me, It is done. I am Alpha and Omega, the beginning and the end. I will give unto him that is athirst of the fountain of the water of life freely.

♦ **Revelation 22:13** "I am the Alpha and the Omega, the Beginning and the Ending, the First and the Last.

♦ **Revelation 22:16** I, Jesus, have sent My angel to testify these things to you over the churches. I am the Root and the Offspring of David, the bright and Morning Star."

The Real Jesus

Jesus of Nazareth is portrayed by the modern religious community as a character far removed from the man of Bible text. His very appearance as a longhaired, bearded, light skinned, blue-eyed, emaciated figure has no basis in any known records. His social status as a poor, homeless, vagabond repairman in beggar's attire is a contradiction of the Biblical record. Such portrayals could not be farther from the truth. The lack of emphasis on his origin as the God of the Old Testament is also more than a simple oversight. To add to this monumental omission is the failure to underscore his return to the role as the God of Israel and as self-proclaimed commander of a fleet of flying vessels. This fleet is set to invade the Earth with the expressed mission of seizing control of the entire planet including all social, governmental, military, financial, academic, and religious entities. Could it be the fact that this truth is too real? Could it be that organized religion, which by Biblical prophecy, is itself threatened and has deemed it expedient to omit certain Biblical truths?

Throughout the Old Testament the Hebrew nation is in the presence of the God, Yhovah. In the New Testament Yhovah appears in human form as the man, Jesus. For a thirty-three year period he presented himself as an Elohiym in human form and for at least three of those years he performed supernatural acts. He declared that he would return to the world at a point in the future and save the planet from destruction and the human race from annihilation. He stated very clearly that he would return with the same flying army he commanded as Yhovah as detailed in Revelation.

Jesus Was The "I AM"

♦ **John 8:58** Jesus said unto them, Verily, verily, I say unto you, Before Abraham was, I am.

He is referring to himself from the Old Testament speaking to Moses:

♦ **Exodus 3:14** And God said unto Moses, I AM THAT I AM: and he said, Thus shalt thou say unto the children of Israel, I AM hath sent me unto you.

Jesus Declared Himself the Son of God

♦ **Matthew 26: 59** Now the chief priests, and elders, and all the council, sought false witness against Jesus, to put him to death; 60 But found none: yea, though many false witnesses came, yet found they none. At the last came two false witnesses, 61 And said, This fellow said, I am able to destroy the temple of God, and to build it in three days. 62 And the high priest arose, and said unto him, Answerest thou nothing? what is it which these witness against thee? 63 But Jesus held his peace, And the high priest answered and said unto him, I adjure thee by the living God, that thou tell us whether thou be the Christ, the Son of God. 64 Jesus saith unto him, Thou hast said: nevertheless I say unto you, Hereafter shall ye see the Son of man sitting on the right hand of power, and coming in the clouds of heaven.

♦ **Mark 14: 61** But he held his peace, and answered nothing. Again the high priest asked him, and said unto him, Art thou the Christ, the Son of the Blessed? 62 And Jesus said, I am: and ye shall see the Son of man sitting on the right hand of power, and coming in the clouds of heaven.

♦ **Luke 22: 66** And as soon as it was day, the elders of the people and the chief priests and the scribes came together, and led him into their council, saying, 67 Art thou the Christ? tell us. And he said unto them, If I tell you, ye will not believe: 68 And if I also ask you, ye will not answer me, nor let me go. 69 Hereafter shall the Son of man sit on the right hand of the power of God. 70 Then said they all, Art thou then the Son of God? And he said unto them, Ye say that I am. 71 And they said, What need we any further witness? for we ourselves have heard of his own mouth.

- Jesus quotes himself as God
  When Jesus, the man, said this:

♦ **John 10:34** Jesus answered them, Is it not written in your law, I said, Ye are gods?

He is quoting himself as Yhovah the God from the Old Testament saying this:

♦ **Psalms 82:6** I have said, Ye are gods; and all of you are children of the most High. **7** But ye shall die like men, and fall like one of the princes.

The Shepherd Connection

The Lord God as the Shepherd

♦ **Ezekiel 34:1** And the word of the LORD came unto me, saying, 2 Son of man, prophesy against the shepherds of Israel, prophesy, and say unto them, Thus saith the Lord GOD unto the shepherds; Woe be to the shepherds of Israel that do feed themselves! should not the shepherds feed the flocks? 3 Ye eat the fat, and ye clothe you with the wool, ye kill them that are fed: but ye feed not the flock. 4 The diseased have ye not strengthened, neither have ye healed that which was sick, neither have ye bound up that which was broken, neither have ye brought again that which was driven away, neither have ye sought that which was lost; but with force and with cruelty have ye ruled them. 5 And they were scattered, because there is no shepherd: and they became meat to all the beasts of the field, when they were scattered. 6 My sheep wandered through all the mountains, and upon every high hill: yea, my flock was scattered upon all the face of the earth, and none did search or seek after them. 7 Therefore, ye shepherds, hear the word of the LORD; 8 As I live, saith the Lord GOD, surely because my flock became a prey, and my flock became meat to every beast of the field, because there was no shepherd, neither did my shepherds search for my flock, but the shepherds fed themselves, and fed not my flock; 9 Therefore, O ye shepherds, hear the word of the LORD; 10 Thus saith the Lord GOD; Behold, I am against the shepherds; and I will require my flock at their hand, and cause them to cease from feeding the flock; neither shall the shepherds feed themselves any more; for I will deliver my flock from their mouth, that they may not be meat for them. 11 For thus saith the Lord GOD; Behold, I, even I, will both search my sheep, and seek them out. 12 As a shepherd seeketh out his flock in the day that he is among his sheep that are scattered; so will I seek out my sheep, and will deliver them out of all places where they have been scattered in the cloudy and dark day. 13 And I will bring them out from the people, and gather them from the countries, and will bring them to their own land, and feed them upon the mountains of Israel by the rivers, and in all the inhabited places of the country. 14 I will feed them in a good pasture, and upon the high mountains of Israel shall their fold be: there shall they lie in a good fold, and in a fat pasture shall they feed upon the mountains of Israel. 15 I will feed my flock, and I will cause them to lie down, saith the Lord GOD. 16 I will seek that which was lost, and bring again that which was driven away, and will bind up that which was broken, and will strengthen that which was sick: but I will destroy the fat and the strong; I will feed them with judgment.

The Lord Jesus as the Shepherd

♦ **John 10:11** I am the good shepherd: the good shepherd giveth his life for the sheep. 12 But he that is an hireling, and not the shepherd, whose own the sheep are not, seeth the wolf coming, and leaveth the sheep, and fleeth: and the wolf catcheth them, and scattereth the sheep. 13 The hireling fleeth, because he is an hireling, and careth not for the sheep. 14 I am the good shepherd, and know my sheep, and am known of mine. 15 As the Father knoweth me, even so know I the Father: and I lay down my life for the sheep. 16 And other sheep I have, which are not of this fold: them also I must bring, and they shall hear my voice; and there shall be one fold, and one shepherd. 17 Therefore doth my Father love me, because I lay down my life, that I might take it again. 18 No man taketh it from me, but I lay it down of myself. I have power to lay it down, and I have power to take it again. This commandment have I received of my Father.

Jesus as a Man

Jesus Had Brothers And Sisters

Jesus had at least four brothers and two sisters. The absence of Joseph in his later life, with no comment of this in Biblical text, indicates that he probably was deceased. The fact that he was the father of at least six children means that he most likely was part of the life of Jesus for many years. The siblings of Jesus are recorded in the following verses:

♦ **Matthew 12:46** While he yet talked to the people, behold, his mother and his brethren stood without, desiring to speak with him 47 Then one said unto him, Behold, thy mother and thy brethren stand without, desiring to speak with thee.

♦ **Matthew 13:55** Is not this the carpenter's son? is not his mother called Mary? and his brethren, James, and Joses, and Simon, and Judas? 56 And his sisters, are they not all with us? Whence then hath this man all these things?

♦ **Mark 3:31** There came then his brethren and his mother, and, standing without, sent unto him, calling him. 32 And the multitude sat about him, and they said unto him, Behold, thy mother and thy brethren without seek for thee.

♦ **Mark 6:3** Is not this the carpenter, the son of Mary, the brother of James, and Joses, and of Juda, and Simon? and are not his sisters here with us? And they were offended at him.

♦ **John 11:3** Therefore his sisters sent unto him, saying, Lord, behold, he whom thou lovest is sick.

Jesus Had a Home

Jesus was a carpenter (**Mark 6:3** Is not this the carpenter, the son of Mary...) and there is no indication that he was chronically unemployed before he began his ministry. Logic dictates that a carpenter, whose profession was very much in demand in his day, would, and could, buy or build a house for himself. And this is confirmed by Biblical text:

♦ **Matthew 9:10** And it came to pass, as Jesus sat at meat in the house, behold, many publicans and sinners came and sat down with him and his disciples.

♦ **Matthew 9:28** And when he was come into the house, the blind men came to him: and Jesus saith unto them, Believe ye that I am able to do this? They said unto him, Yea, Lord.

♦ **Matthew 13:1** The same day went Jesus out of the house, and sat by the sea side.

♦ **Matthew 13:36** Then Jesus sent the multitude away, and went into the house: and his disciples came unto him, saying, Declare unto us the parable of the tares of the field.

♦ **Mark 2:1** And again he entered into Capernaum, after some days; and it was noised that he was in the house.

♦ **Mark 2:15** And it came to pass, that, as Jesus sat at meat in his house, many publicans and sinners sat also together with Jesus and his disciples: for there were many, and they followed him.

♦ **Mark 7:17** And when he was entered into the house from the people, his disciples asked him concerning the parable.

♦ **Mark 9:28** And when he was come into the house, his disciples asked him privately, Why could not we cast him out?

♦ **Mark 10:10** And in the house his disciples asked him again of the same matter.

♦ **Luke 7:6** Then Jesus went with them. And when he was now not far from the house, the centurion sent friends to him, saying unto him, Lord, trouble not thyself: for I am not worthy that thou shouldest enter under my roof:

♦ **John 1:39** He saith unto them, Come and see. They came and saw where he dwelt, and abode with him that day: for it was about the tenth hour.

The Social Standing of Jesus

There is nothing in Biblical text to indicate that Jesus was poor, although, in almost every portrayal in paintings, movies, and from the pulpit he is relegated to beggar's status. This notion can possibly be traced to an often misread parable recorded by Matthew:

♦ **Matthew 25:34** Then shall the King say unto them on his right hand, Come, ye blessed of my Father, inherit the kingdom prepared for you from the foundation of the world: 35 For I was an hungred, and ye gave me meat: I was thirsty, and ye gave me drink: I was a stranger, and ye took me in: 36 Naked, and ye clothed me: I was sick, and ye visited me: I was in prison, and ye came unto me.

Unfortunately, they stop the story there and elaborate about the physical sacrifices of a hard life while ignoring the rest of the parable, which conveys the real message. This parable shows that serving your fellow man is the way to serve Jesus:

♦ **Matthew 25:37** Then shall the righteous answer him, saying, Lord, when saw we thee an hungred, and fed thee? or thirsty, and gave thee drink? 38 When saw we thee a stranger, and took thee in? or naked, and clothed thee? 39 Or when saw we thee sick, or in prison, and came unto thee? 40 And the King shall answer and say unto them, Verily I say unto you, Inasmuch as ye have done it unto one of the least of these my brethren, ye have done it unto me.

Jesus stated very clearly on many occasions that this is the most important aspect of a person's life and the one commandment that he asked his followers to obey. He said that all the laws and the entire prophecies center on this one rule. It is not unusual that this point is passed over considering that buildings and image are the focus of the pulpit. Service to mankind is non-existent or relegated to yearly clothing drives. No apologies to those who claim to be doing more than token service. That is, unless the total focus of the church is on service to those less fortunate, they are not fulfilling the letter or spirit of the law.

There are indications that, rather than poor, Jesus actually had a high social standing normally associated with fiscal security rather than poverty. Considering his true origin, his message, and a lifetime of good works, it would stand to reason that his spiritual Father would bless him with a comfortable life. One of the people in his earthly family was Joseph of Arimathea, his great uncle and the man who retrieved his body after the crucifixion. This man was a wealthy tin merchant dealing with the Roman government and a member of the Sanhedrin, the governing body of the Jews. This man was the uncle of Mary, the mother of Jesus, and a disciple of Jesus. This would give Jesus a close family contact into the higher levels of the society in which he seemed to have associations. The great wedding feast he attended with his mother shows that he moved comfortably in this level.

High in Social Standing:
♦ **John 2:1** And the third day there was a marriage in Cana of Galilee; and the mother of Jesus was there: 2 And both Jesus was called, and his disciples, to the marriage.

Considering that Jesus converted over 60 gallons of water into fine wine, this was no small wedding. He also associated with the controlling figures in society:

28

♦ **Luke 5:29** And Levi made him a great feast in his own house: and there was a great company of publicans and of others that sat down with them.
♦ **Luke 5:36** And one of the Pharisees desired him that he would eat with him. And he went into the Pharisee's house, and sat down to meat.

Did Jesus Have Long Hair?

The depiction of Jesus in paintings and movies is almost a direct contradiction to Bible text and historical reality. The most telling and easily recognizable aspect is the long hair. In a social sense, this would have been an abnormality. Paul, a man highly educated in Jewish laws and customs and in personal contact with the resurrected Jesus, makes it clear that this was not only unacceptable, but also actually shameful. Whether as a religious or social aspect of life, Paul, in his first letter to Corinth, states that it is a shame for a man to have long hair. Are we to assume that Paul is casting aspersions on Jesus? No, the historical reality is that it is highly unlikely that Jesus had long hair.

Not surprisingly, therefore, all portrayals of Jesus prior to the popularization of the Shroud of Turin show a Jesus with short hair and no beard.   After the Shroud was associated with Jesus, all the images produced added long hair and a beard. The first documented exhibition of the Shroud was in 1357, but it was associated with Jesus prior to this. In truth, therefore, the Shroud is the first and only reason that Jesus is pictured with long hair and a beard. Rather presumptuous considering that there is no solid evidence that this is indeed the image of a dead Jesus.

Even attempts to justify the authenticity of this obscure cloth are based on shaky foundations. Many claim that Jesus had long hair and a beard because he was a participant in an extreme religious vow of isolation. This stems from a mistaken assumption that Jesus was a Nazarite. He was not, and there is no indication either in or out of the Bible that he ever was. He was, in fact, a Nazarene, a much different thing. A Nazarite was an individual who went into isolation for three years during which time, among other acts, no razor was allowed to touch his head, thus the long hair and the beard. Even if he had been a Nazarite he still would not have the long hair and a beard as the Nazarites shaved their beards and cut their hair after this period. A Nazarene is a citizen of Nazareth. Jesus was a citizen of Nazareth and, as such, he fulfilled a prophecy. Why would he not just have long hair and a beard anyway? The main reason is that he would stand out like a sore thumb. The male Jews of his day all had short hair and he would have found himself the target of much ridicule. That would be in the Bible and it is not. However, anyone who does portray Jesus as having long hair is portraying him in a shameful way. Beards were reserved for the elders, something else he was not.

It is to be noted that Jesus was a Jew, most of the people in his inner and outer circle of companions and acquaintances were Jews and Paul was a Jew. The condemnation of long hair is, therefore, a Jewish issue in the Bible. The decision whether to have long hair, or not, is an individual choice and an open issue outside of that particular tribe of Israel.

A Man of Talent and Wisdom

Jesus was a carpenter and it is claimed that there are fine houses he built still standing. Certainly he excelled in whatever profession he practiced and, no doubt, was popular and much respected by those with whom he worked and lived. There is a record of 37 of his miracles and verse that indicates that this was only a small potion of the total. Did this miraculous work start suddenly or did it develop over time? We know that at age twelve he greatly impressed the doctors of the law in the temple:

♦ **Luke 2:42** And when he was twelve years old, they went up to Jerusalem after the custom of the feast...... 46 And it came to pass, that after three days they found him in the temple, sitting in the midst of the doctors, both hearing them, and asking them questions. 47 And all that heard him were astonished at his understanding and answers.

Here we see the first sign that this is no ordinary person and that his intelligence and reputation was on an upward spiral:

♦ **Luke 2:52** And Jesus increased in wisdom and stature, and in favour with God and man.

It would not be unrealistic to say that Jesus was probably widely known prior to his ministry and a highly motivated, hard working, and very dynamic person. Should we expect less from a human god?

The Miracles

The Supernatural Actions Of A Human God
Cleansing A Leper - Matt.8:2 * Mark 1:40 * Luke 5:12
Healing The Centurion's Servant - Matt. 8:5 - 13 * Luke 7:1
Healing Of Peter's Mother-In-Law - Matt. 8:14 - 15 * Mark 1:30 * Luke 4:38
Healing The Sick At Evening - Matt. 8:16 * Mark 1:32 * Luke 4:40
Stilling The Storm - Matt. 8:23 - 27 * Mark 4:35 * Luke 8:22
Devils Into A Herd Of Swine - Matt. 8:28 - 34 * Mark 5:1 * Luke 8:26
Healing The Paralytic - Matt. 9:1 - 8 * Mark 2:3 * Luke 5:18
Raising A Ruler's Daughter From The Dead - Matt. 9:18, 23 * Mark 2:3 * Luke 8:40, 49
Healing The Hemorrhaging Woman - Matt. 9:20 - 22 * Mark 5:25   Luke 8:43
Healing The Two Blind Men - Matt. 9:27 - 31
Healing A Possessed, Dumb Man - Matt. 9:32 - 34
Healing A Man's Withered Hand - Matt.12:9 - 21 * Mark 3:1 * Luke 6:6
Possessed, Blind, And Dumb - Matt. 12:22 - 30 * Luke 11:14
Feeding The Five Thousand - Matt.14:13 - 21 * Mark 6:30 35 - 44 * Luke 9:10, 12 - 17 * John 6:10 - 15
Walking On The Sea - Matt.14:22 - 33 * Mark 6:48 * Luke 6:19
Healing The Canaanite Daughter - Matt.15:21 - 28 * Mark 7:24
Feeding The Four Thousand - Matt. 15:29 - 38 * Mark 8:1
Healing Of A Child With A Demon - Matt.17:14 - 20 * Mark 9:17 * Luke 9:38
Taxes In The Mouth Of A Fish - Matt. 17:24 - 27
Healing Two Blind Men By The Way Side - Matt. 20:29 - 34 * Mark 10:46 * Luke 8:35
Withering The Fig Tree - Matt. 21:18 - 22 * Mark 11:12
Casting Out An Unclean Spirit - Mark 1:21 - 28 * Luke 4:33
Healing A Deaf And Dumb Man - Mark 7:31 - 37
Healing The Blind Man At Bethsaida - Mark 8:22 - 26
Escape From The Crowd At Nazareth - Luke 4:14 - 30
Miraculous Catching Of Fishes - Luke 5:1 - 11
The Widow Of Nain - Luke 7:11 - 17
Healing The Infirm, Bowed Woman - Luke 13:10 - 17
Healing The Man With The Dropsy - Luke 14:1 - 6
Cleansing The Ten Lepers - Luke 17:11 - 19
Restoring The Servants Ear - Luke 22:47 - 53
Turning Water Into Wine - John 2:1 - 11
Healing The Nobleman's Son - John 4:46 - 54
Healing The Infirm Man At The Pool Of Bethesda - John 5:1 - 18
Healing The Man Blind From Birth - John 9:1 - 37
The Raising Of Lazarus From The Dead - John 11:1 - 47
The Great Draught Of Fishes - John 21:1 - 14

The Doctrines of Men

The Incredible Gospel of Jesus
and
Humanity's Greatest Quest

Mankind has been on a quest for immortality, unconditional love, absolute truth, perfect wisdom, total freedom, ultimate power, an answer to why the human race is on Earth, and the true destiny of humanity throughout its history. Long hidden by a pious, fear motivating, very narrow, and often contradictory presentation of scripture by "Christian" theology is the fact that all these human treasures are in the Bible. They are not only clearly defined concepts, they are to be inherited by humans, literally guaranteed by the actions of an amazing entity from an incredible race of immortal, universally powerful beings.

The Bible encourages the search for truth, as well as promising reward for its discovery, not the least of which is the epitome of freedom from the physical world. It discourages the pursuit of earthly wealth and power, but strongly encourages that mankind seek treasure of a higher value. The modern church gives no clear guidance as to the true nature of these higher rewards, except a very vague possibility of future residence in a very ethereal place called "heaven". The orthodox concept is vague because the word 'heaven' simply means the sky in the Bible, and the church prefaces entry to this "heaven" with enough exclusion clauses to deter all but the most pious and virtuous. The Bible, on the other hand, is not so vague on the promises it offers, or the true destiny of mankind it clearly presents.

The truth revealed by an intense scriptural quest about who and what the divine beings of the Bible are, is amazing in its own right, while their long-hidden relationship to their highest creation, humanity is almost beyond human perception. It can be easily found in scripture that the major deception, in the "greatest deception", is the ethos of the pulpit effectively concealing the greatest destiny mankind could ever imagine. This long concealed destiny is the "gospel", the incredibly "good news" Jesus, and the Apostles after him, proclaimed to mankind, and the ultimate truth every word in the Bible points toward.

The highest goal to which a human can aspire is to become an immortal, wise, loving, and all-powerful being with complete dedication to a perfect universal force. This, we believe, is the ultimate and true destiny of humanity. What better "good message" could Jesus bring to humanity?

The Gospel of the Royalty

The word "gospel" appears almost 100 times in the New Testament. The word is translated from two similar Greek words, both meaning good news or message. In context, it is referred to as the gospel of Jesus, God, and the kingdom. It is called the everlasting, and the glorious gospel, the gospel of

33

grace and peace, and is associated with mystery and faith. The Bible declares it will be proclaimed, or published to the entire world several times, and Jesus equated it with his own importance.

The kingdom of God is the promise of Jesus to humanity and appears in New Testament scripture almost 150 times. The word kingdom is taken from the Greek word '*basileia*', pronounced bas-il-i'-ah; properly, royalty, and is not a place as portrayed from the orthodox pulpit. The concept of a kingdom, long thought to be synonymous with the mythical place called "heaven", is actually sovereignty, a universal ascendancy, referring to the position of the highest order of beings in existence, the Elohiym, the Gods.

The earthly actions Jesus, the son of El, and head of this universally royal family, will allow the incredible conversion of humans from a physical state, to full eternal inheritance. That inheritance will bring mankind into the majestic family of the Elohiym. The promise of inclusion into this imperial family of the most powerful race of beings in the universe is the only true path of entry into the "kingdom" of the Gods. This is the gospel, the good message Jesus died for, and announced to humanity. This is not only the greatest news ever heard by any human being, but it is the true destiny mankind has been pursuing for millennia.

♦ "For the kingdom of God is not in word, but in power." (**I Corinthians 4:20**)

The Crown of Royalty

The position of membership in a royal family always means the entire family is qualified for a crown. In Britain the royal family is even referred to as "The Crown". The Royal Family of God is no different.

♦ **I Corinthians 9:25** And every man that striveth for the mastery is temperate in all things. Now they do it to obtain a corruptible crown; but we an incorruptible.

♦ **Philippians 4:1** Therefore, my brethren dearly beloved and longed for, my joy and crown, so stand fast in the Lord, my dearly beloved.

♦ **I Thessalonians 2:19** For what is our hope, or joy, or crown of rejoicing? Are not even ye in the presence of our Lord Jesus Christ at his coming?

♦ **II Timothy 4:8** Henceforth there is laid up for me a crown of righteousness, which the Lord, the righteous judge, shall give me at that day: and not to me only, but unto all them also that love his appearing.

♦ **James 1:12** Blessed is the man that endureth temptation: for when he is tried, he shall receive the crown of life, which the Lord hath promised to them that love him.

♦ **I Peter 5: 4** And when the chief Shepherd shall appear, ye shall receive a crown of glory that fadeth not away.

♦ **Revelation 2:10** Fear none of those things which thou shalt suffer: behold, the devil shall cast some of you into prison, that ye may be tried; and ye shall have tribulation ten days: be thou faithful unto death, and I will give thee a crown of life.

♦ **Revelation 3:11** Behold, I come quickly: hold that fast which thou hast, that no man take thy crown.

The Royal Family Connection

The Bible speaks of a family in the sky and makes the announcement that humans will be adopted directly into that family. The family is spoken of by Paul in a letter to the saints at Ephesus:

♦ "For this cause I bow my knees unto the Father of our Lord Jesus Christ, Of whom the whole family in heaven and earth is named," (**Ephesians 3:14 - 15**).

This concept that the family of God is in the sky, heaven, and on Earth as well is represented in an abundance of scriptural references. There are hundreds of verses referenced in this work on the presence of the Gods in the sky from both the Old and New Testaments, and the family on Earth, which is known as the church, is a major focus of the New Testament. Throughout the ministry of Jesus, and the Apostles, humans are called, sons, daughters, children, brethren, brothers, sisters, and offspring of God. They are said to be adopted as heirs with a shared inheritance earned by the firstborn of many begotten, to be born after him. These same humans are called chosen, the elect, and the saints of God, and they are to be physically changed into spiritual beings with status of crowned royalty in the monarchy of the Gods. Humans actually become a part of the household of God: *"Now therefore ye are no more strangers and foreigners, but fellow citizens with the saints, and of the household of God;"* (Ephesians 2:19) Here we present hundreds of scriptural references to a direct family relationship between human beings and the immortal beings of the Bible:

Children of God

The New Testament is replete with references to humans as children of God. They are called children of the Highest, the Father, the prophets, the promise, and the children of light. It says they are peacemakers, richly rewarded, immortal, equal to angels, have a glorious liberty, witnessed by the Spirit, and that all the people on Earth will be blessed by them.
Children of God Verses: See Appendix A

Sons and Daughters of God

In specific verification of a spiritual family relationship, the Bible addresses that kinship among the members of the church. Living human beings are called the sons and daughters of God with this verse leaving no doubt about

the meaning: *"He that overcometh shall inherit all things; and I will be his God, and he shall be my son."* (Revelation 21:7)
Sons and Daughters Verses: See Appendix B

Brothers, Sisters, and Brethren

Further verification of a spiritual family relationship among the members of the church is shown by the way they address each other. The words 'brother' and 'sister' are used in the New Testament both to describe specific persons not directly related by human birth and, generically, to address members of the church as a whole. From the Acts of the Apostles to the Revelation, the word 'brethren' appears almost 200 times, referring to members of the church. Brotherly love and kindness are emphasized and the church is referred to as a 'brotherhood'. Jesus is described as the firstborn of many humans into the royal family of God,

♦ "For whom he did foreknow, he also did predestinate to be conformed to the image of his Son that he might be the firstborn among many brethren." **(Romans 8:29)**

Brothers, Sisters, and Brethren Verses: See Appendix C

Born, Begotten, Offspring, and Firstborn

Entry into this royal family is from godly conception and spiritual birth. Humans are said to be born of God, of the Spirit, and from above. They are called newborn babes and in the same royal lineage as the firstborn, Jesus the Christ, and the true King of the entire planet. Humans are also called offspring of and begotten by God.

Born, Begotten, Offspring, and Firstborn Verses: See Appendix D

Inheritance, Heirs, Joint-heirs, and Adoption

The Bible guarantees an amazing inheritance to humanity on the highest spiritual level. This is an inheritance mankind actually shares with Jesus:

♦ "And if children, then heirs; heirs of God, and joint-heirs with Christ; if so be that we suffer with him, that we may be also glorified together." **(Romans 8:17)** This is an eternal inheritance of everlasting life, spiritual birth into the royal family of God through Christ, salvation, fulfillment of the promises, rewards, and eternal blessing. It was reserved, predestinated, prepared from the foundation of the world, sanctified, confirmed by an oath, incorruptible, undefiled, and guaranteed through adoption by Jesus Christ to himself. And there cannot possibly be a greater inheritance than everything:

♦ "He that overcometh shall inherit all things; and I will be his God, and he shall be my son." **(Revelation 21:7)**

Inheritance, Heirs, Joint-heirs, and Adoption Verses: See Appendix E

Elected, Chosen, and Called

Humans are called the elect for whom the complete destruction of all life

on Earth will be stopped. The elect will be gathered from all areas of the planet. We are called God's elect, guiltless, and will obtain the salvation with eternal glory. Humans are said to be the poor of this world, and rich in faith, chosen out of the world, from before the beginning of the world. Though the world hates them, they are a precious, faithful, chosen generation, a royal priesthood, a holy nation, a peculiar (sacred) people, and heirs of the royalty. The chosen are called according to his purpose, which was given by Christ Jesus before the world began, and announced by the gospel, to the obtaining of the glory of our Lord Jesus, the Christ. Few wise, mighty, or noble men are called. Those called are told to press toward the mark for the prize of the high calling, which is predestinated, justified, glorified, sanctified, worthy, and virtuous. We are called saints with a holy calling to the royalty and glory of the Christ. Through this calling, mankind receives the promise of eternal inheritance, and will inherit a blessing of eternal life and glory, and all things that pertain unto life and godliness will be given to mankind.
Elected, Chosen, and Called Verses: See Appendix F

Saints

To many, a "saint" is a person chosen by the church to receive this honor for great deeds, special powers, and always being very dead. The word appears in the Bible almost a hundred times, and in most instances refers to people that are very much alive. The Bible speaks of poor saints, churches of, collection for, ministry of, perfecting of, supplication for, and want of the saints. It says Jesus will make intercession for the saints, they are sanctified, glorified, righteous, and they will judge the world. They will receive the riches of the glory of Jesus' inheritance and know the mystery, which was hidden from ages and from generations. Jesus, the Christ, is the King of saints and an unknown number of them will appear with him in the last days.

Changed, Converted, and Translated

Men are said to be converted to be healed, their sins will be blotted out, and they will become as little children to enter into the kingdom (royalty) of heaven (the sky). Humans will all be changed into the same image as the glory of the Lord, be in a similar form like his glorious body, and achieve immortality. Humans are to be transferred into kingdom (royalty).
Changed, Converted, and Translated Verses: See Appendix H

A Promise of a Physical Change

Scripture reveals that the change will be physical, with a complete transmutation of the body, from one form to another.
♦ **2 Corinthians 3:17**. Now the Lord is that Spirit: and where the Spirit of the Lord is, there is liberty. 18. But we all, with open face beholding as in a glass the glory of the Lord, are changed into the same image from glory to glory, even as by the Spirit of the Lord.

♦ **Philippians 3:20**. For our conversation is in heaven; from whence also we look for the Saviour, the Lord Jesus Christ: 21. Who shall change our vile body, that it may be fashioned like unto his glorious body, according to the working whereby he is able even to subdue all things unto himself. (conversation = community)

♦ **II Corinthians 5:17** Therefore if any man be in Christ, he is a new creature: old things are passed away; behold, all things are become new.

No Heaven Required

Heaven and the Kingdom

Heaven, incorrectly thought to be a divine retirement home, which is vaguely located somewhere "up there", and "the kingdom", also incorrectly thought to be a "place", are inappropriately labeled as the destination we go "to" if we do whatever the pulpit says to do to "get" there. The Bible completely contradicts this concept. The prophecy "Blessed are the meek: for they shall inherit the earth." (**Matthew 5:5**), is very clear about the true inheritance of those who seek his promise, not heaven but the planet. These two verses show that the Christ not only considered meekness an essential part of his own personality, but that it is also a spiritual trait of great value:

♦ "Take my yoke upon you, and learn of me; for I am meek and lowly in heart: and ye shall find rest unto your souls." (**Matthew 11:29**)

♦ "But let it be the hidden man of the heart, in that which is not corruptible, even the ornament of a meek and quiet spirit, which is in the sight of God of great price." (**I Peter 3:4**)

See Heaven, (Page 140)

Inherit the Earth?

But what does it mean that we will inherit something we are already physically living on? Perhaps the reference Jesus made to our earthly birthright was intended to counter the almost universally accepted concept in the biblically-based church that we go "somewhere" to be with him. This is rather surprising considering the Christ will be here on Earth:

♦ "And I saw thrones, and they sat upon them, and judgment as given unto them: and I saw the souls of them that were beheaded for the witness of Jesus, and for the word of God, and which had not worshipped the beast, neither his image, neither had received his mark upon their foreheads, or in their hands; and they lived and reigned with Christ a thousand years. Blessed and holy is he that hath part in the first resurrection: on such the second death hath no power, but they shall be priests of God and of Christ, and shall reign with him a thousand years. And when the thousand years are expired, Satan shall be loosed out of his prison, And shall go out to deceive the nations which are in the four quarters of the earth, Gog, and Magog, to gather them together to battle: the number of whom is as the sand of the sea." **(Revelation 20:4 - 8)**

♦ "And he that overcometh, and keepeth my works unto the end, to him will I give power over the nations: And he shall rule them with a rod of iron; as the vessels of a potter shall they be broken to shivers: even as I received of my Father." **(Revelation 2:26 - 27)**

This is clearly in the context of "terra firma" and the "nations" he rules over with a rod of iron are nations on the planet Earth.

The Royal Inheritance

The Formula for the Highest of Human Quests.

The Holy Grail, the Fountain of Youth, Atlantis, The Hall of Records, The Spear of Destiny; all pursuits of great import to gain immortality, wisdom, truth, total power, freedom, love, the true meaning of life, and insight into the destiny of humanity. Combined in the pages of the Bible are all these treasures and the key to gain a full share of all for eternity. The promises made to mankind defy every conventional view of possibility, and are gained with the simple action of belief in the royal leader of the family of universally powerful beings who have promised it, Jesus, the Christ, and the Creator. All the superior things mankind has sought, and fought, for are offered in abundance in scripture. In the previous sections of this work we have presented hundreds of verses solidly establishing the promise of an inheritance into the royal family of God as the true gospel Jesus brought to mankind. In this section we offer hundreds of verses detailing the incredible rewards that are received with this eternal inheritance.

Immortality

Immortality is the most sought after of human pursuit. The Fountain of Youth, The Elixir of Life, the mythical Holy Grail, and many other potential sources of eternal life have been the focus of mankind's desire to escape death. Most people are familiar with only one verse in the Bible associated with immortality "For God so loved the world, that he gave his only begotten Son, that whosoever believeth in him should not perish, but have everlasting life." (John 3: 16). What is not well known is that this concept is repeated almost 50 times in the New Testament. Certainly, the heavy emphasis on this by the Christ, as well as the same priority expressed by the Apostles, testifies to its importance in this incredible message intended for humanity.

The almost 50 references to the promise and inheritance of ever lasting, eternal, or immortal life in the New Testament provide, in number alone, proof of its importance to the message of Jesus and his Apostles. It is important to understand that this immortality is easily accessible to humans. All that is required is find a way to get to the Tree of Life:

♦ "And the Lord God said, Behold, the man is become as one of us, to know good and evil: and now, lest he put forth his hand, and take also of the tree of life, and eat, and live for ever:" **(Genesis 3: 22)**.

Human Everlasting and Eternal Life in the New Testament Verses: See Appendix H
Everlasting and Eternal Things in the New Testament Verses: See Appendix I
For Ever in the New Testament Verses: See Appendix J

Old Testament Immortality

The Old Testament is a record of the contacts of a very limited segment of humanity, the Nation of Israel, with a race of beings called the Elohiym, God, and another group of beings serving the Elohiym called the Malak, angels. The concepts these beings passed on to mankind are replete with references to the eternal, everlasting, and things that remain forever. The Old Testament speaks of an everlasting Father, the everlasting God, with everlasting arms, who is is from everlasting, and to everlasting, an everlasting king, and an everlasting kingdom. It mentions an everlasting covenant, dominion, foundation, name, sign, statute, priesthood, possession, and throne. It testifies to an everlasting joy, kindness, light, love, mercy, remembrance, righteousness, and strength. And, it declares there is an everlasting salvation and everlasting life. There is an eternal God and an eternal excellence.

Man is said to have the ability to live forever. Some land is given forever, some land will not be sold forever, and some places are desolate forever. There are covenants, ordinances, statutes, signs, inheritances, memorials, judgments, oaths, kingdoms, kings, princes, and thrones, which last forever, while many other things are established and kept forever, as well as things that perish forever. Things are destroyed forever, priests and their sons minister forever, some generations last forever, some beings are anointed forever. There is love, blessing, friendship, belief, and a peace that will last forever, an ever-burning fire, and places to abide and dwell forever. The Lord will reign forever and ever, he endures, he keeps truth, he rules by his power, and his counsel stands forever, he puts his name on things forever, that name is magnified, glorified, and endures forever, his mercy, truth, commandments, judgments, and righteousness endure for ever, he offers sanctuary, which he has sanctified forever, the word of God will stand forever. Salvation will be forever, saints are preserved, thanks are given, and the earth abides forever, and time will last forever and ever.

Unconditional Love

Of what value would the incredible treasure of eternal life be if it was filled with hatred, apathy, grief, and destruction; all the things present when love is absent? The emphasis on love as a vital part of mankind's relationship to God and the absolute necessity of love in human affairs defines it as the highest priority of the gospel of Jesus. It is defined as the key to all productive results in mankind's relationship with God and the entire spectrum of human affairs. Love of your fellow man is equated with love of God, declared as the "new" commandment, and even loving your enemies is commanded. On love, all the laws and prophecies given to man by God hang, and love fulfills the law. Love is the royal law, the key to freedom, and all things work together for good to them that love God. No one has ever seen or even heard the things which God has prepared for them that love him, nothing can separate us from that love, and love is not just spoken or written, it is shown in action.

- A Description of Love
   As a preface to this scripture it is important to know that in every case the word "charity" is synonymous with love. The word charity comes directly from the Greek word agape, pronounced ag-ah'-pay meaning simply 'love'.
♦ "Though I speak with the tongues of men and of angels, and have not charity, I am become as sounding brass, or a tinkling cymbal. And though I have the gift of prophecy, and understand all mysteries, and all knowledge; and though I have all faith, so that I could remove mountains, and have not charity, I am nothing. And though I bestow all my goods to feed the poor, and though I give my body to be burned, and have not charity, it profiteth me nothing. Charity suffereth long, and is kind; charity envieth not; charity vaunteth not itself, is not puffed up, Doth not behave itself unseemly, seeketh not her own, is not easily provoked, thinketh no evil; Rejoiceth not in iniquity, but rejoiceth in the truth; Beareth all things, believeth all things, hopeth all things, endureth all things. Charity never faileth: but whether there be prophecies, they shall fail; whether there be tongues, they shall cease; whether there be knowledge, it shall vanish away. For we know in part, and we prophesy in part. But when that which is perfect is come, then that which is in part shall be done away. When I was a child, I spake as a child, I understood as a child, I thought as a child: but when I became a man, I put away childish things. For now we see through a glass, darkly; but then face to face: now I know in part; but then shall I know even as also I am known. And now abideth faith, hope, charity, these three; but the greatest of these is charity." (**1 Corinthians 13:1 - 13**)
Love Verses: See Appendix K

Wisdom and Truth
   An eternal future filled with love is a wonderful concept, and when combined with true knowledge and seasoned with understanding, it becomes exciting and vibrant. Wisdom and its components, such as understanding and knowledge, appear over a thousand times in scripture. The Bible delves deeply into the value of wisdom, its benefits and cost, and its source. From Merriam-Webster is the following definition for 'wisdom': 1 a: accumulated philosophic or scientific learning: Knowledge b: ability to discern inner qualities and relationships: Insight c: good sense: Judgment d: generally accepted belief

The Doctrines of Men

Knowledge, the exposure to, and retention of, facts and information, is an essential component of wisdom. Understanding is the ability to properly discern logical associations between, as well as the proper meanings of, facts and information. To many, the concept contained in the phrase "common sense" embodies the true meaning of understanding. These two mental qualities combine together to compose the individual human quality known as wisdom. Knowledge, without the ability to apply or associate it, is simply dormant information. Understanding, without proper knowledge is counter productive and an antithesis to wisdom.

- A description of wisdom in the Old Testament:
♦ "To know wisdom and instruction; to perceive the words of understanding; To receive the instruction of wisdom, justice, and judgment, and equity; To give subtilty to the simple, to the young man knowledge and discretion. A wise man will hear, and will increase learning; and a man of understanding shall attain unto wise counsels: To understand a proverb, and the interpretation; the words of the wise, and their dark sayings. The fear of the LORD is the beginning of knowledge: but fools despise wisdom and instruction." (**Proverbs 1:2 - 7**)
- A description of wisdom in the New Testament:
♦ "Who is a wise man and endued with knowledge among you? let him shew out of a good conversation his works with meekness of wisdom. But if ye have bitter envying and strife in your hearts, glory not, and lie not against the truth. This wisdom descendeth not from above, but is earthly, sensual, devilish. For where envying and strife is, there is confusion and every evil work. But the wisdom that is from above is first pure, then peaceable, gentle, and easy to be intreated, full of mercy and good fruits, without partiality, and without hypocrisy. And the fruit of righteousness is sown in peace of them that make peace." (**James 3:13 - 18**)

- Wisdom is for the asking:
♦ "Ask, and it shall be given you; seek, and ye shall find; knock, and it shall be opened unto you:" (**Matthew 7:7**)
Wisdom Verses: See Appendix L

Total Freedom

Freedom is a common personal desire of the rich and the poor, the weak and the powerful, and the good and the bad. An eternal existence, lived in a tightly structured, heavily restricted way may be acceptable, but certainly not optimal. Humans will be freed from sin, from the law of sin and death, the yoke of bondage; they will also be called to the glorious liberty of the children of God and given the perfect law of liberty.
♦ "And ye shall know the truth, and the truth shall make you free." (**John**

8:32)
Freedom Verses: See Appendix N

Ultimate Power

Pursuit of absolute power has been the goal of humanity since the Creation. This intrinsic trait was the catalyst for the scriptural account of the first sin. Perhaps one of the best-kept secrets concealing the superhuman nature of mankind in Bible based religion is in clear view. The Bible speaks of an incredible and virtually unlimited power inherent in humanity. The key to human power is faith, a word translated from the Greek word pistis, pronounced pis'-tis; persuasion. The way you are persuaded is your faith. Merriam-Webster defines 'persuasion' as an opinion held with complete assurance.

Many believe this is some ethereal force that makes you believe in God and, indeed, it may be triggered directly by God's Spirit. But, a specific definition can be found in Paul's letter to the Hebrews:

♦ "Now faith is the substance of things hoped for, the evidence of things not seen." (**Hebrews 11:1**).

● From the Greek we find these definitions of the prime words in this verse: faith - pistis, pronounced pis'-tis; persuasion / substance - hupostasis, pronounced hoop-os'-tas-is; a setting under (support) / things hoped for - elpizo, pronounced el-pid'-zo; to expect or confide / evidence - elegchos, pronounced el'-eng-khos; proof, conviction. A proper reading of this verse could be: Faith is the support of our expectations and proof of things not seen.

In life, anything we believe, the way we are persuaded, is based on a combination of the things we learn and the experiences we have. Faith is no different, being defined as persuasion. We see this in all aspects of personal performance in life with those taught to have confidence, and experiencing the result of positive self-confidence, being the most successful. Jesus was the most radical proponent of the power of positive thinking, and the first to reveal the true power inherent in human beings. He clearly stated even a minute amount of belief in this power he revealed will give mere humans supernatural power, making them capable of performing feats only limited by the level of belief itself. The followers of Jesus had a problem performing an exorcism on a certain man, which Jesus was easily able to perform. When they inquired why he was able, and they were not, he revealed the incredible power all humans potentially possess:

♦ "And Jesus said unto them, Because of your unbelief: for verily I say unto you, If ye have faith as a grain of mustard seed, ye shall say unto this mountain, Remove hence to yonder place; and it shall remove; and nothing shall be impossible unto you." (**Matthew 17:20**)

"Nothing shall be impossible unto you" is not said in a future tense; after all Jesus was in fact a human at this point, and performing super-human feats.

He was literally saying that if you had the belief, were persuaded, that you could move mountains, an advanced from of psychokenesis, you could move mountains with your mind. And he further declared, by extension, that anything, and everything, you believe you can do is within your power.

♦ **Mark 9:23** Jesus said unto him, If thou canst believe, all things are possible to him that believeth.

♦ **John 14:12** Verily, verily, I say unto you, He that believeth on me, the works that I do shall he do also; and greater works than these shall he do; because I go unto my Father.

♦ **I Corinthians 4:20** For the kingdom of God is not in word, but in power.

♦ **1Corinthians 6:3** Know ye not that we shall judge angels? how much more things that pertain to this life? See Faith: Page 146

Power *Verses: See Appendix O*

The Meaning of Life
A Royal Destiny

How is it that a mere mortal can have the incredible power just by believing they have it as Jesus declares; an all powerful nature considered by orthodox theology to an exclusive power of God? The Bible promises the most incredible rewards for humanity; immortality, unconditional love, absolute wisdom and truth, total freedom, and unlimited power. Are these not the very characteristics attributed to the beings called God in scripture?

• Yhovah, the Lord God, and Creator was very clear about the nature of man:

♦ "I have said, Ye are gods; and all of you are children of the most High." **(Psalms 82:6)**

And when Yhovah, the Lord God, and creator became the human, Jesus, (see the first chapter of John), he repeated it, by quoting himself:

♦ "Jesus answered them, Is it not written in your law, I said, Ye are gods?" **(John 10:34)**

• Yhovah, the Lord God, and Creator of the Old Testament even said he made man to look like an Elohiym:

♦ "And God said, Let us make man in our image, after our likeness: and let them have dominion over the fish of the sea, and over the fowl of the air, and over the cattle, and over all the earth, and over every creeping thing that creepeth upon the earth. So God created man in his own image, in the image of God created he him; male and female created he them." **(Genesis 1:26 - 27)**

• Yhovah also declared that man had reached a level so close to the level of the Elohiym that he must be prevented from becoming an eternal being:

♦ "And the Lord God said, Behold, the man is become as one of us, to know good and evil: and now, lest he put forth his hand, and take also of the tree of life, and eat, and live for ever:" **(Genesis 3:22)**

- Yhovah had to actually place a guarding force to prevent man from getting to the Tree of Life, the source that could make him eternal:
- ♦ "So he drove out the man; and he placed at the east of the garden of Eden Cherubims, and a flaming sword which turned every way, to keep the way of the tree of life." (**Genesis 3:24**)
- As further proof this is true, these verses show what destiny awaits mankind:
- ♦ **Psalms 8:4** What is man, that thou art mindful of him? and the son of man, that thou visitest him? 5 For thou hast made him a little lower than the angels, and hast crowned him with glory and honour. 6 Thou madest him to have dominion over the works of thy hands; thou hast put all things under his feet.
- ♦ **1 Corinthians 15:42**. So also is the resurrection of the dead. It is sown in corruption; it is raised in incorruption: 43. It is sown in dishonour; it is raised in glory: it is sown in weakness; it is raised in power: 44. It is sown a natural body; it is raised a spiritual body. There is a natural body, and there is a spiritual body. 45. And so it is written, The first man Adam was made a living soul; the last Adam was made a quickening spirit. 46. Howbeit that was not first which is spiritual, but that which is natural; and afterward that which is spiritual. 47. The first man is of the earth, earthy: the second man is the Lord from heaven. 48. As is the earthy, such are they also that are earthy: and as is the heavenly, such are they also that are heavenly. 49. And as we have borne the image of the earthy, we shall also bear the image of the heavenly. 50. Now this I say, brethren, that flesh and blood cannot inherit the kingdom of God; neither doth corruption inherit incorruption. 51. Behold, I shew you a mystery; We shall not all sleep, but we shall all be changed, 52. In a moment, in the twinkling of an eye, at the last trump: for the trumpet shall sound, and the dead shall be raised incorruptible, and we shall be changed. 53. For this corruptible must put on incorruption, and this mortal must put on immortality. 54. So when this corruptible shall have put on incorruption, and this mortal shall have put on immortality, then shall be brought to pass the saying that is written, Death is swallowed up in victory.
- ♦ **2 Corinthians 3:17**. Now the Lord is that Spirit: and where the Spirit of the Lord is, there is liberty. 18. But we all, with open face beholding as in a glass the glory of the Lord, are changed into the same image from glory to glory, even as by the Spirit of the Lord.
- ♦ **Philippians 3:20**. For our conversation is in heaven; from whence also we look for the Saviour, the Lord Jesus Christ: 21. Who shall change our vile body, that it may be fashioned like unto his glorious body, according to the working whereby he is able even to subdue all things unto himself.
- ♦ **Hebrews 2:5** For unto the angels hath he not put in subjection the world to come, whereof we speak. 6 But one in a certain place testified, saying, What is man, that thou art mindful of him? or the son of man that thou visitest him? 7 Thou madest him a little lower than the angels; thou crownedst him with glory

and honour, and didst set him over the works of thy hands: 8 Thou hast put all things in subjection under his feet. For in that he put all in subjection under him, he left nothing that is not put under him. But now we see not yet all things put under him.

One of the first questions a child asks at the first concept of the certainty of death is what happens when a human dies. Mankind has devoted uncounted hours of research and anxiety pondering this very question. There are as many theories about the answer to this perpetually elusive concept as there are humans considering it. No doubt great fortunes have been offered in the quest to solve this enigma, and entire cultures are often defined by their answer to this age-old question. What is most enigmatic about this "mystery" is that it is clearly answered, in simple terms, in scripture:

♦ "The days of our years are threescore years and ten; and if by reason of strength they be fourscore years, yet is their strength labour and sorrow; for it is soon cut off, and we fly away."(**Psalms 90:10**)
And here:
♦ "Who knoweth the spirit of man that goeth upward, and the spirit of the beast that goeth downward to the earth?" (**Ecclesiastes 3:21**)

The Ultimate Fail Safe Condition
Power is achieved, bought, stolen, and extorted, yet there is still no limit known to the depths to which members of the human race will sink to acquire it. The quest for power is littered with the bones of its perpetual abuse. The very embodiment of evil in the Bible is the result of a disastrous lust for power on a universal scale. The perfect answer to the control of such power is found in the wonderful destiny humanity is to inherit. By becoming members of the Family of God, the control will come from within. As a member of the royal family of the Gods, fully aware, and dedicated to the source of all power and control, all those receiving such power will receive the absolute control over that power. God will control it because they will be gods.

Salvation is the Gospel

♦ **Mark 8:35** For whosoever will save his life shall lose it; but whosoever shall lose his life for my sake and the gospel's, the same shall save it.
♦ **Romans 1:16** For I am not ashamed of the gospel of Christ: for it is the power of God unto salvation to every one that believeth; to the Jew first, and also to the Greek.
♦ **I Corinthians 15:1** Moreover, brethren, I declare unto you the gospel which I preached unto you, which also ye have received, and wherein ye stand; 2 By which also ye are saved, if ye keep in memory what I preached unto you, unless ye have believed in vain.
♦ **Ephesians 1:13** In whom ye also trusted, after that ye heard the word of

truth, the gospel of your salvation: in whom also after that ye believed, ye were sealed with that holy Spirit of promise,

♦ **2 Timothy 1:9** Who hath saved us, and called us with an holy calling, not according to our works, but according to his own purpose and grace, which was given us in Christ Jesus before the world began, 10 But is now made manifest by the appearing of our Saviour Jesus Christ, who hath abolished death, and hath brought life and immortality to light through the gospel:

♦ **2 Timothy 1:10** But is now made manifest by the appearing of our Saviour Jesus Christ, who hath abolished death, and hath brought life and immortality to light through the gospel:

Salvation From Death

♦ **Matthew 1:21** And she shall bring forth a son, and thou shalt call his name JESUS: for he shall save his people from their sins.

♦ **Romans 6:23** For the wages of sin is death; but the gift of God is eternal life through Jesus Christ our Lord.

♦ **Ephesians 2:5** Even when we were dead in sins, hath quickened us together with Christ, (by grace ye are saved;)

♦ **James 5:20** Let him know, that he which converteth the sinner from the error of his way shall save a soul from death, and shall hide a multitude of sins.

Salvation and Everlasting Life

♦ **Luke 18 26.** And they that heard it said, Who then can be saved? 27. And he said, The things which are impossible with men are possible with God. 28. Then Peter said, Lo, we have left all, and followed thee. 29. And he said unto them, Verily I say unto you, There is no man that hath left house, or parents, or brethren, or wife, or children, for the kingdom of God's sake, 30. Who shall not receive manifold more in this present time, and in the world to come life everlasting.

Salvation, Endurance and Everlasting Life

♦ **Matthew 10:22** And ye shall be hated of all men for my name's sake: but he that endureth to the end shall be saved.(1)

♦ **Mark 13:13** And ye shall be hated of all men for my name's sake: but he that shall endure unto the end, the same shall be saved.

♦ **John 6:27** Labour not for the meat which perisheth, but for that meat which endureth unto everlasting life, which the Son of man shall give unto you: for him hath God the Father sealed.

♦ **James 1:12** Blessed is the man that endureth temptation: for when he is tried, he shall receive the crown of life, which the Lord hath promised to them that love him.

Salvation and Knowledge of the Truth
♦ **1Timothy 2:3** For this is good and acceptable in the sight of God our Saviour; 4 Who will have all men to be saved, and to come unto the knowledge of the truth. 4 Who will have all men to be saved, and to come unto the knowledge of the truth.

Salvation and a Calling to Immortality
♦ **2 Timothy 1:9** Who hath saved us, and called us with an holy calling, not according to our works, but according to his own purpose and grace, which was given us in Christ Jesus before the world began, 10 But is now made manifest by the appearing of our Saviour Jesus Christ, who hath abolished death, and hath brought life and immortality to light through the gospel:

Salvation and Heirs
♦ **Hebrews 1:14** Are they not all ministering spirits, sent forth to minister for them who shall be heirs of salvation?

Salvation and Sons
♦ **Hebrews 2:10** For it became him, for whom are all things, and by whom are all things, in bringing many sons unto glory, to make the captain of their salvation perfect through sufferings.

Salvation for All Flesh, and Eternal Life
♦ **Luke 3:6** And all flesh shall see the salvation of God.
♦ **John 17:2** As thou hast given him power over all flesh, that he should give eternal life to as many as thou hast given him.

Eternal salvation
♦ **Hebrews 5:9** And being made perfect, he became the author of eternal salvation unto all them that obey him;

Salvation, Faith, Belief, Hope, and Everlasting Life
♦ **Mark 16:16** He that believeth and is baptized shall be saved; but he that believeth not shall be damned.
♦ **Mark 9:23** Jesus said unto him, If thou canst believe, all things are possible to him that believeth.
♦ **John 3:15** That whosoever believeth in him should not perish, but have eternal life. 16 For God so loved the world, that he gave his only begotten Son, that whosoever believeth in him should not perish, but have everlasting life.
♦ **John 3:36** He that believeth on the Son hath everlasting life: and he that believeth not the Son shall not see life; but the wrath of God abideth on him.
♦ **John 5:24** Verily, verily, I say unto you, He that heareth my word, and believeth on him that sent me, hath everlasting life, and shall not come into condemnation; but is passed from death unto life.

♦ **John 6:40** And this is the will of him that sent me, that every one which seeth the Son, and believeth on him, may have everlasting life: and I will raise him up at the last day.

♦ **John 6:47** Verily, verily, I say unto you, He that believeth on me hath everlasting life.

♦ **John 7:30** Then they sought to take him: but no man laid hands on him, because his hour was not yet come.

♦ **John 11:25** Jesus said unto her, I am the resurrection, and the life: he that believeth in me, though he were dead, yet shall he live: 26 And whosoever liveth and believeth in me shall never die. Believest thou this?

♦ **Acts 16:30** And brought them out, and said, Sirs, what must I do to be saved? 31 And they said, Believe on the Lord Jesus Christ, and thou shalt be saved, and thy house.

♦ **Romans 8:24** For we are saved by hope: but hope that is seen is not hope: for what a man seeth, why doth he yet hope for? 25 But if we hope for that we see not, then do we with patience wait for it.

♦ **Luke 7:50** And he said to the woman, Thy faith hath saved thee; go in peace.

♦ **Luke 18:42** And Jesus said unto him, Receive thy sight: thy faith hath saved thee.

♦ **Ephesians 2:8** For by grace are ye saved through faith; and that not of yourselves: it is the gift of God:

♦ **1Timothy 3:15** And that from a child thou hast known the holy scriptures, which are able to make thee wise unto salvation through faith which is in Christ Jesus.

♦ **1 Peter 1:5** Who are kept by the power of God through faith unto salvation ready to be revealed in the last time.

♦ **1 Peter 1:9** Receiving the end of your faith, even the salvation of your souls. 10 Of which salvation the prophets have enquired and searched diligently, who prophesied of the grace that should come unto you:

Salvation and Reverence to God

♦ **Acts 13:26** Men and brethren, children of the stock of Abraham, and whosoever among you feareth God, to you is the word of this salvation sent. feareth - phobeo, pronounced fob-eh'-o; to frighten, i.e. (passively) to be alarmed; by analogy, to be in awe of, i.e. revere:

Salvation and Confessing the Lord Jesus

♦ **Romans 10:9** That if thou shalt confess with thy mouth the Lord Jesus, and shalt believe in thine heart that God hath raised him from the dead, thou shalt be saved.

The Doctrines of Men

Salvation and Calling Upon the Name of the Lord
♦ **Romans 10:13** For whosoever shall call upon the name of the Lord shall be saved.

Salvation and Selflessness
♦ **I Corinthians 10:32** Give none offence, neither to the Jews, nor to the Gentiles, nor to the church of God: 33 Even as I please all men in all things, not seeking mine own profit, but the profit of many, that they may be saved.

Jesus as Saviour
♦ **Luke 1:47** And my spirit hath rejoiced in God my Saviour.
♦ **Luke 2:11** For unto you is born this day in the city of David a Saviour, which is Christ the Lord.
♦ **John 4:42** And said unto the woman, Now we believe, not because of thy saying: for we have heard him ourselves, and know that this is indeed the Christ, the Saviour of the world.
♦ **Acts 5:31** Him hath God exalted with his right hand to be a Prince and a Saviour, for to give repentance to Israel, and forgiveness of sins.
♦ **Acts 13:23** Of this man's seed hath God according to his promise raised unto Israel a Saviour, Jesus:
♦ **Acts 5:23** For the husband is the head of the wife, even as Christ is the head of the church: and he is the saviour of the body.
♦ **Philippians 3:20** For our conversation is in heaven; from whence also we look for the Saviour, the Lord Jesus Christ:
♦ **I Timothy 1:1** Paul, an apostle of Jesus Christ by the commandment of God our Saviour, and Lord Jesus Christ, which is our hope;
♦ **I Timothy 2:3** For this is good and acceptable in the sight of God our Saviour;
♦ **I Timothy 4:10** For therefore we both labour and suffer reproach, because we trust in the living God, who is the Saviour of all men, specially of those that believe.
♦ **2 Timothy 1:10** But is now made manifest by the appearing of our Saviour Jesus Christ, who hath abolished death, and hath brought life and immortality to light through the gospel:
♦ **Titus 1:3** But hath in due times manifested his word through preaching, which is committed unto me according to the commandment of God our Saviour; 4 To Titus, mine own son after the common faith: Grace, mercy, and peace, from God the Father and the Lord Jesus Christ our Saviour.
♦ **Titus 2:10** Not purloining, but shewing all good fidelity; that they may adorn the doctrine of God our Saviour in all things.
♦ **Titus 2:13** Looking for that blessed hope, and the glorious appearing of the great God and our Saviour Jesus Christ;

♦ **Titus 3:4** But after that the kindness and love of God our Saviour toward man appeared,

♦ **Titus 3:6** Which he shed on us abundantly through Jesus Christ our Saviour;

♦ **2 Peter 1:1** Simon Peter, a servant and an apostle of Jesus Christ, to them that have obtained like precious faith with us through the righteousness of God and our Saviour Jesus Christ:

♦ **2 Peter 1:11** For so an entrance shall be ministered unto you abundantly into the everlasting kingdom of our Lord and Saviour Jesus Christ.

♦ **2 Peter 2:20** For if after they have escaped the pollutions of the world through the knowledge of the Lord and Saviour Jesus Christ, they are again entangled therein, and overcome, the latter end is worse with them than the beginning.

♦ **2 Peter 3:2** That ye may be mindful of the words which were spoken before by the holy prophets, and of the commandment of us the apostles of the Lord and Saviour:

♦ **2 Peter 3:18** But grow in grace, and in the knowledge of our Lord and Saviour Jesus Christ. To him be glory both now and for ever. Amen.

♦ **I John 4:**14 And we have seen and do testify that the Father sent the Son to be the Saviour of the world.

♦ **Jude 1:25** To the only wise God our Saviour, be glory and majesty, dominion and power, both now and ever. Amen.

The True Gospel

There can be no doubt that the incredible realities of the gospel Jesus brought to mankind are the same treasures humanity has desperately searched for throughout its existence. Scripture absolutely confirms that this great gospel is that humans were created in the image of the Gods, to become gods, with all the characteristics of those Gods and full conversion into that divine race. The highest goal to which a human can aspire is to become an immortal, wise, all-powerful being with complete dedication to a perfect universal force. This, we believe, is the ultimate and true destiny of humanity. We also believe this is the gospel defined in the Greek as "a good message" that Jesus preached, and every word in the Bible leads to. What better "good message" could he bring? While the church will no doubt scream blasphemy and heresy from the rooftops, the biblical realty stands firm in its most important and relevant declaration to the entirety of humanity, the greatest message ever to fall on human ears:

♦ ***"I have said, Ye are gods; and all of you are children of the most High."*** **(Psalms 82:6)**

The Doctrines of Men

The True Nature of Mankind

The Church View:

The Church has as many concepts of the place of mankind in life as there are churches. But, the one thing that is always obvious is that the value of a man is in direct relationship to the weight of his wallet and the weakness of his independence. Ministers often refer to their congregation as the flock, and like sheep, they follow the leader without question and under the constant threat of expulsion. The support of the church, its employees, its property, and bringing in new money is the real purpose of mankind as represented by the main focus of the pulpit. If one learns something along the way, as long as it conforms to church doctrine, it is tolerated, though seldom ever encouraged. Try to test the truth of what is the church's doctrine and you are labeled a heretic, told you are unfaithful, and very often labeled as a threat to the truth you dare to seek. Kept in low esteem by constant ranting from the pulpit, it is only a strong will that allows escape from the chains of harsh doctrine and absolute group conformity.

The Bible View:

The Bible gives man an identity that can be summed up in one short phrase. Humans are gods. This will label a church member as a blasphemer for even considering the concept. Jesus had the same problem when he expressed it publicly. He made the mistake of claiming that he and the Father God were one, which immediately earned him target status at a stoning party. He then informed them that, as Yhovah, he had told their forefathers that they were gods, which would make the stoners gods.

A New Paradigm

Here is the story:
♦ **John 10:29** My Father, which gave them me, is greater than all; and no man is able to pluck them out of my Father's hand. 30 I and my Father are one. 31 Then the Jews took up stones again to stone him. 32 Jesus answered them, Many good works have I shewed you from my Father; for which of those works do ye stone me? 33 The Jews answered him, saying, For a good work we stone thee not; but for blasphemy; and because that thou, being a man, makest thyself God. 34 Jesus answered them, Is it not written in your law, I said, Ye are gods? 35 If he called them gods, unto whom the word of God came, and the scripture cannot be broken; 36 Say ye of him, whom the Father hath sanctified, and sent into the world, Thou blasphemest; because I said, I am the Son of God? 37 If I do not the works of my Father, believe me not. 38 But if I do, though ye believe not me, believe the works: that ye may know, and believe, that the Father is in me, and I in him. 39 Therefore they sought again to take him: but he escaped out of their hand.

As can be seen this did not cool the anger of the crowd in spite of the fact that he was quoting from their own book:

♦ **Psalms 82:6** I have said, Ye are gods; and all of you are children of the most High. 7 But ye shall die like men, and fall like one of the princes.

So as the God of Moses and as the Christ, Jesus made clear the true nature of mankind. Humans are gods.

Humans are Gods

Yhovah even said he made man to look like an Elohiym:

♦ **Genesis 1:26** And God said, Let us make man in our image, after our likeness: and let them have dominion over the fish of the sea, and over the fowl of the air, and over the cattle, and over all the earth, and over every creeping thing that creepeth upon the earth. 27 So God created man in his own image, in the image of God created he him; male and female created he them.

Yhovah declared that man had reached a level so close to the level of the Elohiym that he must be prevented from becoming an eternal being:

♦ **Genesis 3:22** And the Lord God said, Behold, the man is become as one of us, to know good and evil: and now, lest he put forth his hand, and take also of the tree of life, and eat, and live for ever:

Yhovah places a guarding force to prevent man from getting to the source that could make him eternal:

♦ **Genesis 3:24**. So he drove out the man; and he placed at the east of the garden of Eden Cherubims, and a flaming sword which turned every way, to keep the way of the tree of life.

As further proof this is true, these verses show what destiny awaits mankind:

♦ **1 Corinthians 15:42.** So also is the resurrection of the dead. It is sown in corruption; it is raised in incorruption: 43. It is sown in dishonour; it is raised in glory: it is sown in weakness; it is raised in power: 44. It is sown a natural body; it is raised a spiritual body. There is a natural body, and there is a spiritual body. 45. And so it is written, The first man Adam was made a living soul; the last Adam was made a quickening spirit. 46. Howbeit that was not first which is spiritual, but that which is natural; and afterward that which is spiritual. 47. The first man is of the earth, earthy: the second man is the Lord from heaven. 48. As is the earthy, such are they also that are earthy: and as is the heavenly, such are they also that are heavenly. 49. And as we have borne the image of the earthy, we shall also bear the image of the heavenly. 50. Now this I say, brethren, that flesh and blood cannot inherit the kingdom of God; neither doth corruption inherit incorruption. 51. Behold, I shew you a mystery; We shall not all sleep, but we shall all be changed, 52. In a moment, in the twinkling of an eye, at the last trump: for the trumpet shall sound, and the dead shall be raised incorruptible, and we shall be changed. 53. For this corruptible must put on incorruption, and this mortal must put on immortality. 54. So when this corruptible shall have put on incorruption, and this mortal shall have put on immortality, then shall be brought to pass the saying that is written, Death is swallowed up in victory.

♦ **2 Corinthians 3:17**. Now the Lord is that Spirit: and where the Spirit of the Lord is, there is liberty. 18. But we all, with open face beholding as in a glass the glory of the Lord, are changed into the same image from glory to glory, even as by the Spirit of the Lord.

♦ **Philippians 3:20** For our conversation is in heaven; from whence also we look for the Saviour, the Lord Jesus Christ: 21. Who shall change our vile body, that it may be fashioned like unto his glorious body, according to the working whereby he is able even to subdue all things unto himself.

Unlimited Human Power

The power that mankind has within even the physical body is absolutely unlimited, as Jesus demonstrated, and he clearly testified that it was not just his own to possess:

♦ **Matthew 17:14** And when they were come to the multitude, there came to him a certain man, kneeling down to him, and saying, 15 Lord, have mercy on my son: for he is lunatick, and sore vexed: for ofttimes he falleth into the fire, and oft into the water. 16 And I brought him to thy disciples, and they could not cure him. 17 Then Jesus answered and said, O faithless and perverse generation, how long shall I be with you? how long shall I suffer you? bring him hither to me. 18 And Jesus rebuked the devil; and he departed out of him: and the child was cured from that very hour. 19 Then came the disciples to Jesus apart, and said, Why could not we cast him out? 20 And Jesus said unto them, Because of your unbelief: for verily I say unto you, If ye have faith as a grain of mustard seed, ye shall say unto this mountain, Remove hence to yonder place; and it shall remove; and nothing shall be impossible unto you.

♦ **Mark 11:22** And Jesus answering saith unto them, Have faith in God. 23 For verily I say unto you, That whosoever shall say unto this mountain, Be thou removed, and be thou cast into the sea; and shall not doubt in his heart, but shall believe that those things which he saith shall come to pass; he shall have whatsoever he saith. 24 Therefore I say unto you, What things soever ye desire, when ye pray, believe that ye receive them, and ye shall have them.

Man is given rule over the entire planet:

♦ **Genesis 1: 26** And God said, Let us make man in our image, after our likeness: and let them have dominion over the fish of the sea, and over the fowl of the air, and over the cattle, and over all the earth, and over every creeping thing that creepeth upon the earth. 27 So God created man in his own image, in the image of God created he him; male and female created he them. 28 And God blessed them, and God said unto them, Be fruitful, and multiply, and replenish the earth, and subdue it: and have dominion over the fish of the sea, and over the fowl of the air, and over every living thing that moveth upon the earth. 29 And God said, Behold, I have given you every herb bearing seed, which is upon the face of all the earth, and every tree, in the which is the fruit of a tree yielding seed; to you it shall be for meat. 30 And to every beast of the earth, and to every fowl of the air, and to every thing that creepeth upon the earth, wherein there is life, I have given every green herb for meat: and it was so.

♦ **Psalms 8:4** What is man, that thou art mindful of him? and the son of man, that thou visitest him? 5 For thou hast made him a little lower than the angels, and hast crowned him with glory and honour. 6 Thou madest him to have dominion over the works of thy hands; thou hast put all things under his feet.

A Higher Calling

Judging angels:
♦ **1Corinthians 6:3** Know ye not that we shall judge angels? how much more things that pertain to this life?

More in store for mankind:
♦ **Hebrews 2:5** For unto the angels hath he not put in subjection the world to come, whereof we speak. **6** But one in a certain place testified, saying, What is man, that thou art mindful of him? or the son of man that thou visitest him? 7 Thou madest him a little lower than the angels; thou crownedst him with glory and honour, and didst set him over the works of thy hands: 8 Thou hast put all things in subjection under his feet. For in that he put all in subjection under him, he left nothing that is not put under him. But now we see not yet all things put under him.

The actual physical form mankind is destined to take is vague, but evidence exists that if we do look like the Christ as is clearly stated in 2 Corinthians 3:17 above, we will probably have *red skin, white hair, glowing eyes*, and a very loud voice as can be found in these verses:

♦ **Revelation 1:12** And I turned to see the voice that spake with me. And being turned, I saw seven golden candlesticks; 13 And in the midst of the seven candlesticks one like unto the Son of man, clothed with a garment down to the foot, and girt about the paps with a golden girdle. 14 His head and his hairs were white like wool, as white as snow; and his eyes were as a flame of fire; 15 And his feet like unto fine brass, as if they burned in a furnace; and his voice as the sound of many waters.

- And then there is this:
♦ "The days of our years are threescore years and ten; and if by reason of strength they be fourscore years, yet is their strength labour and sorrow; for it is soon cut off, and we fly away."
(Psalms 90:10)

- And this:
♦ "Who knoweth the spirit of man that goeth upward, and the spirit of the beast that goeth downward to the earth?" (**Ecclesiastes 3:21**)

It is this truth, which the church hides from mankind using it to keep the congregations under the iron-fisted rule of the pulpit, while crying that they are lacking faith. If mankind knew of and believed in its true destiny, even in human form, the power would be endless.
Faith Verses: See Appendix O
Power *Verses: See Appendix P*

The Wonder of Humanity

Throughout history, the world has witnessed a side of man that shows he is not just higher than the animals, but higher than what his known physical and mental restrictions should allow. Is mankind endowed with special powers as a race, or are just a chosen few blessed? Do these incredible powers come from an outside source or do they lay dormant within?

Science tells us man is a physical being, but a higher animal than the creatures he supposedly evolved from, just a couple of rungs up some imaginary ladder. The church tells us man is just fire-fodder, with the opportunity to escape that fate if he conforms to a set of standards dictated by that particular church. Education is stuck somewhere in between, teaching what comes out of the debate between the church and science.

History shows us that mankind seems to be something completely removed from the orthodox view. The Bible describes mankind as having a place in the scheme of things mostly ignored by the world's mainstream, but recognized by the facts. Consider the ramifications of these biblical edicts:

Man is a Mirror Image of the Gods

Why is man so different from the other life forms on the planet? Why is he so far up that imaginary ladder? And, how can certain people exhibit such extraordinary powers that are never seen in other animals?
♦ **Genesis 1:26** And God said, Let us make man in our image, after our likeness: and let them have dominion over the fish of the sea, and over the fowl of the air, and over the cattle, and over all the earth, and over every creeping thing that creepeth upon the earth.

Man looks like and acts like the Elohiym or, at least, that's how it started.

Man Can Become Immortal

Is this brief life span of just a few decades the whole of each person's life? Is there a real proverbial fountain of youth?

♦ **Genesis 3:22** And the Lord God said, Behold, the man is become as one of us, to know good and evil: and now, lest he put forth his hand, and take also of the tree of life, and eat, and live for ever:

Man is so much like the Elohiym that if allowed to partake of a particular substance, he would indeed become eternal.

♦ **Genesis 3:24** So he drove out the man; and he placed at the east of the garden of Eden Cherubims, and a flaming sword which turned every way, to keep the way of the tree of life.

The Elohiym had to physically prevent mankind from becoming eternal.

How Close to the Gods?

Are humans just lucky, evolutionary mutants or, worse yet, hapless animals being used as pawns in some higher spiritual game, destined to fry in some eternal oven after the game is over? Or, is the true nature of man higher than his own imagination takes him? Is mankind's real power and destiny suppressed by every form of conditioning society can employ to bury it?

♦ **John 10:34** Jesus answered them, Is it not written in your law, I said, Ye are gods?

As the human Jesus says, in the past he has told men that they are gods.

♦ **Psalms 82:6** I have said, Ye are gods; and all of you are children of the most High. **7** But ye shall die like men, and fall like one of the princes.

As the God of Moses and as the Christ, Yhovah makes clear the true nature of mankind. Humans are gods.

Women in the Bible

"Women are vessels of excrement".
A recorded proclamation by Saint Augustine,
one of the Catholic Church founding fathers

The status of women in history and modern times has been formed and influenced in whole, or in great part, from the religious beliefs of the times. It is not surprising, considering the almost total gender domination of church leadership by men, that this status is somewhere between property and personal slave to those men. Also, the gender domination of power in all levels of society has virtually assured that this status has remained firmly entrenched even in our "enlightened" modern society. With women possessing no power, this religious prejudice is carried into almost every aspect of most women's lives.

It may be by neither law nor truth that women are inferior by their nature, but the evidence that they are denied equality in almost every level of society, in every culture worldwide, is undeniable.

The Women Of Ancient Israel

Women in ancient Israel had their position in society defined in the Hebrew Scriptures and in the interpretation of those scriptures. Their status and freedoms were severely limited by Jewish law and custom in ancient Israel:

- Women were restricted to roles of little or no authority.
- Women were confined to the homes of their fathers or husbands.
- Women were to be inferior to men, under the direct authority of men, their fathers before marriage, or their husband after.
- Women were not allowed to testify in court trials.
- Women could not appear in public venues.
- Women could not talk to strangers.
- Women were required to be doubly veiled when they ventured outside of their homes.

The Glaring Truth

- Women in ancient Israel had a status not unlike that of women in Afghanistan during the grossly oppressive rule of the Taliban.
- An even sadder reality is that in many mainstream "Christian" denominations, if you remove the "double veils in public" aspect, there is very little difference in the treatment of women.

The Explanation Of Old And New

One of the most obvious and most ignored truths of biblical reality is that the word "testament", as used in Old and New Testament, is interchangeable with the word "covenant". The Merriam-Webster Dictionary defines covenant as: a usually formal, solemn, and binding agreement. In our modern world this is known as a "contract". Logic defines "old" as what was, and "new" as what is. In the context of the Bible, the Old Testament is the former contract God made with man, specifically the nation of Israel. The New Testament is the current contract God has made with all mankind.

In the normal course of the affairs of honest contractual dealings in society, the institution of a "new" contract either nullifies or redefines an existing one, with the full force of the former, and the former contract is deemed no more than an historical reference. The doctrinal practice of mainstream Bible-based religion is a strange blending of the old and new contracts that dictates those doctrines. By enforcing some of the old contract's provisions and some of the new contract's stipulations, while ignoring many of the old and most of the new contract's aspects, they have in fact created a completely separate and totally illegitimate third contract. The treatment of women by the mainstream church is based almost solely on the provisions of the old contract which, of course, insures total domination by men resulting in the extreme deprivation of women in every aspect of their lives.

The God who was party to the Old Testament / Contract, became the man Jesus who was party to the New Testament / Contract. It is, therefore, absolute truth that doctrines / provisions of Jesus redefine the old contract with the nation of Israel and those past doctrines are of no effect, being replaced or fulfilled by the new. To deny this is to deny the power and authority of the Holy Spirit which guided Jesus in the formation of this new contract and must be strongly considered in the light of this doctrinal certainty:

♦ **Matthew 21:31** Wherefore I say unto you, All manner of sin and blasphemy shall be forgiven unto men: but the blasphemy against the Holy Ghost shall not be forgiven unto men.

The New Covenant and Women

The dealing of Jesus with the women of his day gives undeniable evidence that the oppressive treatment of women by the edicts of the old contract was ended. Jesus nullified many centuries of oppressive Jewish law and custom. He clearly treated women and men as equals. He ignored numerous Old Testament edicts, which specified inequality. He consistently violated the rules, concerning women, of the three major Jewish religious groups of the day: the Essenes, Pharisees, and Sadducees. The treatment of women by Jesus was nothing short of radical for his day. Here are just a few examples of that revolutionary change:

• Jesus taught female students:

♦ **Luke 10:38** Now it came to pass, as they went, that he entered into a certain village: and a certain woman named Martha received him into her house. 39 And she had a sister called Mary, which also sat at Jesus' feet, and heard his word. 40 But Martha was cumbered about much serving, and came to him, and said, Lord, dost thou not care that my sister hath left me to serve alone? bid her therefore that she help me. 41 And Jesus answered and said unto her, Martha, Martha, thou art careful and troubled about many things: 42 But one thing is needful: and Mary hath chosen that good part, which shall not be taken away from her.

• He called a woman a daughter of Abraham as equal to men.

♦ **Luke 13:16** And ought not this woman, being a daughter of Abraham, whom Satan hath bound, lo, these eighteen years, be loosed from this bond on the sabbath day?

- He accepted women in his inner circle.
♦ **Luke 8:1** And it came to pass afterward, that he went throughout every city and village, preaching and shewing the glad tidings of the kingdom of God: and the twelve were with him, 2 And certain women, which had been healed of evil spirits and infirmities, Mary called Magdalene, out of whom went seven devils, 3 And Joanna the wife of Chuza Herod's steward, and Susanna, and many others, which ministered unto him of their substance.

- He appeared first to a woman after his resurrection.
♦ **Matthew 28:1** In the end of the sabbath, as it began to dawn toward the first day of the week, came Mary Magdalene and the other Mary to see the sepulchre.
♦ **28:9** And as they went to tell his disciples, behold, Jesus met them, saying, All hail. And they came and held him by the feet, and worshipped him.

- Women were present at Jesus' death.
♦ **Matthew 27:55** And many women were there beholding afar off, which followed Jesus from Galilee, ministering unto him: 56 Among which was Mary Magdalene, and Mary the mother of James and Joses, and the mother of Zebedee's children.
♦ **Mark 15:40** There were also women looking on afar off: among whom was Mary Magdalene, and Mary the mother of James the less and of Joses, and Salome; 41 (Who also, when he was in Galilee, followed him, and ministered unto him;) and many other women which came up with him unto Jerusalem.
♦ **John 19:25** Now there stood by the cross of Jesus his mother, and his mother's sister, Mary the wife of Cleophas, and Mary Magdalene.

- Jesus repeatedly expressed concern for widows.
♦ **Luke 20:46** Beware of the scribes, which desire to walk in long robes, and love greetings in the markets, and the highest seats in the synagogues, and the chief rooms at feasts; 47 Which devour widows' houses, and for a shew make long prayers: the same shall receive greater damnation.

- He talked to "foreign" women.
♦ **John 4:7** There cometh a woman of Samaria to draw water: Jesus saith unto her, Give me to drink. 8 (For his disciples were gone away unto the city to buy meat.) 9 Then saith the woman of Samaria unto him, How is it that thou, being a Jew, askest drink of me, which am a woman of Samaria? for the Jews have no dealings with the Samaritans. 10 Jesus answered and said unto her, If thou knewest the gift of God, and who it is that saith to thee, Give me to drink; thou wouldest have asked of him, and he would have given thee living water.

- Jesus changes the male-favored doctrine of divorce:
♦ **Mark 10:11** And he saith unto them, Whosoever shall put away his wife, and marry another, committeth adultery against her. 12 And if a woman shall put away her husband, and be married to another, she committeth adultery.

- After Jesus' resurrection, a women receives the first apostolic commission of any human.
♦ **Matthew 28:5.** And the angel answered and said unto the women, Fear not ye: for I know that ye seek Jesus, which was crucified. 6 He is not here: for he is risen, as he said. Come, see the place where the Lord lay. 7 And go quickly, and tell his disciples that he is risen from the dead; and, behold, he goeth before you into Galilee; there shall ye see him: lo, I have told you.

An Undeniable Conclusion

With just the evidence above, not considering the love and fairness Jesus expressed to all humanity, or his promise of salvation for all humans, the current treatment of women by the mainstream church is not the doctrine or the practice of the Son of God. Women are equal to men, they should be treated with equality and respect in all matters in this world, and no doubt, will be so in the true Kingdom of God.

For a complete listing of the women in the Bible please see Appendix R

Do Humans Possess Supernatural Powers?

♦ **Matthew 17:20** And Jesus said unto them, Because of your unbelief: for verily I say unto you, If ye have faith as a grain of mustard seed, ye shall say unto this mountain, Remove hence to yonder place; and it shall remove; and nothing shall be impossible unto you.

Is Jesus saying that if a person realizes that they have just an infinitesimal level of belief in their own internal power, they are capable of incredible feats of psychokenesis?

♦ **Luke 17:6** And the Lord said, If ye had faith as a grain of mustard seed, ye might say unto this sycamine tree, Be thou plucked up by the root, and be thou planted in the sea; and it should obey you.

Here he is referring to a smaller object, but he is still talking about psychokenesis. And in the verse above, the phase *"and nothing shall be impossible unto you"* shows that there is no limit to the powers of mankind.

Was There Evidence of This Power?

Possessed or empowered? Is the standard dogma of the church, that all people exhibiting unusual powers are possessed by demons, accurate? It is the declaration of the Bible that some of those people have high spiritual power. Is the lack of such supernatural power taking place actually a sign that the church is not a true church? Here is what was going on in the original church community after their power was unleashed:

What About the Rest of the World?

The evidence of unexplained phenomenon radiating from humans is well documented in history and the modern world. Feats of super-human strength or brainpower are evidenced in all societies, at all social levels. Not all the following evidence is spectacular in nature, but it does show a rather diverse perspective of an entity the church calls hapless mortals with a fiery destiny and Jesus calls gods.

Special Talents of Special People

It is a matter of record that many people possess special powers that seem to transcend their gravity bound and physically restricted bodies. Unfortunately, due to church-based and other social stigmas associated with these special talents, the true number of such people is unknown. Many are socially isolated, imprisoned or otherwise institutionalized, or repress these powers to prevent unwanted attention or undeserved harassment. The Bible speaks of spirit possession, exorcism, psychokenesis, out of body experience, spiritual healing, extra sensory perception, and shape shifting.

The Bible also makes it clear that in many cases the early church members possessed many special talents. Many of those talents would find these very members condemned by the church for exhibitions of power bestowed by the God the modern church claims to worship. Many other ancient writings speak of human phenomenon and the Catholic Church is a repository of the supernatural. Media sensationalism has held the human potential for supernatural power at the same sideshow freak level it has occupied through history.

Astral Projection / OBEs / Exoprojection

It is estimated that up to 80% of all those queried report having experienced some form of out of body experiences. There is a worldwide movement to bring this anomaly out of the shadows spear-headed by the International Institute of Projectiology and Conscientiology. They declare someone trained to control his extra physical body could harness his environment's natural energies to levitate, move objects, change the weather or even turn invisible. In his second letter to Corinth, Paul specifically mentions an out of body experience,

♦ **2 Corinthians 12:4:** How that he was caught up into paradise, and heard unspeakable words, which it is not lawful for a man to utter.

Some prophets describe experiences that are similar. Though it is a widely experienced phenomenon, little serious research has been undertaken. Considering the possible ramifications of a true understanding of astral projection, this is inexcusable.

Clairvoyance / Extrasensory Perception / Precognition / Telepathy / Second Sight

ESP goes by many names and is exhibited in many ways. It is, for all practical purposes, an accepted, socially common phenomenon and often cited as the source of even minor coincidence. Family members often have no doubt they have a very solid telepathic relationship with relatives and close friends often have the same experience. It has been projected over great distances and often occurs during emotional crisis and emergency scenarios. It has also been cited as the saving element in life-threatening scenarios.

Levitation

Levitation is a rare phenomenon, but well recognized for its radical physical manifestations. Psychokenesis and levitation are often considered the same anomaly, but have distinct characteristics. Those who levitate defy gravity by floating their own bodies. They do not often exhibit psychokenesis. Psychokinetics defy gravity by lifting other objects and don't often exhibit levitation. Levitation is often a spontaneous event while psychokenesis is seldom an uncontrolled action.

The Catholic Church has many saints that levitate, but also record many excommunications for others who levitate. The two most famous levitators in Catholic history are Saint Teresa of Avila, the character around whose person the vintage television show "The Flying Nun" was formed, and Simon Magus. Simon Magus was judged evil and excommunicated, while Saint Teresa was said to do it in states of rapture and awarded sainthood. Other Catholic levitators include Saint Francis of Paula, Gemma Galgani, a Passionist nun, Joseph of Cupertino, and Saint Benedict.

Other famous levitators include many Tibetan Monks, Milarepa, the great thirteenth century yogi, Daniel Douglas Home, who reportedly levitated regularly over a forty-year period, and the Italian medium, Amedee Zuccarini, who was photographed levitating with his feet twenty feet off of a table.

Glossolalia / Xenoglossia / Tongues

Glossolalia can be classified into two categories, speaking a language everybody understands and speaking a language nobody understands. Both types are mainly associated with ancient and modern Bible based religion. Animism also records glossolalia and the practice is found to have been associated with the Oracle at Delphi, the shrine of Apollo, for centuries. The Charismatic Movement of the modern age is the most recognized example, but Shakers, Quakers, Mormons, and the early Methodists and Presbyterians were all known to speak tongues.

Psychokenesis / Telekinesis

Psychokenesis is the ability to physically effect or alter the location, motion, shape or composition of objects without the use of physical means.

This can range from a feather to the weather in application and has been recorded throughout history in beings from small children to great gods.

At the beginning of the 20th century Rudi Schneider, an early 20th century medium, was well known for his psychokinetic ability to move and change objects. The Israeli psychokinetic, Uri Geller, baffled television audiences with his skills, bending spoons and performing other paranormal feats. Some viewers said their household objects underwent similar changes. Geller was accused of trickery, but such claims went unproven. Nina Kulagina, from Leningrad, was able to move many sizes and types of stationary objects, change of the direction of objects in motion, and project images on photographic film. Ingo Swann, a New York artist and psychic, could change the temperature of an object close to him by one degree. Also, he could affect the magnetic field of a magnetometer. And, Sir Francis Bacon was a champion of research into the practical applications of this anomaly.

The Skeptics Mantra: "All those who believe in psychokenesis, raise my hand."

Radiesthesia / Dowsing / Water-Witching

Radiesthesia is the discovery of hidden water and other metals, minerals, and objects using indicators such as rods and pendulums. In France, it is known as "radiesthesie" and has been used for recovering missing persons and in medical diagnosis. The L' Association de Amis de la Radiesthesie was established in 1930 and the British Society of Dowsers was founded in 1933. A radiesthsist is a person who is very sensitive to certain substances, whose sensitivity is amplified by a rod or pendulum.

Teleradiesthesia / Superpendulism

As with dowsing, there is also the phenomena of teleradiesthesia or superpendulism. This is the phenomena where the sensitive person does not go to the actual location of the sought after object, but a map of the location is brought to him.

Psychometry

Psychometry is a power which enables one to divine facts by handling objects. The most common form of psychometrics is fortunetellers that claim prophetical power by using crystal balls. Palm readers, diviners of tealeaves, and readers of auras are peripheral psychometrics fields.

Microscopic / Telescopic Sight

Telescopic vision is the ability to view objects at great distances normally not negligible to those with normal vision. Microscopic vision is the ability to see items smaller than those with normal vision. In either anomaly, the range distance or size of objects detectable is relative to the abilities of the skilled viewer.

Human Calculators

Over the ages many people have proven complex calculations can be solved in even the minds of those with little or no education.

Photographic Memory / Super Memory / Mnemonics

The ability to retain exact memories of all visual, audio, olfactory, gustatory, or tactile elements of any given experience.

Synesthesia

Synesthesia is the rare ability of a person to experience multiple cross-sensory input, colors have sounds, sounds have smells, etc. Some experience many more sensory inputs from single objects than one would normally experience.

Remote Viewing / Shape Shifting / Metamorphosis / Spiritual Healing / Psychics

In the case of the above named subjects, we have determined that the commercialization and pseudo-spiritualization in these areas render them more entertainment and profit oriented than serious research and will not promote their endeavors.

Special Effects

Auras

A strange, multicolored glow emanating from and surrounding the human body is detected by some claiming to be sensitive to this phenomenon. A process called Kurlian Photography has captured this glow on film. The origin of this phenomenon is widely speculated but it seems likely that it is directly related to the spiritual essence of man. Auras are not exclusive to humans or even to living things. If this phenomenon is connected to the functions of the body, as well as the spirit, lack of formal research is as anomalous as the phenomenon itself.

- A Theory About Chakras and Auras:

Although you may read about auras and chakras, and think them to be two separate objects or manifestations, chakras are a component of an aura, and each interpenetrates the other. Chakras are the means through which a physical body communicates with its aura and vice-versa. You are not a physical body with an aura surrounding you. Rather, your aura and physical body are one unit that together make up only a small portion of the greater you.

Automatic Writing

Automatic Writing is generally believed to be from an outside entity that exhibits itself through uncontrolled use of a pen or pencil, typewriter, computer or in the most well known method, a Ouija board. Messages sometimes come in the form of foreign languages or reverse writing. Many times spaces are not included between words, there is no punctuation or a picture or symbol is part of the writing. In some cases the individual does not recognize the writing as their own. The phenomenon is often classified as having evil origins, particularly in the case of Ouija boards, though it is also considered by some to be a subconscious event. As with all unexplained human anomalies, no formal research is available to explain any aspect of this strange event.

Clairaudience / Channeling

Clairaudience/Channeling are perception of messages in thought forms from an entity that exists in another realm. The Bible and other ancient writings record many instances of anomalous contact with spiritual entities. Modern claims include contact with angels, aliens, ancestors, and Atlanteans. The bottom line is, it is a matter of belief that determines the veracity of the claim. The strong connection to the highly suspect psychic industry should give one cause for caution.

Magnetic People

Human Magnetism is a rare phenomenon that finds certain people attracting metallic objects to their bodies. Everything from sewing needles to frying pans adhere to their bodies and often the bond is so strong the items are hard to remove. There is no known explanation for this anomaly. In some cases the effect extends beyond metal objects to a variety of substances.

Inga Gaiduchenko of the Soviet Union has been likened to a human magnet. It was demonstrated scientifically that pens, dishes, books, and other objects could adhere to her hands. Canadian teenager Caroline Clare became so magnetized after an undiagnosed illness that metal objects stuck to her skin with a force so strong another person was required to remove them. In 1846 a 14-year-old French girl, Angelique Cottin's, mere presence made the needles of compasses spin wildly; objects as heavy as furniture would slide away from her if she tried to touch them, and objects near her would vibrate unnaturally. Though considered a rare human anomaly, a convention for magnetic people in Bulgaria drew 300 participants.

Electric People

People who exhibit the ability to produce electric voltage from their bodies are recorded through history. Others are found that can disrupt electrical appliances, devices, and even streetlights. Some carry such high voltage talents; they often cannot be touched or must avoid all metal surfaces. Most often this unusual talent is involuntary, but many are able to control it and some have even made a career using this power to enthrall audiences. No known cause for the anomaly is evident and is often attributed to the spiritual world.

The Doctrines of Men

Glowing People

The glow from spirits, angels, and gods are common occurrences in ancient writings, paintings, and primitive drawings. Humans have the same talent, some as famous as Moses. Glows from wounds and injured body parts have been recorded.

Spontaneous Human Combustion

Perhaps the strangest and only self-destructive of the human anomalies is spontaneous human combustion. It is most often recorded amongst the elderly, but not exclusive to this age group. Considering the fact that the human body is 85% water, Spontaneous Human Combustion is a physical impossibility, but not the only impossibility of this anomaly. Often the victim is seated in a chair or lying on a bed, which is not even singed, while the body is reduced to ash.

Near Death Experience

A glimpse into life after death is presented by the testimony of many who have slipped over the threshold and quickly returned. The amazing consistency of the eyewitness accounts lead to the inevitable conclusion that death may only be a transfer point rather than the end of life's journey. Near Death Experience is such a widespread human anomaly, it has even generated support groups and major research projects.

Indigo Children

Indigo Children compromise a little known human anomaly defined by children with exceptional and unusual skills normal adolescents do not exhibit. They are the fortunate ones who have held on to higher powers that are in all children, but conditioned out by a society ignorant of the true human potential. As with any individual with special powers or gifts, Indigo children often find a world of rejection and intolerance the common reaction of those not aware. Indigo children exhibit spiritual powers, as well as advanced mental powers, and some powers are yet to be identified.

There is no way to determine how widespread this human phenomenon is. With the social enigma of enforced conformity and low standards, exceptional behavior in children is often ignored or, worse, suppressed. The concept that children should be restricted to a juvenile environment controlled by antiquated standards and profit motivation is deplorable. The demand that all children should learn the same information and achieve the same level of regurgitation of that information is primitive. The expectation that children should be kept entranced by a never ending flow of inane animated characters is the worst form of mind numbing and detrimental conditioning. It is a wonder any children escape the routine

Anomalous Skulls

Anomalous human skulls are a rarity, but no less an enigma. Skulls were found in rural Pennsylvania in the 19th century with horn-like protrusions above the brows. In 1888, in Minnesota, skeletons with skulls containing double rows of teeth in both the upper and lower jaws and low and sloping foreheads were discovered. Elongated, cone-head shaped skulls have been found in South America and a bulbous skull, nicknamed "The Starchild", has been found in Mexico. Whether these are just natural malformations of human skulls or the skulls of extraterrestrial beings is a matter of judgment.

The Incredible Human Body

The God of the Bible says he formed the first human body "out of the dust of the ground" and this concept of human creation is repeated in other ancient writings. Whether he is saying he took natural elements and bioengineered the first man or actually made a model out of mud is a logical question. Evidence shows that the Elohiym has the technology, but the specifics of creation of living things are not detailed. The solid evidence of a perfect method of producing perfect creatures living in perfect biospheres is in the results.

The human body is the finest multifaceted organism in the natural world. When coupled with the most complicated and sophisticated central processing unit ever devised, the human brain, it stands alone as the quintessence of living entities.

- **The Brain**

The human brain is the most complex and orderly arrangement of matter known in the universe. It controls over 100 billion nerve cells and generates more electrical impulses in a single day than all of the world's telephones put together moving at speeds from 150 to 250 miles per hour. This network uses nearly 45 miles of nerves that are powered by more bioelectricity than produced by a 120-volt battery. At least 100,000 different chemical reactions occur in the brain every second. The number of possible different combinations of synaptic connections among neurons in a single human brain is larger than the total number of atomic particles that make up the known universe. The storage capacity is estimated to exceed 4 terabytes. It can store, recognize, and remember 10,000 different odors and differentiate between up to eight million colors and 500 shades of gray. It is estimated that there are between 100 and 200 hundred billion neurons in a brain and seven million brain cells are used each day. A newly formed nerve cell is called a neuroblast.

The brain reaches its maximum weight, three pounds, at age 20, but begins to lose cells at a rate of 50,000 per day by the age of 30. A baby's brain has its full complement of neurons by the sixth month of gestation and grows at a rate of more than 13,000 neurons per second up until this time. The soft mass of the adult brain is motionless but is surrounded by a membrane containing veins and arteries. The brain itself has no feeling; therefore, the pain of a headache comes not from the organ itself, but from the nerve and muscles lining it. The brain is composed of 85% water and, on average, comprises 2 percent of the total body weight, yet it requires 25 percent of all oxygen used, as opposed to 7 percent by the heart. Cholesterol makes up 15 percent of the brain by dry weight. The brain is more active sleeping than it is watching TV.

The short-term memory capacity for most people is between five and nine items or digits. This is one reason that telephone numbers were kept to seven digits. A recent study found that 75 percent of headache patients felt relief when they rubbed capsaicin (the component that makes chili peppers hot) on their nose. A bowl of lime Jell-O, when hooked up to an EEG machine, exhibits activity, which is virtually identical to the brain waves of a healthy adult man or woman. Thomas Edison said, "The chief function of the body is to carry the brain around", however Aristotle believed the main purpose of the human brain was to cool the blood. Even after death, the human brain continues to produce electrical wave signals for up to a day and a half

- **The Heart**

    The heart of an adult beats about 70 to 80 beats per minute, 100,000 times every day, 40 million times a year and in 70 years it will have beaten 2½ billion times. A female heart beats about 10 times per minute faster than a male's. The rate can increase to as much as 200 per minute during heavy exercise. As a pump, it produces enough pressure to shoot a stream 30 feet, produce enough energy in an hour to lift 2000 lb. 3 feet off the ground, and efficiently circulate 50 million gallons over the average lifetime. In one year, the average human heart circulates from 770,000 to 1.6 million gallons of blood through the body. This is enough fluid to fill 200 tank cars, each with a capacity of 8,000 gallons. There are enough tiny blood vessels called capillaries that if placed end to end they would stretch over 2 times around the earth. All this is done with just over a gallon of blood, which circulates 1,000 times in a single day through the body on a daily 60,000-mile journey, 168,000,000 miles in a lifetime. 25 trillion cells travel through the bloodstream, but a stack of 500 would only measure 0.04 inches high. The human heart rests between beats. In an average lifetime of 70 years, the total resting time is estimated to be about 40 years.

    Red blood cells live for a period of only four months and travel between the lungs and other tissues 75,000 times before returning to the bone marrow to die, being replaced by the bone marrow at the rate of 2 to 3 million a second. Men have more blood, 1.5 gallons as compared to 0.875 gallons for women. The most common blood type in the world is Type O accounting for about 46% of the world's population. However, in some areas, other blood groups predominate. The most rare, Type A-H, has been found in less than a dozen people since the type was discovered. According to research, the risk of heart attack is higher on Monday than any other day of the week. A child has 60,000 miles of blood vessels; in an adult there are 100,000. The stethoscope was invented so that doctors could listen to a woman's heart without having to touch her. The native people of the Andes Mountains in South America have 2 to 3 more quarts of blood in their bodies than people who live at lower elevations.

- **The Eyes**

As you focus on each word in this sentence, your eyes swing back and forth 100 times a second, and every second the retina performs 10 billion computer-like calculations. The eyes can perceive more than 1 million simultaneous visual impressions, are able to discriminate among nearly 8 million gradations of color, can distinguish about 500 different shades of gray, and take in more information than the world's largest telescope. Each time the eye blinks, over 200 muscles move and you blink 25 times a minute or over 6 million times each year. The retina inside the eye covers about 650 square millimeters and contains some 137 million light-sensitive cells; 130 million rod cells for black and white vision and 7 million cone cells for color vision. To focus all this, the muscles of the eye move 100,000 times a day. An eye weighs 1.25 ounces. By the age of 60, our eyes have been exposed to more light energy than would be released by a nuclear blast. Sight accounts for 90 to 95 percent of all sensory perceptions.

The human eye sees everything upside down, but the brain turns it right side up, with an average field of vision encompassing a 200-degree wide angle. Your ears and nose continue to grow throughout your entire life but your eyes are the same size from birth to death. A bird's eye takes up about 50 percent of its head; human eyes take up about 5 percent of the head. To be comparable to a bird's eyes, human eyes would have to be the size of baseballs. If you go blind in one eye, you'll loose only one-fifth of your vision, but lose all your depth perception. The only part of the human body that has no blood supply is the cornea; it takes its oxygen directly from the air.

Newborn babies are not blind but have approximately 20/50 vision and can easily discriminate between degrees of brightness. The daughters of a mother who is colorblind and a father who has normal vision will have normal vision. However, the sons will be colorblind. While 7 men in 100 have some form of colorblindness, only 1 woman in 1,000 suffers from it. The most common form of color blindness is a red-green deficiency. People are the only animals in the world who cry tears. Onion Tears are caused by an irritant in onions known as brominates molecules that react with the water on the eye to produces an acid that the eye removes by producing tears. Those stars and colors you see when you close and rub your eyes are called phosphenes.

Two out of three adults in the United Sates wear glasses at some time. While reading a page of print, the eyes do not move continually across the page. They move in a series of jumps, called "fixations," from one clump of words to the next. Though more comfortable with daylight, given enough time to adjust, the human eye can, for a time, see almost as well as an owl's. The sensitivity of the human eye is so keen that on a clear, moonless night, a person standing on a mountain can see a match being struck as far as 50 miles away. Much to their amazement, astronauts in orbit were able to see the wakes of ships. When you have a black eye, you have a bilateral periorbital hematoma. The pupil of the eye expands as much as 45 percent when a person looks at something pleasing.

- **The Ears**

Our hearing is so sensitive it can distinguish between hundreds of thousands of different sounds. Between ages 30 and 70, the ears may be a quarter-inch longer due to the fact that cartilage is one of the few tissues that continue to grow as we age. A human can hear the tick of a watch from 6 meters in very quiet conditions. Sounds too low for human beings to hear are called infrasonic. The easiest sound for the human ear to hear, and those which carry best when pronounced, are, in order, "ah," "aw," "eh," and "oo." Permanent hearing loss can result from prolonged exposure to sounds at 85 decibels (0 decibels is the threshold for hearing). For comparison, a busy street corner is about 80 decibels, a subway train from 20 feet is 100 decibels, a jet plane from 500 feet is 110 decibels, and loud thunder is 120 decibels. A rock band amplified at close range is 140 decibels, more than 100,000 times as loud as the level that will produce permanent hearing loss. The African bushman lives in a quiet, remote environment and has no measurable hearing loss at age 60.

- **The Nose**

The nose cleans, warms or cools, filters, and humidifies over 500 cubic feet of air every day. It monitors and classifies over 10,000 different odors and the sense of smell is so keen that it can detect the odors of certain substances even when they are diluted to 1 part to 30 billion. A human can detect one drop of perfume diffused throughout a three-room apartment. It is totally impossible to sneeze with your eyes open. A sneeze can exceed the speed of 100 mph and when you sneeze, all bodily functions stop, even the heart. Most people by the age of sixty have lost 40 percent of their ability to smell. Your thumb is the same length as your nose.

- **The Mouth**

The average human has about 10,000 taste buds. Those on the tongue are divided into four groups; the tip taste buds sense sweetness; those at the back sense bitterness; the sides sense saltiness and sourness. All the more complex tastes are made up of combinations of the basic four. However, not all taste buds are on the tongue. Some are under the tongue; some are on the inside of the cheeks; some are on the roof of the mouth. Some can even be found on the lips, which are especially sensitive to salt. The sense of taste can detect sweetness in a solution of 1 part sugar to 200 parts water and one gram of salt in 500 liters of water. The average lifespan of a human being's taste bud is 7-10 days. By age sixty, most people have lost half of their taste buds. The strongest muscle in the body is the tongue and every person has a unique tongue print. Pigs, dogs, and some other animals can taste water, but people cannot. Humans don't actually taste water; they taste the chemicals and impurities in the water. 85% of the population can curl their tongue into a tube.

The tooth is the only part of the human body that can't repair itself and tooth enamel is the hardest of all substances manufactured by the human body. Each tooth contains about 55 miles of canals for a total of over 1700 miles. There are 20 baby teeth and 32 adult teeth. False teeth are often radioactive. Approximately 1 million Americans wear some form of denture; half of these dentures are made of a porcelain compound laced with minute amounts of uranium to stimulate fluorescence. Without the uranium additive, the dentures would be a dull green color when seen under artificial light. If you are right-handed, you will tend to chew your food on the right side of the mouth. If you are left-handed, you will tend to chew your food on the left. A pack-a-day smoker will loose approximately 2 teeth every 10 years.

It requires the use of 72 muscles to speak a single word. Whispering is more wearing on your voice than a normal speaking tone. Whispering and shouting stretch the vocal cords. A normal person has two true vocal chords and two false vocal chords, which have no direct role in producing sound. The mouth makes one liter of saliva a day and over a lifetime produces enough to fill two swimming pools. Every time you lick a stamp, you're consuming 1/10 of a calorie. Up to the age of six or seven months, a child can breathe and swallow at the same time. An adult cannot do this. Seeing another person yawn makes it likely that you will yawn yourself. Thinking about, even reading about yawning, can cause a yawn.

- **The Skin**

The largest and heaviest organ is the skin, with a surface area of about 25 square feet and a weight of about 6 pounds. The epidermis, the outermost layer of the skin, sheds itself at a rate of about a million cells every 40 minutes. Humans shed about 600,000 particles of skin every hour, about 1.5 pounds a year, and grow all new outer skin cells about every 27 days, almost 1.000 new skins a lifetime. By 70 years of age, an average person will have lost 105 pounds of skin. Floor dust contains 90% dead skin.

The skin is only about as deep as the tip of a ballpoint pen but the sense of touch is more refined than any device ever created. A human can detect the wing of a bee falling on their cheek from a height of one centimeter. There are 45 miles of nerves in the skin of a human being. When we touch something, we send a message to our brain at 125 mph. In one square inch of skin we have nine feet of blood vessels, 600 pain sensors, four yards of nerve fibers, 1300 nerve cells, 9000 nerve endings, 36 heat sensors, 75 pressure sensors, 650 sweat glands, 60,000 pigment cells, 100 sweat glands, 3 million cells, and an average of 32 million bacteria. Your fingernails grow four times as fast as your toenails.

Perspiration is odorless; it is the bacteria on the skin that creates an odor. The skin of the armpits can harbor up to 516,000 bacteria per square inch, while drier areas, such as the forearm, have only about 13,000 bacteria per square inch. There are about 2 million sweat glands in the average human body. The average adult loses 540 calories with every liter of sweat and men sweat about 40% more than women. There are approximately 250,000 sweat glands in your feet and they sweat as much as 8 ounces of moisture per day. You perspire a total of 1.5 pints a day.

The tips of fingers and the soles of feet are covered by a thick, tough layer of skin called the stratum corneum. Identical twins do not have identical fingerprints. No two sets of prints are alike, including those of identical twins. The fingerprints of koala bears are virtually indistinguishable from those of humans, so much so that they could be confused at a crime scene. Humans are the only primates that don't have pigment in the palms of their hands. A simple, moderately severe sunburn damages the blood vessels to such an extent that it takes four to fifteen months for them to return to their normal condition. First-degree burns affect only the very top layers of the skin; second-degree burns are midway through the skin's thickness. Third-degree burns penetrate and damage the entire thickness of the skin. Varicose veins are stretched, dilated veins whose valves do not work properly.

• The Bones

The average human body has 208 bones, 54 are in the hands; 52 are in the feet, 28 above the neck, 6 are in the ears, and 22 are in the skull. The skeleton of an average 160-pound body weighs about 29 pounds. A newborn baby has 330, but as the child grows, some of the bones join together to give fewer bones in total. Babies are born without kneecaps. They don't appear until the child reaches 2-6 years of age. The longest human bone is the femur or thighbone, which is 48 cm. long. It is so strong that it can support 30 times the weight of a man! The strongest bone in the body, the thighbone, is hollow. Ounce for ounce, it has a greater pressure tolerance and bearing strength than a rod of equivalent size made of cast steel.

The mineral content, porosity, and general makeup of human bone is nearly identical to some species of South Pacific coral. The two are so alike that plastic surgeons are using the coral to replace lost human bone in facial reconstructions. The body has over 100 joints. The average person's hand flexes its finger joints 25 million times during a lifetime. Most people's legs are slightly different lengths. Giraffes and humans have the same number of vertebrae in their necks. The pop you get when you crack your knuckles is actually a bubble of gas bursting generated by imploding synobial fluid. The "funny bone" is not a bone; it is a nerve. The structural plans of a whale's, a dog's, a bird's, and a man's 'arm' are exactly the same.

- **The Muscles**

   The human body has over 600 muscles accounting for 40% of the body's weight and 1/3 of those muscles are used just to blink the eyes. The strongest muscle in the body is the tongue. Jaw muscles can provide about 200 pounds of force for chewing. To focus the eye, muscles move 100,000 times a day. To give the leg muscle the same amount of exercise would require a 50-mile walk. It takes 17 muscles to smile, 43 to frown, and every 2000 frowns create one wrinkle. The longest name for a muscle is: Levator Labii Superioris Alaeque Nasi. It is a two-inch muscle that elevates the tip of the mouth. The simple act of walking requires the use of 200 muscles in the human body. The smallest human muscle is in the ear, which is a little over 1 mm long. If all the muscles in an average body were made into one muscle, it could produce about 2,000 tons force. The longest muscle in the human body is the sartorius. This narrow muscle of the thigh passes obliquely across the front of the thigh and helps rotate the leg to the position assumed in sitting cross-legged. No one truly has double joints. Contortionists are actually able to stretch the fibrous tissues known as ligaments. Ligaments hold organs in place and fasten bones together. Ligaments normally restrict the movements of certain joints, but some folks find that their ligaments are more flexible than others. Between the time of death and the onset of rigor mortis in a human body, the contraction of the muscles can cause the body to turn over on its side.

- **Energy**

   The body gives off the amount of heat equivalent to a 100-watt light bulb and overall produces 25,000 BTUs. 26 calories are burned in a one-minute kiss and banging ones head against a wall will use 150 calories an hour. In a lifetime, the average US resident eats more than 50 tons of food and drinks more than 13,000 gallons of liquid. This includes 8 spiders. 75% of your body heat escapes through your head. The body uses 48 kg of ATP a day (ATP is the energy the body produces during cellular respiration). A person will die from total lack of sleep sooner than from starvation. Death will occur about 10 days without sleep, while starvation takes a few weeks. Small animals, like bats and shrews, consume up to one and one half times their body weight in food every day. For an adult male, this would be like eating 1,000 quarter-pound cheeseburgers a day, or about 50 Thanksgiving dinners a day. Moderate dancing burns 250 to 300 calories an hour. Twenty minutes of moderate dancing will elevate heart rate up to aerobic levels. One study found polkas, swing dancing, and waltzes to be particularly effective for weight loss. If you yelled for 8 years, 7 months and 6 days, you would have produced enough sound energy to heat one cup of coffee. Every human body is naturally radioactive. Our tissues contain traces of the radioactive isotopes Potassium-40 and Carbon-14, which are absorbed by all living organisms from the environment. Every person has nearly 400,000 radioactive atoms disintegrating into other atoms in his or her body each second. Women burn fat more slowly than men, by a rate of about 50 calories a day. Laughing is aerobic. It provides a workout for the diaphragm and increases the body's ability to use oxygen. Laughing lowers levels of stress hormones and strengthens the immune system. Six-year-olds laugh an average of 300 times a day. Adults only laugh 15 to 100 times a day. Most deaths in a hospital are between the times of 4pm and 6pm, the time when the human body is at its weakest. There are 110 calories consumed during an hour of typing, only 30 more than those used while sleeping.

- **Organs and Glands**

Even if the stomach, the spleen, 75 percent of the liver, 80 percent of the intestines, one kidney, one lung, and virtually every organ from the pelvic and groin area are removed, the human body can still survive. The average Human bladder can hold 13 ounces of liquid. There are 35 million digestive glands in the stomach. The pituitary gland, responsible for producing the hormone that regulates growth, is only the size of a pea and weighs little more than a small paper clip. The liver is often called the body's chemical factory and performs over 500 functions. If 80 percent of your liver were to be removed, the remaining part would continue to function. Within a few months, the liver would have reconstituted itself to its original size. The liver is a gland, not an organ. The liver stretches across almost the width of the body, occupying a space about the size of a football. It weighs more than 3 lbs. The kidney consists of over 1 million little tubes, and the total length of the tubes in both kidneys runs to about forty miles.

- **Ingredients**

The body contains hydrogen, copper, zinc, cobalt, calcium, manganese, phosphates, nickel, sulfur, potassium, carbon iron, and silicon. The average human body contains enough: sulfur to kill all fleas on an average dog, carbon to make 900 pencils, potassium to fire a toy cannon, fat to make 7 bars of soap, phosphorus to make 2,200 match heads, water to fill a ten-gallon tank, and enough iron to make a 3 inch nail. The hydrochloric acid of the human digestive process is so strong a corrosive that it easily can eat its way through the iron of an automobile body. Yet, it doesn't endanger the stomach's sticky mucus walls. Smart people have more zinc in their hair. The body's daily requirement of vitamins and minerals is less than a thimbleful.

- **Cells**

The human body consists of about 60 trillion cells, and each cell has about 10,000 times as many molecules as the Milky Way has stars. Except for your brain cells, 50,000 of the cells in your body will have died and been replaced with others, all while you have been reading this sentence. Three hundred million cells die in the human body every minute. The largest cell in the human body is the female reproductive cell, the ovum. The smallest is the male sperm. The average adult has between 40 and 50 billion fat cells.

- **DNA**

All of the DNA in an adult human body could fit inside one ice cube, but if unwound, stretched out and joined end to end, it would reach from the earth to the sun and back again more than 400 times. Scientists estimate that they could fill a 1,000-volume encyclopedia with the coded instructions in the DNA of a single human cell if the instructions could be translated to English.

- **Content**

If you were freeze dried, like coffee, 90% of your weight would be the real you and 10% would be the little critters that call your body their home. If all of the spaces between the nucleuses of the atoms making up an average human body were removed, the person would be the size of half a flea. However, they would still weigh the same.

- **Other Facts**
- Asparagus Urine: The first suspect was proposed in 1891. It was proposed that as your body metabolizes asparagus, it produces a smelly chemical, a metabolite called methanethiol, which your discriminating kidneys see fit to dump into the bladder. Other culprits suspected are S-Methyl Thioesters, or six sulfur-containing compounds. Research says just 22 percent of survey respondents experience asparagus urine, but the problem proved to be one not of producing the stinky urine, but of being able to sniff it out.
- The average human body is worth about 25 dollars.
- People are the only animals in the world who cry tears.
Undertakers report that human bodies do not deteriorate as quickly as they used to. The reason, they believe, is that the modern diet contains so many preservatives that these chemicals tend to prevent the body from decomposing too rapidly after death.
- In the average lifetime, a person will walk the equivalent of 5 times around

the equator.

• The average adult stands 0.4 inch (1 cm) taller in the morning than in the evening because the cartilage in the spine compresses during the day.

• The thumb is such a major player in the human body that it has a special section reserved for it in the brain that is separate from the area that controls the fingers.

* Please note that the facts appearing in the above section were gleaned from scores of resources, over several years, and those sources are not documented. These facts are true and correct to best of the author's knowledge, and are open to correction.

Humanity Incorporated

The Truth About "The Great Deception"

The Church View:

There are many concepts of what the "Great Deception" may be ranging from the Church of Satan to UFOs. Capitalism, corporate greed, and the obsession with possession of wealth are seldom found on the list. Generally, anything that may cause members to question or reject absolute church control over their life fits the bill.

The Bible View:

There are many aspects to the final deception of mankind with corporations being the center of focus. No scripture points toward an invasion, mind control, or holographic images projected into the minds of satanic puppets by alien powers. It is also clear that the mass of mankind will be deceived, that the mainstream church will be following the same drummer, and that the final blame will fall on the world's great mercantile concerns.

The purpose of this work is to present evidence that will cast light on the true nature of the beings described in the pages of the Bible, how they appear, how they interact with humans, who they are, and what their presence means to mankind.

The Bible uses many terms as names for these beings, God, Lord, angels, hosts, and watchers, to name a few. These beings declare that they created all life on this planet, including mankind, and control the biosphere of Earth and what we perceive as the known universe. The Bible also provides evidence that mankind has a direct relationship with these beings and are much higher than all other forms of life on the planet. The highest ranking of these beings, called the Elohiym in the Hebrew, having a direct relationship with mankind and the planet, is a direct representative of the Supreme Being who is the source of all things. This being's name is Yhovah in the Hebrew and is the Lord and the Word in the Old Testament. It is this being who was in control of the actions that brought this world into being, interacted with the humans in the Old Testament, and became the man called Jesus in the New Testament. It is this being that predicted the events directly related to the future of mankind.

It is those predictions that are most important to what the presence of these beings means to mankind. Many of these predictions are general in their content such as wars, earthquakes, signs, and wonders in the sky. But, there are six verses that give specific insight into how mankind will be brought to the brink of self-destruction that can be seen in the events unfolding in our rapidly changing world.

The Doctrines of Men

A series of events unfolding in the beginning of the first decade of the 21st Century is revealing that, indeed, those predictions made almost 2000 years ago are not only possible, but also becoming a stark reality in our modern society. The power elite through a corporate control structure and global financial manipulation will soon have every aspect of human life under direct control using the guise of protection from a worldwide terrorist threat.

The single most destructive reality in our modern world in our historical record, our ancient writings, is the pursuit of wealth and the power it gives. And, throughout history the wealthy elite has used force to maintain that power, giving the masses only enough power to produce that wealth and eliminating all opposition to their despotic quest. Money and the power it facilitates have been the cause of wars, poverty, biosphere devastation, social degradation, political oppression, and the original source of all human and planetary problems. What is now shaping up to be a global monetary control system is clearly predicted in the pages of the Bible.

High Evil in the Corporate World

The world's history is littered with remnants of great societies, gaping scars on the planet, and the bodies of billions of humans, all victims of the relentless pursuit of the power of wealth. Wealth is a clever shape shifter in appearance, but constant in its most despicable effect, avarice. Whether it is golden to the eye, salty to the taste, or oily to the touch, the pursuit of possession for personal gain has created a downward spiral in human condition, the social fabric, and environmental health. At the beginning of the twenty-first century the control by the wealthy elite over every aspect of human life is reaching completeness. It is no longer a dream to pursue, it is now a perpetually growing addiction to its elite possessors, an obsessive quest to those trapped in its lure, and a weapon to control, and fleece the masses.

Now the control mechanism that will insure monitoring and identification of every human on the planet is in place, and riding the crest of the "security at all cost" tide sweeping through the global community. In but a short time, mandatory implantation of the new implantable biochip will be the law of the planet under the guise of the public good. With the terrorist threat dominating every aspect of social reality a new era in global reality has begun. No longer is the future bright with the promise of ever expanding global freedom, peace, and prosperity. The dark shadow of oppression, sinister clouds of war, and gloomy reality of inevitable worldwide economic depression dominate the horizon.

A Warning to Humanity

This is the proclamation of the beginning of the end of the current age of mankind. The Bible warns the world to be careful where the false prophets point, saying the Christ is here, or there, but is very specific where deception can be found:

♦ "And the light of a candle shall shine no more at all in thee; and the voice of the bridegroom and of the bride shall be heard no more at all in thee: for thy merchants were the great men of the earth; for by thy sorceries were all nations deceived." (**Revelation 18:23**) The great merchants of the Earth in the end times are clearly indicted as the culprits behind the complete deception of mankind. There are many concepts in the churches of the world about what the "Great Deception" is, ranging from the Church of Satan to UFOs. Capitalism, corporate greed, and the obsession with possession of wealth are seldom found on the list. Generally, anything that may cause members to question, or reject, absolute church control over their life fits the bill.

The single most destructive reality in our modern world, in our historical record, and from our ancient writings, is the pursuit of wealth and the power it gives. And, throughout history the wealthy elite have used force to maintain that power, giving the masses only enough power to produce that wealth, and eliminating all opposition to their despotic quest. Money and the power it facilitates have been the cause of wars, poverty, biosphere devastation, social degradation, political oppression, and the original source of all human and planetary problems. What is now shaping up to be a global monetary control system is clearly predicted in the pages of the Bible.

Money Is the Key

Follow the Money

♦ 1 Timothy 6:10 For the love of money is the root of all evil: which while some coveted after, they have erred from the faith, and pierced themselves through with many sorrows.

The dismal record of its lure throughout human history more than justifies this pronouncement, but the word "love" must be understood in its original meaning:

• Strong's Exhaustive Concordance renders "love of money" as "avarice" from the word "philarguria" pronounced fil-ar-goo-ree'-ah

• The Merriam-Webster Dictionary defines avarice as "to crave", and the "excessive or insatiable desire for wealth or gain"

It is not, therefore, the simple desire for monetary increase that is the origin of evil, but the unnatural greed that drives the desire to acquire money at all cost, and without regard for the ultimate effect that it has on the planet, or the human race.

An ancient principle used by certain tribes of the indigenous peoples of North America was to make no decision without first taking into consideration the effects it will have on the next seven generations. Corporate decisions are made without regard to the effect on even the current generation. The bottom line controls all decisions in the world's corporate board rooms, and even the hint of the inability to increase that bottom line from quarter to quarter can destroy careers, ruin reputations, and bankrupt major corporations overnight.

The accounting scandals that devastated some of the giants of Wall Street show how honesty and integrity have no place in the race for the riches. Manipulation, misrepresentation, and blatant criminal fraud have now been exposed as the rule, rather than the exception, in corporate conduct. Even more criminal is the government decision to simply slap the hands of the perpetrators a little harder as a way to control the problem. However, considering the entire administration making that decision is a virtual roster of the darlings of the corporate culture, this is not at all surprising. It does show what the result can be when the line between business and government is erased. Corporate interests are clearly in control of the executive branch of the United States government. The only check on the power of the executive branch, the United States Congress, is the blind puppet of the corporate lobby system, thus, nullifying the power of the people over their destiny. With the makeup of the judicial branch of government decided by both the executive and legislative branches, corporate control of the U.S. government is complete. And, that reality has now moved into the global realm.

This work proposes that the very nature of the steady pace by corporations to control all aspects of life is no accident, but has a clear and terrible source. We believe this source has a purpose for this control and that it is openly revealed in scripture.

The Mark of the Beast

Worldwide Financial Control
♦ "And he had power to give life unto the image of the beast, that the image of the beast should both speak, and cause that as many as would not worship the image of the beast should be killed. And he causeth all, both small and great, rich and poor, free and bond, to receive a mark in their right hand, or in their foreheads: And that no man might buy or sell, save he that had the mark, or the name of the beast, or the number of his name." **(Revelation 13:15 - 17)**

No prediction in the Bible is more descriptive or crystal clear in it's meaning than these two verses. A mark, defined as "a scratch or etching", by Strong's Exhaustive Concordance, forcibly placed on the bodies of every human on Earth and used for control of financial transactions worldwide, was not even conceivable until the last century.

With the "terrorist threat" proclaimed by the world's most powerful forces now overshadowing all global events, such tight control over individual identity is not only conceivable now, but also inevitable. The technology is on the market through such companies as Applied Digital Solutions and growing in popularity as the imagined need for unprecedented security worldwide is emphasized in an ever-increasing crescendo. Once this system is in place and becomes a law rather than a concept, total global corporate control will be completed, and the most specific biblical prophecy will be fulfilled.

The Church view of the Mark of the Beast is as vague as its approach to any doctrinal issue; the mark has something to do with the number 666 and will be the mark of Satan's followers. The monetary connection is virtually ignored, and the only purpose noted is that it is a sure ticket to a fiery hell. The Bible view leaves no doubt about its purpose, or its source; it will be required for every human on the planet to conduct any financial transaction. The mark is not the number 666, and there is no indication that mankind will be forced to take this mark. No single prophecy in the Bible is more clearly defined and easy to identify than the Mark of the Beast.

It must be strongly emphasized that the mark is 'not' the number 666; it is specifically noted that this number is the number of a man, and not the mark. Also, there is no indication that mankind will be forced to take this mark, but rather receive it, and that it is a necessity to buy or sell, for all mankind, at all levels of society. The Beast is not specifically identified, and the word "he" in these verses can be translated as "it". This Beast, and the ones preceding it, are considered as powers, not persons. The image, which somehow takes on a life-like presence, is a likeness, an icon or representation of that power.

The Important Points

• The Beast causes an inanimate object, or organization called "an image", to speak, and take on a life-like existence, and forces mankind to pay homage to this "image" under penalty of death. The word image is translated from the Greek word eikon, pronounced i-kone'; a likeness, i.e. (literally) statue, profile, or (figuratively) representation, resemblance. This shows that whatever this image is, it is some sort of representation of the Beast.

• The image, now causes all mankind to receive a mark, defined in the Greek as a "a scratch or etching", in or on their right hand, or their forehead.

• Without this form of identity, the authority of the Beast, or a number of the authority of the Beast, no one is allowed to buy or sell.

• That number is to be totaled, it is the number of the Beast, the number of a human being, and it is 666.

• The living, talking image is is the source of the mark, and has power to force loyalty to itself and death for refusal to worship it.

- The mark is used to control all commerce in all levels of society, and all those doing business must have this mark, or the authority, of the Beast.
- The mark is a something scratched, or etched into the skin, and not the number 666
- The implementation of the mark into the financial sector is "caused", not forced.

Can This Happen Now?

- Only isolated areas of commerce are not totally controlled by computers.
- The world is rapidly becoming a cashless global society.
- Only small portions of the total global monetary flow are in cash transactions.
- The terrorist threat has brought pressure to bear for high security and stricter identification requirements.
- Control of all global financial transactions is being tightened.
- National identification is not just being considered, it is being planned.
- Computers are now capable of voice recognition and speech duplication.
- The technology for implanting every human on the planet with global location and identification devices is on the market, and already cost effective.
- If this "mark" is a necessary aspect of doing business and moving through the society, there will be no need to force anyone to receive it. The only reference to anyone being forced into an action in this context is that those who would not worship the "image" of the beast should be killed.

The Deception of the Corporations and the Powerful Elite

♦ Revelation 18:23 And the light of a candle shall shine no more at all in thee; and the voice of the bridegroom and of the bride shall be heard no more at all in thee: for thy merchants were the great men of the earth; for by thy sorceries were all nations deceived.

Here, the source of the greatest deception in the history of mankind is solidly connected to big business, and the people who control and profit from it. Not alien invaders in UFOs, not Communism, not satanic cults, but the very entities that control virtually every aspect of human society, the corporate empires. Their total disregard for human welfare, and the very planet they occupy, should make that clear, but that is what makes the deception so insidious. They not only control the purse strings and the flow of essential goods and services through control of all major media sources, they also control the information that the world receives. They not only control the physical aspects of life, but the way the society thinks, thus assuring the deception will continue unnoticed and uncontrolled.

Corporate Personhood - Life to the Image

We are living in the age of "global commerce", about this most agree. We are also living at the beginning of an age of "global commercial control", about this, only few are aware. Capitalism, with all its trappings, is the dominant financial model for the entire world. Capitalism has no god, but it is money, the acquiring of it, and the steady increase of the bottom-line that it serves, and is completely dedicated to. Considering the Bible clearly states that total dedication to money, avarice, is the root of all evil, this means the world is serving, and dedicated to an entity, which is an anathema to the very nature of God. And, at the head of this entity, which the world serves, is the cold, immortal, all-powerful corporation.

The Aberrant Nature and Power of the Corporation

What is most disturbing about our capitalist-driven society is the sudden rise to power and prominence over almost every aspect of life by corporations. Merriam-Webster defines a corporation as 1 a obsolete : a group of merchants or traders united in a trade guild b : the municipal authorities of a town or city "2 :a body formed and authorized by law to act as a single person although constituted by one or more persons and legally endowed with various rights and duties including the capacity of succession."

The first corporation was formed in England as a tool to exploit the wealth of vast areas of the world they were colonizing in the 17th Century. As North America was colonized, corporations provided the huge amounts of capital the Monarchy needed to assert sovereignty and control over the colonies. Corporations at that time had a lifespan of a mere 20 years to accomplish their clearly stated goals with fixed capitalization. As a means of encouraging investment massive in risky foreign ventures, the Crown protected investors from legal, as well as financial, responsibility related to their investment, freeing them from any liability for the debts of the corporations. One of the basic principles of common law, the responsibility of the individual business investors, was dropped. It was the power of these corporations, in their attempt to dominate one of the basic staples of the colonies, tea, which sparked the American Revolution.

The Declaration of Independence freed citizens from not only British control over colonial government, but British corporations as well, and for a century after independence Americans kept tight control over corporate power. The early corporations were conceived as institutions serving the public's interest. There were only about 200 corporations operating in the US by the early 19th Century, which were not permitted to engage in the political process, nor were they allowed to own stock in other corporations. They were held to strict adherence to the public interest, and were severely punished, or had their charters revoked for failure to comply with the laws governing them.

This tight control and forced dedication to the public interest ended when the model for modern corporations came to life in 1886. In a strange ruling, or better phrased, the eventual strange outcome of a U. S. Supreme Court decision on the ruling in the Santa Clara County vs. Southern Pacific Railroads, the face of corporate power shifted dramatically. This simple dispute over fences bordering a railroad siding resulted in a radical transformation in the very nature of corporations, or more appropriately, they were given immortal life. In an incredible perversion of the 14th Amendment to the Constitution meant to insure the rights of slaves after the Civil War, the Supreme Court ruled that a private corporation was a actually a "natural person," and entitled to the same rights and privileges as any human being. It not only legally gave life to corporations; it fundamentally changed the United States and the world completely.

At this point we have revealed a little known, but not completely ignored reality about how a seemingly benign commercial entity actually given power equal to, and exceeding that of living human beings. It needs to be understood that this is not an unfounded theory, but a very solid fact based on clear evidence found in the public record. We present several sources that will show how relevant this concept is, and how corporations are now able to control every aspect of human life they choose. We cannot emphasize strongly enough that all who read these words thoroughly inform themselves of the extreme threat this reality presents.

Corporate Personhood Web Links
Corporate Personhood
http://en.wikipedia.org/wiki/Corporate_personhood
Corporate Personhood - Demeaning Our Bill of Rights
http://reclaimdemocracy.org/personhood/
Corporations Are Not Persons
http://www.nancho.net/corperson/cpnader.html
Project Censored - Corporate Personhood Challenged
http://www.projectcensored.org/publications/2004/13.html
The Santa Clara Blues Corporate Personhood versus Democracy
http://www.iiipublishing.com/afd/santaclara.html
POCLAD - Program on Corporations, Law and Democracy
http://www.poclad.org/
Women's International League for Peace and Freedom - Challenge Corporate Power
http://www.wilpf.org/section/campaign/CPOWER.htm
Resource Guide for the Commons
http://www.yesmagazine.org/18Commons/resourcescommons.html
CorpWatch
http://www.corpwatch.org/

Humanity Incorporated

A Guide to the Legal Mechanisms of Corporate Power
http://www.endgame.org/charter-legalmechanisms.html
U.S. Supreme Court - Santa Clara County v. Southern Pacific. RR (1886)
http://www.ratical.org/corporations/SCvSPR1886.html
Reclaim Democracy! Revoke Corporate Corruption of American Democracy
http://www.reclaimdemocracy.org/
Corporations Are Not Persons!
http://lotuscup.com/nothuman.htm
How can a corporation be legally considered a person?
http://www.straightdope.com/columns/030919.html

Corporations Have the Power of Speech

The Image Speaks

The prophecy about the image, which requires the mark for all financial transactions worldwide, is said to be given the power of speech after it is brought to life. This power was given to corporations by no less than a gross usurping of the free speech guaranteed to living human beings under the First Amendment to the Constitution. Now corporations not only have the same rights as living beings, they now can speak with the same force and rights of human beings. In a 1996 Supreme Court ruling they are even guaranteed the unfettered freedom to lie, like living human beings.

- A 1978 Supreme Court ruling enhanced the idea of corporate personhood by declaring that corporations had the free speech right to contribute funds to political causes.
- A 1996 a U.S. Appellate Court ruling struck down a Vermont law that would infringe on corporations' "negative" speech rights, and held it unconstitutional.

As with corporate personhood, corporate free speech is a little known, but not ignored reality. We have provided resources to give further insight into this rather strange concept.

Free Speech for Corporations Web Links

Corporations and Free Speech
http://www.thirdworldtraveler.com/Corporations/Corps_FreeSpeech.htmlFirst Amendment Follies
http://www.thirdworldtraveler.com/Corporations/FirstAmend_Follies.html
Corporations and Free Speech
http://multinationalmonitor.org/mm1998/98may/editorial.html
Negative Free Speech for Corporations
http://reclaimdemocracy.org/personhood/negative_free_speech_corporations.html
Now Corporations Claim The "Right To Lie"
http://www.commondreams.org/views03/0101-07.htm

A "Mark" Determines Who Can Buy or Sell

VeriChip™ - An Exact Fulfillment of Prophecy

A current trend now evidenced in our society is focusing on the new "terrorist threat and the corporate obsession with tracking commerce closely. The ever-present government thrust toward monitoring every move of its citizens makes global control over all finances more than just a remote possibility. Such a system is in place, and becoming a popular choice for the military, the medical profession, and virtually any person, or any organization that needs to track, or identify anything, anywhere.

The leader in global identification for financial purposes using human implants is Applied Digital Solutions. In October 2000, Applied Digital Solutions unveiled a skin-implantable chip called the Digital Angel. Now called "VeriChip™", this devise is a simple skin-implantable chip combining wireless technology, biosensor micro engineering, and heat-sensitive power regeneration. Utilizing a worldwide network of satellites and ground stations, anyone with the proper access can know who you are, where you are, where you have been, and how you are, at any time, anywhere in the world. The implanted chip can transmit data on the implantee's identification, precise location, and vital statistics, such as body temperature, blood sugar content, pulse rate, and even blood pressure.

Applied Digital Solutions and others have touted devices like VeriChip as the ideal technology for instantly monitoring medical patients, tracking livestock conditions and movements, managing the inventory and transit of manufactured goods, locating lost or stolen property, and to provide vital security for those vulnerable to kidnappers. With no alteration, this implant technology could easily become a global identification system used to control the entire world's financial and security needs.

On the VeriChip website you can find "Authorized Centers and Distributors", and a form to Pre-Register for your personal VeriChip, and this announcement that "The ChipMobile is on the Move! Watch for the Chip Mobile coming to your town!"

• You will also find this description of the device:

"VeriChip is a miniaturized, implantable radio frequency identification device (RFID) that has the potential to be used in a variety of security, financial, and other applications. About the size of a grain of rice, each VeriChip product contains a unique verification number and will be available in several formats. The verification number is captured by briefly passing a proprietary scanner over the VeriChip. A small amount of radio frequency energy passes from the scanner energizing the dormant VeriChip, which then emits a radio frequency signal transmitting the verification number."

- And this description of the "Security Identification" applications of the device:

"In the security field, the company is actively developing applications for VeriChip in a variety of security, defense, homeland security and secure-access applications. These opportunities include using VeriChip to control authorized access to government installations and private-sector buildings, nuclear power plants, national research laboratories, correctional facilities, and sensitive transportation resources. VeriChip can enhance airport security, airline security, cruise ship security, intelligent transportation and port congestion management. In these markets, VeriChip could function as a stand-alone, tamper-proof personal verification technology or it could operate in conjunction with other security technologies such as standard ID badges and advanced biometric devices (i.e. retina scanners, thumbprint readers or face recognition devices). The Company recently unveiled VeriPass and VeriTag, which will allow airport and port security personnel to link a VeriChip subscriber to his or her luggage (both during check-in and on the airplane), flight manifest logs and airline or law enforcement software databases. The concept of using VeriChip as a means for secure access could also be extended to include a range of consumer products such as PCs, laptops, cars, cell phones, and even homes and apartments."

- And this telling explanation of the "Financial Identification" applications of the device:

"In the financial arena, the company sees enormous, untapped potential for VeriChip as a personal verification technology that could help to curb identity theft and prevent fraudulent access to banking (especially via ATMs) and credit card accounts. VeriChip's tamper-proof, personal verification technology would provide banking and credit card customers with the added protection of knowing their accounts could not be accessed unless they themselves initiated -- and were physically present during -- the transaction."

- From VeriChip Personal Identification System - Frequently Asked Questions:

Question: How about other uses of VeriChip? Isn't it used for security screening?

Answer: We are promoting VeriChip as a universal means of identification. We expect it to be used in a variety of applications including financial and transportation security, residential and commercial building access, military and government security.

An Amazing Prophecy

There have been many theories about the Mark of the Beast, the most prominent being that it is some sort of implant. The connections this work has made have revealed an undiscovered link to a possible prophesized virus attack on the computer system controlling that mark. This not only verifies the financial connection to the mark but shows another effect it will have in last days.

The relationship between the Mark of the Beast and the VeriChip System could not be more obvious. An implantable microchip that can instantly identify you for financial verification anywhere in the world is exactly what the prophecy describes, and exactly what Applied Digital Solutions produces. Beyond the "Revelation 13" mention of the mark, it appears in the Revelation four other times. It is two of those appearances that provide what may well be a prophecy only possible in the past decade of internet growth, and the insidious practice of producing and infecting an uncounted number of computers with "viruses". The first one speaks of a "sore" related to the mark:

• Revelation 16: 2 And the first went, and poured out his vial upon the earth; and there fell a noisome and grievous sore upon the men which had the mark of the beast, and upon them which worshipped his image.

In this verse, at first glance, an angel pours something out of a vial and a smelly, (noisome), and painful sore breaks out on those who have the mark. Careful examination of two of the words in the verse could give some unexpected insight into what this verse may be describing.

• The word 'noisome' is translated from the word kakos, pronounced kak-os'a primary word; worthless (intrinsically, such; whereas GSN4190 properly refers to effects), i.e. (subjectively) depraved, or (objectively) injurious. Nothing about a malodor here, but considering this mark is all about finance, the concept of "worthless" has meaning in context if it disables the implant's ability to function, meaning that financial transactions could be halted, making the implant "worthless".

• The word 'grievous' is translated from the word poneros, pronounced pon-ay-ros'; hurtful, i.e. evil (properly, in effect or influence, and thus differing from GSN2556, which refers rather to essential character, as well as from GSN4550, which indicates degeneracy from original virtue); figuratively, calamitous; also (passively) ill, i.e. diseased; but especially (morally) culpable, i.e. derelict, vicious, facinorous; neuter (singular) mischief, malice, or (plural) guilt; masculine (singular) the devil, or (plural) sinners. It can be seen from this definition that this word grievous is not "physical" pain, but rather that there is a calamitous and evil "effect". If the implant is, in fact, disabled and no cash, checks, or credit cards are in use, the result could be very disrupting socially. If this implant replaces keys, ID badges, access to computers or secure areas, and other security measures, the effect would effectively shut down not only the economy, but virtually every aspect of life including transportation, utilities, medical services, as well as fire and police departments.

The word sore comes from the Greek word for ulcer, 'helkos', and a common cause for ulcers are viruses. It may only be a strange coincidence that the VeriChip implant is tied to computer technology, however it is a possibility that it may be disabled, and whatever is in the vial could cause a computer virus-like effect, but it is a very intriguing possibility. What would add even more weight to the concept that the implant may be disabled, would be some indication that there is actually an effect demonstrated that financial hardship is caused by the action of this substance the angel poured out of this vial. In two verses following this prophecy about this strange "sore" being inflicted on mankind, there is evidence that this is indeed the case:

• Revelation 16:10 And the fifth angel poured out his vial upon the seat of the beast; and his kingdom was full of darkness; and they gnawed their tongues for pain, 11 And blasphemed the God of heaven because of their pains and their sores, and repented not of their deeds.

• The words ' pain', in verse 10, and 'pains', in verse 11, are both taken from the Greek word ponos, pronounced pon'-os, from the base of GSN3993; toil, i.e. (by implication) anguish. Again we see this is not necessarily physical pain, but the root of this word reveals its origin, and provides clarity of context in this verse. GSN3993, the base for the word 'ponos' is penes, pronounced pen'-ace, from a primary peno (to toil for daily subsistence); starving, i.e. indigent. This would indicate that this "pain" they are vilifying God for, is actually the anguish they are experiencing from extreme poverty. Certainly relevant if the implant is actually disabled and economic chaos results as there will be millions, perhaps even billions, of people with no way or place to buy or obtain food.

A complete reading of this chapter will show that God is not simply tormenting the human race, but that this is in fact quite similar to the plagues of Egypt God inflicted to persuade Pharaoh to release the nation of Israel from his grip. In verse 9 we see the phrase "..and they repented not to give him glory." and in verse 11 this is repeated, "..and they repented not to give him glory." Rather than change their minds, they curse God. This would indicate that though not mentioned, there is some form of communication between humanity and God. And, it would seem that mankind is being offered an opportunity to "surrender", but is repeatedly rejecting those offers in this prophecy.

The Realities

It is, of course, impossible to get the full picture of these events from the few verses that mention the mark, but certain aspects of those events can be understood.

• A condition, not specified, causes mankind, worldwide, to need to receive a "mark" in their hand or forehead for the purpose of conducting financial transactions; buying or selling. Such transactions are not possible without the mark.

• A technology, now existing, and actively promoted, involving the implanting of a device in the hand or the forehead, is designed to be used for security and financial identification applications worldwide.

• The Bible lists a series of actions designed to force humanity to recognize the sovereignty of God over the planet, and in one action there is a substance released that causes a "worthless" and "calamitous" effect on mankind relating directly to the mark.

• During this series of actions, mankind also vilifies God for the anguish of poverty he is inflicted on those with the mark.

In this modern age with the growing dependence on not only electronic finances, but a very definite rush toward the total globalization of commerce, the following scenario could be quite possible, and a logical explanation for the true meaning of these prophecies.

To Set the Stage:

• With the current continuing focus on the global "Terrorist Threat", and the implementation of versions of the U.S. Patriot Act worldwide, security is becoming an obsession.

• The need to track all financial transactions worldwide to control the "Terrorist Threat" is being used to make such tracking a distinct reality.

• Global "Free Trade" policies are the norm rather than the exception, made possible by satellite, and high speed worldwide communications technologies. This makes a global financial network not only possible, but a certainty.

• Society is rapidly moving toward a "cashless" financial reality with credit, debit, and even social service, (food stamp, etc.) cards becoming the preferred means of financial transaction.

• Identity theft, forgery, robbery, and an unending and ever-changing flood of fraudulent schemes designed to steal money, make cash impractical, even plastic is vulnerable to criminal activity.

• A system such as VeriChip is the perfect solution for all these problems and an inevitable choice to provide the ultimate in global monitoring, security access, and financial protection against fraud. It is cheap, easy, and can be completely implemented now.

• If all commerce is dependent on having this implant then there will be no need to "force" anyone to receive it, anymore that anyone is forced to have a driver's license. This will "force" those not wishing to receive the implant into the underground economy, and seriously affect quality of life issues, but it will not "kill" them.

The Result:

• With the above realities being a part of our rush-blindly-to-the-future culture, it is easy to see that any number of events could spark the worldwide use of a VeriChip or similar implant system in the area of financial transaction and security identification.

• The implementation of such a system would create critical dependence on the reliability of Radio Frequency Identification, (RFID), Global Positioning System, (GPS), and Electronics Funds Transfer, (EFT) technology, all connected to a simple implanted chip. This dependence would extend from the grocery store to the gas station, from the drug store to the emergency room. If it requires monetary transaction or proper identification, it will likely be dependent on these vulnerable systems. Everything in the loop; the implant, the scanner that reads it, the transmitter that sends the signal to the satellite, the station controlling the satellite, the satellite itself, the receiver on the ground, the institution controlling the finances or the security agency verifying the identification, all ground transmission lines, and everything all the way back to the entity trying to verify the information, must be working perfectly. One glitch in the loop and the entire system is clogged.

• The Bible makes it clear that humanity will resist the return of the rightful King to his planetary throne. It is clear that humanity will not recognize the return of Jesus and will eventually gather a massive human army against him.

• In the Bible, in the 16th chapter of the Revelation, there is evidence that certain strange plagues are brought upon the planet, and that mankind is given a chance, during these events, to recognize and accept its only true world leader.

• For the rightful heir to the global throne, a logical way of disarming and crippling a world so dependent on such vulnerable and very human technology, would be to disable that technology. Rendering the implant system useless along any point in its path would effectively render the financial holdings of all implantees inaccessible, and their personal value as worthless.

• The result of such a breakdown would be that neither the poor, nor the rich, could buy food, gas, or any other commodities needed for even basic survival. There is no way to determine how transportation of goods and people, police and fire services, health and welfare entities, or government and military organizations would be effected. But considering these all depend on humans with security identification, and the ability to be where they need to be, the result , when added to a useless economic system, would be total chaos.

• The plague of sores on mankind spoken of in Revelation 16 refers to a worthless, evil, and calamitous effect on those having the "mark"'

• Revelation 16 also refers to a vilification of God by those having the "mark" for the anguish of poverty they are suffering.

• We believe the concepts just expressed give strong backing to a possibility that the angel pouring out the vial in Revelations 16:2 will disable the mark / implant, causing worldwide poverty, in just days, and a breakdown in every aspect of life even remotely computerized. The result would be total chaos, especially in the developed world so dependent on technology.

   The government seems unconcerned about privacy issues, advertising abuse, and the obvious potential for population control and, in fact, is certain to be the largest individual customer for the system. The FDA is instituting programs to implant livestock to monitor movement and animal condition to better insure meat quality, while following the movement of military personnel and equipment will be greatly enhanced by service wide use of the system. The government is also moving forward on insuring that GPS technology is present in all wireless communication devices. All cell phones sold in the United States were equipped with advanced wireless tracking technology by the end of 2002.

   When confronted with the obvious privacy concerns, Applied Digital Solutions CEO, Richard Sullivan, stated, "This whole privacy issue is on the table, I would hope that, being part of a free, democratic system, that you have a government that wants to protect people." Sullivan failed to mention that the device is being sold internationally and gave no explanation of how non-democratic governments, who give little thought to protecting their people, would use the technology. Chief project scientist Dr. Peter Zhou, who seems to view the device as a Utopian dream come true stated that Digital Angel "will be a connection from yourself to the electronic world. It will be your guardian, protector. It will bring good things to you. We will be a hybrid of electronic intelligence and our own soul."

   You be the judge of whether this is part of the conspiracy to control the world's population or simply a bizarre and very timely coincidence. The company and the government say it isn't a control system in production, but how credible are the past promises from government and big business? In these times of uncertainty and heightened security worldwide, how easy would it be for that denial to change?

Signs of the Times

♦ "And ye shall hear of wars and rumours of wars: see that ye be not troubled: for all these things must come to pass, but the end is not yet. For nation shall rise against nation, and kingdom against kingdom: and there shall be famines, and pestilences, and earthquakes, in divers places. All these are the beginning of sorrows. Then shall they deliver you up to be afflicted, and shall kill you: and ye shall be hated of all nations for my name's sake. And then shall many be offended, and shall betray one another, and shall hate one another. And many false prophets shall rise, and shall deceive many. And because iniquity shall abound, the love of many shall wax cold. (**Matthew 24:6 - 12**)

No time in history more accurately reflects this and other biblical descriptions of the end times. No entity has more power over human affairs than the global corporate reality in these times. Consider these comparisons:

Jesus on the pursuit of wealth:
♦ "And again I say unto you, It is easier for a camel to go through the eye of a needle, than for a rich man to enter into the kingdom of God." (**Matthew 19:24**)
The whole concept of corporate function is focused on wealth at all cost. By law, corporate officers are required to consider the financial gain of their investors above any, and all other considerations.
♦ "For the love of money is the root of all evil: which while some coveted after, they have erred from the faith, and pierced themselves through with many sorrows." (**1 Timothy 6:10**)
Money, and the unwavering pursuit of it, is the root of all corporate function, law, and structure.

When asked by a ruler what he needed to do to live forever, Jesus gave this answer:
♦ "... Yet lackest thou one thing: sell all that thou hast, and distribute unto the poor, and thou shalt have treasure in heaven: and come, follow me." (**Luke 18:22**)
Such a rash action will only be found in the very worst nightmares of those who worship capitalism and feed at the corporate trough. Surely there are those amongst the rich elite who are benevolent, but none would consider giving everything they own to the poor.

This is the financial model of the first church, as inspired by the Spirit of God:
♦ "And all that believed were together, and had all things common; And sold their possessions and goods, and parted them to all men, as every man had need." (**Acts 2:44 - 45**)

The Doctrines of Men

The concept of the sharing of common wealth amongst all men is an anathema to the corporate world, and vigorously opposed by all governmental entities embracing capitalism, the environment that nurtures corporate power.

The rush for riches is dealt with very clearly in scripture:
♦ "Lay not up for yourselves treasures upon earth, where moth and rust doth corrupt, and where thieves break through and steal:" (**Matthew 6:19**),
♦ "So is he that layeth up treasure for himself, and is not rich toward God." (**Luke 12:21**), and:
♦ "For where your treasure is, there will your heart be also." (**Matthew 6:21**}
The very nature of investing in corporations is the accumulation of wealth on this Earth.

The Bible is also clear about where one should strive to accumulate wealth:
♦ "But lay up for yourselves treasures in heaven, where neither moth nor rust doth corrupt, and where thieves do not break through nor steal:" (**Matthew 6:20**)
In the capitalistic corporate world such a concept is jokingly known as "pie in the sky".

Through John the Apostle, Jesus reveals that a great world entity will give life to an icon that will have the power to kill humans and exercise worldwide financial control.
♦ "And he had power to give life unto the image of the beast, that the image of the beast should both speak, and cause that as many as would not worship the image of the beast should be killed." (**Revelation 13:15**)
Corporations, the icons and proudly held representations of Capitalism, the world's strongest power, which is defended and promoted by the world's greatest militaries, have the same rights and powers as living human beings.

Jesus also revealed that this icon of the great power would have the power of speech (Revelation 13:15, above)
Corporations now have not only the right of free speech; corporations have the right to misrepresent the truth, while exercising that right of free speech.

Jesus tells John that this living, speaking, and very powerful icon will institute a form of control over all financial transactions worldwide, using some type of mark that is given to all humans.
♦ "And he causeth all, both small and great, rich and poor, free and bond, to receive a mark in their right hand, or in their foreheads: And that no man might buy or sell, save he that had the mark, or the name of the beast, or the number of his name. (**Revelation 13:16 - 17**)
Implantable biochip identification technology is rapidly growing as the preferred choice of security in this age of the "Terrorist Threat". Use of this

96

technology is openly being considered as a perfect solution to safe and efficient financial transactions. Global Positioning Technology, GPS, which is the means of conveying the transfer of the information required for this technology, is in place now. It is already used in a number of commercial applications, and can be brought to bear on a global scale to facilitate such global control of all financial transactions immediately.

After the great power is defeated, Jesus reveals that the true source of the deception of humanity has always been the great merchants of the world. (Revelation 18:23)

Global corporations are the "great merchants" of the world. An interesting aspect of the prophecies described in Revelation 18, speak of the center of this, the financial activity, as being Babylon, found in modern day Iraq. Constitutional experts, who have reviewed the new Iraqi constitution, say it will turn the financial infrastructure of the nation into a virtual Corporate Disneyland.

The Satanic Reality

A Serious Caveat

I would like to preface this most important writing with a very serious warning. The concepts contained herein are not meant, in any way, to diminish the danger of the horrendous creature about which it is written. Satan is the most dangerous entity ever to threaten mankind, and if not stopped, he will annihilate the race and destroy the planet we inhabit. No greater peril has, does, or ever will confront the human race.

This writing is intended to enlighten, by putting the threat into proper perspective, and empower those who perceive the true threat with the only defense possible against the power this terrible beast possesses.

♦ **I Peter 5:8** Be sober, be vigilant; because your adversary the devil, as a roaring lion, walketh about, seeking whom he may devour:

The Power of Satan

Satan is touted by the church to be the most powerful entity in the human reality. The constant warnings about Satan's ability to control the minds of humans, and the power he supposedly wields over them to do his bidding, constantly flow like a torrent of terror from the pulpit. The "hell fire and brimstone" reflects, perhaps, no more than the overblown attitude of Satan himself. An objective search of scripture of just how powerful he is will reveal a surprising conclusion. The presence of Satan in scripture is rare, and he is portrayed as a classic example of failure. He has power, but not in the way the church has long claimed.

The church warns of his power to enter your mind, and even your body, without you even knowing it. He is represented as having the ability to actually control your thoughts and actions. To the contrary, the church teaches Jesus can only do this if 'you' decide 'you' want him to. The accepted doctrine is that Satan has complete control of the planet, and his presence is pointed out in everything the church disagrees with, any time in history, and anywhere in the world.

The Power of Jesus

Little, if anything, is ever said about Jesus having anything to do with the worldly affairs of men, except his presence within the church, which, of course, gives them authority over their followers, and justifies demanding money to pay the expenses of that particular church. They admit Jesus "will" rule, though they are vague about where, even though the Bible makes it clear that Jesus will rule on this planet, not in some ethereal place called "heaven".

What this has all led to is the creation of an evil Wizard of Oz-like caricature being used to scare the flock into submission and servitude to, and financial support of, the church. This is a church that changes the teachings of Jesus to suit its own doctrine. It creates a religion filled with ritual, which origins are in the very practices of ancient worship to the false gods Jesus, as the God of Israel, condemned.

Is this fear of Satan justified, or is it smoke and mirrors which actually hides the true deception of this master of deception? While the church is raging about the Devil trying to steal hearts, minds, and money from them, he is hiding behind the perfect image they have so generously provided for him. He is grateful for the image that conceals his true deception so clearly described in the Bible.

Who is Lucifer?

To give a simple example of the ignorance the biblical "authorities" have about scripture is the word "Lucifer". Few, who have had even limited exposure to any Bible-based religions, do not understand, though mistakenly, that this is one of the names of Satan. But, even rarer is the number of those who know the word "Lucifer" was never in the original text of the Book of Isaiah. It does appear in the King James Bible, although incorrectly, but, this is the only time the word appears in the Bible.

♦ **Isaiah 14:12** How art thou fallen from heaven, O Lucifer, son of the morning! how art thou cut down to the ground, which didst weaken the nations!

This word was added by the translators of the King James Bible and is of a Latin origin, not the original Hebrew. The term Lucifer comes not from the Hebrew or the Greek Septuagint translation, but from the 4th Century AD Latin translation of this verse: "quomodo cecidisti de caelo *lucifer* qui mane oriebaris corruisti in terram qui vulnerabas gentes."

The term *lucifer* in Latin was the name for Venus, the morning star. The same word is used in other places in the Latin Vulgate to translate Hebrew terms that mean "bright," especially associated with the sky:

From the Hebrew, Strong's Exhaustive Concordance renders the definition of the original word 'heylel', pronounced hay-lale', as: the morning star: (in the sense of brightness); (Title referring to the king of Babylon). A reading of this verse in context will also show that it is doubtful this verse is even referring to Satan, but rather, to a man.

Many point to the "morning star" in Isaiah as a direct reference to Satan and proof of his connection to this verse. The following verse shows that this term is not exclusive to Satan, but even used by Jesus as a personal description.

♦ **Revelation 22:16** I, Jesus, have sent My angel to testify these things to you over the churches. I am the Root and the Offspring of David, the bright and Morning Star."

Satan's Impact on Humanity

There are only a few instances in the Bible where Satan is described as specifically having a significant impact on the affairs of humans:

♦ **Genesis 3:1** Now the serpent was more subtil than any beast of the field which the Lord God had made. And he said unto the woman, Yea, hath God said, Ye shall not eat of every tree of the garden?

The temptation of Eve by the serpent, although not specifically stated, is believed to be Satan.

♦ **1 Chronicles 21:1** And Satan stood up against Israel, and provoked David to number Israel.

This reference is only a passing reference concerning the census of Israel and seems to have no great impact on mankind.

♦ **Job 1:6** Now there was a day when the sons of God came to present themselves before the Lord, and Satan came also among them.

This is the beginning of Satan's challenge to God to test the faith of Job. It should be noted that Satan's attempt to prove Job was weak failed.

♦ **Zechariah 3:1** And he shewed me Joshua the high priest standing before the angel of the LORD, and Satan standing at his right hand to resist him. 2 And the LORD said unto Satan, The LORD rebuke thee, O Satan; even the LORD that hath chosen Jerusalem rebuke thee: is not this a brand plucked out of the fire?

♦ **5. Matthew 4:1** Then was Jesus led up of the spirit into the wilderness to be tempted of the devil.

Here Satan is trying to turn Jesus from the Father while he is in a very weak state. Again he failed.

♦ **Luke 13:2** And supper being ended, the devil having now put into the heart of Judas Iscariot, Simon's son, to betray him;

Satan uses Judas to betray Jesus, which eventually leads to his death and resurrection. This sets the stage for the victory over death, which brings salvation, and guarantees inheritance into the royal Family of God to all mankind. By helping mankind, a race Satan has been deceiving and intends to destroy, he again fails.

• In the Revelation to John the Apostle the deception of humanity in the last days is detailed over many chapters. It is accepted that this deception and its consequences are from Satan. In the end, Satan fails.

♦ **Revelation 12:7** And there was war in heaven: Michael and his angels fought against the dragon; and the dragon fought and his angels, 8 And prevailed not; neither was their place found any more in heaven. 9. And the great dragon was cast out, that old serpent, called the Devil, and Satan, which deceiveth the whole world: he was cast out into the earth, and his angels were cast out with him.

Here a war in the sky is described and Satan is defeated; another failure. Many think this is the final battle after the last days, but this is contradicted by further disclosures in the Revelation, as well as in a statement by Jesus:

♦ **Revelation 12:12** Therefore rejoice, ye heavens, and ye that dwell in them. Woe to the inhabiters of the earth and of the sea! for the devil is come down unto you, having great wrath, because he knoweth that he hath but a short time.

Since Jesus is on the throne, on the planet, it is obvious Satan will not be allowed to torment mankind. If this is speaking of a "final" battle in the end days, it is completely out of context since the description of tribulation continues for several chapters. The following verses show what the true end of Satan's control over the planet will be:

♦ **Revelation 20:1** And I saw an angel come down from heaven, having the key of the bottomless pit and a great chain in his hand. 2 And he laid hold on the dragon, that old serpent, which is the Devil, and Satan, and bound him a thousand years,

This verse clearly shows that the battle in the sky described in Revelation 12:7 above, is a past event, as Satan certainly would not be able to continue his deception of mankind while he is bound in the bottomless pit. The eyewitness testimony of Jesus shows positively that the battle described in Revelation 12:7 is a past, not a future event.

♦ **Luke 10:18** And he said unto them, I beheld Satan as lightning fall from heaven.

If Jesus saw him fall from the sky, this happened over 2000 years ago and certainly not in the future.

Of the few times Satan is mentioned as having any significant impact on, or influence over, the affairs of mankind he fails miserably in all but one, the temptation of Eve. Considering his actions after this success, which helped to save mankind, even this becomes a failure. He tries, he fails, and he tries again. Considering the condition of the world in this precarious age, one might conclude that he is successful now.

What most do not realize is that by the sacrifice Christ performed for all humanity, he has lost and is now only secretly preparing the human race to fight for him against its own creator. In truth, he has generously written the case for prosecution against himself. In the testimony before the highest court in the universe, which convicts him, will be the ultimate object lesson for mankind that will guide it and keep it safe, free, and progressive forever.

The Real Danger from Satan

The consistent failure of Satan should in no way diminish the threat he poses to mankind. The following two verses contain the identification of the deceiver, and the way he will deceive the world:

Here it is clearly stated Satan will deceive the nations:
♦ **Revelation 20:2** And he laid hold on the dragon, that old serpent, which is the Devil, and Satan, and bound him a thousand years, 3 And cast him into the bottomless pit, and shut him up, and set a seal upon him, that he should deceive the nations no more, till the thousand years should be fulfilled: and after that he must be loosed a little season.

And, this verse clearly connects global corporate power to that deception:
♦ **Revelation 18 23** And the light of a candle shall shine no more at all in thee; and the voice of the bridegroom and of the bride shall be heard no more at all in thee: for thy merchants were the great men of the earth; for by thy sorceries were all nations deceived.

This is the connection between big business and the deception of the nations that positively ascribes that deception directly to Satan.

Knowledge Gives Advantage

The most serious omission from the pulpit is how he manages to deceive the world. A more thorough examination is found in the next section of this work on the true deception, but the Bible is clear that knowledge is the key. Logic tells the wise that there are more ways to influence the affairs of men than direct manipulation. If Satan can control all aspects of human life, from birth to death, he can control the attitudes of society.

♦ **2 Corinthians 2:10** To whom ye forgive any thing, I forgive also: for if I forgave any thing, to whom I forgave it, for your sakes forgave I it in the person of Christ; 11 Lest Satan should get an advantage of us: for we are not ignorant of his devices.

• devices – noema, pronounced no'-ay-mah; a perception, i.e. purpose, or (by implication) the intellect, disposition, itself:

Was Satan a High Angel?

The following verse provides considerable doubt about whether Satan actually was the high angel he is considered to have been:

♦ **John 8; 44**. Ye are of your father the devil, and the lusts of your father ye will do. He was a murderer from the beginning, and abode not in the truth, because there is no truth in him. When he speaketh a lie, he speaketh of his own: for he is a liar, and the father of it.

Is There Protection?

Despite the great power ascribed to Satan, scripture makes it clear that just standing up to him is sufficient to make him flee.

♦ **James 4:7** Submit yourselves therefore to God. Resist the devil, and he will flee from you.

Resist comes from the Greek word 'anthistemi'. pronounced anth-is'-tay-mee; to stand against, i.e. oppose:

The Church

The Church View:

A church is a building that is used for assembly of members of that church, which teaches and practices doctrines, generally determined, and enforced by a master religious organization. The function of the individual church varies according to the edicts of the controlling religious leaders, but follows general guidelines. The indoctrination of the membership in the beliefs of the master religion is a prime function, with absolute loyalty strongly emphasized. This is accomplished with weekly meetings during which the membership is indoctrinated in and conditioned to follow the rules of the religion by a leader variously called a pastor, priest, or minister.

Members are expected to pay a certain percentage of their income to maintain the church building, pay the salaries and living expenses of the church employees, and other costs related to the promotion and functions of the master religion. Seldom is even a small percentage of church income and effort used to serve the community in which the church is situated, or the world in general. Most civic projects are done to present a token image of charity, which is aimed at attracting new members to increase the power of the church in size and financial holdings.

The Bible View:

A group of like-minded people who live in a communal setting and sacrifice all physical belongings to support a work totally devoted to charity. There is a staff, whose job is to feed and clothe the poor and infirmed, and many have the power to perform miracles. One basic law, love for one another, is the guiding principle. Pompous appearance, righteous pronouncements, and the advertising of charitable acts are condemned. There is no command to support any building based organization whose purpose is to serve only the interests of those members accepted into the membership. Pastors, pulpits, and pews were not mentioned, and neither weekly meetings, nor any other scheduled meetings were held or commanded. Those called out of society and into the first church donated all their earthly goods to the group as a whole and it was clearly stated none of the called were in need of anything.

Virtually nothing, which is accepted practice in the modern church, can either be found or supported in scripture, from the building the church is located in to the methods used to support that church. Neither the collection plate, the enforced gathering on Sunday, the open prayer, the support for political candidates, the party behind the pulpit, nor the pulpit itself bear any resemblance to the practice of the first church. Miracles, prophecy, and healing were common amongst the members of the first church.

What Is Religion?

The word religion appears only 4 times in the Bible, three of those times in direct reference to the religion of the Jews. The one time it refers to religion in general is in this verse:

James 1:27 Pure religion and undefiled before God and the Father is this, To visit the fatherless and widows in their affliction, and to keep himself unspotted from the world.

What is the Church?

Does the above verse sound like the standard practice of today's Christian churches or does it sound more like this verse?

♦ " Now I beseech you, brethren, mark them which cause divisions and offences contrary to the doctrine which ye have learned; and avoid them. 18 For they that are such serve not our Lord Jesus Christ, but their own belly; and by good words and fair speeches deceive the hearts of the simple." (**Romans 16:17**)

What Was Peter's Commission?

After the resurrection, Jesus confronted Peter, and with triple emphasis, gave him a very simple and specific command, to feed the people.

♦ **John 21:14** This is now the third time that Jesus shewed himself to his disciples, after that he was risen from the dead. 15 So when they had dined, Jesus saith to Simon Peter, Simon, son of Jonas, lovest thou me more than these? He saith unto him, Yea, Lord; thou knowest that I love thee. He saith unto him, Feed my lambs. 16 He saith to him again the second time, Simon, son of Jonas, lovest thou me? He saith unto him, Yea, Lord; thou knowest that I love thee. He saith unto him, Feed my sheep. 17 He saith unto him the third time, Simon, son of Jonas, lovest thou me? Peter was grieved because he said unto him the third time, Lovest thou me? And he said unto him, Lord, thou knowest all things; thou knowest that I love thee. Jesus saith unto him, Feed my sheep.

The word "feed" is taken from two different words in these verses. In verses 15 and 17 the word translated is bosko, pronounced bos'-ko; to pasture; by extension to, fodder; reflexively, to graze. In verse 16 it is taken from poimaino, pronounced poy-mah'-ee-no; to tend as a shepherd of (figuratively, supervisor). Therefore, the commission is to feed and lead, with double emphasis on the directive to literally feed the followers. Does this not clearly indicate that Jesus clearly chose Peter as the founder of the first church, and is it not obvious that this would also be the focus of the church?

• Helping the poor and indigent is at the very core of the first church's focus and practices.

The First Church

The first chapter of Acts, which is actually the second part of the Book of Luke, details the first actions of the first church. Jesus began the formation of the first church before his crucifixion as can be well established from the gospels. The beginning of Acts shows that this book is details the final actions of Jesus until he was taken up:

♦ **Acts 1:1** The former treatise have I made, O Theophilus, of all that Jesus began both to do and teach, 2 Until the day in which he was taken up, after that he through the Holy Ghost had given commandments unto the apostles whom he had chosen: 3 To whom also he shewed himself alive after his passion by many infallible proofs, being seen of them forty days, and speaking of the things pertaining to the kingdom of God:

The next verses refer to the directive that the apostles and disciples were to wait for a special transfer of spiritual energy to be imparted to them after his ascension:

♦ **Acts 1:4** And, being assembled together with them, commanded them that they should not depart from Jerusalem, but wait for the promise of the Father, which, saith he, ye have heard of me. 5. For John truly baptized with water; but ye shall be baptized with the Holy Ghost not many days hence. 6. When they therefore were come together, they asked of him, saying, Lord, wilt thou at this time restore again the kingdom to Israel? 7 And he said unto them, It is not for you to know the times or the seasons, which the Father hath put in his own power. 8 But ye shall receive power, after that the Holy Ghost is come upon you: and ye shall be witnesses unto me both in Jerusalem, and in all Judaea, and in Samaria, and unto the uttermost part of the earth.

In the next three verses Jesus is beamed aboard a cloud as the apostles have a very close encounter and are told that Jesus would return in the same cloud he just boarded.

♦ **Acts 1:9** And when he had spoken these things, while they beheld, he was taken up; and a cloud received him out of their sight. 10. And while they looked stedfastly toward heaven as he went up, behold, two men stood by them in white apparel; 11. Which also said, Ye men of Galilee, why stand ye gazing up into heaven? this same Jesus, which is taken up from you into heaven, shall so come in like manner as ye have seen him go into heaven.

After the ascension, the group returns to wait for the promise:

♦ **Acts 1:12** Then returned they unto Jerusalem from the mount called Olivet, which is from Jerusalem a sabbath day's journey. 13. And when they were come in, they went up into an upper room, where abode both Peter, and James, and John, and Andrew, Philip, and Thomas, Bartholomew, and Matthew, James the son of Alphaeus, and Simon Zelotes, and Judas the brother of James.

The Spirit of God Enters Mankind and the Miracles Begin:
♦ **Acts 2:1**. And when the day of Pentecost was fully come, they were all with one accord in one place. 2. And suddenly there came a sound from heaven as of a rushing mighty wind, and it filled all the house where they were sitting. 3. And there appeared unto them cloven tongues like as of fire, and it sat upon each of them. 4. And they were all filled with the Holy Ghost, and began to speak with other tongues, as the Spirit gave them utterance. 5. And there were dwelling at Jerusalem Jews, devout men, out of every nation under heaven. 6. Now when this was noised abroad, the multitude came together, and were confounded, because that every man heard them speak in his own language.

The Communal Church

The church establishes a communal lifestyle:
♦ **Acts 2:43** And fear came upon every soul: and many wonders and signs were done by the apostles. 44. And all that believed were together, and had all things common; 45. And sold their possessions and goods, and parted them to all men, as every man had need. 46. And they, continuing daily with one accord in the temple, and breaking bread from house to house, did eat their meat with gladness and singleness of heart,

Communal living is an established church practice:
♦ **Acts 4:**32 And the multitude of them that believed were of one heart and of one soul: neither said any of them that ought of the things which he possessed was his own; but they had all things common. 33. And with great power gave the apostles witness of the resurrection of the Lord Jesus: and great grace was upon them all. 34. Neither was there any among them that lacked: for as many as were possessors of lands or houses sold them, and brought the prices of the things that were sold, 35. And laid them down at the apostles' feet: and distribution was made unto every man according as he had need. 36. And Joses, who by the apostles was surnamed Barnabas, (which is, being interpreted, the son of consolation,) a Levite, and of the country of Cyprus, 37. Having land, sold it, and brought the money, and laid it at the apostles' feet.

Communal honesty is a serious matter:
♦ **Acts 5:1**. But a certain man named Ananias, with Sapphira his wife, sold a possession, 2. And kept back part of the price, his wife also being privy to it, and brought a certain part, and laid it at the apostles' feet. 3. But Peter said, Ananias, why hath Satan filled thine heart to lie to the Holy Ghost, and to keep back part of the price of the land? 4. Whiles it remained, was it not thine own? and after it was sold, was it not in thine own power? why hast thou conceived this thing in thine heart? thou hast not lied unto men, but unto God. 5. And Ananias hearing these words fell down, and gave up the ghost: and great fear came on all them that heard these things. 6. And the young men

106

arose, wound him up, and carried him out, and buried him. 7. And it was about the space of three hours after, when his wife, not knowing what was done, came in. 8. And Peter answered unto her, Tell me whether ye sold the land for so much? And she said, Yea, for so much. 9. Then Peter said unto her, How is it that ye have agreed together to tempt the Spirit of the Lord? behold, the feet of them which have buried thy husband are at the door, and shall carry thee out. 10. Then fell she down straightway at his feet, and yielded up the ghost: and the young men came in, and found her dead, and, carrying her forth, buried her by her husband.

Constantine's Church

Constantine became Emperor of western Rome after Diocletian abdicated in 305 AD. Under Diocletian, 284-305 AD, the Christian faith suffered its worst persecution, but had not been eradicated. Up to this time paganism played an essential role in life and government and religion was considered an area within the governments rule. Constantine was sympathetic to Christianity and tolerant to diversity in religion, but his conversion to Christianity after his rise to power was not due to true religious zeal. Christianity was a more effective way of accomplishing goals his rivals failed to reach under paganism. It was certainly politically advantageous for him to convert. Soon he was not only the head of Rome, but also the head of Christianity. He found that if he portrayed himself as God's appointed Emperor he could accomplish more than claiming himself to be God. What he did in government was God's will, and of course by claiming to be chosen by God, he was a natural as head of the Church.

After solidifying his position to gain complete control of the western portion of the empire in 312, he instituted the Edict of Milan, a "Magna Carta of religious liberty," which eventually changed the Empire's religion and put Christianity on an equal footing with paganism. Almost overnight the position of the Church was reversed from persecuted to legal and accepted. Constantine began to rely on the church for support, and it on him for protection. The Church and the Empire formed an alliance, which remains to this day. Very rapidly, the laws and policies of the Empire and the doctrine of the Church became one with Constantine as the interpreter of both law and policy.

Through a series of Universal Councils, he eliminated dissent and dissenters, changed holy days, and outlawed the Sabbath. The greatest effect he had was destroying any book in the accepted biblical works, (over 80% of the total), he felt did not fit within his concept of Christianity. He completely altered doctrine without regard to biblical edict, set up a church hierarchy of his own design, and established a set of beliefs and practices, which are the basis for all mainstream Bible-based churches. The separation of the Protestants and the Roman Church caused a physical split, but the beliefs and practices established by Constantine remained almost identical. Very little has changed since the 4th century Councils changed the face of Christianity.

An Inspired Church?

In light of the realities outlined above some serious questions need to be asked, and answered.

- Was Constantine, a Roman emperor who embraced pagan religion for years after his Christian "conversion", given a mandate from God to completely change almost every aspect of the church Jesus established?
- Did God inspire Constantine to denounce and criminalize doctrine established in scripture?
- Was it God's will that the Emperor Constantine should blend Christianity with a pagan religion, which God had clearly condemned and outlawed?
- Did God guide a despotic king, with a prime motivation was to firmly establish the "Divine Right of Kings", to translate the Bible into an obscure language of the elite that kept it from the common man?
- Is there any justification that allows the church to ignore clear and specific biblical doctrines and practices?
- Does it please God that the church teaches and practices doctrine that is completely contrary to scripture?
- Is it acceptable to Jesus that churches teach isolationism and prejudice, and are concerned more about the design of their buildings and the size of their Sunday attendance, than the number of poor and indigent people they serve?

If one can answer any of the above questions in the affirmative then this book will be more useful as a paperweight, than a source of knowledge.

If the these questions lead one to a conclusion that the origins of our modern church are not divinely inspired but the result of human edict then this question has been answered:

♦ "And why call ye me, Lord, Lord, and do not the things which I say?" (Luke 6:46)

The Bible of the Church

The Bible is the most widely distributed book in history, with over 5 billion in circulation, and over 100 million sold every year. There are no figures about how often it is read or quoted from in churches, but certainly it must be the most quoted book in history. As overwhelming as these numbers are, very little has changed concerning the information known about what the Bible actually says, despite the centuries it has been in the public domain. (In 1536, William Tyndale was burned at the stake for translating and printing the holy book in English.) This can be attributed to many factors, but two reasons stand out prominently. One very obvious reason is the rather unique language in the King James Bible prevents English speaking readers form having a clear

108

understanding of the context of this rather extensive book. Another more complicated reason is the doctrinal interpretation of the Catholic Church and its spin-off religions generally known as Protestant churches.

Through the centuries the strict conditioning of members of the "Christian" church, by its leaders, has been constant and almost all doctrine and practice of this church is seldom ever questioned. Any such questioning is strictly forbidden and almost always results in castigation, censure, or expulsion from the church. Close examination reveals that there is good reason for this as the very existence of the church is threatened by any objective research into the book it claims as the foundation for its authority.

This book lists the names of hundreds of writings known as the "lost books" of the Bible; those books associated with the Bible, but not included in it. One must make a personal judgment about the authenticity of those books, but to condemn all books not included in the King James Bible as uninspired is to accept the Emperor Constantine and the leaders of the early church he founded as direct representatives of God. This book only uses one ancient writing, the Book of Enoch, which is not included in the Bible, for its clarification on certain realities about the flood and demons.

The Book Used in This Work

The Authorized King James Bible, the King James Bible without the Apocrypha, is the book used for all references in this book other than the ones just mentioned. Many do not know that the Apocrypha books were actually included in the King James translation until the Synod of Dordrecht held in Holland removed them in 1618. There was also a "Translators Preface" and a "Dedicatory Letter from the Translators to King James" also missing from the original translation. Neither the Translators Preface nor the Dedicatory Letter are included here, but can be found on the internet or in most libraries. These two missing sections provide little insight, but the Apocrypha books do contain some 400 years of history missing from the Authorized Version.

The King James Bible is used in this work for two obvious reasons. First it is widely circulated and does not greatly conflict with Catholic Douay Bible, which can also be used in researching this work. The Authorized King James Bible is also the book used for the Strong's Exhaustive Concordance. Strong's is the reference used for translation in this work. Strong's allows for the cross reference of every word in the King James and simple translation from all the original words in that translation. As a work involving over 100 experts and 35 years of dedication, it is unmatched for its accuracy and research value. The modern translations are generally only translations of the King James, thus keeping the mistakes and mistranslations of that book. Any modern translations using any original works are impossible to check for accuracy.

Many claim that the Authorized King James Bible is the inspired work of God, and that all changes and mistranslations are the direct work of God and any research that questions it is wrong. This is not supported by the historical reality. King James did not encourage a translation of the Bible in order to enlighten the common people; his intent was to deny them the marginal notes of the Geneva Bible, the favored Bible of the time. The marginal notes of the Geneva version made it popular with the common people and contained over 300,000 words that questioned many concepts of orthodox religion.

King James I of England was a devout believer in the "divine right of kings", a philosophy claiming a king's power came from God, thus the king then had to answer to no one but God. The reasoning was that if a king was evil, that was a punishment sent from God. The citizens should then suffer in silence. If a king was good, that was a blessing sent from God. If one considers King James himself as inspired by God, the public record must be considered carefully in that judgment.

That record shows King James was a known homosexual, practiced bestiality, proved himself to be a great coward, and was a sadist who personally supervised the torture of those caught up in the witchcraft trials of Scotland.

One very important consideration must be weighed. If there were no translations or commentaries in this work certainly some enlightenment would be missing. But, the verses contained in the original form, as presented directly from the Authorized King James Bible, are sufficient to back the concepts in this work. It also must be understood that as the following doctrines and practices of the church are examined, one glaring reality will become clear. The church ignores the scriptures about those doctrines, properly translated and explained, or not.

> "It ain't the parts of the Bible that I can't understand that bother me, it is the parts that I do understand."
> *Mark Twain*

The Basics

There are 66 books in the Authorized King James Bible containing 1,189 chapters, 41,173 verses, and 774,746 words that were authored by approximately 40 men and women, and written over a period of 1,600 years. The word "Bible" comes from the Greek word "biblia" which means "little books". There are about 6,800 distinct languages in the world; the Bible has been translated (at least in part) into around 3000 of those languages.

The Authors

- The first five books, Genesis through Deuteronomy, were written by Moses.
- Joshua is the author of the book of Joshua.

- Judges was written by the prophet Samuel, as was I Samuel 1-24. The remainder of I Samuel and all of II Samuel was written by Nathan the prophet and Gad.
- I and II Kings were probably written by Jeremiah who compiled older records made by prophets contemporary with the events.
- Isaiah, Jeremiah, Ezekiel, Hosea, Joel, Amos, Obadiah, Jonah, Micah, Nahum, Habakkuk, Zephaniah, Haggai, Zechariah, and Malachi were all prophets who wrote the books bearing their names.
- The Psalms had various authors. David wrote about half; other authors include Asaph or his descendants, the sons of Korah, and Moses.
- Proverbs 1 through 29 belong mostly to Solomon. Chapters 30 and 31 are respectively ascribed to Agur and Lemuel.
- The author of the book of Job was most likely Job himself.
- The Song of Solomon was written by Solomon.
- The book of Ruth is attributed to Samuel.
- Lamentations was written by Jeremiah.
- Ecclesiastes was written by Solomon.
- Esther was written by Mordecai.
- Daniel, Ezra, and Nehemiah wrote the books which bear their names.
- I and II Chronicles were written by Ezra.
- Matthew, Mark, Luke, John, James, I Peter, II Peter, I John, II John, III John, and Jude were written by the men whose names they bear.
- Acts was written by Luke.
- Romans, I and II Corinthians, Galatians, Ephesians, Philippians, Colossians, I and II Thessalonians, I and II Timothy, Titus, Philemon, and Hebrews were all written by Paul.
- The book of Revelation was written by John.

Canon of Scripture

One of the terms used in describing the books that belong in Scripture is the word canon. This comes from the Greek word 'kanon', meaning reed or measurement. A canonical book is one that measures up to the standard of Holy Scripture. Thus, the canon of Scripture refers to the books that are considered the authoritative Word of God. It was the leaders of the early church who determined which books were canonical.

What Criteria Were Used in Determining Which Books Belong in the Bible?

- Prophetic Authorship - For a book to be considered canonical, it must have been written by a prophet or apostle or by one who had a special relationship to such (Mark to Peter, Luke to Paul). Only those who had witnessed the events or had recorded eyewitness testimony could have their writings considered as Holy Scripture.

• Witness of the Spirit - The appeal to the inner witness of the Holy Spirit. Clark Pinnock writes: The Spirit did not reveal a list of inspired books, but left their recognition to a historical process in which He was active, God's people learned to distinguish wheat from chaff, and gold from gravel, as He worked in their hearts (Clark Pinnock, Biblical Revelation)

• Acceptance - The final test is the acceptance of the people of God.

Again it must be realized that it was the leaders of the early church that made all the above determinations about authorship, whether the Holy Spirit approved it, and who the "people of God" were who accepted them. No input was ever accepted from the "common" people.

Who decided which books should be placed in the Bible?

The number of books originally considered for inclusion in the Bible is uncertain. We do know Constantine ordered 50 copies of the Bible to be produced by Eusebius in 325 AD to end any dispute over this, which basically left this important decision to Eusebius alone. This collection set the standard. The first ecclesiastical councils to classify the canonical books were both held in North Africa-at Hippo Regius in 393 and at Carthage in 397.

Jews and Christians use the same Old Testament.

The King James Old Testament consists of thirty-nine books according to the Protestant reckoning, but only twenty-four according to the Jewish reckoning. The books are the same; the difference is in the way they are divided. The division of the Protestants' Bible is as follows: Seventeen historical books: Genesis-Esther, five poetical books Job-Song of Solomon, seventeen prophetical books: Isaiah-Malachi.

The Hebrew Bible numbers these as twenty-four: The Torah or law contains five books, Genesis-Deuteronomy; The Prophets contain eight books, Joshua, Judges, Samuel, Kings, Isaiah, Jeremiah, Ezekiel, and the twelve minor prophets are grouped into one book; The Writings or Kethubim contain eleven books, Psalms, Proverbs, Song of Solomon, Ruth, Lamentations, Ecclesiastes, Esther, Daniel, Ezra-Nehemiah, and Chronicles. The Hebrew Bible combined 1 and 2 Samuel, 1 and 2 Kings, and 1 and 2 Chronicles. The twelve Minor Prophets were combined into one book. Thus, the books are identical. The only difference is in the way they are divided.

The Douay-Rheims Bible

In the Catholic Church, the Bible is the Douay Bible consisting of 73 books. In the Protestant church only the 66 books that were approved by the Synod of Dordrecht in 1618 are in what is known as the Authorized King James Bible.

The Development of the English Language Bible

Most of what we now know as the Old Testament was originally written in Hebrew, and the New Testament largely in common Greek. Since no printing press existed until 1450 AD, all of the original compilations of the Bible were done by hand. The development of the English Bible can be divided into 2 sections; ancient versions and early English versions. Brief descriptions of the significant versions in those time periods follow:

Ancient Versions in other Languages
- The Septuagint Version 285 BC-This was a translation of the Old Testament Hebrew Scriptures into Greek. Probably done in Alexandria.
- The Samaritan Pentateuch-A copy of the Hebrew text done in Samaritan characters.
- The Peshito or Syriac 1st century AD - A common language translation of the entire Bible used in parts of Syria.
- The Codex Sinaiticus 330 AD - A manuscript that contained the Greek Bible, now housed in the British Museum.
- The Codex Vaticanus 340 AD - This manuscript is currently housed in the Vatican library in Rome. It originally contained the whole Bible, but parts have been lost.
- The Vulgate 400 AD - A Roman Catholic scholar in Bethlehem by the name of Jerome translated the entire Bible into Latin. This Bible became the standard in the Catholic church for well over 1,000 years.
- The Codex Alexandrinus 425 AD - This Bible is another Greek translation. Currently housed in the British Museum, it is complete except for 40 leaves.

Early English Versions

All of the earliest attempts at translating the Bible into English were fragmented. For example, Bishop Aldhelm of Sherbourne translated the Psalms into Old English around 709. Venerable Bede, a monk at Jarrow, translated a portion of the Gospel of John. By 900 AD all of the Gospels and most of the Old Testament had been translated into Old English.
- John Wycliffe (1380) - John Wycliffe was the first to plan a complete English translation of the Bible from Latin. His translation was based on the Latin Vulgate. He completed the New Testament prior to his death, and his friends completed the work after his death.
- Printing press invented - 1450
- William Tyndale (1525-1530) - Driven from England by persecution, William Tyndale, shared Wycliffe's desire to produce a Bible that the common English-speaking person could understand. Using the Latin Vulgate and other ancient sources, Tyndale was able to translate the New Testament and Pentateuch before he was martyred.

- Miles Coverdale (1535) - A friend of Tyndale's, Coverdale was able to publish a complete Bible. It is generally believed Coverdale used Tyndale's work in producing his New Testament. This Bible was done to honor King Henry the VIII.
- Matthews Bible (1537) - Despite the name, it is widely accepted that a friend of Tyndale, John Rogus, did most of the work on this Bible. Based largely on Tyndale's previous work, it also contains evidences of Coverdale's work as well. This might well be considered an updated Tyndale Bible.
- The Great Bible (1539) - This Bible takes its name from its great physical size. Based on the Tyndale, Coverdale, and Matthews Bibles, it was used mainly in churches. Often chained to a reading desk in a church, people would come to listen as a minister read from the Great Bible.
- The Geneva Bible (1560) - Produced in Geneva by scholars who had fled persecution in England under Queen Mary, this Bible was based not only on the Great Bible, but also on the other English translations of that day. Though very scholarly, it was a popular Bible because of its small size.
- The Bishops Bible (1568) - This was a revision of the Great Bible and Geneva Bible done under the direction of the Archbishop of Canterbury during the reign of Elizabeth.
- Douay-Rheims Bible (1582-1610) - The New Testament was published in Rheims in 1582 and the Old Testament in Douay in 1610. A revision of the Latin Vulgate, this has become the generally accepted English Version for the Roman Catholic Church.
- King James Version, KJV (1611) - The most popular translation ever produced, this Bible was done during the reign and at the urging of King James the I of England. 47 scholars, divided into 6 groups, worked on this translation. Based largely on the Bishop's Bible, many Hebrew and Greek texts were also studied, as well as all the other available English translations, to insure the best results. By choosing men of many different theological and educational backgrounds, it was hoped individual prejudices of the translators could be minimized. Printed in a handy size and in clear type, the KJV was supposed to please clergy and congregation alike. Despite initial resistance, the KJV became, and still is, the largest selling translation of the Bible.
- Revised Version (1881-1884) - Designed to be a revision of the KJV, the Revised Version had the advantage of being able to access some of the ancient manuscripts. Although this revision was sponsored by the Church of England, many American scholars were invited to participate.

The Lost Books of the Bible

The Church View:

In the Catholic Church, the Bible is the Douay Bible consisting of 73 books. In the Protestant church only the 66 books that were approved by the Synod of Dordrecht in 1618 are in what is known as the Authorized King James Bible.

The Bible View:

Though there is no specific list or accounting of all the books that made up the complete Bible in scripture, there are over 20 books mentioned in the Bible, but not found there. This is proof that many have been removed and there is evidence that many more fell under the same fate.

An Introduction

Human history has allowed precious few ancient religious writings to survive the onslaught of the more aggressive and powerful religious forces, which seek only to gain territory and wealth. Genocide and cultural eradication always go hand in hand with missionary zeal. In many cases every trace of the conquered society's religious writings, practices, icons, and even buildings were destroyed in the name of conversion from worship of gods considered evil, and religious customs labeled as heresies. What generally results from past crusades is the conqueror's religion replacing or predominantly blending with the conquered culture's former religious practice, making its religion almost unrecognizable. Christianity falls into the latter category, having been the victim of the Roman Empire, under the Emperor Constantine, who blended the Christian Church with the institutionalized "pagan" practices of Rome and eliminated any semblance of either the Jewish religious influence or the first church Jesus established during his ministry.

The First Reformation

After solidifying his position to gain complete control of the western portion of the empire in 312, the Emperor Constantine instituted the Edict of Milan, a "Magna Carta of religious liberty," which eventually changed the Empire's religion and put Christianity on an equal footing with paganism. Almost overnight the position of the Christian Church was reversed from persecuted to legal and accepted. Constantine began to rely on the church for support, and it on him for protection. The Church and the Empire formed an alliance, which remains to this day. Very rapidly, the laws and policies of the Empire and the doctrine of the Church became one with Constantine as the interpreter of both law and policy. This was accomplished by eliminating hundreds of books thought to be against "Church" doctrine and watering down what remained by blending Christian beliefs and practice with long established Roman sanctioned pagan worship.

The Doctrines of Men

Constantine believed that the Church and the State should be as close as possible. Constantine tolerated pagan practices, keeping pagan gods on coins and retaining his pagan high priest title "Pontifex Maximus" in order to maintain popularity with his former subjects. In 330 he began an assault on paganism, but used a clever method of persuasion to force people to follow the laws by combining pagan worship with Christianity. He made December 25th, the birthday of the pagan Unconquered Sun god, the official holiday now celebrated as the birthday of Jesus. He also replaced the weekly day of worship by making rest on Saturday unlawful and forcing the new religion to honor the first, not the seventh day, as a day of rest. As a way of defining his concept of the new universal religion, he simply classified everything "Jewish" to be an abomination. Considering almost every aspect of the Bible is "Jewish" by association, every doctrinal biblical principle was changed or eliminated. After 337 Constantine increased his purging of the more obvious aspects of paganism.

Through a series of Universal Councils, he and his successors completely altered doctrine without regard to biblical edict, set up a church hierarchy of his own design, and established a set of beliefs and practices, which are the basis for all mainstream Bible-based churches. The separation of the Protestants and the Roman Church caused a physical split, but the beliefs and practices established by Constantine remained almost identical. Very little has changed since the 4th century Councils changed the face of Christianity. An effective practice instituted was the purging of any book in the formerly accepted biblical works, over 80% of the total, that church leaders felt did not fit within their new concept of Christianity. The doctrines and practices remaining in the surviving books were effectively eradicated by simply changing them by replacing clear scripture with Church-sanctioned doctrine.

Forbidden, Not Lost

Constantine began what was to become a century's long effort to eliminate any book in the original Bible that was considered unacceptable to the new doctrine of the church. At that time, it is believed there were up to 600 books, which comprised the work we now know as the Bible. Through a series of decisions made by the early church leadership, all but 80 of those books, known as the King James Translation of 1611, were purged from the work, with a further reduction by the Protestant Reformation bringing the number to 66 in the "Authorized" King James Bible.

What we now have in Bible-based religion, whether labeled as "Catholic", or Protesting Catholic, known as "Protestant", is unrecognizable from either the Hebrew religion, now known as the Jewish religion, or the church established at Jerusalem by the Apostles and disciples of Jesus. The practices of this first church are not practiced by any major religion and they are almost unknown, despite being clearly outlined in the existing New Testament. In its

116

place are doctrines and practices first established in the first "true" Reformation of Christianity, which was begun by Constantine.

There is much controversy over how many books the Bible should actually contain, but considering the depth and scope of those few works remaining in the "accepted" Bible, we see but a fragment of incredible wisdom and history. A study of the Lost Books of the Bible is incomplete without a clear understanding that this is not a matter of simple loss, but a campaign by the Roman Catholic Church to purge books variously classified as heretical, dangerous, and corruptive. To the public they are "lost"; to the Church they are "forbidden". Although the exact number of books purged is known only to the Church, and not shared knowledge, some can be determined by the discovery of their presence in the church prior to the reformation resulting in what became known as the Roman "Universal" Church. Whatever the number before the purge by the formation of Catholicism by Constantine; even one lost book is a great loss indeed.

We claim no expertise concerning the authenticity of any of the lost books and leave this judgment to the reader. We do, however, strongly reject the self-proclaimed authority of any dogmatically motivated and church-controlled mortals who think themselves qualified to make such decisions. One of the most logical and realistic concepts in the Bible is the caution that one should prove all things. We believe that proving the veracity of a given thing is an individual responsibility, which must not, and should not be the duty of those who think themselves better judges.

The Old Testament Apocryphal Books
"The Apocrypha"

The term "*apocrypha*" comes from a Greek word meaning "hidden" or "secret" and the books were originally considered by the early church as too exalted to be available to the general public. As time progressed, the exalted nature of the books was lost and the books were deemed by some as false. Between the Book of Malachi and Matthew there is a gap of approximately 450 years. It is these books that fill that gap and, in the time of Christ, these books formed part of the Septuagint Greek Bible that was in circulation at that time.

What is missing from most Bibles, and our understanding of it, is what happened in that 450-year gap. Prophets were still writing and reflecting on life in the Holy Land right up until the Romans destroyed the temple of Jerusalem in 70 AD. The world that Jesus entered in 4 BC is not the world that Daniel and Malachi experienced. One of the values of these books is how they reflect the mindset of Judaism and a Roman world that the New Testament writers faced. Malachi and Daniel leave us in Persia; Matthew brings us into a Roman world. The Apocrypha bridges that gap and gently nudges us into the reality of

Roman Palestine. It was only in the fourth century AD that Christians first started to question the "canonicity" of the works, although most survived to be included in the King James translation of the Bible in 1611.

Unknown to almost all of the over two billion people who claim the Bible as their spiritual foundation is that there are several books and two sections missing from all but a few modern versions of that Bible. Perhaps one of the best kept secrets of the modern Protestant church is that the Bible used by that church is not the original King James Bible. That translation, completed in 1611, and the Bibles published for the use of the clergy and the church members until late in the 19th Century, contained 80 books. Although attempts to remove the 14 books, known as the Apocrypha, from the Bible began immediately after the King James translation was completed, they remained in the Bible until the end of the 19th Century. There is no doubt that the 14 books of the Apocrypha were controversial, but it cannot be denied they were included in the original King James Bible.

The concept of the Protestant Church about the Apocrypha is virtually non-existent, with the general understanding that only the Catholic Church uses it. One would be hard-pressed to find any members of the clergy even aware that these books were ever included in the King James Bible. There are 155,683 words and over 5,700 verses contained in 168 chapters now missing from the King James translation of the Bible due to the exclusion of the Apocrypha. Although this only happened just over a hundred years ago, their existence as fully accepted scripture is virtually unknown.

A clear history exists of the inclusion of the Apocrypha in the King James Bible:

• In the year 1615 Archbishop Gorge Abbott, a High Commission Court member and one of the original translators of the 1611 translation, "forbade anyone to issue a Bible without the Apocrypha on pain of one year's imprisonment".

• "It should be observed that the Old Testament thus admitted as authoritative in the Church was somewhat bulkier and more comprehensive than the [Protestant Old Testament] . . . It always included, though with varying degrees of recognition, the so-called Apocrypha or Deutero-canonical books. The use made of the Apocrypha by Tertullian, Hippolytus, Cyprian and Clement of Alexandria is too frequent for detailed references to be necessary". (Early Christian Doctrines, J. Kelly)

• "In 405 Pope Innocent I embodied a list of canonical books in a letter addressed to Exsuperius, bishop of Toulouse; it too included the Apocrypha. The Sixth Council of Carthage (419) Re-enacted the ruling of the Third Council, again with the inclusion of the apocryphal books... "The Sixth Council of Carthage repromulgated in Canon 24 the resolution of the Third

Council regarding the canon of scripture, and added a note directing that the resolution be sent to the bishop of Rome (Boniface I) and other bishops: 'Let this be made known also to our brother and fellow-priest Boniface, or to other bishops of those parts, for the purpose of confirming that Canon [Canon 47 of the Third Council], because we have received from our fathers that these are the books which are to be read in church.'" (The Canon on Scripture, F. F. Bruce)

• "The holy ecumenical and general Council of Trent . . . following the example of the orthodox Fathers, receives and venerates all the books of the Old and New Testament . . . and also the traditions pertaining to faith and conduct . . . with an equal sense of devotion and reverence . . . If, however, any one receive not, as sacred and canonical, the said books entire with all their parts, as they have by custom been read in the Catholic Church, and as they are contained in the old Latin Vulgate, and knowingly and deliberately rejects the aforesaid traditions, let him be accursed." (Decree of the Council of Trent in 1546)

• "In the name of Holy Scripture we do understand those canonical books of the Old and New Testament, of whose authority was never any doubt in the Church. . . And the other books (as Jerome saith) the Church doth read for example of life and instruction of manners: but yet doth it not apply them to establish any doctrine." (Articles of Religion of the Church of England, 1563, Sixth Article)

Most early Bibles contained the Apocrypha; here are just a few:
• 1534 Luther's German translation of the Bible
• 1534 The Coverdale Bible
• 1537 Thomas Matthew Bible
• 1539 The Taverner Bible
• 1541 The "Great" or "Cromwell's" Bible
• 1551 The "Tyndale/ Matthews" Bible
• 1560 The Geneva Bible
• 1568 The Bishops' Bible
• 1610 Catholic Old Testament
• 1611 King James Bible
• 1615 King James Version Robert Barker at London, England
• 1625 A King James Version
• 1717 King George 1st, AKA, The "Vinegar Bible"
• 1782 The Aitken Bible
• 1791 The Family Bible
• 1846 The Illuminated Bible

The Apocrypha are also contained in the following:

- The Septuagint (LXX) - Except II Esdras.
- Codex Alexandrinus (A) - Also contains III & IV Maccabees
- Codex Vaticanus - Except I & II Maccabees and The defaulter of Manassah
- Codex Sinaiticus (Aleph)
- Codex Ephraemi Rescriptus - Includes Wisdom of Solomon and Ecclesiasticus
- Chester Beatty Papyri - Fragments of Ecclesiasticus
- The Dead Sea Scrolls - Some apocryphal writing was found among the Dead Sea Scrolls - interestingly written in Greek.
- Several writings of Church Fathers

Bibles are still available with Apocrypha:

- The Bible: Authorized King James Version with Apocrypha: Published by Oxford University Press; ISBN: 0192835254 (Pub. Date: July 1998)
- KJV Standard Reference Edition With Apocrypha: Published by Cambridge Univ Pr (Bibles); ISBN: 0521509467; Slipcase edition (Pub. Date: August 1997)
- 1611 Edition: a reprint of the 1611 KJV With Apocrypha, Published by Nelson Bible; ISBN: 0840700415; Reissue edition (Pub. Date: June 1, 1982)
- King James Version Lectern Edition: Published by Cambridge Univ Pr (Bibles); ISBN: 0521508169; (Pub. Date: March 1998)
- The Dake Annotated Reference Bible, Standard Edition: King James Version With Apocrypha, Published by Dake Publishing ISBN: 1558290699 (Pub. Date: April 1996)

For 275 years there were efforts to purge the Apocrypha from the Bible:

- "APOCRYPHA, that is, Books which are not to be esteemed like the Holy Scriptures, and yet which are useful and good to read." (Luther Bible, 1534)
- "The books and treatises which among the Fathers of old are not reckoned to be of like authority with the other books of the Bible, neither are they found in the Canon of Hebrew." (Coverdale Bible 1535)
- "The books that follow in order after the Prophets unto the New Testament, are called Apocrypha, that is, books which were not received by a common consent to be read and expounded publicly in the Church, neither yet served to prove any point of Christian religion save in so much as they had the consent of the other scriptures called canonical to confirm the same, or rather whereon they were grounded: but as books proceeding from godly men they were received to be read for the advancement and furtherance of the knowledge of history and for the instruction of godly manners: which books declare that at all times God had an especial care of His Church, and left them not utterly destitute of teachers and means to confirm them in the hope of the promised

Messiah, and also witness that those calamities that God sent to his Church were according to his providence, who had both so threatened by his prophets, and so brought it to pass, for the destruction of their enemies and for the trial of his children." (Geneva Bible, 1560, Preface)

- The Synod of the Reformed Church held at Dordrecht in 1618 condemned the Apocrypha.
- "The books commonly called Apocrypha, not being of divine inspiration, are no part of the Canon of Scripture; and therefore are of no authority in the Church of God, nor to be any otherwise approved, or made use of, than other human writings." (Westminster Confession, 1647)
- The thirty nine Articles of the Church of England in 1562 recognized this and rejected the canonicity of these apocryphal writings which the Roman church had proclaimed.
- In 1880 the American Bible Society voted to remove the "Apocrypha" Books from the King James Version. These 14 Books [There are 155,683 words in over 5,700 verses in 168 Chapters] of the Apocrypha had been part of the King's bible since 1611.
- The "Apocrypha" was officially removed from the English printings of the KJV by the Archbishop of Canterbury in 1885 leaving only 66 books.

An Apocryphal Comparison of the King James and Douay Rheims Bibles:
    The common belief is that even though the Apocryphal books do not appear in the modern King James Bible, they all do appear in the Catholic Douay Rheims Bible. This is not correct as a simple comparison will show.

- **The Apocrypha in the original King James Bible:**
1st Esdras
2nd Esdras
Tobit
Judith
Add to Esther
The Wisdom of Solomon
Ecclesiasticus or the Wisdom of Jesus Son Sirach
Baruch
Letter of Jeremiah
Prayer of Azariah or Song of the Three Young Men
Susanna
Bel and the Dragon
Prayer of Manasseh
1st Macabees
2nd Macabees

- **The Apocrypha in the Douay Rheims Bible:**

1st Esdras
2nd Esdras
Tobias
Judith
Wisdom of Solomon
Ecclisiasticus (The Wisdom of Jesus' Son Sirach)
Baruch
Abdias
Micheas (This is the book of Micah)
Aggeus (This is the book of Haggai)
1st Macabees
2nd Macabees

- **These Apocrypha books are missing from in the Douay Rheims Bible:**

Addition to Esther
Letter of Jeremiah
Prayer of Azariah or Song of the Three Young Men
Susanna
Bel and the Dragon
Prayer of Manasseh

The Other Missing Sections of the Original King James Bible

Two introductory sections were also removed from the original King James Translation. There was a Preface written for the original King James Bible, which is mysteriously missing from that work, called The Translators Preface. There was also a Dedication written for the original King James Bible called The Epistle Dedicatory. These two sections can be accessed on the internet or through the library system.

Books Mentioned, But Not Found, In The Bible

There are many books mentioned in the Bible, but not included.

Book of the Covenant

♦ **Exodus 24:7** And he took the book of the covenant, and read in the audience of the people: and they said, All that the Lord hath said will we do, and be obedient.

There are those that believe the Book of the Covenant is found in Exodus chapters 20 through 23. There are no authoritative sources for this text.

Book of the Wars of the Lord

♦ **Numbers 21:14** Wherefore it is said in the book of the wars of the Lord, What he did in the Red sea, and in the brooks of Arnon,

Certain sources believe that this is to be found by drawing text from several

Old Testament books. There are no authoritative sources for this text.
Book of Jasher
♦ **Joshua 10:13** And the sun stood still, and the moon stayed, until the people had avenged themselves upon their enemies. Is not this written in the book of Jasher? So the sun stood still in the midst of heaven, and hasted not to go down about a whole day.

♦ **2 Samuel 1:18** (Also he bade them teach the children of Judah the use of the bow: behold, it is written in the book of Jasher.)
The Manner of the Kingdom / Book of Statutes
♦ **1 Samuel 10:25** Then Samuel told the people the manner of the kingdom, and wrote it in a book, and laid it up before the Lord. And Samuel sent all the people away, every man to his house.
Book of Samuel the Seer
♦ **1 Chronicles 29:29** Now the acts of David the king, first and last, behold, they are written in the book of Samuel the seer, and in the book of Nathan the prophet, and in the book of Gad the seer,
Nathan the Prophet
♦ **1 Chronicles 29:29** Now the acts of David the king, first and last, behold, they are written in the book of Samuel the seer, and in the book of Nathan the prophet, and in the book of Gad the seer,

♦ **2 Chronicles 9:29** Now the rest of the acts of Solomon, first and last, are they not written in the book of Nathan the prophet, and in the prophecy of Ahijah the Shilonite, and in the visions of Iddo the seer against Jeroboam the son of Nebat?
Acts of Solomon
♦ **1 Kings 11:41** And the rest of the acts of Solomon, and all that he did, and his wisdom, are they not written in the book of the acts of Solomon?
Shemaiah the Prophet
♦ **2 Chronicles 12:15** Now the acts of Rehoboam, first and last, are they not written in the book of Shemaiah the prophet, and of Iddo the seer concerning genealogies? And there were wars between Rehoboam and Jeroboam continually.
Prophecy of Abijah
♦ **2 Chronicles 9:29** Now the rest of the acts of Solomon, first and last, are they not written in the book of Nathan the prophet, and in the prophecy of Ahijah the Shilonite, and in the visions of Iddo the seer against Jeroboam the son of Nebat?
Story of Prophet Iddo
♦ **2 Chronicles 13:22** And the rest of the acts of Abijah, and his ways, and his sayings, are written in the story of the prophet Iddo.

Visions of Iddo the Seer

♦ **2 Chronicles 9:29** Now the rest of the acts of Solomon, first and last, are they not written in the book of Nathan the prophet, and in the prophecy of Ahijah the Shilonite, and in the visions of Iddo the seer against Jeroboam the son of Nebat?

Iddo Genealogies

♦ **2 Chronicles 12:15** Now the acts of Rehoboam, first and last, are they not written in the book of Shemaiah the prophet, and of Iddo the seer concerning genealogies? And there were wars between Rehoboam and Jeroboam continually

Book of Jehu

♦ **2 Chronicles 20:34** Now the rest of the acts of Jehoshaphat, first and last, behold, they are written in the book of Jehu the son of Hanani, who is mentioned in the book of the kings of Israel.

Sayings of the Seers

♦ **2 Chronicles 33:19** His prayer also, and how God was intreated of him, and all his sin, and his trespass, and the places wherein he built high places, and set up groves and graven images, before he was humbled: behold, they are written among the sayings of the seers.

Book of Enoch

♦ **Jude 1:14** And Enoch also, the seventh from Adam, prophesied of these, saying, Behold, the Lord cometh with ten thousands of his saints,

Book of Gad the Seer

♦ **1 Chronicles 29:29** Now the acts of David the king, first and last, behold, they are written in the book of Samuel the seer, and in the book of Nathan the prophet, and in the book of Gad the seer,

Epistle to Corinth

♦ **1 Corinthians 5:9** I wrote unto you in an epistle not to company with fornicators:

Epistle to the Ephesians (Missing)

♦ **Ephesians 3:3** How that by revelation he made known unto me the mystery; (as I wrote afore in few words, 4 Whereby, when ye read, ye may understand my knowledge in the mystery of Christ)

Epistle from Laodicea to the Colossians (Missing)

♦ **Colossians 4:16** And when this epistle is read among you, cause that it be read also in the church of the Laodiceans; and that ye likewise read the epistle from Laodicea.

Nazarene Prophecy Source

♦ **Matthew 2:23** And he came and dwelt in a city called Nazareth: that it might be fulfilled which was spoken by the prophets, He shall be called a Nazarene

Acts of Uziah

♦ **2 Chronicles 26:22** Now the rest of the acts of Uzziah, first and last, did Isaiah the prophet, the son of Amoz, write.

The Annals of King David

♦ **1 Chronicles 27:24** Joab son of Zeruiah began to count the men but did not finish. Wrath came on Israel on account of this numbering, and the number was not entered in the book of the annals of King David.

Jude, the Missing Epistle

♦ **Jude 1:3** Beloved, when I gave all diligence to write unto you of the common salvation, it was needful for me to write unto you, and exhort you that ye should earnestly contend for the faith which was once delivered unto the saints.

Books Removed From the Biblical Collection
A Partial List

There are those that cling to a singular view of all things biblical. If it is not in the King James Bible exactly the way he had it translated, it is a fake, a forgery, or an insidious plot by Satan to corrupt the minds of men. Those works referenced here are not mentioned in the Bible, but are associated with it. Many of the books listed below may be found on the internet by doing a search using the name of the book as a keyword.

We have compiled a list of over 500 books that have been associated with the Bible either through archeological research or historical documentation. There is no guarantee that the books listed here are inspired works, or genuine books actually included in original versions of writings used by, and considered true by the Early Christian Church. The majority of these books are online and can be accessed through the website associated with this book. See "The Website" on page 225

Books Removed From, Or Associated With, The Bible See Appendix R

Bible Misconceptions

As though ignoring and violating biblical doctrine were not enough, many basic misconceptions of actual Bible content exist in mainstream Bible-based religion.   This may seem trivial in the light of the importance of other church contradictions, but they are no less held as truisms and often shape the thoughts and behavior of the membership.

Money is the root of all evil.

Close, but off the mark, is the best way to describe this misquote. The Bible says the love of money is the culprit, not the object itself, with the word love being properly translated as avarice. The actual verse is:

♦ **1 Timothy 6:10** For the love of money is the root of all evil: which while some coveted after, they have erred from the faith, and pierced themselves through with many sorrows.

Spare the rod, spoil the child.

This one seems to imply, don't discipline your children and you are showering them with gifts, hardly a way to raise a well-balanced child. What the Bible does say is that consistent discipline is the key.

♦ **Proverbs 13:24** He that spareth his rod hateth his son: but he that loveth him chasteneth him betimes.

Cleanliness is next to godliness.

This is not in the Bible and no similar verses or concepts are found in the Bible. God does not seem to rate hygiene as a high priority. The origin is John Wesley, from a sermon he gave called "On Dress".

God works in mysterious ways.

Though not found in the Bible, it is one of the rare misquotes that can be supported by scriptural concept. William Cowper actually created this one in the poem "On The Loss of the Royal George".

God helps those that help themselves.

Not only is this not in the Bible, it contradicts the biblical principle of dependence on God.

All sin is equal in God's sight.

This may seem a logical concept, but the wide variation in severity of punishments for different crimes certainly contradicts it.

Jesus was crucified on Friday afternoon, and resurrected on Sunday morning.

The simple problem here is the fact that the Crucifixion happened the day before the Sabbath and the resurrection happened on Sunday morning. It is the ignorance of the fact that there are not one, but two kinds of Sabbaths, Saturday and all the high holy celebrations of the nation of Israel. The Sabbath that Jesus was crucified on was a high Sabbath and there is no indication that Jesus actually rose from the grave Sunday morning, only that the body was discovered missing.

If he was crucified on Friday and arose Sunday it would have negated the prophecies that he would be dead three days and nights. A Friday crucifixion and Sunday resurrection would mean only one day and two nights.
Three Days and Three Nights

♦ **Matthew 12: 39** But he answered and said unto them, An evil and adulterous generation seeketh after a sign; and there shall no sign be given to it, but the sign of the prophet Jonas: 40 For as Jonas was three days and three nights in the whale's belly; so shall the Son of man be three days and three nights in the heart of the earth.

♦ **Mark 8:31** And he began to teach them, that the Son of man must suffer many things, and be rejected of the elders, and of the chief priests, and scribes, and be killed, and after three days rise again.

The Sabbath following the Crucifixion was an annual high Sabbath, not specifically a Saturday.

Preparation for a High Holy Day

♦ **Mark 15:42** And now when the even was come, because it was the preparation, that is, the day before the sabbath, 43 Joseph of Arimathaea, an honourable counsellor, which also waited for the kingdom of God, came, and went in boldly unto Pilate, and craved the body of Jesus. 44 And Pilate marvelled if he were already dead: and calling unto him the centurion, he asked him whether he had been any while dead.

♦ **Luke 23:52** This man went unto Pilate, and begged the body of Jesus. 53 And he took it down, and wrapped it in linen, and laid it in a sepulchre that was hewn in stone, wherein never man before was laid. 54 And that day was the preparation, and the sabbath drew on.

♦ **John 19:31** The Jews therefore, because it was the preparation, that the bodies should not remain upon the cross on the sabbath day, (for that sabbath day was an high day,) besought Pilate that their legs might be broken, and that they might be taken away.

No One Visited the Grave on Saturday

They Rested on Saturday

♦ **Luke 23:56** And they returned, and prepared spices and ointments; and rested the sabbath day according to the commandment.

The body of Jesus was already gone by the dawn on Sunday morning.

♦ **Matthew 28:1** In the end of the sabbath, as it began to dawn toward the first day of the week, came Mary Magdalene and the other Mary to see the sepulchre.

♦ **Mark 16:1** And when the sabbath was past, Mary Magdalene, and Mary the mother of James, and Salome, had bought sweet spices, that they might come and anoint him. 2 And very early in the morning the first day of the week, they came unto the sepulchre at the rising of the sun.

To fulfill the prophecy, the earliest in the week the crucifixion could have taken place was Wednesday, which would mean the body was in the sepulchre Wednesday, Thursday, and Friday night and Thursday, Friday, and Saturday day.

The Non-Biblical Nature of the Modern Church

Though claiming piety and biblical authority, the reality of modern church conduct is sadly lacking in scriptural foundation, and often runs contrary to biblical principle. Finding any resemblance to the first church is a futile pursuit. Here are but a few of the discrepancies:

• All the High Sabbaths, or festivals, outlined in the Bible are ignored and are replaced with ancient pagan holidays such as Easter, Christmas, and Halloween.

• Money is solicited, and often demanded, to allegedly support the work of the church, which has little, if anything, to do with the original commission of the church. Such practice is not authorized in biblical law and may possibly be a gross violation if extracted as a tithe.

• Meetings are held on Sunday without biblical authority and setting aside the last day of the week for rest is ignored. There is no biblical command to meet in any building, on any day of the week, in force. The fact that the first day of the week is a day set aside by pagan religions to worship an assortment of sun gods only increases the violation. In the year 321, Constantine the Great ruled that the first day of the week, 'the venerable day of the sun', should be a day of rest. The personal pronouncements of a mere mortal do not negate the rules of God.

• Ministers and deacons in churches do not fulfill duties outlined in biblical text for these positions.

• Socialism, the core principle, and well-documented practice, of the first church, is condemned by its pretender.

• Miracles and abnormal powers in people are condemned as witchcraft without regard to the reality that such were common phenomenon in the first church.

• Churches openly support political issues that contradict biblical principle and use church resources for these activities.

• Churches openly support war and nationalism and use church resources for these activities.

• Churches demand adherence to an old divine contract made with the twelve tribes of Israel by persons who are not members of the nation of Israel.

• Churches ignore the new contract made with the entire world.

• Churches exhibit an extreme level of hypocrisy by following only those laws it chooses and ignoring those it violates, while claiming total obedience to all biblical law.

• Church buildings, officers, staff, customs, public and private practices, finances, celebrations, rules, solicitations, associations, appearances, and stated missions are without biblical foundation.

• Feeding, clothing, and housing the poor, a basic biblical principle, and the core teaching of Jesus, is seldom practiced and then with only a token effort and a minute percentage of the church funding and resources. In most cases of such rare exhibitions of charity, religious indoctrination is exacted as the cost for these services.

- Bigotry, with respect to race, gender, political belief, religion, national origin, sexual orientation, financial status, social conduct, and philosophy is commonly practiced or tolerated in either overt or covert manifestations.

- Mind control and dogmatic conditioning is encouraged, blind acceptance is expected, obedience is demanded, and all dissension and inquiry are condemned. Biblical demands for proof of doctrine are ignored. Loving your fellow man is restricted to those the church approves.

Church Members

As can be seen from the above verses the modern church bears no resemblance to the first church. A study of the principles Jesus taught would, of course, mean the church was engaged in helping the poor and indigent, as well as the healing by those possessed with this gift. The roles that the members of the church played were quite different from the members of today's pew fillers and plate passers:

♦ **1 Corinthians 12: 1**. Now concerning spiritual gifts, brethren, I would not have you ignorant. 2. Ye know that ye were Gentiles, carried away unto these dumb idols, even as ye were led. 3. Wherefore I give you to understand, that no man speaking by the Spirit of God calleth Jesus accursed: and that no man can say that Jesus is the Lord, but by the Holy Ghost. 4. Now there are diversities of gifts, but the same Spirit. 5. And there are differences of administrations, but the same Lord. 6. And there are diversities of operations, but it is the same God which worketh all in all. 7. But the manifestation of the Spirit is given to every man to profit withal. 8. For to one is given by the Spirit the word of wisdom; to another the word of knowledge by the same Spirit; 9. To another faith by the same Spirit; to another the gifts of healing by the same Spirit; 10. To another the working of miracles; to another prophecy; to another discerning of spirits; to another divers kinds of tongues; to another the interpretation of tongues:

♦ **1 Corinthians 12:27**. Now ye are the body of Christ, and members in particular. 28. And God hath set some in the church, first apostles, secondarily prophets, thirdly teachers, after that miracles, then gifts of healings, helps, governments, diversities of tongues. 29. Are all apostles? are all prophets? are all teachers? are all workers of miracles? 30. Have all the gifts of healing? do all speak with tongues? do all interpret? 31. But covet earnestly the best gifts: and yet shew I unto you a more excellent way.

The Power of the Church Members

♦ **Acts 2:43** And fear came upon every soul: and many wonders and signs were done by the apostles.

♦ **Acts 5:12** And by the hands of the apostles were many signs and wonders wrought among the people; (and they were all with one accord in Solomon's porch.

♦ **Acts 6:8** And Stephen, full of faith and power, did great wonders and miracles among the people.

♦ **Acts 8:6** And the people with one accord gave heed unto those things which Philip spake, hearing and seeing the miracles which he did.

♦ **Acts 8:3** Then Simon himself believed also: and when he was baptized, he continued with Philip, and wondered, beholding the miracles and signs which were done.

♦ **Acts 14:3** Long time therefore abode they speaking boldly in the Lord, which gave testimony unto the word of his grace, and granted signs and wonders to be done by their hands.

♦ **Acts 15:12** Then all the multitude kept silence, and gave audience to Barnabas and Paul, declaring what miracles and wonders God had wrought among the Gentiles by them.

♦ **Acts 19:11** And God wrought special miracles by the hands of Paul:

♦ **Romans 15:19** Through mighty signs and wonders, by the power of the Spirit of God; so that from Jerusalem, and round about unto Illyricum, I have fully preached the gospel of Christ.

♦ **I Corinthians 12:8** For to one is given by the Spirit the word of wisdom; to another the word of knowledge by the same Spirit; 9 To another faith by the same Spirit; to another the gifts of healing by the same Spirit; 10 To another the working of miracles; to another prophecy; to another discerning of spirits; to another divers kinds of tongues; to another the interpretation of tongues:

♦ **I Corinthians 12:28** And God hath set some in the church, first apostles, secondarily prophets, thirdly teachers, after that miracles, then gifts of healings, helps, governments, diversities of tongues. 29 Are all apostles? are all prophets? are all teachers? are all workers of miracles?

♦ **2 Corinthians 12:12** Truly the signs of an apostle were wrought among you in all patience, in signs, and wonders, and mighty deeds.

♦ **Galations 3:5** He therefore that ministereth to you the Spirit, and worketh miracles among you, doeth he it by the works of the law, or by the hearing of faith?

♦ **Hebrews 2:4** God also bearing them witness, both with signs and wonders, and with divers miracles, and gifts of the Holy Ghost, according to his own will?

A Serious Question

Do we see this kind of supernatural activity in the modern mainstream church? If not, why not?

Is the Modern Church the True Church?

It is clear that not all supernatural phenomena are evil. The words miracle and miracles appear 36 times in the Bible, 33 times they refer to good miracles. Three times they refer to miracles being performed by one man, the Anti-Christ. The word wonder appears 55 times; 51 times they refer to good wonders, 2 times to the Anti-Christ, 2 times to false christs and prophets. It would seem that the good supernatural phenomenon far outweighs the bad by a hefty margin.

So why is this generally given the label of evil by the church, even though it was totally accepted by the first church? Could it be that the modern church rejects the reality of the Church Jesus inspired as they do the communal nature of that same church? Branding all super natural events as evil is no different than branding the socialistic lifestyle of the early church as communist atheism. Both were embraced by the first church, both are condemned by the modern church. Add to this the differences in the law, church structure, prejudice, finances and the very purpose for existence, and the validity of the modern church comes up very short. One begins to wonder, considering the glaring opposites, what forces brought the modern church into being?

The Doctrines of Men

Doctrines and Practices of the Church

Church Symbols

The many questions about the integrity of the church extend well beyond its less than divinely inspired origins. The very appearance the church presents to public has its origin in the same manmade and pagan inspired concepts as the foundations upon which it was established.

The Church Building

The very existence of a building for sole purpose of weekly worship is without scriptural foundation, nor is the practice of weekly worship itself. The weekly practice of keeping the Sabbath, the last day of the week, as a day of rest is biblical, but gathering together to worship on any day is not. This practice was instituted by the Emperor Constantine when he actually outlawed the practice of resting on the Sabbath. This will be discussed further in this chapter in "The Holy Days"

The Church Steeple

The presence of steeples on top of church buildings is the classic testament to the pagan origins of virtually every aspect of the church. The Bible specifically condemns having such things anywhere near any area where there is an altar to the real God, and certainly any Ch4ristian would consider a church as such.

♦ **Deuteronomy 16: 21** Thou shalt not plant thee a grove of any trees near unto the altar of the Lord thy God, which thou shalt make thee.

The word grove is taken from ammuwd, pronounced am-mood'; a column (as standing) and tree comes from ets, pronounced ates; a tree (from its firmness); hence, wood.

This is speaking to ancient custom of erecting wooden columns at pagan worship sites. This edict is repeated here:

♦ **Leviticus 26:1** Ye shall make you no idols nor graven image, neither rear you up a standing image, neither shall ye set up any image of stone in your land, to bow down unto it: for I am the Lord your God.

The Cross

The cross has similar origins in ancient worship, and history shows that the cross was in use centuries before Christ. In the British Museum is a statue of the Assyrian king Samsi-Vul, son of Shalmaneser with an almost perfect Maltese cross around his neck and a similar cross on an accompanying figure of Ashur-nasir-pal. The ancient Greek goddess Diana is pictured with a cross over her head, in much the same way the "Virgin Mary" is represented by many medieval artists. Bacchus, the Greek god of wine, is often pictured wearing a headdress adorned with crosses. Different types of crosses were used

133

in the Mesoamerican cultures centuries before the Europeans arrived and he Egyptians and Hindus used cross symbols in abundance. There is absolutely no evidence that God's true Church ever used the cross symbol for any purpose. Nowhere does the Bible command its use and archaeologists have not found any Christian use of the symbol before that time. The Christian use of the cross did not begin until the time of Constantine, over three centuries after Christ when, after claiming to have a vision of a cross in a dream, the cross was adopted by Constantine to be the prime Christian symbol. "Thus the Labarum (the cross) took its origin, and under this glorious banner Constantine overcame his adversary near the Milvian Bridge, on 28 October, 312" (The Catholic Encyclopedia) The cross therefore became an Easter icon at the Council of Nicaea, in A.D. 325, when Constantine decreed that the Cross was the symbol of the Crucifixion and the official symbol of Christianity.

The Tithe

The Church View:

Ten percent of your income should be given to the church to be spent as the church decides. Some churches exact a second tithe, which is used to support a festival or conference each year for a total of 20 percent. Others exact a third tithe for the poor, which is spent as the church decides for a total of 30 percent.

The Bible View:

Ten percent of your food yield should be saved and used for a feast and converted into money for a spending spree each year. Every third year you must take ten percent of your food yield and feed the priests and the poor. If the church was a tabernacle, which it isn't, and ministers were priests, who they aren't, and were performing the duties clearly laid out in scripture, which they don't, all they could legally receive according to scripture is ten percent of your income every three years and that must also be used to feed the needy.

The tithe is one tenth of the agricultural yield that is taken to a designated site to be consumed and used for a general spending spree each year. Every third year the tithe is used to provide food for the priests and all those in need.

There is no indication whether the gift tithe is an extra ten percent or just designated for a different purpose every three years. The tithing law is found in the Book of Deuteronomy:

- The tithe is one tenth of the agricultural yield.
♦ **Deuteronomy 14:22** Thou shalt truly tithe all the increase of thy seed, that the field bringeth forth year by year.

- The tithe is to be brought to a designated place and consumed or converted into money and spent as one desires.

134

♦ **Deuteronomy 14:23** And thou shalt eat before the Lord thy God, in the place which he shall choose to place his name there, the tithe of thy corn, of thy wine, and of thine oil, and the firstlings of thy herds and of thy flocks; that thou mayest learn to fear the Lord thy God always. 24 And if the way be too long for thee, so that thou art not able to carry it; or if the place be too far from thee, which the Lord thy God shall choose to set his name there, when the Lord thy God hath blessed thee: 25 Then shalt thou turn it into money, and bind up the money in thine hand, and shalt go unto the place which the Lord thy God shall choose: 26 And thou shalt bestow that money for whatsoever thy soul lusteth after, for oxen, or for sheep, or for wine, or for strong drink, or for whatsoever thy soul desireth: and thou shalt eat there before the Lord thy God, and thou shalt rejoice, thou, and thine household,

- Every third year a tenth of the agricultural increase is to be given to the priests and the poor.

♦ **Deuteronomy 14:27** And the Levite that is within thy gates; thou shalt not forsake him; for he hath no part nor inheritance with thee.
28 At the end of three years thou shalt bring forth all the tithe of thine increase the same year, and shalt lay it up within thy gates: 29 And the Levite, (because he hath no part nor inheritance with thee,) and the stranger, and the fatherless, and the widow, which are within thy gates, shall come, and shall eat and be satisfied; that the Lord thy God may bless thee in all the work of thine hand which thou doest.

♦ **Deuteronomy 26:12** When thou hast made an end of tithing all the tithes of thine increase the third year, which is the year of tithing, and hast given it unto the Levite, the stranger, the fatherless, and the widow, that they may eat within thy gates, and be filled;

The tithe is to be used to feed the priests, travelers, and the poor at the tither's home. There is no place in the Bible stating that ten percent of your income should be given for any kind of religious purpose every year other than a feast and any doctrines or practices that demand such funds are committing extortion if they attempt to justify this with scripture. These are the other verses in the Bible dealing with the tithe:

- Tithe is of agricultural origin.

♦ **Leviticus 27:30** And all the tithe of the land, whether of the seed of the land, or of the fruit of the tree, is the LORD's: it is holy unto the LORD. 31 And if a man will at all redeem ought of his tithes, he shall add thereto the fifth part thereof. 32 And concerning the tithe of the herd, or of the flock, even of whatsoever passeth under the rod, the tenth shall be holy unto the LORD.

- Tithe rules for priests.

♦ **Numbers 18:24** But the tithes of the children of Israel, which they offer as an heave offering unto the LORD, I have given to the Levites to inherit: therefore I have said unto them, Among the children of Israel they shall have no inheritance. 25 And the LORD spake unto Moses, saying, 26 Thus speak unto the Levites, and say unto them, When ye take of the children of Israel the tithes which I have given you from them for your inheritance, then ye shall offer up an heave offering of it for the LORD, even a tenth part of the tithe.

- Rules for eating the tithe.
♦ **Deuteronomy12:17** Thou mayest not eat within thy gates the tithe of thy corn, or of thy wine, or of thy oil, or the firstlings of thy herds or of thy flock, nor any of thy vows which thou vowest, nor thy freewill offerings, or heave offering of thine hand: 18 But thou must eat them before the LORD thy God in the place which the LORD thy God shall choose, thou, and thy son, and thy daughter, and thy manservant, and thy maidservant, and the Levite that is within thy gates: and thou shalt rejoice before the LORD thy God in all that thou puttest thine hands unto.

- Tithes to priests.
♦ **2 Chronicles 31:4** Moreover he commanded the people that dwelt in Jerusalem to give the portion of the priests and the Levites, that they might be encouraged in the law of the LORD. 5 And as soon as the commandment came abroad, the children of Israel brought in abundance the firstfruits of corn, wine, and oil, and honey, and of all the increase of the field; and the tithe of all things brought they in abundantly. 6 And concerning the children of Israel and Judah, that dwelt in the cities of Judah, they also brought in the tithe of oxen and sheep, and the tithe of holy things which were consecrated unto the LORD their God, and laid them by heaps.
♦ **Nehemiah 10:37** And that we should bring the firstfruits of our dough, and our offerings, and the fruit of all manner of trees, of wine and of oil, unto the priests, to the chambers of the house of our God; and the tithes of our ground unto the Levites, that the same Levites might have the tithes in all the cities of our tillage. 38 And the priest the son of Aaron shall be with the Levites, when the Levites take tithes: and the Levites shall bring up the tithe of the tithes unto the house of our God, to the chambers, into the treasure house.
♦ **Nehemiah 12:44** And at that time were some appointed over the chambers for the treasures, for the offerings, for the firstfruits, and for the tithes, to gather into them out of the fields of the cities the portions of the law for the priests and Levites: for Judah rejoiced for the priests and for the Levites that waited.
♦ **Nehemiah 13:5** And he had prepared for him a great chamber, where aforetime they laid the meat offerings, the frankincense, and the vessels, and the tithes of the corn, the new wine, and the oil, which was commanded to be given to the Levites, and the singers, and the porters; and the offerings of the priests.

♦ **Nehemiah 13:12** Then brought all Judah the tithe of the corn and the new wine and the oil unto the treasuries.

♦ **Hebrews 7:5** And verily they that are of the sons of Levi, who receive the office of the priesthood, have a commandment to take tithes of the people according to the law, that is, of their brethren, though they come out of the loins of Abraham: 6 But he whose descent is not counted from them received tithes of Abraham, and blessed him that had the promises. 7 And without all contradiction the less is blessed of the better. 8 And here men that die receive tithes; but there he receiveth them, of whom it is witnessed that he liveth. 9 And as I may so say, Levi also, who receiveth tithes, payed tithes in Abraham.

• Tithes to priests every three years.

♦ **Amos 4:4** Come to Bethel, and transgress; at Gilgal multiply transgression; and bring your sacrifices every morning, and your tithes after three years:

• Failure to tithe to the priests is a crime.

♦ **Malachi 3:8** Will a man rob God? Yet ye have robbed me. But ye say, Wherein have we robbed thee? In tithes and offerings.9 Ye are cursed with a curse: for ye have robbed me, even this whole nation. 10 Bring ye all the tithes into the storehouse, that there may be meat in mine house, and prove me now herewith, saith the LORD of hosts, if I will not open you the windows of heaven, and pour you out a blessing, that there shall not be room enough to receive it. 11 And I will rebuke the devourer for your sakes, and he shall not destroy the fruits of your ground; neither shall your vine cast her fruit before the time in the field, saith the LORD of hosts.

• Tithing is not to boast about.

♦ **Matthew 23:23** Woe unto you, scribes and Pharisees, hypocrites! for ye pay tithe of mint and anise and cummin, and have omitted the weightier matters of the law, judgment, mercy, and faith: these ought ye to have done, and not to leave the other undone.

♦ **Luke 11:42** But woe unto you, Pharisees! for ye tithe mint and rue and all manner of herbs, and pass over judgment and the love of God: these ought ye to have done, and not to leave the other undone.

♦ **Luke 18:11** The Pharisee stood and prayed thus with himself, God, I thank thee, that I am not as other men are, extortioners, unjust, adulterers, or even as this publican. 12 I fast twice in the week, I give tithes of all that I possess. 13 And the publican, standing afar off, would not lift up so much as his eyes unto heaven, but smote upon his breast, saying, God be merciful to me a sinner. 14 I tell you, this man went down to his house justified rather than the other: for every one that exalteth himself shall be abased; and he that humbleth himself shall be exalted.

The Tax Exempt Status of the Church

When a church is formed it applies for and receives IRS status as a 501(c)(3) corporation. This status allows contributions made to the church to be deductible by the donors, and the church to be exempt from paying taxes. This is seldom questioned except in cases where churches cross the line between Church and State usually by overt support or opposition to political candidates or issues. The very concept that a church has the right to be exempt from paying taxes is never questioned, but the Bible is very clear on the issue. Jesus was asked the question, answered it very clearly, and his answer is completely ignored by the church. Three of the four gospels recount the incident that brought this question before the ultimate judge of all things related to the church. Here is the answer from Matthew, Mark, and Luke:

♦ **Matthew 22:15** Then went the Pharisees, and took counsel how they might entangle him in his talk. 16 And they sent out unto him their disciples with the Herodians, saying, Master, we know that thou art true, and teachest the way of God in truth, neither carest thou for any man: for thou regardest not the person of men. 17 Tell us therefore, What thinkest thou? Is it lawful to give tribute unto Caesar, or not? 18 But Jesus perceived their wickedness, and said, Why tempt ye me, ye hypocrites? 19 Shew me the tribute money. And they brought unto him a penny. 20 And he saith unto them, Whose is this image and superscription? 21 They say unto him, Caesar's. Then saith he unto them, Render therefore unto Caesar the things which are Caesar's; and unto God the things that are God's. 22 When they had heard these words, they marvelled, and left him, and went their way.

♦ **Mark 12:13** And they send unto him certain of the Pharisees and of the Herodians, to catch him in his words. 14 And when they were come, they say unto him, Master, we know that thou art true, and carest for no man: for thou regardest not the person of men, but teachest the way of God in truth: Is it lawful to give tribute to Caesar, or not? 15 Shall we give, or shall we not give? But he, knowing their hypocrisy, said unto them, Why tempt ye me? bring me a penny, that I may see it. 16 And they brought it. And he saith unto them, Whose is this image and superscription? And they said unto him, Caesar's. 17 And Jesus answering said unto them, Render to Caesar the things that are Caesar's, and to God the things that are God's. And they marvelled at him.

♦ **Luke 20:20** And they watched him, and sent forth spies, which should feign themselves just men, that they might take hold of his words, that so they might deliver him unto the power and authority of the governor. 21 And they asked him, saying, Master, we know that thou sayest and teachest rightly, neither acceptest thou the person of any, but teachest the way of God truly: 22 Is it lawful for us to give tribute unto Caesar, or no? 23 But he perceived their craftiness, and said unto them, Why tempt ye me? 24 Shew me a penny. Whose image and superscription hath it? They answered and said, Caesar's. 25 And he said unto them, Render therefore unto Caesar the things which be Caesar's, and unto God the things which be God's. 26 And they could not take hold of his words before the people: and they marvelled at his answer, and held their peace.

Consider a simple question. If one could stand before Jesus and ask the question, "Should those who follow Christ pay taxes to the government currently in power?" What would be his answer? You be the judge of whether the church is correct in seeking tax exemption.

A Holy Spirit – A Holy Ghost

The Church View:

The Holy Ghost or Holy Spirit is a supreme eternal being separate from either the Father or Jesus and is part of a equal trinity with those two beings.

The Bible View:

The Holy Ghost, or Holy Spirit, is the essence of God the Father, and is the source of all love, life, and faith. There is no scriptural evidence to support the concept that the Holy Ghost or Holy Spirit is an individual being. There is clear historical evidence that the belief in a "Trinity" is a traditionally accepted concept rather than a doctrine supported by scripture.

The concept of the Holy Spirit or Holy Ghost as an individual entity that is part of a Trinity, including the Father and Jesus, is a dogma not supported in biblical text. A "trinity" was never mentioned by the prophets, or the apostles, and was actually contradicted by the words of Jesus himself. The concept of the Holy Spirit or Holy Ghost as a force projected by God, and as a form of spiritual contact and power, is well supported in Biblical text, and clearly described as a source of power and guidance by prophets and apostles alike. It is well documented in theological environs that this doctrine is shaky, at best, and only accepted as doctrine through a constant presence in doctrinal development; it is a tradition, not biblical doctrine. In simple terms, it is from man, not the Bible. Such a powerful entity with equal status to the Supreme Elohiym would certainly have at least a name or some description of its individual personality. It is almost always described as the device of the will of the Elohiym rather than a supreme partner in an exclusive triad of this supreme race. The names Holy Ghost and Holy Spirit are from the same words.

A Gross Mistranslation

• Evidence of the dogmatic directives driving the King James translation can be found in this glaring example:

♦ **1 John 5:7** For there are three that bear record in heaven, the Father, the Word, and the Holy Ghost: and these three are one. 8 And there are three that bear witness in earth, the spirit, and the water, and the blood: and these three agree in one.

In verse 7, the phrases "*the Father, the Word, and the Holy Ghost:*" and "*and these three are one*" have both been added by the translators, as was the phrase "*And there are three that bear witness.*" in verse 8. This was a blatant attempt by the Bishop of London, the supervisor of the translation project under King James, to inject the human based tradition of the Trinity into biblical text. No words that can be translated into these added phrases could be found in the original text. It is a fraud. The words are not found in any of the oldest, and most reliable manuscripts, nor in any of the ancient translations.

The concept of a triad in the godhead was not known in the original church the Christ established, and only appeared in "church" doctrine when the Emperor Constantine began his wholesale overhaul of biblical doctrine. It was made official in 381 A.D by the Council of Constantinople, which defined the godhead as three gods in one. From the Council transcripts we find this statement: "You, we and all who are not bent on subverting the word of the true faith should give this creed our approval. It is the most ancient and is consistent with our baptism. It tells us how to believe in the name of the Father and of the Son and of the holy Spirit: believing also, of course, that the Father, the Son and the holy Spirit have a single Godhead and power and substance, a dignity deserving the same honour and a co-eternal sovereignty, in three most perfect hypostases, or three perfect persons." The Council of Nice refers to this "institution" of the trinity into church doctrine as backing concepts formed in 325 A.D. This Council, convened by the Emperor Constantine, formulated the Nicene Creed. In every form, and from every aspect, the concept of the Holy Spirit / Ghost as an independent entity, or personality, and part of a "trinity" is a human, not a biblical, doctrine.

In truth, the doctrine of the "Trinity" is one of the most blatant, and easily documented examples of the hypocrisy Jesus spoke of when he stated:
♦ "Ye hypocrites, well did Esaias prophesy of you, saying, This people draweth nigh unto me with their mouth, and honoureth me with their lips; but their heart is far from me. But in vain they do worship me, teaching for doctrines the commandments of men.", (**Matthew 15:7-9**).

Heaven

Heaven is the Sky, Not a Divine Retirement Home

All these clouds, whirlwinds, pillars, vessels, chariots and pavilions are seen hovering in, coming down from or rising into heaven. The thunders, trumpets and voices that are heard are heard from heaven. All the men who leave the ground, and all the angels and metallic, glowing beings that come down to the ground do so either to, or from, heaven. All the lightning, streams of fire, brimstone, and other destructive things mentioned have their origin in heaven. Even the wars are fought in heaven are all thought to be from another place, or dimension. Since all these things are seen in relationship to heaven, the way the word 'heaven' is used is the key to understanding these phenomena and must be explained. The word heaven is used over 500 times in the Bible. In the Old Testament 'heaven' is translated almost exclusively from two different words. The Hebrew word '*shamayim*', which is defined as 'the sky', the place where the clouds and stars are, or '*shamayin*', the Aramaic word of the same definition, are the prime origins of the word "heaven.

The Old Testament
In the Old Testament 'heaven' is translated from other words only five times in the following verses:
- **Psalms 68:4:** it is translated from the Hebrew, arabah, ' the desert '
- **77:18:** the word is galgal, Hebrew for ' wheel or whirlwind '
- **89:6 & 37:** it is translated from the word shachaq, Hebrew for ' powder or thin vapor '.
- **Isaiah 5:30:** heaven is translated from ariyph, Hebrew for ' the sky '

The New Testament
The New Testament defines 'heaven' from the Greek word 'ouranos' meaning 'the sky' in all but 7 instances :
- **Philippians 2:10:** from the Greek, epouranos, ' above the sky, celestial
- **Revelation   8:13, 14:6, 19:1, 11, 14, and 17:** from the Greek word mesouranema, meaning mid-sky

The infrequency of the word 'sky'in the Bible must also be looked at in the overall study of this concept. The words sky and skies only appear 11 times in all 66 books. The words for things that normally appear in the sky such as clouds, stars, whirlwinds, storms, lightning, birds, rain, hail, and wind appear over 600 times. Heaven is the word the translators of the King James Bible in the early 1600's purposefully translated into the original words biblical authors used for the physical sky, not some ethereal plane.

The King James Bible was translated for King James of England who lived in a royal castle, surrounded by royal people, all speaking a royal language; a very proper form of court English. The Court English employed entirely different words to describe things, thus, confusing the commoners as to the meaning of certain words. You was *thee*, raiment was *clothing,* and sky was *heaven*. Therefore, in all but the above noted instances, the word heaven should be read as sky. Heaven is the sky, and sky fits in every instance.

Heaven is not the place with the 'pearly gates' or the 'streets of gold ' as the pulpit would have you believe. That is the New Jerusalem and is described in Revelation. Heaven is not said to be a reward for paying your tithes or a final destination for certain church members. Heaven is where God flies, the same place the birds fly. Heaven is where God lives because that is where his throne is and his throne flies. And, if any more proof is needed, just consider the inheritance of the beatitudes. Matthew 5:5 states clearly "Blessed are the meek: for they shall inherit the earth." not heaven. The heaven of the pulpit is a simplistic, human conceptualization, not a Biblically based reality.

Hell

The Church View:

It is represented by the church to mean a place of eternal, fiery torture for those who don't believe in the Christ as Saviour, and in extreme cases, those who question the authority of the church. This obviously means that the majority of humanity is destined for eternal, fiery torture. Not very fair for a loving and forgiving God, but then the church does not seem to deeply embrace fairness or forgiveness. A vengeful and unforgiving God more suits a pulpit that spews eternal, fiery condemnations for everything from style of dress to political affiliation as a matter of standard practice. Hell also fulfills the strongest motivational force for the church in its arsenal of flock control, fear. There are no statistics on how many people attend church, not out of belief in God, but more out of conditioned fear of a fiery torture. It would be a good bet that if fear of hell were eliminated, church revenues would drastically shrink.

The Bible View:

In most instances "hell" is translated from words which mean a hole in the ground into which bodies are placed after death. Other instances leave it highly unlikely that hell is a place exclusively created for the eternal torture of unbelievers.

Of all biblical concepts, hell is one of the most mysterious and feared. The word "hell" appears 54 times in the Bible, 30 times in the Old Testament, 24 in the New Testament. In the Old Testament, hell is taken from the word, Sh'owl, pronounced sheh-ole' or Sh'ol; Hades or the world of the dead (as if a subterranean retreat), Sheol, including its accessories and inmates: KJV--grave, hell, pit. It is interchangeable with the word grave or a pit. Basically, hell is a hole in the ground where bodies are buried. A thorough study of its appearance in Old Testament scripture will show it is not referred to as place of eternal fiery damnation.

142

In the New Testament it is taken from three words. First, we will examine the one from which the fiery place of eternal torture, so often associated with this word, is taken, Ghenna. It may surprise many to realize that we actually know where this place is, not an ethereal place where Satan dwells, but actually the Jerusalem city dump.

The word is Geena, pronounced gheh'-en-nah of Hebrew origin; valley of the son of Hinnom; ge-henna, or Ge-Hinnom, a valley of Jerusalem, used figuratively as a name for the place or state of everlasting punishment:

The actual place referred to is Hinnom, a deep, narrow ravine separating Mount Zion from the so-called "Hill of Evil Counsel" to the southwest of Jerusalem.

Hinnom is first mentioned here:

♦ **Joshua 15:8**. And the border went up by the valley of the son of Hinnom unto the south side of the Jebusite; the same is Jerusalem: and the border went up to the top of the mountain that lieth before the valley of Hinnom westward, which is at the end of the valley of the giants northward:

It was formerly the place where the idolatrous Jews burned their children alive as a sacrifice to Moloch and Baal. A particular part of the valley was called Tophet, the "fire-stove" or furnace, where the children were burned. After the Exile, in order to show their abhorrence of the locality, the Jews made this valley the receptacle of the refuse of the city. As with refuse, in those times it was burned to keep down vermin, the obvious offensive odors, to maximize space, and a fire was kept constantly burning there. Excavations carried out at this site from 1975 to 1980 by an archaeological mission turned up remains of nine burial caves around the ravine. In earlier excavations of the actual dump, it was found that the fire was still smoldering after centuries.

Here we have all the elements of the modern concept of Hell. A place of death, a burial area, destruction, anything placed in this fiery pit was consumed, a fiery furnace, where in the past children were burned alive, and unquenchable and everlasting fire, which is burning to this day.

• Here are the instances where Ghenna is used:

♦ **Matthew 5:22** But I say unto you, That whosoever is angry with his brother without a cause shall be in danger of the judgment: and whosoever shall say to his brother, Raca, shall be in danger of the council: but whosoever shall say, Thou fool, shall be in danger of hell fire.

♦ **Matthew 5:29** And if thy right eye offend thee, pluck it out, and cast it from thee: for it is profitable for thee that one of thy members should perish, and not that thy whole body should be cast into hell. 30 And if thy right hand offend thee, cut it off, and cast it from thee: for it is profitable for thee that one of thy members should perish, and not that thy whole body should be cast into hell.

143

♦ **Matthew 10: 28** And fear not them which kill the body, but are not able to kill the soul: but rather fear him which is able to destroy both soul and body in hell.

♦ **Matthew 18:9** And if thine eye offend thee, pluck it out, and cast it from thee: it is better for thee to enter into life with one eye, rather than having two eyes to be cast into hell fire.

♦ **Matthew 23:15** Woe unto you, scribes and Pharisees, hypocrites! for ye compass sea and land to make one proselyte, and when he is made, ye make him twofold more the child of hell than yourselves.

♦ **Matthew 23:33** Ye serpents, ye generation of vipers, how can ye escape the damnation of hell?

♦ **Mark 9:43** And if thy hand offend thee, cut it off: it is better for thee to enter into life maimed, than having two hands to go into hell, into the fire that never shall be quenched: 44 Where their worm dieth not, and the fire is not quenched. 45 And if thy foot offend thee, cut it off: it is better for thee to enter halt into life, than having two feet to be cast into hell, into the fire that never shall be quenched: 46 Where their worm dieth not, and the fire is not quenched. 47 And if thine eye offend thee, pluck it out: it is better for thee to enter into the kingdom of God with one eye, than having two eyes to be cast into hell fire:

♦ **Luke 12:5** But I will forewarn you whom ye shall fear: Fear him, which after he hath killed hath power to cast into hell; yea, I say unto you, Fear him.

♦ **James 3:6** And the tongue is a fire, a world of iniquity: so is the tongue among our members, that it defileth the whole body, and setteth on fire the course of nature; and it is set on fire of hell.

• The next word is familiar to most, the Greek word Hades. And, as with the Hebrew word Sheol, it is interchangeable with the word grave. There is a serious problem trying to designate this as a place of eternal fiery torture rather than a burial place, the problem being, mainly, that Jesus spent three days in Hades after his crucifixion. Since it is clear that this place was actually a sepulchre, not a furnace, and that Jesus committed no sin to warrant such punishment; it would justify the logical conclusion that this is the grave. Attempting to insinuate that Jesus had to go to this fiery Hell to defeat it presupposes that such a place exists without solid scriptural evidence. Jesus performed his ultimate miracle by defeating death, not fire. In the case of Lazarus, it must be noted that this is a parable and is used in a metaphoric sense as with the use of the word Ghenna.

The word hell is translated from is haides, pronounced hah'-dace; properly, unseen, i.e. "Hades" or the place (state) of departed souls: KJV--grave, hell.

• Here are the instances where the word Hades is used:

♦ **Matthew 11:23** And thou, Capernaum, which art exalted unto heaven, shalt be brought down to hell: for if the mighty works, which have been done in thee, had been done in Sodom, it would have remained until this day.

♦ **Mark 16:18** And I say also unto thee, That thou art Peter, and upon this rock I will build my church; and the gates of hell shall not prevail against it.

♦ **Luke 10:15** And thou, Capernaum, which art exalted to heaven, shalt be thrust down to hell.

♦ **Luke 16:23** And in hell he lift up his eyes, being in torments, and seeth Abraham afar off, and Lazarus in his bosom.

♦ **Acts 2:27** Because thou wilt not leave my soul in hell, neither wilt thou suffer thine Holy One to see corruption.

♦ **Acts 2:31** He seeing this before spake of the resurrection of Christ, that his soul was not left in hell, neither his flesh did see corruption.

♦ **Revelation 1:18** I am he that liveth, and was dead; and, behold, I am alive for evermore, Amen; and have the keys of hell and of death.

♦ **Revelation 6:8** And I looked, and behold a pale horse: and his name that sat on him was Death, and Hell followed with him. And power was given unto them over the fourth part of the earth, to kill with sword, and with hunger, and with death, and with the beasts of the earth.

♦ **Revelation 20:13** And the sea gave up the dead which were in it; and death and hell delivered up the dead which were in them: and they were judged every man according to their works. 14 And death and hell were cast into the lake of fire. This is the second death. 15 And whosoever was not found written in the book of life was cast into the lake of fire.

• The third word translated into hell is only used once and refers to the place of imprisonment for the angels that are described here:

♦ **Genesis 6:4**. There were giants in the earth in those days; and also after that, when the sons of God came in unto the daughters of men, and they bare children to them, the same became mighty men which were of old, men of renown.

Enoch gives a detailed description of this place and can more easily be understood by reviewing the section in this book about the Flood. The word is Tartaroo, pronounced tar-tar-o'-o from Tartaros (the deepest abyss of Hades); to incarcerate in eternal torment.

Here is the verse and its relation to the angels of the flood:

♦ **2 Peter 2:4** For if God spared not the angels that sinned, but cast them down to hell, and delivered them into chains of darkness, to be reserved unto judgment; 5 And spared not the old world, but saved Noah the eighth person, a preacher of righteousness, bringing in the flood upon the world of the ungodly;

If one chooses to embrace the concept of an eternity of suffering in a furnace, that is one's prerogative, but it is not a biblical concept based on a strong foundation. It can be speculated and implied, but there is ample evidence against this concept.

Faith

The Church View:

Faith is an unquestioned trust in God you receive by going to church, accepting what you are told from the pulpit, and of course, paying your dues. Any doubts or questions are considered as a lack of faith.

The Bible View:

Persuasion that man is more than a physical entity and is part of a much larger and higher purpose. Even a minute amount of this belief will give mere humans supernatural power, making them capable of performing feats only limited by the level of belief itself. A tiny amount of this belief can allow a person to literally move mountains and gave the miracles of the first members of the church world great power. It is obvious that that persuasion comes from exposure to evidence given to man through an opening of the mind to these proofs by God.

The word most often translated into 'faith', (*223 out of 229 times in the NT*), is pistis, pronounced pis'-tis, from peitho; persuasion, i.e. credence; moral conviction.. The word of origin is peitho Pronounced pi'-tho a primary verb; to convince (by argument, true or false); by analogy, to pacify or conciliate (by other fair means); reflexively or passively, to assent (to evidence or authority), to rely (by inward certainty):

This means that faith is belief based on evidence that persuades one to believe. Paul verifies this in his letter to the Hebrew church:
See Faith Verses: Appendix N

Faith is Substance and Evidence

♦ **Hebrews 11:1** Now faith is the substance of things hoped for, the evidence of things not seen.

The word evidence is translated from elegchos, pronounced el'-eng-khos; proof, conviction. This is consistent with the charge that we are to prove, and literally put to the test, to approve all things before we accept them.

Prove all things.

♦ **1 Thessalonians 5:21** Prove all things; hold fast that which is good.

♦ **Romans 12:2** And be not conformed to this world: but be ye transformed by the renewing of your mind, that ye may prove what is that good, and acceptable, and perfect, will of God.

In both the verses the word translated is dokimazo, pronounced dok-im-ad'-zo; to test (literally or figuratively); by implication, to approve.

♦ **2 Corinthians 13:5** Examine yourselves, whether ye be in the faith; prove your own selves. Know ye not your own selves, how that Jesus Christ is in you, except ye be reprobates?

Faith is a Gift
♦ **Ephesians 2:8** For by grace are ye saved through faith; and that not of yourselves: it is the gift of God:

Proof Is Freely Given, If One Simply Looks For It.
♦ **Matthew 7:7** Ask, and it shall be given you; seek, and ye shall find; knock, and it shall be opened unto you:

How is it that a mere mortal can have the incredible power Jesus describes just by believing they have it? How powerful is a human being? Yhovah was very clear about the nature of man:
♦ **Psalms 82:6** I have said, Ye are gods; and all of you are children of the most High.

And when Yhovah became the human, Jesus, he repeated it, by quoting himself:
♦ **John 10:34** Jesus answered them, Is it not written in your law, I said, Ye are gods?

Even though the Bible does say humans were made lower than the angels, does that mean this will be their permanent station?
♦ **1Corinthians 6:3** Know ye not that we shall judge angels? how much more things that pertain to this life?

From what the Bible presents, there is but one logical conclusion. Faith is the belief that humans are gods, created to be gods, by the creator God, Yhovah. If this is true, is it any wonder that Jesus said humans have the power to move mountains with just an infinitesimal amount of belief in such an awesome reality?

A complete review of all the verses that record the word faith will show that the above verses are not contradicted. Nowhere is it stated that one should not question or test the evidence. Nowhere is it stated that faith is not the way the persons possessing it are persuaded. And, it is shown that the increase in faith of the members of the first church gave them undeniable super-human power.

Faith is Belief in God's Power
♦ **Matthew 6:30** Wherefore, if God so clothe the grass of the field, which to day is, and to morrow is cast into the oven, shall he not much more clothe you, O ye of little faith?
♦ **Matthew 8:26** And he saith unto them, Why are ye fearful, O ye of little faith? Then he arose, and rebuked the winds and the sea; and there was a great calm.
♦ **Romans 4:5** But to him that worketh not, but believeth on him that justifieth the ungodly, his faith is counted for righteousness.

147

♦ **Romans 4:20** He staggered not at the promise of God through unbelief; but was strong in faith, giving glory to God;

♦ **Romans 9:32** Wherefore? Because they sought it not by faith, but as it were by the works of the law. For they stumbled at that stumblingstone;

♦ **Romans 14:23** And he that doubteth is damned if he eat, because he eateth not of faith: for whatsoever is not of faith is sin.

♦ **1 Corinthians 2:5** That your faith should not stand in the wisdom of men, but in the power of God.

♦ **1 Corinthians 15:14** And if Christ be not risen, then is our preaching vain, and your faith is also vain.

♦ **1 Corinthians 15:17** And if Christ be not raised, your faith is vain; ye are yet in your sins.

♦ **Galatians 3:22** But the scripture hath concluded all under sin, that the promise by faith of Jesus Christ might be given to them that believe.

♦ **Galatians 5:5** For we through the Spirit wait for the hope of righteousness by faith.

♦ **Ephesians 3:12** In whom we have boldness and access with confidence by the faith of him.

♦ **2 Thessalonians 1:11** Wherefore also we pray always for you, that our God would count you worthy of this calling, and fulfil all the good pleasure of his goodness, and the work of faith with power:

♦ **Timothy 4:1** Now the Spirit speaketh expressly, that in the latter times some shall depart from the faith, giving heed to seducing spirits, and doctrines of devils;

♦ **Hebrews 11:3** Through faith we understand that the worlds were framed by the word of God, so that things which are seen were not made of things which do appear.

♦ **Hebrews 11:6** But without faith it is impossible to please him: for he that cometh to God must believe that he is, and that he is a rewarder of them that diligently seek him. 7 By faith Noah, being warned of God of things not seen as yet, moved with fear, prepared an ark to the saving of his house; by the which he condemned the world, and became heir of the righteousness which is by faith. 8 By faith Abraham, when he was called to go out into a place which he should after receive for an inheritance, obeyed; and he went out, not knowing whither he went. 9 By faith he sojourned in the land of promise, as in a strange country, dwelling in tabernacles with Isaac and Jacob, the heirs with him of the same promise:

♦ **Hebrews 11:13** These all died in faith, not having received the promises, but having seen them afar off, and were persuaded of them, and embraced them, and confessed that they were strangers and pilgrims on the earth.

♦ **Hebrews 11:33** Who through faith subdued kingdoms, wrought righteousness, obtained promises, stopped the mouths of lions.

Faith Comes From Learning

♦ **Romans 10:17** So then faith cometh by hearing, and hearing by the word of God.

♦ **Galatians 3:2** This only would I learn of you, Received ye the Spirit by the works of the law, or by the hearing of faith?

♦ **Galatians 3:5** He therefore that ministereth to you the Spirit, and worketh miracles among you, doeth he it by the works of the law, or by the hearing of faith?

Faith Can Give Unlimited Power

♦ **Matthew 14:31** And immediately Jesus stretched forth his hand, and caught him, and said unto him, O thou of little faith, wherefore didst thou doubt?

♦ **Matthew 17:20** And Jesus said unto them, Because of your unbelief: for verily I say unto you, If ye have faith as a grain of mustard seed, ye shall say unto this mountain, Remove hence to yonder place; and it shall remove; and nothing shall be impossible unto you.

♦ **Matthew 21:21** Jesus answered and said unto them, Verily I say unto you, If ye have faith, and doubt not, ye shall not only do this which is done to the fig tree, but also if ye shall say unto this mountain, Be thou removed, and be thou cast into the sea; it shall be done. 22 And all things, whatsoever ye shall ask in prayer, believing, ye shall receive.

♦ **Mark 11:22** And Jesus answering saith unto them, Have faith in God. 23 For verily I say unto you, That whosoever shall say unto this mountain, Be thou removed, and be thou cast into the sea; and shall not doubt in his heart, but shall believe that those things which he saith shall come to pass; he shall have whatsoever he saith. 24 Therefore I say unto you, What things soever ye desire, when ye pray, believe that ye receive them, and ye shall have them.

♦ **Luke 8:25** And he said unto them, Where is your faith? And they being afraid wondered, saying one to another, What manner of man is this! for he commandeth even the winds and water, and they obey him.

♦ **Luke 17:5** And the apostles said unto the Lord, Increase our faith. 6 And the Lord said, If ye had faith as a grain of mustard seed, ye might say unto this sycamine tree, Be thou plucked up by the root, and be thou planted in the sea; and it should obey you.

♦ **Acts 6:7** And the word of God increased; and the number of the disciples multiplied in Jerusalem greatly; and a great company of the priests were obedient to the faith. 8 And Stephen, full of faith and power, did great wonders and miracles among the people.

♦ **Romans 3:3** For what if some did not believe? shall their unbelief make the faith of God without effect?

Faith Heals

♦ **Matthew 9:2** And, behold, they brought to him a man sick of the palsy, lying on a bed: and Jesus seeing their faith said unto the sick of the palsy; Son, be of good cheer; thy sins be forgiven thee.

♦ **Matthew 9:22** But Jesus turned him about, and when he saw her, he said, Daughter, be of good comfort; thy faith hath made thee whole. And the woman was made whole from that hour.

♦ **Matthew 9:29** Then touched he their eyes, saying, According to your faith be it unto you.

♦ **Matthew 15:28** Then Jesus answered and said unto her, O woman, great is thy faith: be it unto thee even as thou wilt. And her daughter was made whole from that very hour.

♦ **Mark 5:34** And he said unto her, Daughter, thy faith hath made thee whole; go in peace, and be whole of thy plague.

♦ **Luke 18:42** And Jesus said unto him, Receive thy sight: thy faith hath saved thee.

♦ **Acts 13:9** The same heard Paul speak: who stedfastly beholding him, and perceiving that he had faith to be healed,

♦ **James 5:15** And the prayer of faith shall save the sick, and the Lord shall raise him up; and if he have committed sins, they shall be forgiven him.

Faith and the Law

♦ **Romans 3:28** Therefore we conclude that a man is justified by faith without the deeds of the law.

♦ **Romans 4:13** For the promise, that he should be the heir of the world, was not to Abraham, or to his seed, through the law, but through the righteousness of faith. 14 For if they which are of the law be heirs, faith is made void, and the promise made of none effect:

♦ **Galatians 2:16** Knowing that a man is not justified by the works of the law, but by the faith of Jesus Christ, even we have believed in Jesus Christ, that we might be justified by the faith of Christ, and not by the works of the law: for by the works of the law shall no flesh be justified.

♦ **Galatians 3:5** He therefore that ministereth to you the Spirit, and worketh miracles among you, doeth he it by the works of the law, or by the hearing of faith?

♦ **Galatians 3:11** But that no man is justified by the law in the sight of God, it is evident: for, The just shall live by faith. 12 And the law is not of faith: but, The man that doeth them shall live in them.

♦ **Galatians 3:23** But before faith came, we were kept under the law, shut up unto the faith which should afterwards be revealed. 24 Wherefore the law was our schoolmaster to bring us unto Christ, that we might be justified by faith. 25 But after that faith is come, we are no longer under a schoolmaster.

♦ **Philippians 3:9** And be found in him, not having mine own righteousness, which is of the law, but that which is through the faith of Christ, the righteousness which is of God by faith:

Faith and Love
♦ **Galatians 5:6** For in Jesus Christ neither circumcision availeth any thing, nor uncircumcision; but faith which worketh by love.
♦ **Galatians 5:22** But the fruit of the Spirit is love, joy, peace, longsuffering, gentleness, goodness, faith,
♦ **Ephesians 3:17** That Christ may dwell in your hearts by faith; that ye, being rooted and grounded in love,
♦ **Ephesians 6:23** Peace be to the brethren, and love with faith, from God the Father and the Lord Jesus Christ.
♦ **Colossians 1:4** Since we heard of your faith in Christ Jesus, and of the love which ye have to all the saints,
♦ **1 Timothy 1:14** And the grace of our Lord was exceeding abundant with faith and love which is in Christ Jesus.

Children Of God And Abraham
♦ **Galatians 3:7** Know ye therefore that they which are of faith, the same are the children of Abraham.
♦ **Galatians 3:26** For ye are all the children of God by faith in Christ Jesus.

The Law

The Church View:
The church should follow whatever laws found in the Bible the leaders of that particular church decide should be enforced and whatever other laws they make. These laws are to be enforced without regard to whether they do, or do not, have any biblical authority.

The Bible View:
The laws of the Old Testament that were only given to the Nation of Israel are oppressive and impossible to follow.

♦ "Now therefore why tempt ye God, to put a yoke upon the neck of the disciples, which neither our fathers nor we were able to bear?" {Acts 15:10}

The Hypocrisy of Church Law
It is hard to fathom how the mainstream Bible based church has arrived at the choice of doctrinal concepts it now follows. Through a series of decisions by the early church leadership, almost every law and principle has been changed or discarded altogether. When doctrine could not be modified or abandoned, new doctrine was created to suit the need. Every aspect of church structure is added, from the buildings it inhabits to the pastor that leads it.

The Doctrines of Men

These are additions not to be found in scripture.

The doctrine of choosing a day to call its members to worship has been added, there is no day for the church to meet for worship in scripture. While adding a day for worship, the church discarded the day specifically commanded as a day of rest, actually making the act of resting on the seventh day an offense. The High Sabbaths that God commanded were also abandoned while ancient pagan celebrations were added and they were altered to suit the needs of the church.

The very financial foundation of the church, the tithing laws, have been grossly corrupted and abused. They would be judged as extortion by fraudulent means if a court of law could challenge them. Not only is the means of exacting tribute from the membership wrong, the use for which the funding is spent is wrong.

Most importantly, the New Testament edicts clearly pronounced as doctrine have been altogether ignored. The church proudly uses the name and sacrifice of Jesus while teaching and practicing doctrines contrary to the doctrines he personally taught. Not surprising is the fact that Jesus recognized and warned against this enigma even in his own time:

♦ **Matthew 15:7** Ye hypocrites, well did Esaias prophesy of you, saying, 8 This people draweth nigh unto me with their mouth, and honoureth me with their lips; but their heart is far from me. 9 But in vain they do worship me, teaching for doctrines the commandments of men. 10 And he called the multitude, and said unto them, Hear, and understand: 11 Not that which goeth into the mouth defileth a man; but that which cometh out of the mouth, this defileth a man. 12 Then came his disciples, and said unto him, Knowest thou that the Pharisees were offended, after they heard this saying? 13 But he answered and said, Every plant, which my heavenly Father hath not planted, shall be rooted up. 14 Let them alone: they be blind leaders of the blind. And if the blind lead the blind, both shall fall into the ditch.

♦ **Luke 6:46** And why call ye me, Lord, Lord, and do not the things which I say? 47 Whosoever cometh to me, and heareth my sayings, and doeth them, I will shew you to whom he is like: 48 He is like a man which built an house, and digged deep, and laid the foundation on a rock: and when the flood arose, the stream beat vehemently upon that house, and could not shake it: for it was founded upon a rock 49 But he that heareth, and doeth not, is like a man that without a foundation built an house upon the earth; against which the stream did beat vehemently, and immediately it fell; and the ruin of that house was great.

A simple study of the laws laid down in the Old Testament will clearly demonstrate that the church does not even attempt to follow all the laws found there. Yet, with false authority, they pick and chose what they determine are laws the membership should follow, and how those laws should be interpreted without even the slightest regard to the principles and details of the laws they enforce.

The Oppressive Laws

As non-Jewish members began to enter the first church, some of the more rigid members demanded that all new male members, Hebrew or not, be circumcised, young and old. This prompted a debate during which the harshness and unobtainable nature of the Jewish Law is pointed out:

♦ **Acts 15:5** But there rose up certain of the sect of the Pharisees which believed, saying, That it was needful to circumcise them, and to command them to keep the law of Moses. 6 And the apostles and elders came together for to consider of this matter. 7 And when there had been much disputing, Peter rose up, and said unto them, Men and brethren, ye know how that a good while ago God made choice among us, that the Gentiles by my mouth should hear the word of the gospel, and believe. 8 And God, which knoweth the hearts, bare them witness, giving them the Holy Ghost, even as he did unto us; 9 And put no difference between us and them, purifying their hearts by faith. 10 Now therefore why tempt ye God, to put a yoke upon the neck of the disciples, which neither our fathers nor we were able to bear?

The Change

After the matter of compliance with the Jewish laws is heard, James announces the decision not to require the new members to follow the whole of the law, but to honor only four minor laws:

♦ **Acts 15:13** And after they had held their peace, James answered, saying, Men and brethren, hearken unto me: 14 Simeon hath declared how God at the first did visit the Gentiles, to take out of them a people for his name. 15 And to this agree the words of the prophets; as it is written, 16 After this I will return, and will build again the tabernacle of David, which is fallen down; and I will build again the ruins thereof, and I will set it up: 17 That the residue of men might seek after the Lord, and all the Gentiles, upon whom my name is called, saith the Lord, who doeth all these things. 18 Known unto God are all his works from the beginning of the world. 19 Wherefore my sentence is, that we trouble not them, which from among the Gentiles are turned to God: 20 But that we write unto them, that they abstain from pollutions of idols, and from fornication, and from things strangled, and from blood.

The Change Becomes Doctrine

The apostles and elders decide that this change should be immediately announced to all the members and do so with hand-carried letters:

♦ **Acts 15:22** Then pleased it the apostles and elders with the whole church, to send chosen men of their own company to Antioch with Paul and Barnabas; namely, Judas surnamed Barsabas and Silas, chief men among the brethren: 23 And they wrote letters by them after this manner; The apostles and elders and brethren send greeting unto the brethren which are of the Gentiles in Antioch and Syria and Cilicia. 24 Forasmuch as we have heard, that certain which went out from us have troubled you with words, subverting your souls, saying, Ye must be circumcised, and keep the law: to whom we gave no such commandment: 25 It seemed good unto us, being assembled with one accord, to send chosen men unto you with our beloved Barnabas and Paul, 26 Men that have hazarded their lives for the name of our Lord Jesus Christ. 27 We have sent therefore Judas and Silas, who shall also tell you the same things by mouth. 28 For it seemed good to the Holy Ghost, and to us, to lay upon you no greater burden than these necessary things; 29 That ye abstain from meats offered to idols, and from blood, and from things strangled, and from fornication: from which if ye keep yourselves, ye shall do well. Fare ye well.

♦ **Acts 21:21** And they are informed of thee, that thou teachest all the Jews which are among the Gentiles to forsake Moses, saying that they ought not to circumcise their children, neither to walk after the customs. 22 What is it therefore? the multitude must needs come together: for they will hear that thou art come. 23 Do therefore this that we say to thee: We have four men which have a vow on them; 24 Them take, and purify thyself with them, and be at charges with them, that they may shave their heads: and all may know that those things, whereof they were informed concerning thee, are nothing; but that thou thyself also walkest orderly, and keepest the law. 25 As touching the Gentiles which believe, we have written and concluded that they observe no such thing, save only that they keep themselves from things offered to idols, and from blood, and from strangled, and from fornication.

The Prime Directive

Throughout the ministry of Jesus, the single most important principle that was emphasized is love. He declared this to be the basis of all law and prophecy.

♦ **Matthew 22:35**. Then one of them, which was a lawyer, asked him a question, tempting him, and saying, 36. Master, which is the great commandment in the law? 37. Jesus said unto him, Thou shalt love the Lord thy God with all thy heart, and with all thy soul, and with all thy mind. 38. This is the first and great commandment. 39. And the second is like unto it, Thou shalt love thy neighbour as thyself.

♦ **Mark 12:28**. And one of the scribes came, and having heard them reasoning together, and perceiving that he had answered them well, asked him, Which is the first commandment of all? 29. And Jesus answered him, The first of all the commandments is, Hear, O Israel; The Lord our God is one Lord: 30. And thou shalt love the Lord thy God with all thy heart, and with all thy soul, and with all thy mind, and with all thy strength: this is the first commandment. 31. And the second is like, namely this, Thou shalt love thy neighbour as thyself. There is none other commandment greater than these.

♦ **John 13:34**. A new commandment I give unto you, That ye love one another; as I have loved you, that ye also love one another. 35. By this shall all men know that ye are my disciples, if ye have love one to another.

♦ **John 15:12** This is my commandment, That ye love one another, as I have loved you. 13. Greater love hath no man than this, that a man lay down his life for his friends

The Law is a Curse

♦ **Galatians 3:10**. For as many as are of the works of the law are under the curse: for it is written, Cursed is every one that continueth not in all things which are written in the book of the law to do them. 11. But that no man is justified by the law in the sight of God, it is evident: for, The just shall live by faith. 12. And the law is not of faith: but, the man that doeth them shall live in them. 13. Christ hath redeemed us from the curse of the law, being made a curse for us: for it is written, Cursed is every one that hangeth on a tree:

♦ **2 Corinthians 3:3**. Forasmuch as ye are manifestly declared to be the epistle of Christ ministered by us, written not with ink, but with the Spirit of the living God; not in tables of stone, but in fleshy tables of the heart.

The Golden Rule is the Law

♦ **Matthew 7:12**. Therefore all things whatsoever ye would that men should do to you, do ye even so to them: for this is the law and the prophets.

The Good Samaritan Defines the Law

♦ **Luke 10:25** And, behold, a certain lawyer stood up, and tempted him, saying, Master, what shall I do to inherit eternal life? 26 He said unto him, What is written in the law? how readest thou? 27 And he answering said, Thou shalt love the Lord thy God with all thy heart, and with all thy soul, and with all thy strength, and with all thy mind; and thy neighbour as thyself. 28 And he said unto him, Thou hast answered right: this do, and thou shalt live. 29 But he, willing to justify himself, said unto Jesus, And who is my neighbour? 30 And Jesus answering said, A certain man went down from Jerusalem to Jericho, and fell among thieves, which stripped him of his raiment, and wounded him, and departed, leaving him half dead. 31 And by chance there came down a certain priest that way: and when he saw him, he passed by on the other side. 32 And likewise a Levite, when he was at the place, came and looked on him, and passed by on the other side. 33 But a certain Samaritan, as he journeyed, came where he was: and when he saw him, he had compassion on him, 34 And went to him, and bound up his wounds, pouring in oil and wine, and set him on his own beast, and brought him to an inn, and took care of him. 35 And on the morrow when he departed, he took out two pence, and gave them to the host, and said unto him, Take care of him; and whatsoever thou spendest more, when I come again, I will repay thee. 36 Which now of these three, thinkest thou, was neighbour unto him that fell among the thieves?

37 And he said, He that shewed mercy on him. Then said Jesus unto him, Go, and do thou likewise.

The Law and the Truth
♦ **John 1:17** For the law was given by Moses, but grace and truth came by Jesus Christ.

Not Under the Law
♦ **Romans 6:14** For sin shall not have dominion over you: for ye are not under the law, but under grace.

Who Can Enforce the Law?
♦ **John 8:5** Now Moses in the law commanded us, that such should be stoned: but what sayest thou? 6 This they said, tempting him, that they might have to accuse him. But Jesus stooped down, and with his finger wrote on the ground, as though he heard them not. 7 So when they continued asking him, he lifted up himself, and said unto them, He that is without sin among you, let him first cast a stone at her.
♦ **Acts 13:39** And by him all that believe are justified from all things, from which ye could not be justified by the law of Moses.
♦ **John 7:19** Did not Moses give you the law, and yet none of you keepeth the law? Why go ye about to kill me?

An In-Depth View of the Law
A thorough explanation of the true implications of the law, this can be found by a complete and careful reading of the Epistle to the Romans chapters 2 through 8

It would seem from what has been presented that the strict adherence to Hebrew law demanded by churches is in direct defiance of the authority of the apostles. As such, it is also a contradiction of Jesus himself. This, of course, does not refer to members of the Jewish faith. For those who are quick to point out that Jesus followed the law, it should be remembered that he was a Jew and the edict presented above was directed at the non-Jewish members of the church.

Prayer

The Church View:
Public prayer is encouraged in all public venues and practiced at all church oriented functions.

The Bible View:
Prayer is private, public prayer is condemned, repeated prayer is vain and unnecessary.

From the Expert: Prayer is Private!

Without reservation, the final authority on prayer is Jesus. This is his treatise on the merits of public, private, and scripted prayer:

Public Prayer

♦ **Matthew 6:5** And when thou prayest, thou shalt not be as the hypocrites are: for they love to pray standing in the synagogues and in the corners of the streets, that they may be seen of men. Verily I say unto you, They have their reward.

Private Prayer

♦ **Matthew 6: 6** But thou, when thou prayest, enter into thy closet, and when thou hast shut thy door, pray to thy Father which is in secret; and thy Father which seeth in secret shall reward thee openly.

♦ **Matthew 23:14** Woe unto you, scribes and Pharisees, hypocrites! for ye devour widows' houses, and for a pretence make long prayer: therefore ye shall receive the greater damnation.

Scripted Prayer

♦ **Matthew 6:7** But when ye pray, use not vain repetitions, as the heathen do: for they think that they shall be heard for their much speaking. 8 Be not ye therefore like unto them: for your Father knoweth what things ye have need of, before ye ask him.

In these verses Jesus condemns the accepted prayer practices of almost all modern day Bible-based churches. Public prayer is hypocritical, narcissistic, and ineffective, and practiced or scripted prayer is vain and unnecessary. The single most often repeated and public prayer consists of the next five verses, and is known as the Lord's Prayer.

The "Lord's Prayer
A Public Prayer - Or a Lesson?

Did Jesus immediately contradict himself, and utter a public prayer after condemning the practice? Not when one considers the first six words: *"After this manner therefore pray ye…"* This makes it clear that what follows is not a prayer, but a guide. Following the denouncement of complicated and repetitive prayer, this is an outline of a simple prayer and certainly not a spontaneous prayer.

The Outline

♦ **Matthew 6:9** After this manner therefore pray ye: Our Father which art in heaven, Hallowed be thy name. 10 Thy kingdom come, Thy will be done in earth, as it is in heaven. 11 Give us this day our daily bread. 12 And forgive us our debts, as we forgive our debtors. 13 And lead us not into temptation, but deliver us from evil: For thine is the kingdom, and the power, and the glory, for ever. Amen.

The Lesson Confirmed

In Luke this outline is clearly shown to be a lesson in how to pray and not a prayer and he actually stops praying before he gives the lesson:

♦ **Luke 1:1** And it came to pass, that, as he was praying in a certain place, when he ceased, one of his disciples said unto him, Lord, teach us to pray, as John also taught his disciples. 2 And he said unto them, When ye pray, say, Our Father which art in heaven, Hallowed be thy name. Thy kingdom come. Thy will be done, as in heaven, so in earth. 3 Give us day by day our daily bread. 4 And forgive us our sins; for we also forgive every one that is indebted to us. And lead us not into temptation; but deliver us from evil.

Private Prayer In Practice

The practice of praying privately is demonstrated in biblical text:

♦ **Matthew 14:23** And when he had sent the multitudes away, he went up into a mountain apart to pray: and when the evening was come, he was there alone.

♦ **Matthew 26:36** Then cometh Jesus with them unto a place called Gethsemane, and saith unto the disciples, Sit ye here, while I go and pray yonder.

♦ **Mark 6:46** And when he had sent them away, he departed into a mountain to pray.

♦ **Mark 14:32** And they came to a place which was named Gethsemane: and he saith to his disciples, Sit ye here, while I shall pray.

♦ **Luke 6:12** And it came to pass in those days, that he went out into a mountain to pray, and continued all night in prayer to God.

♦ **Luke 22:45** And when he rose up from prayer, and was come to his disciples, he found them sleeping for sorrow,

♦ **Acts 10:9** On the morrow, as they went on their journey, and drew nigh unto the city, Peter went up upon the housetop to pray about the sixth hour:

♦ **1 Corinthians 7:5** Defraud ye not one the other, except it be with consent for a time, that ye may give yourselves to fasting and prayer; and come together again, that Satan tempt you not for your incontinency.

Charity and Fasting

A quick study of both charitable giving and fasting will show that these practices are to be done in private as well:

♦ **Matthew 6:1** Take heed that ye do not your alms before men, to be seen of them: otherwise ye have no reward of your Father which is in heaven. 2 Therefore when thou doest thine alms, do not sound a trumpet before thee, as the hypocrites do in the synagogues and in the streets, that they may have glory of men. Verily I say unto you, They have their reward. 3 But when thou doest alms, let not thy left hand know what thy right hand doeth: 4 That thine alms may be in secret: and thy Father which seeth in secret himself shall reward thee openly.

♦ **Matthew 6:16** Moreover when ye fast, be not, as the hypocrites, of a sad countenance: for they disfigure their faces, that they may appear unto men to fast. Verily I say unto you, They have their reward. 17 But thou, when thou fastest, anoint thine head, and wash thy face; 18 That thou appear not unto men to fast, but unto thy Father which is in secret: and thy Father, which seeth in secret, shall reward thee openly.

The Holy Days

The Church View:

Sunday, the first day of the week, is the day of worship, and you are commanded to attend church on that day. The birth of Jesus is to be celebrated on Christmas Day, and the death of Jesus is to be celebrated on Easter Day.

The Bible View:

Saturday is the seventh day of the week, and mankind is commanded to rest on that day. There is no command to gather at a building for worship on any day any where in scripture. There are specific days in the Old Testament, called festivals, or high Sabbaths, which the members of the nation of Israel are commanded to observe. There are no indications that the members of the first church observed these days. There are no commands to observe either the birth or death of Jesus.

This section contains only the three most prominent church holy day contradictions, Sunday, Christmas, and Easter. The pages needed to describe the number and diversity of celebrations not sanctioned by scripture, but honored by the different Bible based religions, would require another entire book. The space required to describe the celebrations actually sanctioned in scripture is one sentence. Quite simply, not a single one of the High Sabbaths commanded by God to be observed is honored by the mainstream Christian Church.

The weekly day of worship, Sunday, and the two yearly holidays, Easter and Christmas, observed by the church have no foundation in scripture. They are, in fact, the creations of men and condemned by God.

The Sabbath and Sunday

• The question of the why we are commanded to rest on the Sabbath, but don't, is very simple. God commanded the seventh day of the week as a day of rest. The church outlawed resting on the seventh day.

• The reason why we gather to worship on Sunday, though there is no scriptural edict to do so, is equally simple. God did not declare any day as a day to meet and worship. The church declared the first day as a day to meet and worship.

The Doctrines of Men

- The Bible is very clear about the sanctity of the Sabbath, not as day of worship, but a day of rest.
- Constantine the Great changed the day of rest on March 7, 321 AD by declaring, "All judges and city people and the craftsmen shall rest upon the Venerable Day of the Sun."
- From the Council of Laodicea in Phrygia Pacatiana 364 A.D, Canon XXIX.: "Christians must not judaize by resting on the Sabbath, but must work on that day, rather honouring the Lord's Day; and, if they can, resting then as Christians. But if any shall be found to be judaizers, let them be anathema from Christ."
- These verses are a direct condemnation of the actions taken to outlaw the Sabbath by the early church:
♦ **Exodus 20:8** Remember the sabbath day, to keep it holy. 9 Six days shalt thou labour, and do all thy work: 10 But the seventh day is the sabbath of the LORD thy God: in it thou shalt not do any work, thou, nor thy son, nor thy daughter, thy manservant, nor thy maidservant, nor thy cattle, nor thy stranger that is within thy gates: 11 For in six days the LORD made heaven and earth, the sea, and all that in them is, and rested the seventh day: wherefore the LORD blessed the sabbath day, and hallowed it.
♦ **Hebrews 4:4** For he spake in a certain place of the seventh day on this wise, And God did rest the seventh day from all his works. 5 And in this place again, if they shall enter into my rest. 6 Seeing therefore it remaineth that some must enter therein, and they to whom it was first preached entered not in because of unbelief: 7 Again, he limiteth a certain day, saying in David, To day, after so long a time; as it is said, To day if ye will hear his voice, harden not your hearts. 8 For if Jesus had given them rest, then would he not afterward have spoken of another day. 9 There remaineth therefore a rest to the people of God

Christmas

Christmas is not only a big advertising opportunity today; it was actually created as an advertising campaign. There is no biblical edict to celebrate the birth of Jesus and certainly it is clear that he was not born at the time of the winter solstice. The celebration of the winter solstice has been a part of most ancient cultures throughout history. The celebration of this event is actually an advertising campaign used by early church leaders to lure non-Christians into the church.

- The Mesopotamian culture, thousands of years before the birth of Jesus, had winter solstice that included many of the trappings of Christmas. These included the 12 days of Christmas, the bright fires, the Yule log, the giving of gifts, carnivals, parades with floats, carolers, the holiday feasts, all dedicated to the god Marduk.

- The Persians and the Babylonians celebrated a similar festival called the Sacaea. Part of that celebration included the exchanging of places, the slaves would become the masters and the masters were to obey.
- Scandinavian cultures celebrated the winter solstice including a festival called Yuletide including a feast, which would be served around a fire burning with the Yule log. They also decorated trees with fruit.
- In Scandinavia, during the winter months, the sun would disappear for many days. After thirty-five days, scouts would be sent to the mountaintops to look for the return of the sun. When the first light was seen, the scouts would return with the good news. A great festival would be held, called the Yuletide, and a special feast would be served around a fire burning with the Yule log. Great bonfires would also be lit to celebrate the return of the sun. In some areas people would tie apples to branches of trees to remind themselves that spring and summer would return.

The most direct relation these winter solstice festivals have to what is now called Christmas is the Roman celebration called Saturnalia, which took place on December 25th. The Roman festival marking the "birthday of the unconquered sun, Natalis Solis Invicti"; celebrates the winter solstice, when the days begin to lengthen. The problem for the early church leaders is that Saturnalia was in direct competition with the church, right on their home turf, Rome.

Many campaigns were launched to outlaw and eradicate this pagan practice, but this proved to be a difficult task. The lure of such interesting celebrations to Christians alarmed the church to such a degree that they took a step that forever changed the face of Christian practice. They decided that by integrating the previously forbidden customs into a new celebration honoring the Christian Son of God, they would lure the pagans into the Christian fold.

In 137 AD the Bishop of Rome declared for the first time that the birth of the Christ Child would be celebrated and the Bishop of Rome, Julius I, ordered the date of December 25th as the official day in 350 AD. Saint Boniface substituted a fir tree for the pagan oak in the eighth century as a symbol of faith. Martin Luther fostered the Christmas tree cult by using a candlelit tree as a symbol of Christ's heavenly home

This is one of the many examples of the church adopting ancient traditions to worship God, an example of the practice Jesus specifically condemned:
♦ **Mark 7: 7** Howbeit in vain do they worship me, teaching for doctrines the commandments of men. 8 For laying aside the commandment of God, ye hold the tradition of men, as the washing of pots and cups: and many other such like things ye do. 9 And he said unto them, Full well ye reject the commandment of God, that ye may keep your own tradition.

The Christmas Tree

The single most recognizable symbol of Christmas, the Christmas tree, is not only an ancient winter solstice symbol; the use of it for the purpose of worship is specifically condemned in scripture:

♦ **Jeremiah 10:2** Thus saith the LORD, Learn not the way of the heathen, and be not dismayed at the signs of heaven; for the heathen are dismayed at them. 3 For the customs of the people are vain: for one cutteth a tree out of the forest, the work of the hands of the workman, with the axe. 4 They deck it with silver and with gold; they fasten it with nails and with hammers, that it move not. 5 They are upright as the palm tree, but speak not: they must needs be borne, because they cannot go. Be not afraid of them; for they cannot do evil, neither also is it in them to do good.

Houses decorated with greenery and lights, gifts given to children and the poor, decorating evergreen trees as symbols of survival, fires and lights, symbols of warmth and lasting life, the Yule log and Yule cakes, mistletoe, holly, and virtually every aspect of the modern Christmas celebration are not biblical in origin. They are instead a cleverly contrived collection of ancient winter solstice customs and commercial promotions used to hold church memberships high and gain great profits for Big Business.

Easter

There is no biblical edict to celebrate the crucifixion or resurrection of Christ on a particular day with worship services. Christian missionaries from the church in Rome are the authors of this celebration. While attempting to draw the Saxons into the church without provoking wholesale slaughter, they used bait and switch tactics to accomplish their mission. It would have been suicide for the Christian missionaries to celebrate their holy days with observances that did not coincide with celebrations that already existed. To save lives, the missionaries, in a devious clandestine manner, spread their religious message slowly throughout the populations by allowing them to continue to celebrate pagan feasts, but to do so in a Christian manner. Even the name of the ancient celebration, Eastre was adopted and eventually changed to its modern spelling, Easter.

To make it official, during the Council of Nicaea, in 325 AD, Constantine declared Easter would replace Passover and be observed the annual Sunday following the full moon after the vernal equinox. Not surprising, this coincided with the date for the ancient day to honor Eostre, a goddess of spring and renewal. The emperor was also responsible for starting the traditional Easter Parade when he ordered every citizen to wear his or her best clothing to observe the Holy Day.

The Easter Egg

The Romans, Gauls, Chinese, Egyptians, and Persians all cherished the egg as a symbol of the universe and the rebirth of the earth. During many rite-of-Spring festivals, the egg represented the long, hard winter was over; the earth burst forth and was reborn just as the egg miraculously burst forth with life. Egyptians and Greeks buried eggs in their tombs to ward off evil; pregnant, young Roman women carried an egg on their persons to foretell the sex of their unborn children. A Roman proverb states, "All life comes from an egg". The myths of several Eastern and Middle Eastern cultures maintain that the earth itself was hatched from a giant egg.

The Easter Bunny

The name Easter is derived from Oestar, or Eostre, a goddess of spring and renewal. The rabbit or hare was the symbol of fertility, new life, and of the moon in ancient Egypt. Also the ancient Egyptians called the hare Wenu, an insignia of the rising of the sun, Ra, and of the resurrecting powers of Osiris. The Germans brought the symbol of the Easter rabbit to America. It was widely ignored by other Christians until shortly after the Civil War. In fact, Easter itself was not widely celebrated in America until after that time.

The Vernal Equinox

In the Greek mythology, Demeter and Persephone convey the idea of a goddess returning seasonally from the nether regions to the light of the day. This is in conjunction with the vernal equinox, March 21, when nature is in resurrection after the winter. The festival of Eostre was celebrated at the vernal equinox, when the day and night are of equal duration.

Creation

The Church View:

God the Father, one god, one entity, created the world, alone, in a time period lasting exactly six, twenty-four hour days. The world we know and the biosphere now existing.

The Bible View:

Yhovah, the Lord of Hosts, the God of Israel, who became Jesus the Christ, created the world in six, twenty-four hour Earth days, which equates to an unspecified amount of godly time, with the help of an unknown number of other entities. It was not the first, possibly not even the second, and not the last, but the current creation.

The least known verse relative to the creation is this:

♦ **Genesis 2:1** Thus the heavens and the earth were finished, and all the host of them.

The word *host* is taken from 'tsaba', which literally means an army. The word *them* was added. This army is spoken of almost 300 times from the creation to Armageddon with Yhovah as its supreme commander. Although it does function as a fighting army, this verse shows that combat is only one of its functions. The inclusion of the army in the final verse of creation shows that they were involved in the creation. There is no way to get a firm total on the number of entities in this army, but there are indications that definitely put the numbers in the millions. The first verse shows that there is an actual fleet of vehicles:

♦ **Psalms 68:17** The chariots of God are twenty thousand, even thousands of angels: the Lord is among them, as in Sinai, in the holy place.

The vehicles of Elohiym number a myriad of thousands. The Hebrew word translated into the word twenty means "myriad". This second verse shows that the number of entities, by implication, is from millions to infinite:

♦ **Revelation 5:11** And I beheld, and I heard the voice of many angels round about the throne and the beasts and the elders: and the number of them was ten thousand times ten thousand, and thousands of thousands;

Ten thousand = myriads. Thousands = one thousand.

What is apparent is that there were thousands of vehicles and millions of beings present at the creation process. Considering that Yhovah states this was all done in a short span of human time is more understandable with a high tech fleet present. But, is the human time span truly relevant to the entities involved? The following verses indicate that time may have no bearing on the creation process at all.

Time of the Gods

This verse shows that time is different, if not altogether irrelevant, to the Elohiym:

♦ **Psalms 90:4** For a thousand years in thy sight are but as yesterday when it is past, and as a watch in the night.

Again, time is shown to be of no effect to the nature of the Elohiym:

♦ **2 Peter 3:8** But, beloved, be not ignorant of this one thing, that one day is with the Lord as a thousand years, and a thousand years as one day.

Throughout the Bible there are instances of manipulation of natural forces, from simple alteration of plant life to halting the rotation of the planet.

Evolution and Theistic Evolution

Evolution is society's alternative to the creation concept. Though based on primitive knowledge of the planet and virtually no evidence, it is surprising that the supposedly "enlightened" academic and scientific community give it any credibility at all. Theories about theories are given high priority in our educational and cultural conditioning. No other scientific endeavor is founded on such shaky ground and the foundations of this theory are deteriorated on almost a daily basis. No problem for evolutionists, they just adjust the theory.

Design without a designer, order without planning, structure without engineering is unreal. To consider that a system of such magnitude and perfection is simply the result of mind-boggling series of chaotic chance mutations is without logic. Looking for links to a mythical chain and creating theories to bolster theories is only confusing. Trying to explain something from nothing is intellectual obsession, not high scientific process.

The Bible and other ancient writings that touch upon the subject say it was planned, designed, and engineered. Every aspect of the natural world proves it. To state otherwise is gross deception, not scientific pursuit.

More Than One Creation

In Jeremiah we find clear evidence that this biosphere is not the first complete planetary terra-forming project done on this planet:

♦ **Jeremiah 4:23** I beheld the earth, and, lo, it was without form, and void; and the heavens, and they had no light. 24 I beheld the mountains, and, lo, they trembled, and all the hills moved lightly. 25 I beheld, and, lo, there was no man, and all the birds of the heavens were fled. 26 I beheld, and, lo, the fruitful place was a wilderness, and all the cities thereof were broken down at the presence of the LORD, and by his fierce anger. 27 For thus hath the LORD said, The whole land shall be desolate; yet will I not make a full end. 28 For this shall the earth mourn, and the heavens above be black; because I have spoken it, I have purposed it, and will not repent, neither will I turn back from it.

If this previous creation did not include the strange collection of fauna and flora, which included dinosaurs clearly evidenced in the geological record, our biosphere is at least the third creation. This would account for the existence of, and validate, the histories of many cultures going back many thousands of years before the accepted creation "timeline" and anomalous archeological finds known as "out of place artifacts".

♦ **Isaiah 65:17** For, behold, I create new heavens and a new earth: and the former shall not be remembered, nor come into mind.

It is not clear whether this refers to the past or present creation, but does provide clarification in either case.

Not The Last Creation

♦ **Revelation 21:1** And I saw a new heaven and a new earth: for the first heaven and the first earth were passed away; and there was no more sea. 2 And I John saw the holy city, new Jerusalem, coming down from God out of heaven, prepared as a bride adorned for her husband. 3 And I heard a great voice out of heaven saying, Behold, the tabernacle of God is with men, and he will dwell with them, and they shall be his people, and God himself shall be with them, and be their God. 4 And God shall wipe away all tears from their eyes; and there shall be no more death, neither sorrow, nor crying, neither shall there be any more pain: for the former things are passed away. 5 And he that sat upon the throne said, Behold, I make all things new. And he said unto me, Write: for these words are true and faithful.

This prophecy occurs after the thousand-year period following the return of the Christ. Considering the current polluted and depleted condition of our biosphere and the clear indications that that thousand-year reign will occur on this planet, it is only logical that a certain level of biosphere modification must occur after the return of Christ. The devastating prophecies of the Revelation to John will worsen that condition even further to the point that the total annihilation of all life will be imminent.

♦ **Matthew 24:32** And except those days should be shortened, there should no flesh be saved: but for the elect's sake those days shall be shortened.

It does not fit into the loving nature of God or the benefit of mankind that the planet would not be quickly healed and brought back to a pristine state for this 1000 year period as rapidly as possible. This could mean a major re-creation of the planet will occur to achieve that end.

The Conclusion

The biosphere we inhabit is at least the second creation, or terra-forming project, that occurred on this planet and possibly only the current one in an unknown number of many past creations. It will be partially re-terra-formed to accommodate the 1000 years period following the return of the Christ and completely re-created following that period. The time involved cannot be accurately determined due to the anomalous relationship of divine beings to time, but in the perspective humans have to time this has occurred in clearly defined human periods. There is also no evidence biblically that the Creator used the purely hypothetical "Theory of Evolution", a concept known as "Theistic Evolution" to accomplish these massive terra-forming projects.

The Flood

The Church View:

The flood was caused by the corrupt actions of mankind.

The Bible View:

The flood was caused by the corrupt actions of angels.

The first eight verses of the sixth chapter of Genesis describe an incredible series of events that, when taken in their entirety, leave a gaping hole in the church's view of mankind's past. Unmentioned from the pulpit is mankind's former close relationship with the Elohiym and the devastation of a terrible action by the angels. The circumstance that caused Yhovah such regret is a master key to understanding many of the enigmas of the Bible, human history, and much of what is known in our world as the paranormal.

The Flood of Noah is perhaps the best known of the Old Testament Bible stories; yet, the cause of the worst catastrophe in human history is veiled in mystery. The relationship between the Nephilim (called giants, mighty men, and men of renown) and the flood is not revealed from the pulpit. The relationship of the Nephilim to the devils of the New Testament is seldom considered.

Why did Yhovah decide to destroy all life?

The Genesis account of the beginning of worldwide devastation:

♦ **Genesis 6:1** And it came to pass, when men began to multiply on the face of the earth, and daughters were born unto them, 2 That the sons of God saw the daughters of men that they were fair; and they took them wives of all which they chose. 3 And the LORD said, My spirit shall not always strive with man, for that he also is flesh: yet his days shall be an hundred and twenty years. 4 There were giants in the earth in those days; and also after that, when the sons of God came in unto the daughters of men, and they bare children to them, the same became mighty men which were of old, men of renown. 5 And God saw that the wickedness of man was great in the earth, and that every imagination of the thoughts of his heart was only evil continually. 6 And it repented the LORD that he had made man on the earth, and it grieved him at his heart. 7 And the LORD said, I will destroy man whom I have created from the face of the earth; both man, and beast, and the creeping thing, and the fowls of the air; for it repenteth me that I have made them. 8 But Noah found grace in the eyes of the LORD.

The orthodox doctrinal line, which falsely explains the devastating decision Yhovah made, is that mankind simply achieved a level of consistent evil that caused its demise. Found in eight verses, Genesis 6: 1 -8, is a group of concepts which, considered individually or as a whole, present a plethora of doubts about accepted doctrinal accuracy and completeness.

- Mankind begins to be fruitful and multiply.
- Angels are shown to be in very close contact with men.
- Yhovah is shown to be in close contact with men.
- Angels begin to freely mate with women.
- Women give birth to a race of giants.
- Yhovah decides to cease his close contact with men.
- Evil becomes the central focus of mankind.
- Yhovah regrets the creation of all life on Earth.
- Yhovah decides to bring an end to human civilization.
- Yhovah decides to eliminate all life on the planet.

- Fortunately for mankind, only one man on the planet finds favor with Yhovah.

It doesn't get any closer to the edge than that. Without the favor Noah had, life, as we know it, would never have occurred. Perhaps this is why there are hundreds of accounts of the flood worldwide, with hundreds of Noah figures to match. And why, in the face of overwhelming geological evidence that a flood did indeed occur, does science cling so tightly to shaky theoretical alternatives?

Breaking down the individual concepts and considering them in their relation to the whole will give a clearer perspective of the final impact on humanity.

Humanity Multiplies

♦ **Genesis 6:1** And it came to pass, when men began to multiply on the face of the earth, and daughters were born unto them.

This is as it should be. Prior to the end of this age Man is told to be fruitful and multiply in the first chapter of Genesis:

♦ **Genesis 1:22** And God blessed them, saying, Be fruitful, and multiply, and fill the waters in the seas, and let fowl multiply in the earth.

♦ **Genesis 1:28** And God blessed them, and God said unto them, Be fruitful, and multiply, and replenish the earth, and subdue it: and have dominion over the fish of the sea, and over the fowl of the air, and over every living thing that moveth upon the earth.

Since this is apparently what mankind is commanded to do, then of course it, of itself, is not the cause of the evil that has caused Yhovah's regret. There is no way to know the population figures, but hundreds of cultures worldwide record the event. It certainly took all these cultures by surprise and most evidence of those cultures vanished in a watery quagmire. Considering the wealth of evidence that remains, there must have been an incredible explosion in human culture and diversity.

A Relationship with the Gods

♦ **Genesis 6:2** That the sons of God saw the daughters of men that they were fair; and they took them wives of all which they chose.

Most ancient cultures speak of a close relationship with the gods. Here we will deal with the specific details recorded by Moses, but it should be remembered that there are many versions of man's close ties to the gods by many authors worldwide. The similarities between these accounts give rise to a serious question. Was all this activity concentrated in one tiny geographical area? Logic and corroborating evidence would make this a ridiculous assumption.

The account in the Bible of the Family of man and his dispersal worldwide starts with his expulsion from the Garden of Eden. The concept of a human culture does not begin biblically until the mention of the acts of Cain in the fourth chapter of Genesis:

♦ **Genesis 4:16** And Cain went out from the presence of the Lord, and dwelt in the land of Nod, on the east of Eden. 17 And Cain knew his wife; and she conceived, and bare Enoch: and he builded a city, and called the name of the city, after the name of his son, Enoch.

The end of the fourth chapter gives us our only clue concerning this close relationship with the Elohiym and the angels.

♦ **Genesis 4: 26**. And to Seth, to him also there was born a son; and he called his name Enos: then began men to call upon the name of the Lord.

Unfortunately, that is the extent of the Bible's coverage of mankind's history before the flood with only the genealogy from Adam to Noah to fill in the gaps. Cain builds a city, men begin a relationship with God, and then it's over. But, there is a source that provides enlightenment to this unknown age. It comes from the third generation of Adam, Cain's firstborn, Enoch.

The Missing Antediluvian Age

With only a few words from Moses and brief general descriptions from Matthew and Luke, there is little to point to the true cause of man's evil binge before the flood:

♦ **Matthew 24:37** But as the days of Noe were, so shall also the coming of the Son of man be. 38 For as in the days that were before the flood they were eating and drinking, marrying and giving in marriage, until the day that Noe entered into the ark, 39 And knew not until the flood came, and took them all away; so shall also the coming of the Son of man be.

♦ **Luke 17:26** And as it was in the days of Noe, so shall it be also in the days of the Son of man. 27 They did eat, they drank, they married wives, they were given in marriage, until the day that Noe entered into the ark, and the flood came, and destroyed them all.

There is a source that sheds considerable light on the cause of mankind's demise, and presents a scenario so unorthodox it is no wonder it was rejected by the church. Here, in brief, is what Enoch has to say about the reason for mankind's near demise:

Enoch's Revelation

There is a source that sheds considerable light on the cause of mankind's demise and presents a scenario so unorthodox; it is no wonder the church rejected it. It is the Book of Enoch.

- Enoch was so close to God, the Bible says God took him:
♦ **Genesis 5: 24** And Enoch walked with God: and he was not; for God took him.

- Paul recalls his favor with God:
♦ **Hebrews 11:15** By faith Enoch was translated that he should not see death; and was not found, because God had translated him: for before his translation he had this testimony, that he pleased God.

- The book of Enoch is quoted in the Bible:
♦ **Jude 1:14** And Enoch also, the seventh from Adam, prophesied of these, saying, Behold, the Lord cometh with ten thousands of his saints.

The Book of Enoch Purged

Why isn't his book in the Bible? The Book of Enoch was recognized centuries before Christ, it was accepted by early Christians, and early Christian literature contains many references to it. The book was an accepted part of the scriptures up to the middle of the third century when the church leadership decided to ban it during the Council of Laodicea. Along with 40 other books it was banned as a scriptural source and was lost for over a thousand years. It was not until the late 1700s that a copy surfaced.

The obvious reason for this mass book banning was that these books did not agree with the beliefs of the church leaders. During the same Council, this leadership declared the keeping of the Sabbath a sin. The simple reality was scripture did not determine what dogma was accepted; rather dogma determined what scripture was accepted. This may have occurred centuries ago, but the modern day church practices the same contradiction.

Enoch is Taken

It is recorded that Enoch lived for 365 years, but that is a relative figure because apparently Yhovah took him on board and didn't bring him back. In Hebrews 11:5 the word 'translate' is used 3 times:
♦ "By faith Enoch was *translated* that he should not see death; and was not found, because God had *translated* him: for before his *translation* he had this testimony, that he pleased God". (Hebrews 11:5)

The words from which "translate" is rendered mean" to transport". It is clear that he was physically transported and it is the amazing odyssey that Enoch records after, "God took him", that reveals the true cause of early mankind's demise. Enoch had a revelation given to him just as John received thousands of years later on the Isle of Patmos.

Here, in brief, is what Enoch has to say about what caused such a radical action as a worldwide flood:

- The angels were in such close contact with mankind that they actually taught men previously unknown knowledge. This is a practical explanation about why there is no apparent evolution of early culture, just a sudden burst of knowledge with no evident progression of learning. It not only seems that our ancestors were taught advanced skills, but the records of many ancient cultures testify to that reality.
- Certain angels actually organized a plot to inbreed with human women and swore an evil oath to seal the devastating conspiracy. The ringleaders are named and the number of conspirators is given. Many ancient writings speak of such a relationship with divine or extraterrestrial beings.
- The offspring of this plot were giants. World anthropological and historical documentation, as well as the biblical record, testify to the existence of giants throughout the ages.

See the section on Giants, (Page 178)

- The giants apparently had appetites that matched their size. These hybrid monsters ate all man could produce, and when man could not produce enough, they began to eat humans. They also began to consume all they could acquire from nature, and when this ran out they turned on each other.
- The rampant destruction of the natural environment by the giant hybrids and the corruption of mankind caused the decision to flood the planet.
- When the flood killed the giants, their spirits separated from their bodies as spirit beings whose sole purpose is to torture and devastate man until the judgment day.
- The angels who perpetrated the invasive act are imprisoned, but the spirits of their illicit offspring are roaming the planet.

Enoch and the Flood -A Liaison to Angels

After taking Enoch, God appointed him as liaison to the imprisoned angels that had perpetrated the corruption of, and inbreeding with mankind. This gave him direct knowledge of the cause and effect of this act and witness to the events that followed. Not only are the criminals named, but also the true nature of the devils recorded in the Bible is revealed. This is a revelation concealed from mankind by the actions of other men, a decision that keeps the most evil of forces hidden from view. Many of the strange events and entities witnessed in ancient and modern times remain unexplained without this knowledge.

Following are the verses from the Book of Enoch that relate to the Flood, the angels that caused this worldwide disaster, and the destructive spirits that now inhabit Earth. Though many ancient writings refer to a worldwide flood, none is more concise and descriptive of the root causes of this disaster than the writings of Enoch.

The Angels Plot Against Mankind

♦ **Enoch 6:1** And it came to pass when the children of men had multiplied that in those days were born unto them beautiful and comely daughters. 2 And the angels, the children of the heaven, saw and lusted after them, and said to one another: 'Come, let us choose us wives from among the children of men 3 and beget us children.' And Semjaza, who was their leader, said unto them: 'I fear ye will not 4 indeed agree to do this deed, and I alone shall have to pay the penalty of a great sin.' And they all answered him and said: 'Let us all swear an oath, and all bind ourselves by mutual imprecations 5 not to abandon this plan but to do this thing.' Then sware they all together and bound themselves 6 by mutual imprecations upon it. And they were in all two hundred; who descended in the days of Jared on the summit of Mount Hermon, and they called it Mount Hermon, because they had sworn 7 and bound themselves by mutual imprecations upon it. And these are the names of their leaders: Samlazaz, their leader, Araklba, Rameel, Kokablel, Tamlel, Ramlel, Danel, Ezeqeel, Baraqijal, 8 Asael, Armaros, Batarel, Ananel, Zaq1el, Samsapeel, Satarel, Turel, Jomjael, Sariel. These are their chiefs of tens.

Inbreeding Begins

♦ **7:1** And all the others together with them took unto themselves wives, and each chose for himself one, and they began to go in unto them and to defile themselves with them,

An Education in Secret Arts Begins

♦ **7:1** .....and they taught them charms 2 and enchantments, and the cutting of roots, and made them acquainted with plants.....

Voracious, Giant, Man-eating, Cannibal Mutants Are Born

♦ **7:2** .....And they 3 became pregnant, and they bare great giants, whose height was three thousand ells: Who consumed 4 all the acquisitions of men. And when men could no longer sustain them, the giants turned against 5 them and devoured mankind. And they began to sin against birds, and beasts, and reptiles, and 6 fish, and to devour one another's flesh, and drink the blood. Then the earth laid accusation against the lawless ones.

Weapon Making and Metallurgy Are Taught

♦ **8:1** And Azazel taught men to make swords, and knives, and shields, and breastplates, and made known to them the metals of the earth and the art of working them, and bracelets, and ornaments, and the use of [1]antimony, [1]antimony, a trivalent and pentavalent metalloid element that is commonly metallic silvery white, crystalline, and brittle and that is used especially as a constituent of alloys and semiconductors

Cosmetics and Jewelry Are Taught
♦ **8:1**.....and the beautifying of the eyelids, and all kinds of costly stones, and all **2** colouring tinctures...

Society is Corrupted
♦ **8:2**.....And there arose much godlessness, and they committed fornication, and they **3** were led astray, and became corrupt in all their ways.

Sorcery, Astrology, and Astronomy
♦ **8:3**.....Semjaza taught enchantments, and root-cuttings, 'Armaros the resolving of enchantments, Baraqijal (taught) astrology, Kokabel the constellations, Ezeqeel the knowledge of the clouds, Araqiel the signs of the earth, Shamsiel the signs of the sun, and Sariel the course of the moon. And as men perished, they cried, and their cry went up to heaven . . .

The Corruption is Exposed
♦ **9:1** And then Michael, Uriel, Raphael, and Gabriel looked down from heaven and saw much blood being **2** shed upon the earth, and all lawlessness being wrought upon the earth. And they said one to another: 'The earth made without inhabitant cries the voice of their cryingst up to the gates of heaven. **3** And now to you, the holy ones of heaven, the souls of men make their suit, saying, "Bring our cause **4** before the Most High."' And they said to the Lord of the ages: 'Lord of lords, God of gods, King of kings, and God of the ages, the throne of Thy glory (standeth) unto all the generations of the **5** ages, and Thy name holy and glorious and blessed unto all the ages! Thou hast made all things, and power over all things hast Thou: and all things are naked and open in Thy sight, and Thou seest all **6** things, and nothing can hide itself from Thee. Thou seest what Azazel hath done, who hath taught all unrighteousness on earth and revealed the eternal secrets which were (preserved) in heaven, which **7** men were striving to learn: And Semjaza, to whom Thou hast given authority to bear rule over his associates. And they have gone to the daughters of men upon the earth, and have slept with the **9** women, and have defiled themselves, and revealed to them all kinds of sins. And the women have **10** borne giants, and the whole earth has thereby been filled with blood and unrighteousness. And now, behold, the souls of those who have died are crying and making their suit to the gates of heaven, and their lamentations have ascended: and cannot cease because of the lawless deeds which are **11** wrought on the earth. And Thou knowest all things before they come to pass, and Thou seest these things and Thou dost suffer them, and Thou dost not say to us what we are to do to them in regard to these.'

Noah Informed
♦ **10:1** Then said the Most High, the Holy and Great One spake, and sent Uriel to the son of Lamech, **2** and said to him: Go to Noah and tell him in my name

173

"Hide thyself!" and reveal to him the end that is approaching: that the whole earth will be destroyed, and a deluge is about to come 3 upon the whole earth, and will destroy all that is on it. And now instruct him that he may escape 4 and his seed may be preserved for all the generations of the world.

Giants Become Evil Spirits

♦ !5:1 And He answered and said to me, and I heard His voice: 'Fear not, Enoch, thou righteous 2 man and scribe of righteousness: approach hither and hear my voice. And go, say to the Watchers of heaven, who have sent thee to intercede for them: "You should intercede" for men, and not men 3 for you: Wherefore have ye left the high, holy, and eternal heaven, and lain with women, and defiled yourselves with the daughters of men and taken to yourselves wives, and done like the children 4 of earth, and begotten giants (as your) sons? And though ye were holy, spiritual, living the eternal life, you have defiled yourselves with the blood of women, and have begotten (children) with the blood of flesh, and, as the children of men, have lusted after flesh and blood as those also do who die 5 and perish. Therefore have I given them wives also that they might impregnate them, and beget 6 children by them, that thus nothing might be wanting to them on earth. But you were formerly 7 spiritual, living the eternal life, and immortal for all generations of the world. And therefore I have not appointed wives for you; for as for the spiritual ones of the heaven, in heaven is their dwelling. 8 And now, the giants, who are produced from the spirits and flesh, shall be called evil spirits upon 9 the earth, and on the earth shall be their dwelling. Evil spirits have proceeded from their bodies; because they are born from men and from the holy Watchers is their beginning and primal origin; 10 they shall be evil spirits on earth, and evil spirits shall they be called. [As for the spirits of heaven, in heaven shall be their dwelling, but as for the spirits of the earth which were born upon the earth, on the earth shall be their dwelling.] 11 And the spirits of the giants afflict, oppress, destroy, attack, do battle, and work destruction on the earth, and cause trouble: they take no food, but nevertheless 12 hunger and thirst, and cause offences. And these spirits shall rise up against the children of men and against the women, because they have proceeded from them.
See Devils and Strange Spirits: Appendix Q

The previous concepts from scripture and the Book of Enoch show clearly that the blame for the Flood, which is used by the Church to shame mankind into believing it was responsible, is false. It also shoves the existence of giants under the rug, and hides the true origin and nature of demons. Perhaps this is one of the prime reason reasons Enoch was purged from the Bible.

The Revelation

The Theories

The theories about the meaning of the prophecies Jesus revealed to John on the Isle of Patmos are too numerous to calculate. There are several aspects that dominate the various scenarios presented, which scripture does not support, and it is those we will address. It is of the utmost importance that the readers not make the mistake many have made before, which has allowed so many myths to be accepted. The problem is that so many simply accept the word of those theorists without studying the foundations of their concepts.

The most popular belief is that the Revelation is the future story of the rise of the Antichrist to world power, his actions to demand loyalty, the creation of a world government and world religion, the rebuilding of the temple at Jerusalem, the rapture, a great battle at Armageddon, the final battle that defeats Satan, Jesus taking the throne, and a new earth being created.

Here are the major points most often presented concerning the prophecies of the Revelation to John:

- The Antichrist is the central figure of the end times.
- The Antichrist will establish a world government.
- The Antichrist will bring peace to the world.
- The Antichrist will stand in the Holy of Holies in the rebuilt Temple at Jerusalem.
- The Antichrist will either declare himself as the Messiah or be declared the Messiah by a new World Church.
- The Antichrist is the author of the "Great Deception".
- The Mark of the Beast will be an identifying sign of loyalty to the Antichrist.
- The Mark of the Beast is 666.
- A new World Church will be established.
- The Temple at Jerusalem will be rebuilt.
- The False Prophet plays a major role in the end times events.
- The Jews will accept Jesus as the Messiah before he returns.
- There are two specific groups of 144,000 people each "raptured".
- The Beast is a human.
- The Beast is the Antichrist.
- There will be a "Great Battle" at Armageddon.
- Satan will be defeated in a "Great Battle" in heaven just before he is imprisoned in chains.

The Beast

One of the first problems in the orthodox view of the "beast" is that it is a person. Many believe this, but scripture and theological study reveal that this is more likely, an organization, or group of nations. The word from which the word beast is taken means "dangerous animal". In our modern society an animal is considered "dangerous" for several reasons, not the least of which is posing a threat to human life or physical harm to humans or their property.

Since the beast is mentioned in a social, rather than a natural context, we can assume that whatever the beast is, it is probably not an actual animal, but more likely some other entity that exhibits the traits of a dangerous animal. The connection of the Mark to global commerce, the institution of that Mark by the image the Beast creates, and the identification of the global corporations as the deceiver of the world place those corporations in the direct spotlight as a prime suspect. See The Mark of the Beast Page ***

In a recent book, and movie, titled "The Corporation", the concept of corporate personhood, and its ramifications socially, were closely examined. A person who is considered dangerous to the society as a whole very often exhibit traits that are defined as psychopathic, and would make that person a threat to society. In the book, "The Corporation", a leading expert in forensic psychology was asked to determine how the corporate personality, with its questionable humanlike power under the status of corporate personhood, would be rated psychologically. His conclusion is that the corporation, as legally structured, by the actions it is mandated to take, and considering its well-publicized performance socially, would qualify it as a severe psychopath.

Psychologist Dr. Robert Hare, a leading expert in the study of psychopathic behavior, has developed a checklist of psychopathic traits and these are but a few that represent the aberrant behavior of corporations.

• The corporation is irresponsible because in an attempt to satisfy the corporate goal, everybody else is put at risk.

• Corporations try to manipulate everything, including public opinion.

• Corporations are grandiose, always insisting that "we're number one, we're the best."

• Corporations refuse to accept responsibility for their own actions and are unable to feel remorse.

The following is his well-known and implemented psychopathy checklist in its entirety. The reader can easily see that considering what we know about the global behavior of corporations, there are very few aspects of psychopathic behavior corporations do not match.

1. Glibness / superficial charm
2. Grandiose sense of self-worth
3. Need for stimulation/proneness to boredom
4. Pathological lying
5. Conning/manipulative
6. Lack of remorse or guilt
7. Shallow affect

8. Callous/lack of empathy
9. Parasitic lifestyle
10. Poor behavioral controls
11. Promiscuous sexual behavior
12. Early behavior problems
13. Lack of realistic, long-term plans
14. Impulsivity
15. Irresponsibility
16. Failure to accept responsibility for own actions
17. Many short-term relationships
18. Juvenile delinquency
19. Revocation of conditional release
20. Criminal versatility

The Antichrist

There is no reference to a "leader", a person who will "claim to be God", some charismatic leader that will take over as a world ruler, or anything resembling that in the prophecies Jesus revealed to John. The phrase antichrist, or the plural of it, only appears four times in scripture, the antichrist is not referred to in the Revelation, and was actually described as a living human being during the time he was mentioned:

♦ "And every spirit that confesseth not that Jesus Christ is come in the flesh is not of God: and this is that spirit of antichrist, whereof ye have heard that it should come; and even now already is it in the world. " (I John 4:3)
The other verses mentioning the antichrist in scripture are:

♦ I John 2:18 Little children, it is the last time: and as ye have heard that antichrist shall come, even now are there many antichrists; whereby we know that it is the last time.

♦ I John 2:22 Who is a liar but he that denieth that Jesus is the Christ? He is antichrist, that denieth the Father and the Son.

♦ II John 1:7 For many deceivers are entered into the world, who confess not that Jesus Christ is come in the flesh. This is a deceiver and an antichrist.

Bottom-line; the stories you have heard about this very charismatic man taking over the world, proclaiming himself the Savior, and being the one to make people take the mark are pure tradition and have no foundation in scripture.

Antichrist Association Syndrome

There is a strange disorder affecting the amateur theological world which causes those afflicted to believe that every verse about any unsavory character in the Bible, no matter how vague the association, absolutely must be a prophetical reference to the Antichrist. Context is not considered, obvious references to people living at the time are ignored, and all sense of

177

investigative integrity is put aside to clump these verses into the confusing Antichrist pigeonhole. It would seem that the only description of any evildoer in scripture is the Antichrist, no matter that there actually might be other evildoers out there.

The antichrist, as an individual with this specific identity, is not to be found in the Bible. In order to keep the Antichrist in the forefront of importance to their theories, the proponents of his greatness use several verses outside the Revelation. The key passages used are Daniel 7, 8, 11; Matthew 24; II Thessalonians 2; and Revelation 13, 17 and 18.

Daniel 7

The use of this chapter centers on the fourth beast being the Antichrist:
♦ Daniel 7:24. And the ten horns out of this kingdom are ten kings that shall arise: and another shall rise after them; and he shall be diverse from the first, and he shall subdue three kings. 25. And he shall speak great words against the most High, and shall wear out the saints of the most High, and think to change times and laws: and they shall be given into his hand until a time and times and the dividing of time.

While it is obvious that this ruler will certainly be a very dangerous and important character, we find that his descriptions fit the Emperor Constantine, the ruler who virtually assured the complete alteration of the church and the truth to be buried for centuries, like a glove.

• Constantine outlawed the keeping of the weekly Sabbath, and all High Sabbaths, substituting different festivals from pagan practice in their stead, and changing the times those celebrations are held to the times the pagans held the ancient festivals.

• Constantine forbid the keeping of a "Jewish" law, virtually changing or removing every biblical law from practice.

• Constantine's established papal monarchy gained sovereign rule of the Western Empire and, through its Crusades, subdued the Heruli, the Ostrogoths, and the Vandals, whose kings resisted papal control.

• Constantine was not known to physically harm any Christians as a common practice. He did, however, force them to relinquish their centuries old beliefs and celebrate pagan festivals. The phrase " wear out" is taken from the Greek word "bla", pronounced bel-aw'; to afflict (but used only in a mental sense).

Daniel 8 & 11

A careful read of these chapters will provide no solid proof that these chapters are either speaking of the end times, an antichrist, or even the same entities described in any of the other two chapters.

178

Matthew 24

This chapter is used because it mentions the abomination of desolation, false christs, and false prophets. We have expanded on the identity of these three below, and they do not refer to a great world leader in the end times, but actually several beings, probably appearing in their time.

2 Thessalonians 2

♦ 2 Thessalonians 2:8 And then shall that Wicked be revealed, whom the Lord shall consume with the spirit of his mouth, and shall destroy with the brightness of his coming: 9 Even him, whose coming is after the working of Satan with all power and signs and lying wonders,

To presume this is an end time prophecy denies the fact that whatever is troubling them, (2 Thessalonians 1:6), was discussed before, (2 Thessalonians 2:5), and was happening at the time this was written, (2 Thessalonians 2:7). When describing the individual mentioned, he is spoken of as having already committed his blasphemous acts, or was doing them at the time, not that he would only do those things in the future.

The end of the letter brings this conclusion:

♦ "Finally, brethren, pray for us, that the word of the Lord may have free course, and be glorified, even as it is with you: And that we may be delivered from unreasonable and wicked men: for all men have not faith." (2 Thessalonians 3:1 - 2).

And this is the judgment about how to deal with the problem discussed in the letter:

♦ "Now we command you, brethren, in the name of our Lord Jesus Christ, that ye withdraw yourselves from every brother that walketh disorderly, and not after the tradition which he received of us." (2 Thessalonians 3:1 - 2).

Revelation 13

The liberal use of the words he, him, and his throughout this chapter in relation to the beast were the choice of the translators and are all translated from a word which could also be rendered as it. The descriptions used to identify the appearance and actions of the beast further indicate that this is not an individual world ruler, but a very powerful organization with global control, eventually facilitated by the use of a mark to control global commerce.

Revelation 17

Rather than an individual, this chapter speaks of several kings under a single ruler. It is surprising that the ruling Antichrist proponents use this chapter when it, in fact, does identify a world ruling power:

♦ Revelation 17:18. And the woman which thou sawest is that great city, which reigneth over the kings of the earth.

The ruler of the world is a city, not an individual called the Antichrist, and the true deceivers are clearly identified in the chapter they commonly and mistakenly use from the Revelation to prove the rule of the antichrist.

Revelation 18

Although no individual is even mentioned in this chapter, they site verses out of context from it. One verse they do not use shows why the mark is to be used to control all global financial transactions, because the true deceivers are the source of global commerce.

♦ Revelation 18: 23. And the light of a candle shall shine no more at all in thee; and the voice of the bridegroom and of the bride shall be heard no more at all in thee: for thy merchants were the great men of the earth; for by thy sorceries were all nations deceived.

The Dragon

We can definitely identify the Dragon as Satan from these verses:

♦ "And he laid hold on the dragon, that old serpent, which is the Devil, and Satan, and bound him a thousand years," (Revelation 20:2)

♦ "And the great dragon was cast out, that old serpent, called the Devil, and Satan, which deceiveth the whole world: he was cast out into the earth, and his angels were cast out with him." (Revelation 20:9)

The Dragon is clearly the controlling force behind the Beast, but is only shown in a role of power behind those action, not directly as any kind of world leader, nor is the dragon described as taking on any kind of human role. He uses the Beast, and the Image of the Beast, to fulfill his goals. He is the power behind them and the actions they take.

The entire twelfth chapter of the Revelation is about the Dragon. When read carefully, an amazing number of paradigms are revealed in just this one chapter.

• The identity of the Dragon as Satan is clarified.

• Satan's association with the powers that are the foundation of the Beast is confirmed.

• Satan is described as coming down from the sky and waiting for Mary to give birth to Jesus, with the intention to kill him.

• Jesus and Mary are taken out of harms way and protected.

• The "Great Battle Time Warp" occurs. We have seen Satan lay in wait to destroy Jesus at his birth and fail in his attempt. The very next thing, after the mother and child are taken to safety, the Bible describes is that Michael, and his forces, attack and defeat Satan. Here many end-time theorists have pulled this battle out of its clear chronological order, as immediately after the birth of Christ, and claim that it occurs thousands of years later. If the chapter stopped here and nothing more concerning the matter was described, this might be possible. But, it continues.

- Satan and his forces are defeated and permanently thrown down to the surface of the planet.
- His defeat is celebrated in the sky and a warning is proclaimed to all the planet's inhabitants that he is angry, and in a hurry.
- The "Great Battle Time Warp" theory is now debunked, as we see Satan going after Mary, clearly described as an action he took after he was defeated and exiled to terra firma. This means that the battle had to take place during Mary's life.
- Mary is again rescued from Satan's assaults and he then goes after the remnant of her seed, presumed to be the first church, the persecution and slaughter of which is a matter of the historical record.

We present the entire twelfth chapter to show the clear chronological order of these events and the paradigms that are so clear, but never considered:

♦ Revelation 12:1 And there appeared a great wonder in heaven; a woman clothed with the sun, and the moon under her feet, and upon her head a crown of twelve stars: 2 And she being with child cried, travailing in birth, and pained to be delivered. 3 And there appeared another wonder in heaven; and behold a great red dragon, having seven heads and ten horns, and seven crowns upon his heads. 4 And his tail drew the third part of the stars of heaven, and did cast them to the earth: and the dragon stood before the woman which was ready to be delivered, for to devour her child as soon as it was born. 5 And she brought forth a man child, who was to rule all nations with a rod of iron: and her child was caught up unto God, and to his throne. 6 And the woman fled into the wilderness, where she hath a place prepared of God, that they should feed her there a thousand two hundred and threescore days. 7 And there was war in heaven: Michael and his angels fought against the dragon; and the dragon fought and his angels, 8 And prevailed not; neither was their place found any more in heaven. 9 And the great dragon was cast out, that old serpent, called the Devil, and Satan, which deceiveth the whole world: he was cast out into the earth, and his angels were cast out with him. 10 And I heard a loud voice saying in heaven, Now is come salvation, and strength, and the kingdom of our God, and the power of his Christ: for the accuser of our brethren is cast down, which accused them before our God day and night. 11 And they overcame him by the blood of the Lamb, and by the word of their testimony; and they loved not their lives unto the death. 12 Therefore rejoice, ye heavens, and ye that dwell in them. Woe to the inhabiters of the earth and of the sea! for the devil is come down unto you, having great wrath, because he knoweth that he hath but a short time. 13 And when the dragon saw that he was cast unto the earth, he persecuted the woman which brought forth the man child. 14 And to the woman were given two wings of a great eagle, that she might fly into the wilderness, into her place, where she is nourished for a time, and times, and half a time, from the face of the serpent. 15 And the serpent cast out of his mouth water as a flood after the woman, that he might cause her to be carried away of the flood. 16 And the earth helped the woman, and the earth opened her mouth, and swallowed up the flood which the dragon cast out of his mouth. 17 And the dragon was wroth with the woman, and went to make war with the remnant of her seed, which keep the commandments of God, and have the testimony of Jesus Christ.

The Abomination of Desolation

The verse about the "abomination of desolation, spoken of by Daniel the prophet" in Matthew 24:15 and Mark 13:14, gives no indication that this verse is referring to a man, nor is this specifically identified as the Temple at Jerusalem. The verse in Daniel that the other New Testament verses are referring to is:

♦ "And from the time that the daily sacrifice shall be taken away, and the abomination that maketh desolate set up, there shall be a thousand two hundred and ninety days." (Daniel 12:11).

Again, the original has no reference to a man or the temple.

The Number of a "Man"

The other reference is about the number of a man:

♦ "Here is wisdom. Let him that hath understanding count the number of the beast: for it is the number of a man; and his number is Six hundred threescore and six." (Revelation 13:18).

The word "of" can mean for, the word man can be men and the "his" was added by the translators. This could just as easily be translated as "for it is the number for men; and the number is Six hundred threescore and six." And, of course, it gives nothing specific to any person or actions he will take. If we allow that this verse is speaking to a particular person having this number somehow in his name, there is a very serious gap in scripture. Beyond this verse there is no mention of any particular man to be found in the Revelation. If this is some mysterious man, nothing more is said about him in scripture.

The False Prophet

There is a false prophet mentioned three times in the Revelation; twice referring to his imprisonment, but he is not referred to as a leader.

♦ Revelation 16:13 And I saw three unclean spirits like frogs come out of the mouth of the dragon, and out of the mouth of the beast, and out of the mouth of the false prophet.

♦ Revelation 19:20 And the beast was taken, and with him the false prophet that wrought miracles before him, with which he deceived them that had received the mark of the beast, and them that worshipped his image. These both were cast alive into a lake of fire burning with brimstone.

♦ Revelation 20: 10 And the devil that deceived them was cast into the lake of fire and brimstone, where the beast and the false prophet are, and shall be tormented day and night for ever and ever.

The only other references to a false prophet in scripture are here:

♦ Matthew 7:15 Beware of false prophets, which come to you in sheep's clothing, but inwardly they are ravening wolves.

♦ Matthew 24:11 And many false prophets shall rise, and shall deceive many.

♦ Matthew 24:24 For there shall arise false Christs, and false prophets, and shall shew great signs and wonders; insomuch that, if it were possible, they shall deceive the very elect.

♦ Mark 13:22 For false Christs and false prophets shall rise, and shall shew signs and wonders, to seduce, if it were possible, even the elect.

♦ Luke 6:26 Woe unto you, when all men shall speak well of you! for so did their fathers to the false prophets.

♦ Acts 13:6 And when they had gone through the isle unto Paphos, they found a certain sorcerer, a false prophet, a Jew, whose name was Barjesus:

♦ II Peter 2:1 But there were false prophets also among the people, even as there shall be false teachers among you, who privily shall bring in damnable heresies, even denying the Lord that bought them, and bring upon themselves swift destruction.

♦ I John 4:1 Beloved, believe not every spirit, but try the spirits whether they are of God: because many false prophets are gone out into the world.

It should be noted that most of the verses above speak of these false prophets as living at the time. Matthew 24:24 and Mark 13:22 also represent the only times the term "false christ" appears.

Blind-sided By God?

Seemingly without any explanation God begins to attack the planet, wreaking ecological havoc, and killing billions of people.

The eighth chapter of the Revelation starts out with "voices, thunderings, and lightnings, and an earthquake", then hail and fire mingled with blood, burning up a third part of trees and "all green grass was burnt up". A third part of the sea then turns to blood and this kills one-third of all sea life. The rivers and springs are then poisoned killing many people. The sun, the moon, and the stars begin to shine for only two-thirds of the night and day.

Continuing into the ninth chapter; from out of the Earth come hordes of creatures, strange, stinging creatures called "locusts", which do not eat plants, but do begin to torment mankind and continue this for five months. These creatures are controlled by an angel of the bottomless pit named Abaddon and the description shows that they are anything but locusts. Verse 6 shows how serious this problem is: "And in those days shall men seek death, and shall not find it; and shall desire to die, and death shall flee from them.". Then four angels that have been restrained in the Euphrates River assemble an "army" made up of creatures stranger and more deadly than the "locusts' that previously attacked men. The result is that one third of the planet's human population die from the attacks of these creatures.

Now, out of the clear blue, comes the references to the population remaining who are refusing to repent of a whole laundry list of offenses, starting with the worship of the things they manufacture.

♦ Revelation 9:20 And the rest of the men which were not killed by these plagues yet repented not of the works of their hands, that they should not worship devils, and idols of gold, and silver, and brass, and stone, and of wood: which neither can see, nor hear, nor walk: 21 Neither repented they of their murders, nor of their sorceries, nor of their fornication, nor of their thefts.

They have just gone through a whole series of attacks of every sort imaginable, billions are dead, and the planet lies in destruction. Why would repentance now become an issue unless they had been told to repent before the attacks began? Does it make sense for God to kill off a third of the population, devastate the planet, and then demand that they repent after they have already been punished or without telling them why they are under attack?

Before the plagues begin the scripture starts with this:

♦ Revelation 8:5. And the angel took the censer, and filled it with fire of the altar, and cast it into the earth: and there were voices, and thunderings, and lightnings, and an earthquake.

The word "voices" here is taken from the same word in these verses:

♦ Revelation 1:10. I was in the Spirit on the Lord's day, and heard behind me a great voice, as of a trumpet, 11. Saying, I am Alpha and Omega, the first and the last:

It comes from the Greek word phone, pronounced fo-nay', through the idea of disclosure; a tone (articulate, bestial or artificial); by implication, an address (for any purpose), saying or language. Could it be that before the plagues these voices were disclosing or addressing mankind about what is to come and the need to follow the directions of God?

The eighth chapter of the Revelation ends with this verse:

♦ "And I beheld, and heard an angel flying through the midst of heaven, saying with a loud voice, Woe, woe, woe, to the inhabiters of the earth by reason of the other voices of the trumpet of the three angels, which are yet to sound!" (Revelation 8:13).

Though not specific in content, this clearly states that an angel flying low in the sky is broadcasting a warning to humanity about the three next disasters to come. The last of the next three events will cost the lives of about 2 billion people by today's population figures. It is unlikely that the only thing the angel is saying is "Woe, woe, woe" but perhaps this is a short way to say the angel revealed what all three disasters would bring. This could also be a point at which humanity is offered a chance to repent.

We see this again in connection with the next disasters that occur after the testimony of the witnesses:

♦ Revelation 16:18. And there were voices, and thunders, and lightnings; and there was a great earthquake, such as was not since men were upon the earth, so mighty an earthquake, and so great.

We can only trust that logic, and the fairness God has shown by warning civilization in the past to stop or pay the price, as scripture shows, must apply here as well. We certainly find this true for the second round of disasters that hit humanity. The warning comes in the form of two witnesses who spend 3 ½ years on the planet defying attempts to kill them and working great miracles.

The next round of events to plague mankind is found in the 16th chapter and comes after these witnesses are killed and resurrected. It starts with what is called a "noisesome sore", which is thoroughly examined in the book under An Amazing Prophecy on Page 96. The oceans are poisoned, killing all life in them, followed by all the rivers turning to blood. This is followed by a burst of heat from the sun which causes men to get badly burned. Here again it says mankind curses God and refuses to repent and give God the glory. The world goes dark and something causes mankind great pain. Again they curse God and refuse to repent.

The Euphrates River dries up and three unclean spirits convince the world to gather an army to fight God at Armageddon. The results of this battle are not described until the 19th chapter, but at the time they are gathering, the greatest earthquake in history hits the planet. After that a hailstorm strikes with the hail stones having a weight of a talent, or almost 95 pounds. Again mankind curses God.

Throughout the plagues mankind experiences, it is described as refusing to repent and recognize the rule of Jesus. In the end the world gathers a great army to fight the returning Christ. How far would we have to stretch our speculation to consider that the people refusing to submit have the slightest clue that they are cursing and defying the Creator? The only reason they would go to these lengths would be if they were completely deceived about who was attacking them. If the clouds Jesus returns in, and from which all these plagues are originating, do not look like clouds as the church teaches they should, mankind could easily be persuaded that it was an alien invasion.

What threat would cause such resistance and unite the world to organize a great army to resist it, other than the fear that mankind is about to be destroyed or enslaved? Certainly you could not get such a global consensus to fight against the returning Christ. There can be little doubt that the world will be seriously deceived about who they are gathering to fight.

The only other individual humans described in the prophecies from the Revelation are the two witnesses of Revelation 11, two women; one Mary, and the other, a great city. The only group of humans mentioned as being evil are merchants.

As you will no doubt agree, we have challenged perhaps every concept most people believe is to be found in the Revelation to John. And, we have pointed out some very serious contradictions to those beliefs. We have carefully searched for any references to the orthodox concepts, and particularly for any mention of the actions of a man as world leader, or as a pretender to the Christ, and can find none. These are the main points we have discovered about the Revelation:

- The antichrist plays no role in the Revelation and is not associated with the visions of Daniel.
- The False Prophet plays a minor role.
- The Beast is not referred to as a human, and is described more realistically as a group of nations or powers.
- There is no great human world leader mentioned that will bring peace, convince mankind he is the Christ, form a world government, or display any control worldwide.
- The only specific humans mentioned in the prophecies of the Revelation are Jesus, his mother Mary, and the two witnesses.
- Satan is not described in human form, nor is he described using any specific humans to do his bidding.
- No human or other living being is specifically described as standing in the Temple at Jerusalem in the last days.
- The blending of the visions of Daniel with the prophecies given to John is shaky at best, and can be very misleading.

There are 404 verses in the Revelation and we have searched them all. The first 5 books are introductory and contain letters to the churches of John's day, so that brings the number down to about 300. Anyone willing to take the time to read the book with the thought of proving or disproving these facts could do so in a relatively short period of time.

The Beings of the Bible

The Angels

Angels are the messengers and most physically present of the spiritual beings in the eternal world of the Elohiym. The word used in the Old Testament is Malak, pronounced mal-awk' and means to dispatch as a deputy; a messenger; specifically, of God. They serve the Elohiym, though obviously not in absolute perfection, as conveyors of thought and action. They are not gods. They are protectors of the Elohiym and mankind. They are not described as having wings, halos, harps, or having the appearance of the orthodox portrayal as commonly seen in paintings and other representations. Angels can appear in flying vehicles or on terra firma and are often in some form of brilliant uniform. There are at least 2 ranks of angels with the archangels being superior in rank. Satan was, of course, an angel, apparently of very high rank though in earlier times he attempted to take over the throne of the Elohiym. Angels appear almost 200 times in the Bible, so the entries in this section deal with those references that relate to appearances in the sky, vehicles, and close encounters.

The concept that man was made "*a little lower than the angels*" as stated in Psalms 8:4 is based on a mistranslation. The word angel is taken from the same word as Elohiym. Therefore, this is properly rendered " a little lower than the Gods". This is repeated in Hebrews 2:5 and in this case, 'angels' is properly translated. However, a statement that shows the angels were not given the high level of responsibility bestowed upon man prefaces this. This puts the ranking of angels in limbo until the true nature of man is clearly stated by Yhovah in Psalms:

♦ **Psalms 82: 6**, I have said, Ye are gods; and all of you are children of the most High.

Jesus quotes himself in emphasizing this fact in John:

♦ **John 10:34** Jesus answered them, "Is it not written in your law, I said, Ye are gods?"

In Luke he speaks on the nature of man after his spiritual change,

♦ **Luke 20:36** Neither can they die any more: for they are equal unto the angels; and are the children of God, being the children of the resurrection."

♦ **1 Corinthians 6:3** Know ye not that we shall judge angels? how much more things that pertain to this life?"

It seems that the angels rank at least equal to man, but are not the children of God and will be judged by men after a spiritual change. This, of course, is up to the opinion of the reader. An interesting perspective on this can be found in Hebrews, chapters 1 and 2.

Angels are never described with wings, halos, or harps. They are not gods.

Devils
And Unclean, Evil Or Familiar Spirits

Devils in the Bible are today known as demons, although the word 'demon' does not appear in Biblical text. The one consistent characteristic trait is that they almost always possess a human body with less than desirable physical and mental consequences. These devils are the Nephilim, the spirits of the giants that were progeny of the human / angelic union that resulted in the Flood. The term fallen angels is not in the Bible although it is recorded that Satan is fallen and it would be presumed that it makes his cohorts fallen angels as well. The question that this poses is whether or not the devils that possess humans and animals are the beings known as Satan's angels or the Nephilim of the flood? For an understanding of the origin of the Nephilim see The Flood, (Page 168)

We have collected the verses in the dealing with these beings:
See Devils and Strange Spirits: Appendix Q

The Giants

The Bible speaks of giants as the offspring of a plot by angels to inbreed with mankind. This first implies that angels had a direct, ongoing relationship with humans as is referred to in Genesis 6:3 when Yhovah says he will end this close association. In Genesis, the flood is pronounced immediately after the giants are mentioned, although not directly referred to as a direct result of the phenomenon of the giants. The verses following this brief mention of giants would seem to indicate that the giants and the flood were seemingly unrelated and are dealt with as such by the pulpit.

The early Catholic Church found it necessary to eliminate the book written by Enoch. The Book of Enoch goes into great detail about the plot by certain angels and that plot's direct relation to the flood. What Enoch relates is a story of deceit, mutant beings out of control, cannibalism, and a decision by Yhovah to end the carnage perpetrated by these mutants which was leading to the decimation of life on Earth. It also shows that though the physical bodies of these mutants were destroyed, their eternal spirits remained intact and are directly connected to the demons encountered by Jesus.

Two Giant Races

It is important to notice that within the first mention of giants in the Bible that this statement is made:

♦ **Genesis 6:4** There were giants in the earth in those days; and also after that.

The "also after that" is clearly represented as meaning "after the Flood" as the giants appear in scriptural narration after that event. They are described as very tall, up to 16 feet, having more fingers and toes than humans, and associated with war. One is even described as a king and entire regional areas are recognized as their habitat. The word Nephilim is the plural Hebrew pronunciation of the word from which giants and giant were taken and does not appear in the Bible. The word Nephil comes from nphiyl, pronounced nef-eel', a bully or tyrant.

Where the word 'Rephaim', 'Rapha' and, in some places, the word 'dead' is used in the verses presented here, they are all taken from the word rapha', pronounced raw-faw', meaning, in the sense of invigorating; a giant, lax, (figuratively) a ghost (as dead; in plural only): In the case of the word dead, it is generally accepted that this is referring to the spirits of the dead giants destroyed by the Flood. The Rephaim are believed to be a race of giants separate from the Nephilim of Genesis 6:4. In two verses the translators used the word 'Rephaim' where the word for the Nephilim appears and these verses are noted.

There is much evidence in history that clearly show giants have been with us far beyond ancient times. Here are the verses in the Bible that describe giants:

♦ **Genesis 6:1** And it came to pass, when men began to multiply on the face of the earth, and daughters were born unto them, 2 That the sons of God saw the daughters of men that they were fair; and they took them wives of all which they chose. 3 And the LORD said, My spirit shall not always strive with man, for that he also is flesh: yet his days shall be an hundred and twenty years. 4 There were giants in the earth in those days; and also after that, when the sons of God came in unto the daughters of men, and they bare children to them, the same became mighty men which were of old, men of renown.

♦ **Genesis 14:5** And in the fourteenth year came Chedorlaomer, and the kings that were with him, and smote the Rephaims in Ashteroth Karnaim, and the Zuzims in Ham, and the Emims in Shaveh Kiriathaim,

♦ **Genesis 15:20** And the Hittites, and the Perizzites, and the Rephaims,

♦ **Numbers 13:33** And there we saw the giants, the sons of Anak, which come of the giants: and we were in our own sight as grasshoppers, and so we were in their sight.

♦ **Deuteronomy 1:28** Whither shall we go up? our brethren have discouraged our heart, saying, The people is greater and taller than we; the cities are great and walled up to heaven; and moreover we have seen the sons of the Anakims there

♦ **Deuteronomy 2:10** The Emims dwelt therein in times past, a people great, and many, and tall, as the Anakims; 11 Which also were accounted giants, as the Anakims; but the Moabites called them Emims.

♦ **Deuteronomy 2:20** (That also was accounted a land of giants: giants dwelt therein in old time; and the Ammonites call them Zamzummims; 21 A people great, and many, and tall, as the Anakims; but the LORD destroyed them before them; and they succeeded them, and dwelt in their stead:

♦ **Deuteronomy 3:11** For only Og king of Bashan remained of the remnant of giants; behold his bedstead was a bedstead of iron; is it not in Rabbath of the children of Ammon? nine cubits was the length thereof, and four cubits the breadth of it, after the cubit of a man. 12 And this land, which we possessed at that time, from Aroer, which is by the river Arnon, and half mount Gilead, and the cities thereof, gave I unto the Reubenites and to the Gadites. 13 And the rest of Gilead, and all Bashan, being the kingdom of Og, gave I unto the half tribe of Manasseh; all the region of Argob, with all Bashan, which was called the land of giants.

(This bed is 6' feet wide 14 feet long and King Og's height is estimated at least 12 feet.)

♦ **Deuteronomy 9:2** A people great and tall, the children of the Anakims, whom thou knowest, and of whom thou hast heard say, Who can stand before the children of Anak!

♦ **Joshua 11:21** And at that time came Joshua, and cut off the Anakims from the mountains, from Hebron, from Debir, from Anab, and from all the mountains of Judah, and from all the mountains of Israel: Joshua destroyed them utterly with their cities. 22 There was none of the Anakims left in the land of the children of Israel: only in Gaza, in Gath, and in Ashdod, there remained.

♦ **Joshua 12:4** And the coast of Og king of Bashan, which was of the remnant of the giants, that dwelt at Ashtaroth and at Edrei,

♦ **Joshua 13:12** All the kingdom of Og in Bashan, which reigned in Ashtaroth and in Edrei, who remained of the remnant of the giants: for these did Moses smite, and cast them out.

♦ **Joshua 14:12** Now therefore give me this mountain, whereof the Lord spake in that day; for thou heardest in that day how the Anakims were there, and that the cities were great and fenced: if so be the Lord will be with me, then I shall be able to drive them out, as the Lord said.

♦ **Joshua 15:8** And the border went up by the valley of the son of Hinnom unto the south side of the Jebusite; the same is Jerusalem: and the border went up to the top of the mountain that lieth before the valley of Hinnom westward, which is at the end of the valley of the giants northward:

♦ **Joshua 15:13** And unto Caleb the son of Jephunneh he gave a part among the children of Judah, according to the commandment of the Lord to Joshua, even the city of Arba the father of Anak, which city is Hebron. 14 And Caleb drove thence the three sons of Anak, Sheshai, and Ahiman, and Talmai, the children of Anak.

♦ **Joshua 17:15** And Joshua answered them, If thou be a great people, then get thee up to the wood country, and cut down for thyself there in the land of the Perizzites and of the giants, if mount Ephraim be too narrow for thee.

♦ **Joshua 18:16** And the border came down to the end of the mountain that lieth before the valley of the son of Hinnom, and which is in the valley of the giants on the north, and descended to the valley of Hinnom, to the side of Jebusi on the south, and descended to Enrogel,

♦ **Joshua 21:11** And they gave them the city of Arba the father of Anak, which city is Hebron, in the hill country of Judah, with the suburbs thereof round about it.

Cherubim

There is no way to be sure that the cherubim described in the Bible are actually beings. To the contrary, they are described as having mechanical characteristics and are most likely devices. They are duplicated in the Temple as ornamentation in spite of the admonition not to create sacred images. They are most often described as having a protective role as well as to facilitate aerial transportation.

Cloaking cherubim

♦ **Genesis 3:24** So he drove out the man; and he placed at the east of the garden of Eden Cherubim, and a flaming sword which turned every way, to keep the way of the tree of life.

The cherubim, which appears to be some sort of device rather than a being, is placed to protect the Tree of life in the garden. This device or devices is described as flashing and either rotating or having a constant 360-degree range of coverage. The cherubim are mentioned many times throughout the Bible. They are described as having protective properties and as having the capability of performing various tasks. Flaming = flashing.

Yhovah Rides A Cherub And Flies

♦ **2 Samuel 22:11** And he rode upon a cherub, and did fly: and he was seen upon the wings of the wind.

Yhovah rides on a 'cherub' and flies on the edge of the wind. This could indicate a smooth, soaring-like flight, much like a glider. Wings = extreme edge

Chariot Of The Cherubim

♦ **1 Chronicles 28:18** And for the altar of incense refined gold by weight; and gold for the pattern of the chariot of the Cherubims, that spread out their wings, and covered the ark of the covenant of the Lord.

Is this to be a representation of Yhovah's flying vehicles?

Yhovah Flies A Cherub On The Wind

♦ **Psalms 18:10** And he rode upon a cherub, and did fly: yea, he did fly upon the wings of the wind.

Yhovah flies a cherub rapidly on the wings of the wind. Second fly = to dart or fly rapidly.

Up From The Cherubim

♦ **Isaiah 9:3** And the glory of the God of Israel was gone up from the cherub, whereupon he was, to the threshold of the house. And he called to the man clothed with linen, which had the writer's inkhorn by his side

The glory rises above the cherubim.

A Sapphire Throne

♦ **Ezekiel 10:1** Then I looked, and, behold, in the firmament that was above the head of the cherubims there appeared over them as it were a sapphire stone, as the appearance of the likeness of a throne.

Ezekiel is describing an expanse on top of the four devices that is a structure like a gem in the form of a canopy.

Wheels And Glowing Objects

♦ **Ezekiel 10:2** And he spake unto the man clothed with linen, and said, Go in between the wheels, even under the cherub, and fill thine hand with coals of fire from between the cherubims, and scatter them over the city. And he went in my sight.

A being, clothed in white, tells Ezekiel to go to the center of the devices.

Stationed Cherubims

♦ **Ezekiel 10:3** Now the cherubims stood on the right side of the house, when the man went in; and the cloud filled the inner court.

Wheels And Cherubim

♦ **Ezekiel 10:6** And it came to pass, that when he had commanded the man clothed with linen, saying, Take fire from between the wheels, from between the cherubims; then he went in, and stood beside the wheels.

There are glowing objects between the wheels.

Moving Devices On Cherubim

♦ **Ezekiel 10:7** And one cherub stretched forth his hand from between the cherubims unto the fire that was between the cherubims, and took thereof, and put it into the hands of him that was clothed with linen: who took it, and went out.

The indication that the cherubim literally grabs a glowing object and literally hands it to the being clothed in linen could be Ezekiel's interpretation of the movements of a mechanical device. See next verse.

Hand-Like Devices On Cherubim

♦ **Ezekiel 10:8** And there appeared in the cherubims the form of a man's hand under their wings.

Form = shape.

Seraphim

♦ **Numbers 8:15** Who led thee through that great and terrible wilderness, wherein were fiery serpents, and scorpions, and drought, where there was no water; who brought thee forth water out of the rock of flint;

   Seraphim dwell in a great and terrible wilderness.

♦ **Numbers 21:6** And the Lord sent fiery serpents among the people, and they bit the people; and much people of Israel died. 7 Therefore the people came to Moses, and said, We have sinned, for we have spoken against the Lord, and against thee; pray unto the Lord, that he take away the serpents from us. And Moses prayed for the people. 8 And the Lord said unto Moses, Make thee a fiery serpent, and set it upon a pole: and it shall come to pass, that every one that is bitten, when he looketh upon it, shall live.

   Seraphim are unleashed on the nation. Fiery serpents = seraphim.

Elders

A Celestial Council Around The Throne

♦ **Revelation 4:4** And round about the throne were four and twenty seats: and upon the seats I saw four and twenty elders sitting, clothed in white raiment; and they had on their heads crowns of gold.

   Elders = a Sanhedtrist, member of the ruling council.

♦ **Revelation 5:11** And I beheld, and I heard the voice of many angels round about the throne and the beasts and the elders: and the number of them was ten thousand times ten thousand, and thousands of thousands;

   Ten thousand = myriads. Thousands = one thousand. See Psalms 68:17

Men

A Copper Being

♦ **Isaiah 40:3** And he brought me thither, and, behold, there was a man, whose appearance was like the appearance of brass, with a line of flax in his hand, and a measuring reed; and he stood in the\gate.

   Ezekiel encounters a man who appeared as copper colored metal.

A Man Appears

♦ **Isaiah 43:6** And I heard him speaking unto me out of the house; and the man stood by me.

   A being appears beside Ezekiel.

Appearance Of A Man

♦ **Daniel 8:15** And it came to pass, when I, even I Daniel, had seen the vision, and sought for the meaning, then, behold, there stood before me as the appearance of a man.

   A being that looked like a man appears before Daniel.

The Transfiguration Cloud

♦ **Mark 9:4** And there appeared unto them Elias with Moses: and they were talking with Jesus. 5 And Peter answered and said to Jesus, Master, it is good for us to be here: and let us make three tabernacles; one for thee, and one for Moses, and one for Elias. 6 For he wist not what to say; for they were sore afraid. 7 And there was a cloud that overshadowed them: and a voice came out of the cloud, saying, This is my beloved Son: hear him. 8 And suddenly, when they had looked round about, they saw no man any more, save Jesus only with themselves.

This is known as the "Transfiguration". Jesus tells his apostles that some of them will see the realm of God before they die. Jesus is praying and his appearance changes. His clothes became pure white and gleaming. Two men appear with Jesus and a cloud enveloped them with a brilliant haze and suddenly the two men disappear.

A Young Man In The Tomb

♦ **Mark 16:3** And they said among themselves, Who shall roll us away the stone from the door of the sepulchre? 4 And when they looked, they saw that the stone was rolled away: for it was very great. 5 And entering into the sepulchre, they saw a young man sitting on the right side, clothed in a long white garment; and they were affrighted. 6 And he saith unto them, Be not affrighted: Ye seek Jesus of Nazareth, which was crucified: he is risen; he is not here: behold the place where they laid him.

The Transfiguration And Bright Lights

♦ **Luke 9:29** And as he prayed, the fashion of his countenance was altered, and his raiment was white and glistering. 30 And, behold, there talked with him two men, which were Moses and Elias: 31 Who appeared in glory, and spake of his decease which he should accomplish at Jerusalem. 32 But Peter and they that were with him were heavy with sleep: and when they were awake, they saw his glory, and the two men that stood with him. 33 And it came to pass, as they departed from him, Peter said unto Jesus, Master, it is good for us to be here: and let us make three tabernacles; one for thee, and one for Moses, and one for Elias: not knowing what he said.

The transfiguration is the account of an aerial visitation to Jesus by two beings that discuss the coming crucifixion.

Two Men In White Apparel

♦ **Acts 1:10** And while they looked stedfastly toward heaven as he went up, behold, two men stood by them in white apparel; 11 Which also said, Ye men of Galilee, why stand ye gazing up into heaven? this same Jesus, which is taken up from you into heaven, shall so come in like manner as ye have seen him go into heaven.

Two men, who suddenly appeared, stated that Jesus, who they just saw ascending into the sky, would return from the sky in the same manner as that which they had just witnessed.

The Beings of the Bible

A Man In Radiant Clothing
♦ **Acts 10:30** And Cornelius said, Four days ago I was fasting until this hour; and at the ninth hour I prayed in my house, and, behold, a man stood before me in bright clothing,

A man, in radiant clothing, suddenly appears.

Saints

Ten Thousand Saints
♦ **Deuteronomy 33:2** And he said, The Lord came from Sinai, and rose up from Seir unto them; he shined forth from mount Paran, and he came with ten thousands of saints: from his right hand went a fiery law for them.

In the phrase ' fiery law for them ', law for them was added. It should say from his right hand went a fire. The saints may be the first mention of the army that Yahweh commands

Watchers

A Watcher from the Sky
♦ **Daniel 4:13**   I saw in the visions of my head upon my bed, and, behold, a watcher and an holy one came down from heaven;

A watcher comes down from the sky.

♦ **Daniel 4:23** And whereas the king saw a watcher and an holy one coming down from heaven, and saying, Hew the tree down, and destroy it; yet leave the stump of the roots thereof in the earth, even with a band of iron and brass, in the tender grass of the field; and let it be wet with the dew of heaven, and let his portion be with the beasts of the field, till seven times pass over him;

Nebuchadnezzar is seeing this in a vision.

Other Beings

Bright, Shining River
♦ **Daniel 7:10** A fiery stream issued and came forth from before him: thousand thousands ministered unto him, and ten thousand times ten thousand stood before him: the judgment was set, and the books were opened.

A beam of light shown from him, millions served him, and hundreds of millions were in his presence.

A Golden Being
♦ **Daniel 10:5** Then I lifted up mine eyes, and looked, and behold a certain man clothed in linen, whose loins were girded with fine gold of Uphaz:

A being, dressed in linen and gold, appears. Girded = dressed.

Flying Horses
♦ **Joel 2:4** The appearance of them is as the appearance of horses; and as horsemen, so shall they run. **5** Like the noise of chariots on the tops of

mountains shall they leap, like the noise of a flame of fire that devoureth the stubble, as a strong people set in battle array.

Horses= swift.

Strange Beings On Strange Horses

♦ **Revelation 9:17** And thus I saw the horses in the vision, and them that sat on them, having breastplates of fire, and of jacinth, and brimstone: and the heads of the horses were as the heads of lions; and out of their mouths issued fire and smoke and brimstone.

It is not clear whether these are actually horses or devices.

Beings That Live In The Sky

♦ **Revelation 12:12** Therefore rejoice, ye heavens, and ye that dwell in them. Woe to the inhabiters of the earth and of the sea! for the devil is come down unto you, having great wrath, because he knoweth that he hath but a short time.

Those that are already in the sky are lucky because Satan knows his time is short and he is in a rage.

Hosts - The Army of Yhovah

The reason for the title "The Army of Yhovah" is that almost 300 times the God of the Old Testament is referred to as the Lord of hosts. The word host is taken from, *tsaba', pronounced tsaw-baw'; a mass of persons (or figuratively, things), especially reg. organized for war (an army).* This army has an armada of many thousands of chariots and millions of beings called the Malak or angels. The chariots of God are also called chariots of fire and are described as flying. It is also clearly stated that the clouds are his chariots. Since Jesus is Yhovah of the Old Testament and because he will return coming in the clouds, it is doubtless that those clouds are the flying chariots of fire of 2 Kings.

The Army Of Yhovah

♦ **Genesis 2:1** Thus the heavens and the earth were finished, and all the host of them.

This verse shows another aspect of the nature of these supreme beings, they have an army. The word host is taken from 'tsaba', which literally means an army. This army is spoken of almost 300 times from the creation to Armageddon with the God Yhovah as its supreme commander. Although it is a fighting army, this verse shows combat is one of its functions.

God's Army

♦ **Genesis 32:1** And Jacob went on his way, and the angels of God met him. 2 And when Jacob saw them, he said, This is God's host: and he called the name of that place Mahanaim.

host = machaneh pronounced makh-an-eh', an encampment (of travellers or troops); hence, an army

The Beings of the Bible

A Captain Of Yhovah's Army

♦ **Joshua 5:13** And it came to pass, when Joshua was by Jericho, that he lifted up his eyes and looked, and, behold, there stood a man over against him with his sword drawn in his hand: and Joshua went unto him, and said unto him, Art thou for us, or for our adversaries? 14 And he said, Nay; but as captain of the host of the Lord am I now come. And Joshua fell on his face to the earth, and did worship, and said unto him, What saith my lord unto his servant?

A high-ranking member of the Army of Yhovah hovering over him confronts Joshua.

Battle In The Stars

♦ **Judges 5:20** They fought from heaven; the stars in their courses fought against Sisera.

Unclear as to significance but this verse seems to be talking about a stellar battle.

Armies Of The Living God

♦ **1 Samuel 17:26** And David spake to the men that stood by him, saying, What shall be done to the man that killeth this Philistine, and taketh away the reproach from Israel? for who is this uncircumcised Philistine, that he should defy the armies of the living God?

The Army Of The Sky By The Throne

♦ **1 Kings 22:19** And he said, Hear thou therefore the word of the Lord: I saw the Lord sitting on his throne, and all the host of heaven standing by him on his right hand and on his left.

Yhovah is on his throne and the army of the sky are by his side. Hosts = army.

Spinning Chariots Of Fire Take Elijah

♦ **2 Kings 2:11** And it came to pass, as they still went on, and talked, that, behold, there appeared a chariot of fire, and horses of fire, and parted them both asunder; and Elijah went up by a whirlwind into heaven. 12 And Elisha saw it, and he cried, My father, my father, the chariot of Israel, and the horsemen thereof. And he saw him no more: and he took hold of his own clothes, and rent them in two pieces.

Elijah and Elisha are talking and suddenly a bright, flying vehicle and a cavalry of bright, flying objects appear and Elijah ascends into the sky by a spinning-flying vehicle. The word translated into horses, 'cuwc' means rapid movement or flight. This cavalry of glowing vehicles is most likely the army spoken of where the word 'hosts' appears.

Chariots of Fire

♦ **2 Kings 6:17** And Elisha prayed, and said, Lord, I pray thee, open his eyes, that he may see. And the Lord opened the eyes of the young man; and he saw: and, behold, the mountain was full of horses and chariots of fire round about

Elisha. 18 And when they came down to him, Elisha prayed unto the Lord, and said, Smite this people, I pray thee, with blindness. And he smote them with blindness according to the word of Elisha.

The King of Syria has surrounded the city of Dothan where Elisha is and Elisha asks Yhovah to help him. Suddenly the sky was filled with rapidly moving, bright, flying objects all around Elisha. One or more flying objects descend to the ground and Elisha asks Yhovah to cause blindness to befall the surrounding army, which he does. The army is captured and later Yhovah restores their sight.

Army of God

♦ **1 Chronicles 12: 22** For at that time day by day there came to David to help him, until it was a great host, like the host of God.

The Sky Army And The Throne

♦ **2 Chronicles 18:18** Again he said, Therefore hear the word of the Lord; I saw the Lord sitting upon his throne, and all the host of heaven standing on his right hand and on his left.

Yhovah is described as sitting on his throne, the army of the sky beside him.

Sky Army Command

♦ **Nehemiah 9:6** Thou, even thou, art Lord alone; thou hast made heaven, the heaven of heavens, with all their host, the earth, and all things that are therein, the seas, and all that is therein, and thou preservest them all; and the host of heaven worshippeth thee.

The army of the sky pays homage to Yhovah the creator and protector of all the skies.

The Number Of Yhovah's "Armies"

♦ **Job 25:3** Is there any number of his armies? and upon whom doth not his light arise?

Biblical Paranormal Evidence

Presented here are a few of what divine miracles to some are, and paranormal events to others. There are many times more the number of anomalous events that appear in the Bible and here in this work.

"Any sufficiently advanced technology is indistinguishable from magic"
Arthur C. Clark

Old Testament Evidence

Men Blinded Through Walls
♦ **Genesis 19:10** But the men put forth their hand, and pulled Lot into the house to them, and shut to the door. 11 And they smote the men that were at the door of the house with blindness, both small and great: so that they wearied themselves to find the door.

Telepathic Contact
♦ **Genesis 20:3** But God came to Abimelech in a dream by night, and said to him, Behold, thou art but a dead man, for the woman which thou hast taken; for she is a man's wife.

Physical Transmutation
♦ **Exodus 7:2** And the Lord said unto him, What is that in thine hand? And he said, A rod. 3 And he said, Cast it on the ground. And he cast it on the ground, and it became a serpent; and Moses fled from before it. 4 And the Lord said unto Moses, Put forth thine hand, and take it by the tail. And he put forth his hand, and caught it, and it became a rod in his hand:
♦ **Numbers 17:8** And it came to pass, that on the morrow Moses went into the tabernacle of witness; and, behold, the rod of Aaron for the house of Levi was budded, and brought forth buds, and bloomed blossoms, and yielded almonds.

Invisibility
♦ **Numbers 22:31** Then the Lord opened the eyes of Balaam, and he saw the angel of the Lord standing in the way, and his sword drawn in his hand: and he bowed down his head, and fell flat on his face.

Voice Projection
♦ **Numbers 22:28** And the Lord opened the mouth of the ass, and she said unto Balaam, What have I done unto thee, that thou hast smitten me these three times?

Immortal Clothing
♦ **Deuteronomy 8:4** Thy raiment waxed not old upon thee, neither did thy foot swell, these forty years.

♦ **Deuteronomy 29:5** And I have led you forty years in the wilderness: your clothes are not waxen old upon you, and thy shoe is not waxen old upon thy foot.

Super Human Strength
♦ **Judges 16:3** And Samson lay till midnight, and arose at midnight, and took the doors of the gate of the city, and the two posts, and went away with them, bar and all, and put them upon his shoulders, and carried them up to the top of an hill that is before Hebron.

Conjuring Up the Dead
♦ **1 Samuel 28: 6** And when Saul inquired of the Lord, the Lord answered him not, neither by dreams, nor by Urim, nor by prophets.7 Then said Saul unto his servants, Seek me a woman that hath a familiar spirit, that I may go to her, and inquire of her. And his servants said to him, Behold, there is a woman that hath a familiar spirit at Endor. 8 And Saul disguised himself, and put on other raiment, and he went, and two men with him, and they came to the woman by night: and he said, I pray thee, divine unto me by the familiar spirit, and bring me him up, whom I shall name unto thee. 9 And the woman said unto him, Behold, thou knowest what Saul hath done, how he hath cut off those that have familiar spirits, and the wizards, out of the land: wherefore then layest thou a snare for my life, to cause me to die? 10 And Saul sware to her by the Lord, saying, As the Lord liveth, there shall no punishment happen to thee for this thing. 11 Then said the woman, Whom shall I bring up unto thee? And he said, Bring me up Samuel. 12 And when the woman saw Samuel, she cried with a loud voice: and the woman spake to Saul, saying, Why hast thou deceived me? for thou art Saul.

Audio Projection
♦ **2 Kings 7:5** And they rose up in the twilight, to go unto the camp of the Syrians: and when they were come to the uttermost part of the camp of Syria, behold, there was no man there. 6 For the Lord had made the host of the Syrians to hear a noise of chariots, and a noise of horses, even the noise of a great host: and they said one to another, Lo, the king of Israel hath hired against us the kings of the Hittites, and the kings of the Egyptians, to come upon us.

An Apparition
♦ **Job 4:12** Now a thing was secretly brought to me, and mine ear received a little thereof. 13 In thoughts from the visions of the night, when deep sleep falleth on men, 14 Fear came upon me, and trembling, which made all my bones to shake. 15 Then a spirit passed before my face; the hair of my flesh stood up: 16 It stood still, but I could not discern the form thereof: an image was before mine eyes, there was silence, and I heard a voice, saying, 17 Shall mortal man be more just than God? shall a man be more pure than his maker?

Contact with the Dead

♦ **Job 4:8** For inquire, I pray thee, of the former age, and prepare thyself to the search of their fathers: 9 (For we are but of yesterday, and know nothing, because our days upon earth are a shadow:) 10 Shall not they teach thee, and tell thee, and utter words out of their heart?

A Book of Woes and a Hand

♦ **Ezekiel 2:9** And when I looked, behold, an hand was sent unto me; and, lo, a roll of a book was therein; 10 And he spread it before me; and it was written within and without: and there was written therein lamentations, and mourning, and woe.

Dream Interpretation

♦ **Daniel 5:10** Now the queen by reason of the words of the king and his lords came into the banquet house: and the queen spake and said, O king, live for ever: let not thy thoughts trouble thee, nor let thy countenance be changed: 11 There is a man in thy kingdom, in whom is the spirit of the holy gods; and in the days of thy father light and understanding and wisdom, like the wisdom of the gods, was found in him; whom the king Nebuchadnezzar thy father, the king, I say, thy father, made master of the magicians, astrologers, Chaldeans, and soothsayers; 12 Forasmuch as an excellent spirit, and knowledge, and understanding, interpreting of dreams, and shewing of hard sentences, and dissolving of doubts, were found in the same Daniel, whom the king named Belteshazzar: now let Daniel be called, and he will shew the interpretation.

New Testament Evidence

Angelic Protection

♦ **Matthew 4:6** And saith unto him, If thou be the Son of God, cast thyself down: for it is written, He shall give his angels charge concerning thee: and in their hands they shall bear thee up, lest at any time thou dash thy foot against a stone.

Levitation

♦ **Matthew 14:24** But the ship was now in the midst of the sea, tossed with waves: for the wind was contrary. 25 And in the fourth watch of the night Jesus went unto them, walking on the sea. 26 And when the disciples saw him walking on the sea, they were troubled, saying, It is a spirit; and they cried out for fear. 27 But straightway Jesus spake unto them, saying, Be of good cheer; it is I; be not afraid. 28 And Peter answered him and said, Lord, if it be thou, bid me come unto thee on the water. 29 And he said, Come. And when Peter was come down out of the ship, he walked on the water, to go to Jesus.

Telekinesis

♦ **Matthew 17:20** And Jesus said unto them, Because of your unbelief: for verily I say unto you, If ye have faith as a grain of mustard seed, ye shall say unto this mountain, Remove hence to yonder place; and it shall remove; and nothing shall be impossible unto you.

♦ **Matthew 21:18** Now in the morning as he returned into the city, he hungered. 19 And when he saw a fig tree in the way, he came to it, and found nothing thereon, but leaves only, and said unto it, Let no fruit grow on thee henceforward for ever. And presently the fig tree withered away.

Invisibility

♦ **Luke 4:29** And rose up, and thrust him out of the city, and led him unto the brow of the hill whereon their city was built, that they might cast him down headlong. 30 But he passing through the midst of them went his way,

Physical Transmutation

♦ **John 2:7** Jesus saith unto them, Fill the waterpots with water. And they filled them up to the brim. 8 And he saith unto them, Draw out now, and bear unto the governor of the feast. And they bare it. 9 When the ruler of the feast had tasted the water that was made wine, and knew not whence it was: (but the servants which drew the water knew;) the governor of the feast called the bridegroom, 10 And saith unto him, Every man at the beginning doth set forth good wine; and when men have well drunk, then that which is worse: but thou hast kept the good wine until now.

Healing Waters

♦ **John 5:1** After this there was a feast of the Jews; and Jesus went up to Jerusalem. 2 Now there is at Jerusalem by the sheep market a pool, which is called in the Hebrew tongue Bethesda, having five porches. 3 In these lay a great multitude of impotent folk, of blind, halt, withered, waiting for the moving of the water. 4 For an angel went down at a certain season into the pool, and troubled the water: whosoever then first after the troubling of the water stepped in was made whole of whatsoever disease he had.

A Voice from the Sky

♦ **John 12:27** Now is my soul troubled; and what shall I say? Father, save me from this hour: but for this cause came I unto this hour. 28 Father, glorify thy name. Then came there a voice from heaven, saying, I have both glorified it, and will glorify it again. 29 The people therefore, that stood by, and heard it, said that it thundered: others said, An angel spake to him. 30 Jesus answered and said, This voice came not because of me, but for your sakes.

Metamorphosis
♦ **John 20:17** Jesus saith unto her, Touch me not; for I am not yet ascended to my Father: but go to my brethren, and say unto them, I ascend unto my Father, and your Father; and to my God, and your God.

Merriam-Webster: Metamorphosis: 1 a : change of physical form, structure, or substance especially by supernatural means b : a striking alteration in appearance, character, or circumstances. (Merriam-Webster)
• Compare Jesus' appearance after the Ascension: Revelation 1:14 His head and his hairs were white like wool, as white as snow; and his eyes were as a flame of fire; 15 And his feet like unto fine brass, as if they burned in a furnace; and his voice as the sound of many waters.

A Strange Shaking
♦ **Acts 4:31** And when they had prayed, the place was shaken where they were assembled together; and they were all filled with the Holy Ghost, and they spake the word of God with boldness. 32 And the multitude of them that believed were of one heart and of one soul: neither said any of them that ought of the things which he possessed was his own; but they had all things common.

Shadow Healing
♦ **Acts 5:15** Insomuch that they brought forth the sick into the streets, and laid them on beds and couches, that at the least the shadow of Peter passing by might overshadow some of them.

A Trance
♦ **Acts 10:9** On the morrow, as they went on their journey, and drew nigh unto the city, Peter went up upon the housetop to pray about the sixth hour: 10 And he became very hungry, and would have eaten: but while they made ready, he fell into a trance,

Psychokenesis
♦ **Acts 12:5** Peter therefore was kept in prison: but prayer was made without ceasing of the church unto God for him. 6 And when Herod would have brought him forth, the same night Peter was sleeping between two soldiers, bound with two chains: and the keepers before the door kept the prison. 7 And, behold, the angel of the Lord came upon him, and a light shined in the prison: and he smote Peter on the side, and raised him up, saying, Arise up quickly. And his chains fell off from his hands. 8 And the angel said unto him, Gird thyself, and bind on thy sandals. And so he did. And he saith unto him, Cast thy garment about thee, and follow me. 9 And he went out, and followed him; and wist not that it was true which was done by the angel; but thought he saw a vision. 10 When they were past the first and the second ward, they came unto the iron gate that leadeth unto the city; which opened to them of his own

accord: and they went out, and passed on through one street; and forthwith the angel departed from him.

Healing Cloth
♦ **Acts 19:11** And God wrought special miracles by the hands of Paul: 12 So that from his body were brought unto the sick handkerchiefs or aprons, and the diseases departed from them, and the evil spirits went out of them.

Spiritual Power
♦ **1 Corinthians 12:8** For to one is given by the Spirit the word of wisdom; to another the word of knowledge by the same Spirit; 9 To another faith by the same Spirit; to another the gifts of healing by the same Spirit; 10 To another the working of miracles; to another prophecy; to another discerning of spirits; to another divers kinds of tongues; to another the interpretation of tongues:
♦ **1 Corinthians 12:28** And God hath set some in the church, first apostles, secondarily prophets, thirdly teachers, after that miracles, then gifts of healings, helps, governments, diversities of tongues.

Out of Body Experience
♦ **2 Corinthians 12:2** I knew a man in Christ above fourteen years ago, (whether in the body, I cannot tell; or whether out of the body, I cannot tell: God knoweth;) such an one caught up to the third heaven. 3 And I knew such a man, (whether in the body, or out of the body, I cannot tell: God knoweth;) 4 How that he was caught up into paradise, and heard unspeakable words, which it is not lawful for a man to utter.

Sorcery and Enchantments

♦ **Exodus 7:11** Then Pharaoh also called the wise men and the sorcerers: now the magicians of Egypt, they also did in like manner with their enchantments.
♦ **Exodus 7:23** And the magicians of Egypt did so with their enchantments: and Pharaoh's heart was hardened, neither did he hearken unto them; as the LORD had said.
♦ **Exodus 8:7** And the magicians did so with their enchantments, and brought up frogs upon the land of Egypt.
♦ **Exodus 8:18** And the magicians did so with their enchantments to bring forth lice, but they could not: so there were lice upon man, and upon beast.
♦ **Numbers 24:1** And when Balaam saw that it pleased the LORD to bless Israel, he went not, as at other times, to seek for enchantments, but he set his face toward the wilderness
♦ **Isaiah 47:9** But these two things shall come to thee in a moment in one day, the loss of children, and widowhood: they shall come upon thee in their perfection for the multitude of thy sorceries, and for the great abundance of thine enchantments. 10 For thou hast trusted in thy wickedness: thou hast said,

None seeth me. Thy wisdom and thy knowledge, it hath perverted thee; and thou hast said in thine heart, I am, and none else beside me. 12 Stand now with thine enchantments, and with the multitude of thy sorceries, wherein thou hast laboured from thy youth; if so be thou shalt be able to profit, if so be thou mayest prevail. 13 Thou art wearied in the multitude of thy counsels. Let now the astrologers, the stargazers, the monthly prognosticators, stand up, and save thee from these things that shall come upon thee.

♦ **Acts 8:9** But there was a certain man, called Simon, which beforetime in the same city used sorcery, and bewitched the people of Samaria, giving out that himself was some great one: 10 To whom they all gave heed, from the least to the greatest, saying, This man is the great power of God. 11 And to him they had regard, because that of long time he had bewitched them with sorceries.

♦ **Revelation 9:21** Neither repented they of their murders, nor of their sorceries, nor of their fornication, nor of their thefts.

♦ **Revelation 18:23** And the light of a candle shall shine no more at all in thee; and the voice of the bridegroom and of the bride shall be heard no more at all in thee: for thy merchants were the great men of the earth; for by thy sorceries were all nations deceived.

Magic and Astrology

♦ **Daniel 1:20** And in all matters of wisdom and understanding, that the king enquired of them, he found them ten times better than all the magicians and astrologers that were in all his realm.

♦ **Daniel 2:2** Then the king commanded to call the magicians, and the astrologers, and the sorcerers, and the Chaldeans, for to shew the king his dreams. So they came and stood before the king.

♦ **Daniel 2:27** Daniel answered in the presence of the king, and said, The secret which the king hath demanded cannot the wise men, the astrologers, the magicians, the soothsayers, shew unto the king;

♦ **Daniel 4:7** Then came in the magicians, the astrologers, the Chaldeans, and the soothsayers: and I told the dream before them; but they did not make known unto me the interpretation thereof.

♦ **Daniel 5:7** The king cried aloud to bring in the astrologers, the Chaldeans, and the soothsayers. And the king spake, and said to the wise men of Babylon, Whosoever shall read this writing, and shew me the interpretation thereof, shall be clothed with scarlet, and have a chain of gold about his neck, and shall be the third ruler in the kingdom.

♦ **Daniel 5:11** There is a man in thy kingdom, in whom is the spirit of the holy gods; and in the days of thy father light and understanding and wisdom, like the wisdom of the gods, was found in him; whom the king Nebuchadnezzar thy father, the king, I say, thy father, made master of the magicians, astrologers, Chaldeans, and soothsayers;

♦ **Daniel 5:15** And now the wise men, the astrologers, have been brought in before me, that they should read this writing, and make known unto me the interpretation thereof: but they could not shew the interpretation of the thing:

Witches And Wizards

♦ **Exodus 22:18** Thou shalt not suffer a witch to live.

♦ **Deuteronomy 18:10** There shall not be found among you any one that maketh his son or his daughter to pass through the fire, or that useth divination, or an observer of times, or an enchanter, or a witch. 11 Or a charmer, or a consulter with familiar spirits, or a wizard, or a necromancer. 12 For all that do these things are an abomination unto the LORD: and because of these abominations the LORD thy God doth drive them out from before thee. 14 For these nations, which thou shalt possess, hearkened unto observers of times, and unto diviners: but as for thee, the LORD thy God hath not suffered thee so to do.

♦ **1 Samuel 15:23** For rebellion is as the sin of witchcraft, and stubbornness is as iniquity and idolatry. Because thou hast rejected the word of the LORD, he hath also rejected thee from being king.

♦ **2 Chronicles 33:6** And he caused his children to pass through the fire in the valley of the son of Hinnom: also he observed times, and used enchantments, and used witchcraft, and dealt with a familiar spirit, and with wizards: he wrought much evil in the sight of the LORD, to provoke him to anger.

♦ **2 Kings 21:6** And he made his son pass through the fire, and observed times, and used enchantments, and dealt with familiar spirits and wizards: he wrought much wickedness in the sight of the LORD, to provoke him to anger.

♦ **Leviticus 19:31** Regard not them that have familiar spirits, neither seek after wizards, to be defiled by them: I am the LORD your God.

♦ **Leviticus 20:6** And the soul that turneth after such as have familiar spirits, and after wizards, to go a whoring after them, I will even set my face against that soul, and will cut him off from among his people.

♦ **1 Samuel 28:3** Now Samuel was dead, and all Israel had lamented him, and buried him in Ramah, even in his own city. And Saul had put away those that had familiar spirits, and the wizards, out of the land.

♦ **1 Samuel 28:9** And the woman said unto him, Behold, thou knowest what Saul hath done, how he hath cut off those that have familiar spirits, and the wizards, out of the land: wherefore then layest thou a snare for my life, to cause me to die?

♦ **2 Kings 23:24** Moreover the workers with familiar spirits, and the wizards, and the images, and the idols, and all the abominations that were spied in the land of Judah and in Jerusalem, did Josiah put away, that he might perform the words of the law which were written in the book that Hilkiah the priest found in the house of the LORD.

♦ **Isaiah 8:19** And when they shall say unto you, Seek unto them that have familiar spirits, and unto wizards that peep, and that mutter: should not a people seek unto their God? for the living to the dead?

♦ **Isaiah 19:3** And the spirit of Egypt shall fail in the midst thereof; and I will destroy the counsel thereof: and they shall seek to the idols, and to the charmers, and to them that have familiar spirits, and to the wizards.

♦ **Galatians 5:19** Now the works of the flesh are manifest, which are these; Adultery, fornication, uncleanness, lasciviousness, 20 Idolatry, witchcraft, hatred, variance, emulations, wrath, strife, seditions, heresies, 21 Envyings, murders, drunkenness, revellings, and such like: of the which I tell you before, as I have also told you in time past, that they which do such things shall not inherit the kingdom of God.

Divination

♦ **2 Kings 17:17** And they caused their sons and their daughters to pass through the fire, and used divination and enchantments, and sold themselves to do evil in the sight of the LORD, to provoke him to anger.

♦ **Jeremiah 14:14** Then the LORD said unto me, The prophets prophesy lies in my name: I sent them not, neither have I commanded them, neither spake unto them: they prophesy unto you a false vision and divination, and a thing of nought, and the deceit of their heart. 15 Therefore thus saith the LORD concerning the prophets that prophesy in my name, and I sent them not, yet they say, Sword and famine shall not be in this land; By sword and famine shall those prophets be consumed.

♦ **Ezekiel 12:24** For there shall be no more any vain vision nor flattering divination within the house of Israel.

♦ **Ezekiel 13:6** They have seen vanity and lying divination, saying, The LORD saith: and the LORD hath not sent them: and they have made others to hope that they would confirm the word. 7 Have ye not seen a vain vision, and have ye not spoken a lying divination, whereas ye say, The LORD saith it; albeit I have not spoken?

♦ **Ezekiel 21:21** For the king of Babylon stood at the parting of the way, at the head of the two ways, to use divination: he made his arrows bright, he consulted with images, he looked in the liver. 22 At his right hand was the divination for Jerusalem, to appoint captains, to open the mouth in the slaughter, to lift up the voice with shouting, to appoint battering rams against the gates, to cast a mount, and to build a fort. 23 And it shall be unto them as a false divination in their sight, to them that have sworn oaths: but he will call to remembrance the iniquity, that they may be taken.

♦ **Acts 16:16** And it came to pass, as we went to prayer, a certain damsel possessed with a spirit of divination met us, which brought her masters much gain by soothsaying: 17 The same followed Paul and us, and cried, saying,

These men are the servants of the most high God, which shew unto us the way of salvation. 18 And this did she many days. But Paul, being grieved, turned and said to the spirit, I command thee in the name of Jesus Christ to come out of her. And he came out the same hour.

Familiar and Unclean Spirits

Cures From Disease and Evil Spirits

♦ **Luke 6:18** And they that were vexed with unclean spirits: and they were healed.

♦ **Luke 7:21** And in that same hour he cured many of their infirmities and plagues, and of evil spirits; and unto many that were blind he gave sight.

♦ **Luke 8:2** And certain women, which had been healed of evil spirits and infirmities, Mary called Magdalene, out of whom went seven devils,

♦ **Acts 5:16** There came also a multitude out of the cities round about unto Jerusalem, bringing sick folks, and them which were vexed with unclean spirits: and they were healed every one.

♦ **Acts 8:5** Then Philip went down to the city of Samaria, and preached Christ unto them. 6 And the people with one accord gave heed unto those things which Philip spake, hearing and seeing the miracles which he did. 7 For unclean spirits, crying with loud voice, came out of many that were possessed with them: and many taken with palsies, and that were lame, were healed.

♦ **Acts 8:7** For unclean spirits, crying with loud voice, came out of many that were possessed with them: and many taken with palsies, and that were lame, were healed.

♦ **Acts 10:38** How God anointed Jesus of Nazareth with the Holy Ghost and with power: who went about doing good, and healing all that were oppressed of the devil; for God was with him.

♦ **Acts 19:12** So that from his body were brought unto the sick handkerchiefs or aprons, and the diseases departed from them, and the evil spirits went out of them. 13 Then certain of the vagabond Jews, exorcists, took upon them to call over them which had evil spirits the name of the LORD Jesus, saying, We adjure you by Jesus whom Paul preacheth. 14 And there were seven sons of one Sceva, a Jew, and chief of the priests, which did so. 15 And the evil spirit answered and said, Jesus I know, and Paul I know; but who are ye? 16 And the man in whom the evil spirit was leaped on them, and overcame them, and prevailed against them, so that they fled out of that house naked and wounded.

Familiar And Unclean Spirits Verses See: Appendix Q

Ghosts

♦ **Genesis 25:8** Then Abraham gave up the ghost, and died in a good old age, an old man, and full of years; and was gathered to his people.

♦ **Genesis 25:17** And these are the years of the life of Ishmael, an hundred and thirty and seven years: and he gave up the ghost and died; and was gathered unto his people.

♦ **Genesis 35:29** And Isaac gave up the ghost, and died, and was gathered unto his people, being old and full of days: and his sons Esau and Jacob buried him.

♦ **Genesis 49:33** And when Jacob had made an end of commanding his sons, he gathered up his feet into the bed, and yielded up the ghost, and was gathered unto his people.

♦ **Job 3:11** Why died I not from the womb? why did I not give up the ghost when I came out of the belly?

♦ **Job 14:10** But man dieth, and wasteth away: yea, man giveth up the ghost, and where is he?

♦ **Lamentations 1:19** I called for my lovers, but they deceived me: my priests and mine elders gave up the ghost in the city, while they sought their meat to relieve their souls.

♦ **Matthew 27:50** Jesus, when he had cried again with a loud voice, yielded up the ghost.

♦ **Mark 15:37** And Jesus cried with a loud voice, and gave up the ghost.

♦ **Mark 15:39** And when the centurion, which stood over against him, saw that he so cried out, and gave up the ghost, he said, Truly this man was the Son of God.

♦ **Luke 23:46** And when Jesus had cried with a loud voice, he said, Father, into thy hands I commend my spirit: and having said thus, he gave up the ghost.

♦ **John 19:30** When Jesus therefore had received the vinegar, he said, It is finished: and he bowed his head, and gave up the ghost.

♦ **Acts 5:5** And Ananias hearing these words fell down, and gave up the ghost: and great fear came on all them that heard these things.

♦ **Acts 5:10** Then fell she down straightway at his feet, and yielded up the ghost: and the young men came in, and found her dead, and, carrying her forth, buried her by her husband.

♦ **Acts 12:23** And immediately the angel of the Lord smote him, because he gave not God the glory: and he was eaten of worms, and gave up the ghost.

The Doctrines of Men

Cryptozoology

The Biblical Bestiary

The Church View:
  The strange creatures described in the Bible are either visions or just overstated or excited descriptions of normal animals

The Bible View:
  The strange creatures described in the Bible are clearly described in a natural context and appear with the accurate descriptions of other well-known creatures.

Cryptozoology: "the study of the lore concerning legendary animals especially in order to evaluate the possibility of their existence." *Merriam-Webster*

  The word "cryptozoology" did not appear in the English language until 1969, but it has sparked the imagination and spawned debate throughout modern history. With the uncompromising attitude of modern science and the enterprise of the sensationalist tabloid industry, it has long been the brunt of official ridicule.

  A classic example of scientific refusal to accept anything out of the ordinary is the infamous "Platypus Fraud". When first seen in 1797 near Sydney Australia, it generated local excitement, but scientific denial. The duck-billed, web-footed, beaver-tailed, egg-laying, warm-blooded amphibian was declared a fraud and written off as a clever taxidermist trick by science. Though somewhat more sophisticated now, science is no less skeptical, denying a wealth of cultural evidence in ancient writings that the creatures of ancient lore may have been more than myth.

  One of the more prominent ancient writings clearly presenting evidence of anomalous creatures is also the world's longest running bestseller, the Bible. In the pages of the Bible are found dragons, unicorns, cockatrices, and leviathans

Dragons

♦ **Deuteronomy 32:23** Their wine is the poison of dragons, and the cruel venom of asps.
♦ **Nehemiah 2:13** And I went out by night by the gate of the valley, even before the dragon well, and to the dung port, and viewed the walls of Jerusalem, which were broken down, and the gates thereof were consumed with fire.
♦ **Job 30:29** I am a brother to dragons, and a companion to owls.
♦ **Psalms 44:19** Though thou hast sore broken us in the place of dragons, and covered us with the shadow of death.

211

♦ **Psalms 74:13** Thou didst divide the sea by thy strength: thou brakest the heads of the dragons in the waters.

♦ **Psalms 91:3** Thou shalt tread upon the lion and adder: the young lion and the dragon shalt thou trample under feet.

♦ **Psalms 148:7** Praise the LORD from the earth, ye dragons, and all deeps:

♦ **Isaiah 13:22** And the wild beasts of the islands shall cry in their desolate houses, and dragons in their pleasant palaces: and her time is near to come, and her days shall not be prolonged.

♦ **Isaiah 27:1** IIn that day the LORD with his sore and great and strong sword shall punish leviathan the piercing serpent, even leviathan that crooked serpent; and he shall slay the dragon that is in the sea.

♦ **Isaiah 34:13** And thorns shall come up in her palaces, nettles and brambles in the

♦ **Isaiah 35:7** And the parched ground shall become a pool, and the thirsty land springs of water: in the habitation of dragons, where each lay, shall be grass with reeds and rushes.

♦ **Isaiah 43:20** The beast of the field shall honour me, the dragons and the owls: because I give waters in the wilderness, and rivers in the desert, to give drink to my people, my chosen.

♦ **Jeremiah 9:11** And I will make Jerusalem heaps, and a den of dragons; and I will make the cities of Judah desolate, without an inhabitant.

♦ **Jeremiah 10:22** Behold, the noise of the bruit is come, and a great commotion out of the north country, to make the cities of Judah desolate, and a den of dragons.

♦ **Jeremiah 14:6** And the wild asses did stand in the high places, they snuffed up the wind like dragons; their eyes did fail, because there was no grass.

♦ **Jeremiah 49:33** And Hazor shall be a dwelling for dragons, and a desolation for ever: there shall no man abide there, nor any son of man dwell in it.

♦ **Jeremiah 51:34** Nebuchadrezzar the king of Babylon hath devoured me, he hath crushed me, he hath made me an empty vessel, he hath swallowed me up like a dragon, he hath filled his belly with my delicates, he hath cast me out.

♦ **Jeremiah 51:37** And Babylon shall become heaps, a dwellingplace for dragons, an astonishment, and an hissing, without an inhabitant.

♦ **Ezekiel 23:3** Speak, and say, Thus saith the Lord GOD; Behold, I am against thee, Pharaoh king of Egypt, the great dragon that lieth in the midst of his rivers, which hath said, My river is mine own, and I have made it for myself.

♦ **Micah 1:8** Therefore I will wail and howl, I will go stripped and naked: I will make a wailing like the dragons, and mourning as the owls.

♦ **Malachi 1:3** And I hated Esau, and laid his mountains and his heritage waste for the dragons of the wilderness.

Unicorns

♦ **Numbers 23:22** God brought them out of Egypt; he hath as it were the strength of an unicorn.

♦ **Numbers 24:8** God brought him forth out of Egypt; he hath as it were the strength of an unicorn: he shall eat up the nations his enemies, and shall break their bones, and pierce them through with his arrows

♦ **Deuteronomy 33:17** His glory is like the firstling of his bullock, and his horns are like the horns of unicorns: with them he shall push the people together to the ends of the earth: and they are the ten thousands of Ephraim, and they are the thousands of Manasseh.

♦ **Job 39:10** will he harrow the valleys after thee? **11** Wilt thou trust him, because his strength is great? or wilt thou leave thy labour to him? **12** Wilt thou believe him, that he will bring home thy seed, and gather it into thy barn?

♦ **Psalms 22:21** Save me from the lion's mouth: for thou hast heard me from the horns of the unicorns.

♦ **Psalms 29:6** He maketh them also to skip like a calf; Lebanon and Sirion like a young unicorn.

♦ **Psalms 92:10** But my horn shalt thou exalt like the horn of an unicorn: I shall be anointed with fresh oil.

♦ **Isaiah 34:7** And the unicorns shall come down with them, and the bullocks with the bulls; and their land shall be soaked with blood, and their dust made fat with fatness.

Leviathan:
A Fire-Breathing, Smoke-Snorting, Stone-Hearted Sea Monster

♦ **Job 41:1** Canst thou draw out leviathan with an hook? or his tongue with a cord which thou lettest down? 2 Canst thou put an hook into his nose? or bore his jaw through with a thorn? 3 Will he make many supplications unto thee? will he speak soft words unto thee? 4 Will he make a covenant with thee? wilt thou take him for a servant for ever? 5 Wilt thou play with him as with a bird? or wilt thou bind him for thy maidens? 6 Shall the companions make a banquet of him? shall they part him among the merchants? 7 Canst thou fill his skin with barbed irons? or his head with fish spears? 8 Lay thine hand upon him, remember the battle, do no more. 9 Behold, the hope of him is in vain: shall not one be cast down even at the sight of him? 10 None is so fierce that dare stir him up: who then is able to stand before me? 11 Who hath prevented me, that I should repay him? whatsoever is under the whole heaven is mine. 12 I will not conceal his parts, nor his power, nor his comely proportion. 13 Who can discover the face of his garment? or who can come to him with his double bridle? 14 Who can open the doors of his face? his teeth are terrible round about. 15 His scales are his pride, shut up together as with a close seal. 16 One is so near to another, that no air can come between them. 17 They are joined one to another, they stick together, that they cannot be sundered. 18 By his neesings a light doth shine, and his eyes are like the eyelids of the morning. 19 Out of his mouth go burning lamps, and sparks of fire leap out. 20 Out of his nostrils goeth smoke, as out of a seething pot or caldron. 21 His breath kindleth coals, and a flame goeth out of his mouth. 22 In his neck remaineth strength, and sorrow is turned into joy before him. 23 The flakes of his flesh are joined together: they are firm in themselves; they cannot be moved. 24 His heart is as firm as a stone; yea, as hard as a piece of the nether millstone. 25 When he raiseth up himself, the mighty are afraid: by reason of breakings they purify themselves. 26 The sword of him that layeth at him cannot hold: the spear, the dart, nor the habergeon. 27 He esteemeth iron as straw, and brass as rotten wood. 28 The arrow cannot make him flee: slingstones are turned with him into stubble. 29 Darts are counted as stubble: he laugheth at the shaking of a spear. 30 Sharp stones are under him: he spreadeth sharp pointed things upon the mire. 31 He maketh the deep to boil like a pot: he maketh the sea like a pot of ointment. 32 He maketh a path to shine after him; one would think the deep to be hoary. 33 Upon earth there is not his like, who is made without fear. 34 He beholdeth all high things: he is a king over all the children of pride.

♦ **Psalms 74:14**Thou brakest the heads of leviathan in pieces, and gavest him to be meat to the people inhabiting the wilderness.

♦ **Psalms 104:26** There go the ships: there is that leviathan, whom thou hast made to play therein.

♦ **Isaiah 27:1** In that day the LORD with his sore and great and strong sword shall punish leviathan the piercing serpent, even leviathan that crooked serpent; and he shall slay the dragon that is in the sea.

The Behemoth

♦ **Job 40:15** Behold now behemoth, which I made with thee; he eateth grass as an ox. 16 Lo now, his strength is in his loins, and his force is in the navel of his belly. 17 He moveth his tail like a cedar: the sinews of his stones are wrapped together. 18 His bones are as strong pieces of brass; his bones are like bars of iron. 19 He is the chief of the ways of God: he that made him can make his sword to approach unto him. 20 Surely the mountains bring him forth food, where all the beasts of the field play. 21 He lieth under the shady trees, in the covert of the reed, and fens. 22 The shady trees cover him with their shadow; the willows of the brook compass him about. 23 Behold, he drinketh up a river, and hasteth not: he trusteth that he can draw up Jordan into his mouth. 24 He taketh it with his eyes: his nose pierceth through snares.

Some say this is a hippo or an elephant, neither of which have tails as big as trees

214

Flying, Fiery Serpents

♦ **Numbers 21:6** And the LORD sent fiery serpents among the people, and they bit the people; and much people of Israel died. 7 Therefore the people came to Moses, and said, We have sinned, for we have spoken against the LORD, and against thee; pray unto the LORD, that he take away the serpents from us. And Moses prayed for the people. 8 And the LORD said unto Moses, Make thee a fiery serpent, and set it upon a pole: and it shall come to pass, that every one that is bitten, when he looketh upon it, shall live.

♦ **Deuteronomy 8:15** Who led thee through that great and terrible wilderness, wherein were fiery serpents, and scorpions, and drought, where there was no water; who brought thee forth water out of the rock of flint;

♦ **Isaiah 14:29** Rejoice not thou, whole Palestina, because the rod of him that smote thee is broken: for out of the serpent's root shall come forth a cockatrice, and his fruit shall be a fiery flying serpent.

♦ **Isaiah 30:6** The burden of the beasts of the south: into the land of trouble and anguish, from whence come the young and old lion, the viper and fiery flying serpent, they will carry their riches upon the shoulders of young asses, and their treasures upon the bunches of camels, to a people that shall not profit them.

The Cockatrice

♦ **Isaiah 11:8** And the sucking child shall play on the hole of the asp, and the weaned child shall put his hand on the cockatrice' den.

♦ **Isaiah 14:29** Rejoice not thou, whole Palestina, because the rod of him that smote thee is broken: for out of the serpent's root shall come forth a cockatrice, and his fruit shall be a fiery flying serpent.

♦ **Isaiah 59:5** They hatch cockatrice' eggs, and weave the spider's web: he that eateth of their eggs dieth, and that which is crushed breaketh out into a viper.

♦ **Jeremiah8:17** For, behold, I will send serpents, cockatrices, among you, which will not be charmed, and they shall bite you, saith the LORD.

The Doctrines of Men

In Conclusion

The concepts presented in this work are a serious challenge to the status quo of the doctrines and practices that are accepted by all mainstream Bible-based religions. This work was not begun to compile an in-depth, scripturally evidenced, and all-encompassing case against those religions, but that is the glaring result. There are a few well-circulated contradictions of church conduct such as the pagan origins of holidays revered by the church, and the sleazy side of certain "shepherds of the flock" that discredit church integrity. The exclusive inward view, and intrusive public actions of the pulpit, also cast a shadow of doubt on the power of those who presume to be leaders of the church. But, never has such a salient and scripturally verified case against a broad range of church practices been gathered.

There are a dozen major theological subjects, and scores of concepts within those subjects, in this work. Each of those concepts brings into question the teachings and practices of the church in those areas. Much more could be added, but the number of contradictions, and the weight of scriptural evidence proving their erroneous nature, is sufficient to question the very foundations of church authority.

This work poses a broad range of questions which challenge the origins of the majority of church doctrines and practices. The scriptural edict to "prove all things", (I Thessalonians 5:21), demands answers to those questions posed. The church uses the doctrines it teaches to form the thoughts and actions of its followers. It demands loyalty, and receives financial support, based on those teachings, which also affect the way those learning them deal with the world around them.

Considering one-third of humanity is under the influence of Bible-based churches, the foundation of that influence must be open to scrutiny. If that foundation is based on untruths, contradictions, and manmade doctrine, rather than solid scriptural footing, the authority of those churches is false.

It is not our place to condemn, and there is no realistic consideration that neither this work, nor any other power, will change even a single teaching of the church. There will be those who condemn, and those that will applaud this work, but, one mind enlightened, one life liberated, or even one spark of hope generated justifies its existence. There is no organization associated with this work and there is no movement or goal driving it, other than a mission to present the truth as scripture reveals it.

God

Scripture reveals a very real and immortal race called the Elohiym with a tangible physical presence and absolute power extending from terra forming entire planets, and the creation of an intense biosphere teeming with complicated life forms, to the control of a universe that has no boundaries. The second highest ranking being of this family of supreme beings, the first son of the source of all life, was the Lord God, called in the Hebrew, Yhovah the Elohiym, and the guiding force behind the creation. This same being was the God directly dealing with mankind, was known as the God of the nation of Israel, and entered into the human race to save that race from destruction and to insure a higher destiny for humanity. It has been clearly documented that mankind was made to look like, and become, the Elohiym.

Jesus

The Lord God, the creator of the human race, entered physically into that race through a miraculous birth and became the man called Jesus of Nazareth. He was a well-respected member of his community, owned homes, had brothers and sisters, and socialized with the leaders of his society. His ministry, and his mission, was completely focused on the love between those humans he encountered, taught, and healed. He brought a positive declaration and solid promise that he would save humanity from future destruction and adopt mankind into the immortal race of the Elohiym. He conquered death as a sacrifice for mankind, which fulfilled the ultimate destiny of mankind.

The Gospel

The good news Jesus brought to this world was the announcement and fulfillment of a guaranteed joint-inheritance with him into the Family of God. He promised that humans will be spiritually changed and born into children, actual sons and daughters, of the Father who sent Jesus. This inheritance would convert those mortals into brothers and sisters by spiritual adoption with the ultimate power of the Elohiym they will become.

As heirs with Jesus, humans will receive the unimaginable gifts of immortality, unconditional love, wisdom and truth, unlimited power, and total freedom. This adoption will come with a crown of royalty and rulership with Jesus. The true meaning of life is this gospel and the salvation from death, which Jesus, the Christ, conquered.

Mankind

The most complex creature on this planet has not reached that advanced state by luck or some ethereal selection process of "Mother Nature", but by the design of the powerful beings that created it. Human beings were created by the Lord God, in the image of the Elohiym, to become joint-heirs with the Lord Jesus into the royal eternal Family of the Elohiym. Humans possess an incredible underlying power restricted only by the knowledge of, and belief in, that power, even in a seemingly limited physical state. The Gospel of Jesus testifies strongly that this power is inherent in all humans by the gift of guaranteed ascension to a godly state. Evidence worldwide bears witness to many aspects of this power being exhibited by individuals throughout our history. Scripture testifies that Jesus, and the members of the church he founded, had supernatural powers. The Bible reveals the key to complete happiness and fulfillment in life, and the prime principle in the conduct in all human affairs is love. Unconditional love toward all people without prejudice, complete equality in social and financial standing in all human affairs, and a focus on unlimited service to all men and women is what Jesus taught.

The Great Deception

All scripture leads chronologically towards a time when worldwide financial control, mass social deception, bizarre planetary upheaval, and horrific human disaster will dominate the affairs of mankind. The Bible identifies both Satan and global corporations as the social deceivers. Global financial control has been the goal of big business for centuries, and the search for commercial wealth has resulted in the devastation of several entire cultures. No doubt, the planet has suffered greatly under the weight of human progress sponsored by big business, as the frequency and severity of disasters is rapidly increasing, with many concluding that it is on the brink of complete upheaval now.

The complete dedication by the business world to profit as the only guiding principle in corporate conduct is an anathema to principles taught by Jesus. Avarice, materialism, covetousness, consumptive obsession, and unfettered increase in wealth are the doctrines of the religion of a capitalist society, and contrary to scriptural doctrines, not the least of which is this:
"For the love of money is the root of all evil..." (I Timothy 6:10).

There is nothing a corporation cannot do, and there is no freedom it should not have. This is becoming the mindset of politicians worldwide, and causing great consternation for any who dare question unlimited corporate freedom and criminal act., Through manipulation of rights guaranteed to humans, corporations now have equivalent freedom, including freedom of speech. Because of the corporate structure, the stockholders are free from responsibility, for corporate acts cannot be effectively controlled. That same corporate structure insures, by law, that the profit of the stockholders is the prime concern of the officers controlling the corporation. A powerful entity with freedom exceeding a human; as it is a creation of lesser parts with no responsibility, and those lesser parts though human, cannot be punished under the corporate umbrella. This has given corporations unprecedented control over the regulations that govern them, the governments that enforce those regulations, and the lawmakers making those regulations law.

Satan has been moving the world towards total destruction for millennia, but not as a demon possessing souls of hapless humans, or enticing members from church congregations. He is deceptively, but directly involved in the day to day affairs of mankind using financial, military, political, social, scientific, academic, and false religious influence, not spiritual mind control. He was not called Lucifer, made very few appearances scripturally, is a miserable failure, and can be controlled, simply by understanding how he is influencing mankind and resisting that influence.

The Church

From scripture nothing can be found that justifies either the physical or the organizational structures of the church and doctrinal rationalization for its utilization and observances. The buildings and practices for which those buildings are used have no basis in scripture. But, the purpose and practices of the church Jesus established are clearly defined. The only definition of religion is to serve those in need and keep your self unblemished from worldly things. The last words of Jesus to Peter, the apostle he said he would build his church upon, were to feed the people, and this edict was repeated three times for emphasis. Healing and feeding people in need were regular practices for Jesus and the Apostles. The entire ministry of Jesus is centered on his love for mankind and their love for each other. Love toward, and service to, all mankind was the mission of Jesus and the mission of the church he founded. This is not the priority of the church. It may be the stated purpose ,but not the prime focus or practice.

Scripture reveals that the very first act of the church was to place all the worldly goods of individuals into common possession with all other members of the church. This practice, though clearly described and verified in scripture is perceived as an anathema by the modern church and rejected as godless communism. All efforts to opt out of the capitalist model are considered and the church supports any, and all, methods to stamp it out. The strongest motivation for military support by the church is its vehement rejection of anything that even seems to resemble socialism.

Communal living is associated with cultism and drugs by the church. Bad portrayals of the youth movements of the 60's, which spawned the modern communal living phenomenon, as being dominated by illicit sex, mind-wrecking drug trips, and ruined lives, are held up as proof of its evil effects. The communal actions of the first church are either ignored completely, or explained as a sacrifice the early church had to make. The fact that the scripture says that none had need in the church or that it was clearly inspired by the Spirit of God is never factored into any presentation of this glaring doctrinal church contradiction.

In Conclusion

The influence of Constantine over Christianity is well documented, and the radical change of doctrines and practices he made, and his successors refined and enforced, has resulted in a church with a scripturally barren foundation. These church "fathers" eliminated, replaced, altered, or created virtually every practice, every concept, every doctrine, and virtually every recognizable element of the church Jesus founded. The doctrines the church teaches, the concepts they believe, and customs and rituals they practice, all have origins in the decisions made by men, contrary to the scripture they claim as their authority.

The King James Bible is taken word for word, as completely accurate and divinely inspired without any effort to verify its accuracy. Never is the questionable character or the power oriented motivation of the king who ordered and controlled this translation called into question. The most respected companion work to the Bible, the Strong's Exhaustive Concordance, was a labor that took seven times longer to produce than the work it translates and indexes, and involved twice the scholars. It reveals the true meanings of the rare King's English, exposes the additions of the court appointed translators, and unravels the mistranslations. Yet, it is little known to the laity, never used on the pulpit, and seldom used in pastoral research.

The power exhibited by the members of the first church is not cryptically hidden in scripture, it is clearly described. The absence of these powers in the modern church is never considered as of having any relevance. Any individual possessing any of the powers within the stoic church environment would be suspected of a different kind of possession. Certain religions claim the speaking of tongues, which are no more than sounds or words no one understands, not known languages spoken in the Bible. Rarely is there found legitimate instances of healing in a church environment, but not as common occurrence in the church as a whole.

Though seemingly innocent, some of the concepts thought to exist in the Bible are actually contradictions of scripture. A classic example is that God helps those who help themselves. Logic dictates that life would be pretty dull and difficult for anybody who waited for everything to be done for them. But, this simple phrase implies that mankind is not dependent on God and actually implies that such reliance is wrong. These common traditional beliefs should certainly be dealt with rather than ignored.

The love of money, which is specifically defined as the source of all evil, is defined as avarice, an obsession with, and dedication to, wealth. This obsession with wealth is not condemned, or even shunned by the church; it is embraced, encouraged, and proudly displayed in the buildings, employee and leadership compensation, financial holdings, and the advertising budgets of the churches. The standard justification for the looting and slaughter throughout history is either religious belief or national values based on religious beliefs.

221

There is strong indication that the church will accept, rather than reject, the deception.

It is no wonder that when one more element is factored into the equation, the church is solidly locked into the cycle of the deception. The church is only as wealthy as its membership, and one of its manmade doctrines is that God will materially bless those who live the way God wants them to live. They fail to point out several problems with this doctrine.

True, God will reward those who serve him, but the reward comes not in this life, nor should one seek fortune in this life, on this Earth. Jesus clearly said to reject wealth, and that it was an impediment to salvation. They also do mention that they are sitting in pews, located in a church building, listening to a pastor who is speaking to a meeting on the first day of the week; none of which are described, in scripture, as part of church function. The church's teachings on, and encouragement of, personal wealth among its members is part of the deception.

The Doctrines of the Church

There is not a great deal one can say about the obvious disregard the church has for scripture, and the doctrines and practices actually found in the Bible. Although there is a great deal of ritual and a host of laws, observances, and practices, most were Hebrew law, not required of non-Hebrew cultures. This is specifically shown in the interaction of the church with others not of the tribes of the nation of Israel.

Although these Hebrew laws and practices are not actually properly followed by the modern church, the laity, and no doubt the leadership as well, believe they are following the Bible. An open view will show that all these laws and practices are of manmade origins and that, in fact, the church is "teaching for doctrines the commandments of men."

We have revealed a concept that without the overwhelming scriptural truth would seem quite paradoxical. Could the church possibly be so blind that these obvious truths are completely hidden from them, while in full view? The rejection of Jesus by the Sanhedrin, the governing religious body in his reality, was an example of such blindness, even though Jesus was constantly working incredible miracles and even raising the dead in their presence. They were called "blind leaders of the blind" and "blind guides" in scripture. And, there is no doubt the religious leaders of this day will deny the glaring contradictions they are faced with by the evidence presented against them in scripture. They are not blind because they cannot see, they are blind because they cannot believe what they see is real. What they do believe is a set of beliefs and edicts created by men, and completely conditioned into their minds for seventeen centuries. They teach, practice, believe, and defend the doctrines of men.

In Conclusion

- Neither the buildings the church constructs, the steeples that often crown those structures, nor the crosses, symbols, or "holy" images that adorn those vaulted edifices have any foundation or semblance in scripture. These are all the creations of men.
- The tithe is for celebration and the care of the needy and the priests of the tribe of Levi, not land, buildings, building funds, and church employees. This tithe is being usurped by men to support a church structure created by men.
- The tax exempt status of the church is contrary to the edicts of Jesus, and shifts any practical recognition of his leadership and power over the church to the state. It is men seeking to maximize income to be used for purposes determined by other men
- The weekly worship services practiced by the church is the edict of a man, and never commanded in scripture.
The weekly day of rest, not practiced by the church was outlawed by a man, and is commanded in scripture.
- The "holy" days practiced in Bible-based churches are pagan in origin, have no foundation semblance in scripture. A man outlawed the observance of the true High Sabbaths of scripture.
- Heaven, the promise of the church, is the sky, not the reward for following the edicts of the church. The heaven of the church is a concept of men, not scripture.
- Hell, the threat of the church, is the grave, not the punishment for not following the edicts of the church. The hell of the church is a concept of men, not scripture.
- The Flood, the church's proof of the evil nature of mankind, was not caused by the sins of mankind, but an angelic conspiracy, and is ignored as the source of demons. The complete descriptions of this event were purged from the church by men.
- Prayer is commanded to be done in private, not openly, never ordered to accompany almost every religious activity, never evidenced in scripture, and open prayer is condemned as hypocritical and insincere. Open prayer is the custom of men, practice found in the Bible.

These doctrinal contradictions are at the very core of the doctrine and practice, as well as the foundation of authority and power, of the church. Combined with the other areas of church doctrine, this leaves a final question. Is there anything, relating to modern Bible-based religious practice, or belief, which actually does have its origin in scripture? Again, there is no movement behind this work with the goal of changing anything, nor is that possible. The deception is complete and few will escape its shadow or its control. Nothing short of direct intervention by the forces of God will wrest that control from those who claim themselves to be shepherds of the flock.

The Website

Though a broad spectrum of concepts have been presented in this work, there is much more to be revealed as one delves deeper into its roots and lesser known practices. We have created a website for this book and will expand the range of information as our research uncovers it. There are links to many resources for further research, and tools for general biblical research. You will also find an email address; your questions or comments are welcome.

The Doctrines of Men - A Terrible Truth

www.doctrinesofmen.com

The Appendices

Appendix A - Children of God

Matthew 5:9 Blessed are the peacemakers: for they shall be called the children of God.
Matthew 5:45 That ye may be the children of your Father which is in heaven: for he maketh his sun to rise on the evil and on the good, and sendeth rain on the just and on the unjust.
Matthew 18:3 And said, Verily I say unto you, Except ye be converted, and become as little children, ye shall not enter into the kingdom of heaven.
Luke 6:35 But love ye your enemies, and do good, and lend, hoping for nothing again; and your reward shall be great, and ye shall be the children of the Highest: for he is kind unto the unthankful and to the evil.
Luke 20:36 Neither can they die any more: for they are equal unto the angels; and are the children of God, being the children of the resurrection.
John 11:52 And not for that nation only, but that also he should gather together in one the children of God that were scattered abroad.
Acts 3:25 Ye are the children of the prophets, and of the covenant which God made with our fathers, saying unto Abraham, And in thy seed shall all the kindreds of the earth be blessed.
Romans 8:21 Because the creature itself also shall be delivered from the bondage of corruption into the glorious liberty of the children of God.
Romans 8:16 The Spirit itself beareth witness with our spirit, that we are the children of God: 17 And if children, then heirs; heirs of God, and joint-heirs with Christ; if so be that we suffer with him, that we may be also glorified together.
Romans 8:21 Because the creature itself also shall be delivered from the bondage of

corruption into the glorious liberty of the children of God.

Romans 9:8 That is, They which are the children of the flesh, these are not the children of God: but the children of the promise are counted for the seed.

Romans 9:26 And it shall come to pass, that in the place where it was said unto them, Ye are not my people; there shall they be called the children of the living God.

Galatians 3:26 For ye are all the children of God by faith in Christ Jesus.

Galatians 4:28 Now we, brethren, as Isaac was, are the children of promise.

Hebrews 2:13 And again, I will put my trust in him. And again, Behold I and the children which God hath given me. 14 Forasmuch then as the children are partakers of flesh and blood, he also himself likewise took part of the same; that through death he might destroy him that had the power of death, that is, the devil;

I John 3:10 In this the children of God are manifest, and the children of the devil: whosoever doeth not righteousness is not of God, neither he that loveth not his brother.

I John 5:2 By this we know that we love the children of God, when we love God, and keep his commandments.

* Children of light

John 12:36 While ye have light, believe in the light, that ye may be the children of light. These things spake Jesus, and departed, and did hide himself from them.

Ephesians 5:8 For ye were sometimes darkness, but now are ye light in the Lord: walk as children of light:

I Thessalonians 5:5 Ye are all the children of light, and the children of the day: we are not of the night, nor of darkness.

Appendix B - Sons and Daughters of God

John 1: 12. But as many as received him, to them gave he power to become the sons of God, even to them that believe on his name:

Revelation 21:7 He that overcometh shall inherit all things; and I will be his God, and he shall be my son.

Acts 17: 28. For in him we live, and move, and have our being; as certain also of your own poets have said, For we are also his offspring. 29. Forasmuch then as we are the offspring of God, we ought not to think that the Godhead is like unto gold, or silver, or stone, graven by art and man's device.

Romans 8: 14. For as many as are led by the Spirit of God, they are the sons of God. 15. For ye have not received the spirit of bondage again to fear; but ye have received the Spirit of adoption, whereby we cry, Abba, Father. 16. The Spirit itself beareth witness with our spirit, that we are the children of God: 17. And if children, then heirs; heirs of God, and joint-heirs with Christ; if so be that we suffer with him, that we may be also glorified together. 18. For I reckon that the sufferings of this present time are not worthy to be compared with the glory which shall be revealed in us. 19. For the earnest expectation of the creature waiteth for the manifestation of the sons of God.

Hebrews 12:7 If ye endure chastening, God dealeth with you as with sons; for what son is he whom the father chasteneth not?

I John 3:1 Behold, what manner of love the Father hath bestowed upon us, that we should be called the sons of God: therefore the world knoweth us not, because it knew him not. 2 Beloved, now are we the sons of God, and it doth not yet appear what we shall be: but we know that, when he shall appear, we shall be like him; for we shall see him as he is.

Philippians 2:15 That ye may be blameless and harmless, the sons of God, without rebuke, in the midst of a crooked and perverse nation, among whom ye shine as lights in the world;

Galatians 4:5 To redeem them that were under the law, that we might receive the adoption of sons. 6 And because ye are sons, God hath sent forth the Spirit of his Son into your hearts, crying, Abba, Father.7 Wherefore thou art no more a servant, but a son; and if a son, then an heir of God through Christ.

* Sons and daughters

II Corinthians 6:18 And will be a Father unto you, and ye shall be my sons and daughters, saith the Lord Almighty.

* Sons unto glory

Hebrews 2:10 For it became him, for whom are all things, and by whom are all things, in bringing many sons unto glory, to make the captain of their salvation perfect through sufferings.

Appendix C - Brothers, Sisters, Brethren, Brotherly, and Brotherhood

* Brother

Acts 9:17 And Ananias went his way, and entered into the house; and putting his hands on him said, Brother Saul, the Lord, even Jesus, that appeared unto thee in the way as thou camest, hath sent me, that thou mightest receive thy sight, and be filled with the Holy Ghost.

Acts 21:20 And when they heard it, they glorified the Lord, and said unto him, Thou seest, brother, how many thousands of Jews there are which believe; and they are all zealous of the law:

Acts 22:13 Came unto me, and stood, and said unto me, Brother Saul, receive thy sight. And the same hour I looked up upon him.

Romans 14:10 But why dost thou judge thy brother? or why dost thou set at nought thy brother? for we shall all stand before the judgment seat of Christ.

Romans 14:13 Let us not therefore judge one another any more: but judge this rather, that no man put a stumblingblock or an occasion to fall in his brother's way.

Romans 16:23 Gaius mine host, and of the whole church, saluteth you. Erastus the chamberlain of the city saluteth you, and Quartus a brother.

I Corinthians 1:1 Paul called to be an apostle of Jesus Christ through the will of God, and Sosthenes our brother,

I Corinthians 6:5 I speak to your shame. Is it so, that there is not a wise man among you? no, not one that shall be able to judge between his brethren? 6 But brother goeth to law with brother, and that before the unbelievers.

I Corinthians 7:12 But to the rest speak I, not the Lord: If any brother hath a wife that believeth not, and she be pleased to dwell with him, let him not put her away.

I Corinthians 8:11 And through thy knowledge shall the weak brother perish, for whom Christ died?

I Corinthians 16:12 As touching our brother Apollos, I greatly desired him to come unto you with the brethren: but his will was not at all to come at this time; but he will come when he shall have convenient time.

II Corinthians 1:1 Paul, an apostle of Jesus Christ by the will of God, and Timothy our brother, unto the church of God which is at Corinth, with all the saints which are in all Achaia:

II Corinthians 8:18 And we have sent with him the brother, whose praise is in the gospel throughout all the churches;

II Corinthians 8:22 And we have sent with them our brother, whom we have oftentimes proved diligent in many things, but now much more diligent, upon the great confidence which I have in you.

II Corinthians 12:18 I desired Titus, and with him I sent a brother. Did Titus make a gain of you? walked we not in the same spirit? walked we not in the same steps?

Ephesians 6:21 But that ye also may know my affairs, and how I do, Tychicus, a beloved brother and faithful minister in the Lord, shall make known to you all things:

Colossians 1:1 Paul, an apostle of Jesus Christ by the will of God, and Timotheus our brother,

Colossians 4:7 All my state shall Tychicus declare unto you, who is a beloved brother, and a faithful minister and fellowservant in the Lord:

Colossians 4:9 With Onesimus, a faithful and beloved brother, who is one of you. They shall make known unto you all things which are done here.

I Thessalonians 3:2 And sent Timotheus, our brother, and minister of God, and our fellowlabourer in the gospel of Christ, to establish you, and to comfort you concerning your faith:

I Thessalonians 4:6 That no man go beyond and defraud his brother in any matter: because that the Lord is the avenger of all such, as we also have forewarned you and testified.

I Thessalonians 4:9 But as touching brotherly love ye need not that I write unto you: for ye yourselves are taught of God to love one another.

Hebrews 8:11 And they shall not teach every man his neighbour, and every man his brother, saying, Know the Lord: for all shall know me, from the least to the greatest.

Hebrews 13:23 Know ye that our brother Timothy is set at liberty; with whom, if he come shortly, I will see you.

James 1:9 Let the brother of low degree rejoice in that he is exalted:

I Peter 5:12 By Silvanus, a faithful brother unto you, as I suppose, I have written briefly, exhorting, and testifying that this is the true grace of God wherein ye stand.

I John 3:10 In this the children of God are manifest, and the children of the devil: whosoever doeth not righteousness is not of God, neither he that loveth not his brother.

Revelation 1:9 I John, who also am your brother, and companion in tribulation, and in the kingdom and patience of Jesus Christ, was in the isle that is called Patmos, for the word of God, and for the testimony of Jesus Christ.

* Sisters

Romans 16:1 I commend unto you Phebe our sister, which is a servant of the church which is at Cenchrea:

II John 1:13 The children of thy elect sister greet thee. Amen.

Brethren

Romans 8:29 For whom he did foreknow, he also did predestinate to be conformed to the image of his Son, that he might be the firstborn among many brethren.

Hebrews 2:11 For both he that sanctifieth and they who are sanctified are all of one: for which cause he is not ashamed to call them brethren, 12 Saying, I will declare thy name unto my brethren, in the midst of the church will I sing praise unto thee.
I Peter 1:22 Seeing ye have purified your souls in obeying the truth through the Spirit unto unfeigned love of the brethren, see that ye love one another with a pure heart fervently:
* Brotherhood
I Peter 2:17 Honour all men. Love the brotherhood. Fear God. Honour the king.
* Brotherly
Romans 12:10 Be kindly affectioned one to another with brotherly love; in honour preferring one another;
I Thessalonians 4:9 But as touching brotherly love ye need not that I write unto you: for ye yourselves are taught of God to love one another.
Hebrews 13:1 Let brotherly love continue.
II Peter 1:7 And to godliness brotherly kindness; and to brotherly kindness charity.

Appendix D - Born, Begotten, Offspring, Firstborn, and Babes
* Born
John 1:12 But as many as received him, to them gave he power to become the sons of God, even to them that believe on his name: 13 Which were born, not of blood, nor of the will of the flesh, nor of the will of man, but of God.
John 3:3 Jesus answered and said unto him, Verily, verily, I say unto thee, Except a man be born again, he cannot see the kingdom of God.
again - anothen, pronounced an'-o-then; from above
John 3:5 Jesus answered, Verily, verily, I say unto thee, Except a man be born of water and of the Spirit, he cannot enter into the kingdom of God.
John 3:6 That which is born of the flesh is flesh; and that which is born of the Spirit is spirit.
John 3:7 Marvel not that I said unto thee, Ye must be born again.
again - anothen, pronounced an'-o-then; from above
John 3:8 The wind bloweth where it listeth, and thou hearest the sound thereof, but canst not tell whence it cometh, and whither it goeth: so is every one that is born of the Spirit.
John 8:41 Ye do the deeds of your father. Then said they to him, We be not born of fornication; we have one Father, even God.
I Peter 1:23 Being born again, not of corruptible seed, but of incorruptible, by the word of God, which liveth and abideth for ever.
I John 2:29 If ye know that he is righteous, ye know that every one that doeth righteousness is born of him.
I John 3:9 Whosoever is born of God doth not commit sin; for his seed remaineth in him: and he cannot sin, because he is born of God.
I John 4:7 Beloved, let us love one another: for love is of God; and every one that loveth is born of God, and knoweth God.
I John 5:1 Whosoever believeth that Jesus is the Christ is born of God: and every one that loveth him that begat loveth him also that is begotten of him.

The Doctrines of Men

I John 5:4 For whatsoever is born of God overcometh the world: and this is the victory that overcometh the world, even our faith.

I John 5:18 We know that whosoever is born of God sinneth not; but he that is begotten of God keepeth himself, and that wicked one toucheth him not.

* Begotten

I. Corinthians 4:15 For though ye have ten thousand instructers in Christ, yet have ye not many fathers: for in Christ Jesus I have begotten you through the gospel.

Hebrews 1:4 Being made so much better than the angels, as he hath by inheritance obtained a more excellent name than they. 5 For unto which of the angels said he at any time, Thou art my Son, this day have I begotten thee? And again, I will be to him a Father, and he shall be to me a Son?

I Peter 1:3 Blessed be the God and Father of our Lord Jesus Christ, which according to his abundant mercy hath begotten us again unto a lively hope by the resurrection of Jesus Christ from the dead,

I John 5:1 Whosoever believeth that Jesus is the Christ is born of God: and every one that loveth him that begat loveth him also that is begotten of him.

I John 5:18 We know that whosoever is born of God sinneth not; but he that is begotten of God keepeth himself, and that wicked one toucheth him not.

* Firstborn

Romans 8:29 For whom he did foreknow, he also did predestinate to be conformed to the image of his Son, that he might be the firstborn among many brethren.

Hebrews 12:23 To the general assembly and church of the firstborn, which are written in heaven, and to God the Judge of all, and to the spirits of just men made perfect,

* Offspring

Acts 17: 28. For in him we live, and move, and have our being; as certain also of your own poets have said, For we are also his offspring. 29. Forasmuch then as we are the offspring of God, we ought not to think that the Godhead is like unto gold, or silver, or stone, graven by art and man's device.

* Babes

I Peter 2:2 As newborn babes, desire the sincere milk of the word, that ye may grow thereby:

Matthew 11:25 At that time Jesus answered and said, I thank thee, O Father, Lord of heaven and earth, because thou hast hid these things from the wise and prudent, and hast revealed them unto babes.

Matthew 21:16 And said unto him, Hearest thou what these say? And Jesus saith unto them, Yea; have ye never read, Out of the mouth of babes and sucklings thou hast perfected praise?

Luke 10:21 In that hour Jesus rejoiced in spirit, and said, I thank thee, O Father, Lord of heaven and earth, that thou hast hid these things from the wise and prudent, and hast revealed them unto babes: even so, Father; for so it seemed good in thy sight.

I Corinthians 3:1 And I, brethren, could not speak unto you as unto spiritual, but as unto carnal, even as unto babes in Christ.

Appendix E - Inheritance, Heirs, Joint-heirs, and Adoption
* Inheritance

Matthew 19:29 And every one that hath forsaken houses, or brethren, or sisters, or father, or mother, or wife, or children, or lands, for my name's sake, shall receive an hundredfold, and shall inherit everlasting life.

Matthew 25:34 Then shall the King say unto them on his right hand, Come, ye blessed of my Father, inherit the kingdom prepared for you from the foundation of the world:

Mark 10:17 And when he was gone forth into the way, there came one running, and kneeled to him, and asked him, Good Master, what shall I do that I may inherit eternal life?

Acts 20:32 And now, brethren, I commend you to God, and to the word of his grace, which is able to build you up, and to give you an inheritance among all them which are sanctified.

Acts 26:18 To open their eyes, and to turn them from darkness to light, and from the power of Satan unto God, that they may receive forgiveness of sins, and inheritance among them which are sanctified by faith that is in me.

Romans 8:17 And if children, then heirs; heirs of God, and joint-heirs with Christ; if so be that we suffer with him, that we may be also glorified together.

Galatians 3:29 And if ye be Christ's, then are ye Abraham's seed, and heirs according to the promise.

Galatians 4:7 Wherefore thou art no more a servant, but a son; and if a son, then an heir of God through Christ.

Ephesians 1:11 In whom also we have obtained an inheritance, being predestinated according to the purpose of him who worketh all things after the counsel of his own will:

Ephesians 1:14 Which is the earnest of our inheritance until the redemption of the purchased possession, unto the praise of his glory.

Ephesians 1:18 The eyes of your understanding being enlightened; that ye may know what is the hope of his calling, and what the riches of the glory of his inheritance in the saints,

Colossians 1:12 Giving thanks unto the Father, which hath made us meet to be partakers of the inheritance of the saints in light:

Colossians 3:24 Knowing that of the Lord ye shall receive the reward of the inheritance: for ye serve the Lord Christ.

Titus 3:7 That being justified by his grace, we should be made heirs according to the hope of eternal life.

Hebrews 1:4 Being made so much better than the angels, as he hath by inheritance obtained a more excellent name than they.

Hebrews 1:14 Are they not all ministering spirits, sent forth to minister for them who shall be heirs of salvation?

Hebrews 6:12 That ye be not slothful, but followers of them who through faith and patience inherit the promises.

Hebrews 6:17 Wherein God, willing more abundantly to shew unto the heirs of promise the immutability of his counsel, confirmed it by an oath:

Hebrews 9:15 And for this cause he is the mediator of the new testament, that by means of death, for the redemption of the transgressions that were under the first

testament, they which are called might receive the promise of eternal inheritance.
James 2:5 Hearken, my beloved brethren, Hath not God chosen the poor of this world rich in faith, and heirs of the kingdom which he hath promised to them that love him?
I Peter 1:3 Blessed be the God and Father of our Lord Jesus Christ, which according to his abundant mercy hath begotten us again unto a lively hope by the resurrection of Jesus Christ from the dead, 4 To an inheritance incorruptible, and undefiled, and that fadeth not away, reserved in heaven for you,
I Peter 3:7 Likewise, ye husbands, dwell with them according to knowledge, giving honour unto the wife, as unto the weaker vessel, and as being heirs together of the grace of life; that your prayers be not hindered.
I Peter 3:9 Not rendering evil for evil, or railing for railing: but contrariwise blessing; knowing that ye are thereunto called, that ye should inherit a blessing.
Revelation 21:7 He that overcometh shall inherit all things; and I will be his God, and he shall be my son.
* Joint-heirs
Romans 8:17 And if children, then heirs; heirs of God, and joint-heirs with Christ; if so be that we suffer with him, that we may be also glorified together.
* Adoption
Romans 8:15 For ye have not received the spirit of bondage again to fear; but ye have received the Spirit of adoption, whereby we cry, Abba, Father.
Romans 8:23 And not only they, but ourselves also, which have the firstfruits of the Spirit, even we ourselves groan within ourselves, waiting for the adoption, to wit, the redemption of our body.
Galatians 4:5 To redeem them that were under the law, that we might receive the adoption of sons. 6 And because ye are sons, God hath sent forth the Spirit of his Son into your hearts, crying, Abba, Father.7 Wherefore thou art no more a servant, but a son; and if a son, then an heir of God through Christ.
Ephesians 1:5 Having predestinated us unto the adoption of children by Jesus Christ to himself, according to the good pleasure of his will,

Appendix F - Elected, Chosen, Called, Call, and Calling
* Elect
Matthew 24:22 And except those days should be shortened, there should no flesh be saved: but for the elect's sake
Matthew 24:24 For there shall arise false Christs, and false prophets, and shall shew great signs and wonders; insomuch that, if it were possible, they shall deceive the very elect.
Matthew 24:31 And he shall send his angels with a great sound of a trumpet, and they shall gather together his elect from the four winds, from one end of heaven to the other.
Mark 13:20 And except that the Lord had shortened those days, no flesh should be saved: but for the elect's sake, whom he hath chosen, he hath shortened the days.
Mark 13:22 For false Christs and false prophets shall rise, and shall shew signs and wonders, to seduce, if it were possible, even the elect.
Mark 13:27 And then shall he send his angels, and shall gather together his elect from the four winds, from the uttermost part of the earth to the uttermost part of heaven.

Romans 8:33 Who shall lay any thing to the charge of God's elect? It is God that justifieth.

Colossians 3: 12 Put on therefore, as the elect of God, holy and beloved, bowels of mercies, kindness, humbleness of mind, meekness, longsuffering;

II Timothy 2:10 Therefore I endure all things for the elect's sakes, that they may also obtain the salvation which is in Christ Jesus with eternal glory.

Titus 1:1 Paul, a servant of God, and an apostle of Jesus Christ, according to the faith of God's elect, and the acknowledging of the truth which is after godliness;

elect - eklektos, pronounced ek-lek-tos'; select

* Chosen

Matthew 20:16 So the last shall be first, and the first last: for many be called, but few chosen (1).

Matthew 22:14 For many are called, but few are chosen (1).

Mark 13:20 And except that the Lord had shortened those days, no flesh should be saved: but for the elect's sake, whom he hath chosen (2), he hath shortened the days.

John 15:19 If ye were of the world, the world would love his own: but because ye are not of the world, but I have chosen (2) you out of the world, therefore the world hateth you.

Ephesians 1:4 According as he hath chosen (2) us in him before the foundation of the world, that we should be holy and without blame before him in love:

II Thessalonians 2:13 But we are bound to give thanks alway to God for you, brethren beloved of the Lord, because God hath from the beginning chosen (3) you to salvation through sanctification of the Spirit and belief of the truth:

James 2:5 Hearken, my beloved brethren, Hath not God chosen the poor of this world rich in faith, and heirs of the kingdom which he hath promised to them that love him?

I Peter 2:4 To whom coming, as unto a living stone, disallowed indeed of men, but chosen (1) of God, and precious,

I Peter 2:9 But ye are a chosen (1) generation, a royal priesthood, an holy nation, a peculiar people; that ye should shew forth the praises of him who hath called you out of darkness into his marvellous light;

peculiar -hagios, pronounced hag'-ee-os; sacred

Revelation 17:14 These shall make war with the Lamb, and the Lamb shall overcome them: for he is Lord of lords, and King of kings: and they that are with him are called, and chosen (1), and faithful.

(1) eklektos, pronounced ek-lek-tos'; select, (2) eklegomai, pronounced ek-leg'-om-ahee; to select, (3) haireomai, pronounced hahee-reh'-om-ahee; to take for oneself

* Called

Matthew 20:16 So the last shall be first, and the first last: for many be called (1), but few chosen.

Matthew 22:14 For many are called (1), but few are chosen.

Romans 8:28 And we know that all things work together for good to them that love God, to them who are the called (1) according to his purpose.

Romans 8:30 Moreover whom he did predestinate, them he also called (2): and whom he called (2), them he also justified: and whom he justified, them he also glorified.

Romans 9:24 Even us, whom he hath called (2), not of the Jews only, but also of the Gentiles?

The Doctrines of Men

I Corinthians 1:2 Unto the church of God which is at Corinth, to them that are sanctified in Christ Jesus, called (1) to be saints, with all that in every place call upon the name of Jesus Christ our Lord, both their's and our's:

I Corinthians 1:9 God is faithful, by whom ye were called (1) unto the fellowship of his Son Jesus Christ our Lord.

I Corinthians 1:26 For ye see your calling, brethren, how that not many wise men after the flesh, not many mighty, not many noble, are called (3) :

I Corinthians 7:17 But as God hath distributed to every man, as the Lord hath called (2) every one, so let him walk. And so ordain I in all churches.

Ephesians 4:4 There is one body, and one Spirit, even as ye are called (2) in one hope of your calling;

I Thessalonians 2:12 That ye would walk worthy of God, who hath called (2) you unto his kingdom and glory.

II Thessalonians 2:14 Whereunto he called (2) you by our gospel, to the obtaining of the glory of our Lord Jesus Christ.

I Timothy 6:12 Fight the good fight of faith, lay hold on eternal life, whereunto thou art also called (2), and hast professed a good profession before many witnesses.

II Timothy 1:9 Who hath saved us, and called (2) us with an holy calling (3), not according to our works, but according to his own purpose and grace, which was given us in Christ Jesus before the world began,

Hebrews 9:15 And for this cause he is the mediator of the new testament, that by means of death, for the redemption of the transgressions that were under the first testament, they which are called (2) might receive the promise of eternal inheritance.

I Peter 1:15 But as he which hath called (2) you is holy, so be ye holy in all manner of conversation;

I Peter 2: 9 But ye are a chosen generation, a royal priesthood, an holy nation, a peculiar people; that ye should shew forth the praises of him who hath called (2) you out of darkness into his marvellous light;

I Peter 2:21 For even hereunto were ye called (2): because Christ also suffered for us, leaving us an example, that ye should follow his steps:

I Peter 3:9 Not rendering evil for evil, or railing for railing: but contrariwise blessing; knowing that ye are thereunto called (2), that ye should inherit a blessing.

I Peter 5:10 But the God of all grace, who hath called (2) us unto his eternal glory by Christ Jesus, after that ye have suffered a while, make you perfect, stablish, strengthen, settle you.

II Peter 1:3 According as his divine power hath given unto us all things that pertain unto life and godliness, through the knowledge of him that hath called (2) us to glory and virtue:

Revelation 17:14 These shall make war with the Lamb, and the Lamb shall overcome them: for he is Lord of lords, and King of kings: and they that are with him are called (1), and chosen, and faithful, (1) kletos, pronounced klay-tos'; invited, (2) kaleo, pronounced, kal-eh'-o, to "call" (properly, aloud, but used in a variety of applications, dir. or otherwise), (3) klesis, pronounced klay'-sis; an invitation

* Call

Matthew 9:13 But go ye and learn what that meaneth, I will have mercy, and not sacrifice: for I am not come to call (1) the righteous, but sinners to repentance.

Mark 2:17 When Jesus heard it, he saith unto them, They that are whole have no need of the physician, but they that are sick: I came not to call (1) the righteous, but sinners to repentance.

Luke 5:32 I came not to call (1) the righteous, but sinners to repentance.

Acts 2:39 For the promise is unto you, and to your children, and to all that are afar off, even as many as the LORD our God shall call (2).

(1) kaleo, pronounced, kal-eh'-o, to "call" (properly, aloud, but used in a variety of applications, dir. or otherwise)

(2) proskaleomai, pronounced pros-kal-eh'-om-ahee; to call toward oneself

* Calling

I Corinthians 1:26 For ye see your calling (1), brethren, how that not many wise men after the flesh, not many mighty, not many noble, are called:

I Corinthians 7:20 Let every man abide in the same calling (1) wherein he was called.

Ephesians 4:4 There is one body, and one Spirit, even as ye are called in one hope of your calling (1);

Philippians 3:14 I press toward the mark for the prize of the high calling (1) of God in Christ Jesus.

II Thessalonians 1:11 Wherefore also we pray always for you, that our God would count you worthy of this calling (1), and fulfil all the good pleasure of his goodness, and the work of faith with power:

II Timothy 1:9 Who hath saved us, and called us with an holy calling (1), not according to our works, but according to his own purpose and grace, which was given us in Christ Jesus before the world began,

Hebrews 3:1 Wherefore, holy brethren, partakers of the heavenly calling (1), consider the Apostle and High Priest of our profession, Christ Jesus;

II Peter 1:10 Wherefore the rather, brethren, give diligence to make your calling (1) and election sure: for if ye do these things, ye shall never fall:

(1) klesis, pronounced klay'-sis; an invitation

Appendix G - Converted, Changed, and Translated

* Converted

Matthew 13:15 For this people's heart is waxed gross, and their ears are dull of hearing, and their eyes they have closed; lest at any time they should see with their eyes and hear with their ears, and should understand with their heart, and should be converted(1), and I should heal them.

Matthew 18:3 And said, Verily I say unto you, Except ye be converted (2), and become as little children, ye shall not enter into the kingdom of heaven.

Mark 4:12 That seeing they may see, and not perceive; and hearing they may hear, and not understand; lest at any time they should be converted (1), and their sins should be forgiven them.

Luke 22:32 But I have prayed for thee, that thy faith fail not: and when thou art converted (1), strengthen thy brethren.

John 12:40 He hath blinded their eyes, and hardened their heart; that they should not see with their eyes, nor understand with their heart, and be converted (1), and I should heal them.

The Doctrines of Men

Acts 3:19 Repent ye therefore, and be converted (1), that your sins may be blotted out, when the times of refreshing shall come from the presence of the Lord.

Acts 28:27 For the heart of this people is waxed gross, and their ears are dull of hearing, and their eyes have they closed; lest they should see with their eyes, and hear with their ears, and understand with their heart, and should be converted(1), and I should heal them.

(1) epistrepho, pronounced ep-ee-stref'-o; to revert (literally, figuratively or morally):
(2) strepho, pronounced stref'-o; to twist, i.e. turn quite around or reverse (literally or figuratively):

* Changed

I Corinthians 15:51 Behold, I shew you a mystery; We shall not all sleep, but we shall all be changed, 52 In a moment, in the twinkling of an eye, at the last trump: for the trumpet shall sound, and the dead shall be raised incorruptible, and we shall be changed. 53 For this corruptible must put on incorruption, and this mortal must put on immortality. 54 So when this corruptible shall have put on incorruption, and this mortal shall have put on immortality, then shall be brought to pass the saying that is written, Death is swallowed up in victory.

II Corinthians 3:18 But we all, with open face beholding as in a glass the glory of the Lord, are changed into the same image from glory to glory, even as by the Spirit of the LORD.

Philippians 3:21 Who shall change our vile body, that it may be fashioned like unto his glorious body, according to the working whereby he is able even to subdue all things unto himself.

fashioned - summorphos, pronounced soom-mor-fos'; jointly formed, i.e. (figuratively) similar:

* Translated

Colossians 1:13 Who hath delivered us from the power of darkness, and hath translated us into the kingdom of his dear Son:

Translated: methistemi, pronounced meth-is'-tay-mee; to transfer,

Appendix H - Human Everlasting and Eternal Life In the New Testament

Matthew 19:16 And, behold, one came and said unto him, Good Master, what good thing shall I do, that I may have eternal life?

Matthew 19:29 And every one that hath forsaken houses, or brethren, or sisters, or father, or mother, or wife, or children, or lands, for my name's sake, shall receive an hundredfold, and shall inherit everlasting life.

Matthew 25:46 And these shall go away into everlasting punishment: but the righteous into life eternal.

Mark 10:17 And when he was gone forth into the way, there came one running, and kneeled to him, and asked him, Good Master, what shall I do that I may inherit eternal life?

Mark 10:30 But he shall receive an hundredfold now in this time, houses, and brethren, and sisters, and mothers, and children, and lands, with persecutions; and in the world to come eternal life.

Luke 10:25 And, behold, a certain lawyer stood up, and tempted him, saying, Master, what shall I do to inherit eternal life?

Luke 18:18 And a certain ruler asked him, saying, Good Master, what shall I do to inherit eternal life?

Luke 18: 29 And he said unto them, Verily I say unto you, There is no man that hath left house, or parents, or brethren, or wife, or children, for the kingdom of God's sake, 30 Who shall not receive manifold more in this present time, and in the world to come life everlasting.

John 3: 15 That whosoever believeth in him should not perish, but have eternal life.

John 3: 16 For God so loved the world, that he gave his only begotten Son, that whosoever believeth in him should not perish, but have everlasting life.

John 3: 36 He that believeth on the Son hath everlasting life: and he that believeth not the Son shall not see life; but the wrath of God abideth on him.

John 4:14 But whosoever drinketh of the water that I shall give him shall never thirst; but the water that I shall give him shall be in him a well of water springing up into everlasting life.

John 4:36 And he that reapeth receiveth wages, and gathereth fruit unto life eternal: that both he that soweth and he that reapeth may rejoice together.

John 5:24 Verily, verily, I say unto you, He that heareth my word, and believeth on him that sent me, hath everlasting life, and shall not come into condemnation; but is passed from death unto life.

John 5:39 Search the scriptures; for in them ye think ye have eternal life: and they are they which testify of me.

John 6:27 Labour not for the meat which perisheth, but for that meat which endureth unto everlasting life, which the Son of man shall give unto you: for him hath God the Father sealed.

John 6: 40 And this is the will of him that sent me, that every one which seeth the Son, and believeth on him, may have everlasting life: and I will raise him up at the last day.

John 6: 47 Verily, verily, I say unto you, He that believeth on me hath everlasting life.

John 6:51 I am the living bread which came down from heaven: if any man eat of this bread, he shall live for ever: and the bread that I will give is my flesh, which I will give for the life of the world.

John 6:54 Whoso eateth my flesh, and drinketh my blood, hath eternal life; and I will raise him up at the last day.

John 6:58 This is that bread which came down from heaven: not as your fathers did eat manna, and are dead: he that eateth of this bread shall live for ever.

John 6:68 Then Simon Peter answered him, Lord, to whom shall we go? thou hast the words of eternal life.

John 10:28 And I give unto them eternal life; and they shall never perish, neither shall any man pluck them out of my hand.

John 12:25 He that loveth his life shall lose it; and he that hateth his life in this world shall keep it unto life eternal.

John 12:50 And I know that his commandment is life everlasting: whatsoever I speak therefore, even as the Father said unto me, so I speak.

John 17:2 As thou hast given him power over all flesh, that he should give eternal life to as many as thou hast given him. 3 And this is life eternal, that they might know thee the only true God, and Jesus Christ, whom thou hast sent.

The Doctrines of Men

Acts 13: 48 And when the Gentiles heard this, they were glad, and glorified the word of the Lord: and as many as were ordained to eternal life believed.

Romans 2:7 To them who by patient continuance in well doing seek for glory and honour and immortality, eternal life:

Romans 5:21 That as sin hath reigned unto death, even so might grace reign through righteousness unto eternal life by Jesus Christ our Lord.

Romans 6:22 But now being made free from sin, and become servants to God, ye have your fruit unto holiness, and the end everlasting life. 23 For the wages of sin is death; but the gift of God is eternal life through Jesus Christ our Lord.

I. Corinthians 15:53 For this corruptible must put on incorruption, and this mortal must put on immortality. 54 So when this corruptible shall have put on incorruption, and this mortal shall have put on immortality, then shall be brought to pass the saying that is written, Death is swallowed up in victory.

Galatians 6:8 For he that soweth to his flesh shall of the flesh reap corruption; but he that soweth to the Spirit shall of the Spirit reap life everlasting.

I. Timothy 1:16 Howbeit for this cause I obtained mercy, that in me first Jesus Christ might shew forth all longsuffering, for a pattern to them which should hereafter believe on him to life everlasting.

I Timothy 2:10 Therefore I endure all things for the elect's sakes, that they may also obtain the salvation which is in Christ Jesus with eternal glory.

I Timothy 6:12 Fight the good fight of faith, lay hold on eternal life, whereunto thou art also called, and hast professed a good profession before many witnesses.

I Timothy 6:19 Laying up in store for themselves a good foundation against the time to come, that they may lay hold on eternal life.

II Timothy 1:10 But is now made manifest by the appearing of our Saviour Jesus Christ, who hath abolished death, and hath brought life and immortality to light through the gospel:

Titus 1:2 In hope of eternal life, which God, that cannot lie, promised before the world began;

Titus 3:7 That being justified by his grace, we should be made heirs according to the hope of eternal life.

Hebrews 5:9 And being made perfect, he became the author of eternal salvation unto all them that obey him;

I John 1:2 (For the life was manifested, and we have seen it, and bear witness, and shew unto you that eternal life, which was with the Father, and was manifested unto us;)

I John 2: 25 And this is the promise that he hath promised us, even eternal life.

I John 5:11 And this is the record, that God hath given to us eternal life, and this life is in his Son. 12 He that hath the Son hath life; and he that hath not the Son of God hath not life. 13 These things have I written unto you that believe on the name of the Son of God; that ye may know that ye have eternal life, and that ye may believe on the name of the Son of God.

I John 5:20 And we know that the Son of God is come, and hath given us an understanding, that we may know him that is true, and we are in him that is true, even in his Son Jesus Christ. This is the true God, and eternal life.

Jude 1:21 Keep yourselves in the love of God, looking for the mercy of our Lord Jesus Christ unto eternal life.

Appendix I - Everlasting and Eternal Things In the New Testament

Romans 1:20 For the invisible things of him from the creation of the world are clearly seen, being understood by the things that are made, even his eternal power and Godhead; so that they are without excuse:

Romans 16:26 But now is made manifest, and by the scriptures of the prophets, according to the commandment of the everlasting God, made known to all nations for the obedience of faith:

II Corinthians 4: 17 For our light affliction, which is but for a moment, worketh for us a far more exceeding and eternal weight of glory; eternal life: 18 While we look not at the things which are seen, but at the things which are not seen: for the things which are seen are temporal; but the things which are not seen are eternal.

II Corinthians 5:1 For we know that if our earthly house of this tabernacle were dissolved, we have a building of God, an house not made with hands, eternal in the heavens.

Ephesians 3:11 According to the eternal purpose which he purposed in Christ Jesus our Lord:

II Thessalonians 2: 16 Now our Lord Jesus Christ himself, and God, even our Father, which hath loved us, and hath given us everlasting consolation and good hope through grace,

I Timothy 1:17 Now unto the King eternal, immortal, invisible, the only wise God, be honour and glory for ever and ever. Amen.

I Timothy 6:16 Who only hath immortality, dwelling in the light which no man can approach unto; whom no man hath seen, nor can see: to whom be honour and power everlasting. Amen.

II Timothy 2:10 Therefore I endure all things for the elect's sakes, that they may also obtain the salvation which is in Christ Jesus with eternal glory.

Hebrews 6:2 Of the doctrine of baptisms, and of laying on of hands, and of resurrection of the dead, and of eternal judgment.

Hebrews 9:12 Neither by the blood of goats and calves, but by his own blood he entered in once into the holy place, having obtained eternal redemption for us.

Hebrews 9:14 How much more shall the blood of Christ, who through the eternal Spirit offered himself without spot to God, purge your conscience from dead works to serve the living God?

Hebrews 9:15 And for this cause he is the mediator of the new testament, that by means of death, for the redemption of the transgressions that were under the first testament, they which are called might receive the promise of eternal inheritance.

Hebrews 13:20 Now the God of peace, that brought again from the dead our Lord Jesus, that great shepherd of the sheep, through the blood of the everlasting covenant,

I Peter 1:23 Being born again, not of corruptible seed, but of incorruptible, by the word of God, which liveth and abideth for ever.

I Peter 5:10 But the God of all grace, who hath called us unto his eternal glory by Christ Jesus, after that ye have suffered a while, make you perfect, establish, strengthen, settle you.

I John 2: 17 And the world passeth away, and the lust thereof: but he that doeth the will of God abideth for ever.

I John 3:15 Whosoever hateth his brother is a murderer: and ye know that no murderer hath eternal life abiding in him.

Jude 1:6 And the angels which kept not their first estate, but left their own habitation, he hath reserved in everlasting chains under darkness unto the judgment of the great day.

Revelation 14:6 And I saw another angel fly in the midst of heaven, having the everlasting gospel to preach unto them that dwell on the earth, and to every nation, and kindred, and tongue, and people,

Appendix J - For Ever In the New Testament

Matthew 6:13 And lead us not into temptation, but deliver us from evil: For thine is the kingdom, and the power, and the glory, for ever. Amen.

Matthew 21:19 And when he saw a fig tree in the way, he came to it, and found nothing thereon, but leaves only, and said unto it, Let no fruit grow on thee henceforward for ever. And presently the fig tree withered away.

Luke 1:33 And he shall reign over the house of Jacob for ever; and of his kingdom there shall be no end.

Luke 1:55 As he spake to our fathers, to Abraham, and to his seed for ever.

John 12:34 The people answered him, We have heard out of the law that Christ abideth for ever: and how sayest thou, The Son of man must be lifted up? who is this Son of man?

John 14:16 And I will pray the Father, and he shall give you another Comforter, that he may abide with you for ever;

Romans 1:25 Who changed the truth of God into a lie, and worshipped and served the creature more than the Creator, who is blessed for ever. Amen.

Romans 9:5 Whose are the fathers, and of whom as concerning the flesh Christ came, who is over all, God blessed for ever. Amen.

Romans 11:36 For of him, and through him, and to him, are all things: to whom be glory for ever. Amen.

Romans 16:27 To God only wise, be glory through Jesus Christ for ever. Amen.

II Corinthians 9:9 (As it is written, He hath dispersed abroad; he hath given to the poor: his righteousness remaineth for ever.

Galatians 1:5 To whom be glory for ever and ever. Amen.

Philippians 4:20 Now unto God and our Father be glory for ever and ever. Amen.

I Timothy 1:17 Now unto the King eternal, immortal, invisible, the only wise God, be honour and glory for ever and ever. Amen.

II Timothy 4:18 And the Lord shall deliver me from every evil work, and will preserve me unto his heavenly kingdom: to whom be glory for ever and ever. Amen.

Philemon 1:15 For perhaps he therefore departed for a season, that thou shouldest receive him for ever;

Hebrews 1: 8 But unto the Son he saith, Thy throne, O God, is for ever and ever: a sceptre of righteousness is the sceptre of thy kingdom.

Hebrews 5:6 As he saith also in another place, Thou art a priest for ever after the order of Melchisedec.

Hebrews 6:20 Whither the forerunner is for us entered, even Jesus, made an high priest for ever after the order of Melchisedec.

Hebrews 7:17 For he testifieth, Thou art a priest for ever after the order of Melchisedec.

Hebrews 7:21 (For those priests were made without an oath; but this with an oath by him that said unto him, The Lord sware and will not repent, Thou art a priest for ever after the order of Melchisedec:)

Hebrews 10:12 But this man, after he had offered one sacrifice for sins for ever, sat down on the right hand of God;

Hebrews 10:14 For by one offering he hath perfected for ever them that are sanctified.

Hebrews 13:8 Jesus Christ the same yesterday, and to day, and for ever.

Hebrews 13:21 Make you perfect in every good work to do his will, working in you that which is wellpleasing in his sight, through Jesus Christ; to whom be glory for ever and ever. Amen.

I Peter 1:25 But the word of the Lord endureth for ever. And this is the word which by the gospel is preached unto you.

I Peter 4:11 If any man speak, let him speak as the oracles of God; if any man minister, let him do it as of the ability which God giveth: that God in all things may be glorified through Jesus Christ, to whom be praise and dominion for ever and ever. Amen.

I Peter 5:11 To him be glory and dominion for ever and ever. Amen.

II Peter 2:17 These are wells without water, clouds that are carried with a tempest; to whom the mist of darkness is reserved for ever.

II Peter 3:18 But grow in grace, and in the knowledge of our Lord and Saviour Jesus Christ. To him be glory both now and for ever. Amen.

II John 1:2 For the truth's sake, which dwelleth in us, and shall be with us for ever.

Jude 1:13 Raging waves of the sea, foaming out their own shame; wandering stars, to whom is reserved the blackness of darkness for ever.

Jude 1:25 To the only wise God our Saviour, be glory and majesty, dominion and power, both now and ever. Amen.

Revelation 1:6 And hath made us kings and priests unto God and his Father; to him be glory and dominion for ever and ever. Amen.

Revelation 4:9 And when those beasts give glory and honour and thanks to him that sat on the throne, who liveth for ever and ever, 10 The four and twenty elders fall down before him that sat on the throne, and worship him that liveth for ever and ever, and cast their crowns before the throne, saying,

Revelation 5:13 And every creature which is in heaven, and on the earth, and under the earth, and such as are in the sea, and all that are in them, heard I saying, Blessing, and honour, and glory, and power, be unto him that sitteth upon the throne, and unto the Lamb for ever and ever. 14 And the four beasts said, Amen. And the four and twenty elders fell down and worshipped him that liveth for ever and ever.

Revelation 10:6 And sware by him that liveth for ever and ever, who created heaven, and the things that therein are, and the earth, and the things that therein are, and the sea, and the things which are therein, that there should be time no longer:

Revelation 11:15 And the seventh angel sounded; and there were great voices in heaven, saying, The kingdoms of this world are become the kingdoms of our Lord, and of his Christ; and he shall reign for ever and ever.

Revelation 14:11 And the smoke of their torment ascendeth up for ever and ever: and they have no rest day nor night, who worship the beast and his image, and whosoever receiveth the mark of his name.

Revelation 15:7 And one of the four beasts gave unto the seven angels seven golden vials full of the wrath of God, who liveth for ever and ever.

Revelation 20:10 And the devil that deceived them was cast into the lake of fire and brimstone, where the beast and the false prophet are, and shall be tormented day and night for ever and ever.

Revelation 22:5 And there shall be no night there; and they need no candle, neither light of the sun; for the Lord God giveth them light: and they shall reign for ever and ever.

Appendix K - Love In the New Testament

Matthew 5:44 But I say unto you, Love your enemies, bless them that curse you, do good to them that hate you, and pray for them which despitefully use you, and persecute you;

Matthew 22: 36. Master, which is the great commandment in the law? 37. Jesus said unto him, Thou shalt love the Lord thy God with all thy heart, and with all thy soul, and with all thy mind. 38. This is the first and great commandment. 39. And the second is like unto it, Thou shalt love thy neighbour as thyself. 40. On these two commandments hang all the law and the prophets**

Mark 12:30 And thou shalt love the Lord thy God with all thy heart, and with all thy soul, and with all thy mind, and with all thy strength: this is the first commandment. 31 And the second is like, namely this, Thou shalt love thy neighbour as thyself. There is none other commandment greater than these. 32. And the scribe said unto him, Well, Master, thou hast said the truth: for there is one God; and there is none other but he: 33. And to love him with all the heart, and with all the understanding, and with all the soul, and with all the strength, and to love his neighbour as himself, is more than all whole burnt offerings and sacrifices.

Luke 6:27 But I say unto you which hear, Love your enemies, do good to them which hate you,

Luke 6:35 But love ye your enemies, and do good, and lend, hoping for nothing again; and your reward shall be great, and ye shall be the children of the Highest: for he is kind unto the unthankful and to the evil.

Luke 10:25 And, behold, a certain lawyer stood up, and tempted him, saying, Master, what shall I do to inherit eternal life?

26 He said unto him, What is written in the law? how readest thou? 27 And he answering said, Thou shalt love the Lord thy God with all thy heart, and with all thy soul, and with all thy strength, and with all thy mind; and thy neighbour as thyself.

John 13:34 A new commandment I give unto you, That ye love one another; as I have loved you, that ye also love one another. 35 By this shall all men know that ye are my disciples, if ye have love one to another.

John 14:15 If ye love me, keep my commandments.

John 14:21 He that hath my commandments, and keepeth them, he it is that loveth me: and he that loveth me shall be loved of my Father, and I will love him, and will manifest myself to him.

John 14:23 Jesus answered and said unto him, If a man love me, he will keep my words: and my Father will love him, and we will come unto him, and make our abode with him. 24 He that loveth me not keepeth not my sayings: and the word which ye hear is not mine, but the Father's which sent me.

John 15:9 As the Father hath loved me, so have I loved you: continue ye in my love. 10 If ye keep my commandments, ye shall abide in my love; even as I have kept my Father's commandments, and abide in his love. 11 These things have I spoken unto you, that my joy might remain in you, and that your joy might be full. 12 This is my commandment, That ye love one another, as I have loved you.

John 15:17 These things I command you, that ye love one another.

John 21:15 So when they had dined, Jesus saith to Simon Peter, Simon, son of Jonas, lovest thou me more than these? He saith unto him, Yea, Lord; thou knowest that I love thee. He saith unto him, Feed my lambs. 16 He saith to him again the second time, Simon, son of Jonas, lovest thou me? He saith unto him, Yea, Lord; thou knowest that I love thee. He saith unto him, Feed my sheep. 17 He saith unto him the third time, Simon, son of Jonas, lovest thou me? Peter was grieved because he said unto him the third time, Lovest thou me? And he said unto him, Lord, thou knowest all things; thou knowest that I love thee. Jesus saith unto him, Feed my sheep.

Romans 5:5 And hope maketh not ashamed; because the love of God is shed abroad in our hearts by the Holy Ghost which is given unto us.

Romans 5:8 But God commendeth his love toward us, in that, while we were yet sinners, Christ died for us.

Romans 8:28 And we know that all things work together for good to them that love God, to them who are the called according to his purpose.

Romans 8:35 Who shall separate us from the love of Christ? shall tribulation, or distress, or persecution, or famine, or nakedness, or peril, or sword?

Romans 8:38 For I am persuaded, that neither death, nor life, nor angels, nor principalities, nor powers, nor things present, nor things to come, 39 Nor height, nor depth, nor any other creature, shall be able to separate us from the love of God, which is in Christ Jesus our Lord.

Romans 12:9 Let love be without dissimulation. Abhor that which is evil; cleave to that which is good.

Romans 13: 8 Owe no man any thing, but to love one another: for he that loveth another hath fulfilled the law. 9 For this, Thou shalt not commit adultery, Thou shalt not kill, Thou shalt not steal, Thou shalt not bear false witness, Thou shalt not covet; and if there be any other commandment, it is briefly comprehended in this saying, namely, Thou shalt love thy neighbour as thyself. 10 Love worketh no ill to his neighbour: therefore love is the fulfilling of the law.

I Corinthians 2:9 But as it is written, Eye hath not seen, nor ear heard, neither have entered into the heart of man, the things which God hath prepared for them that love him.

1 Corinthians 13:1. Though I speak with the tongues of men and of angels, and have not charity, I am become as sounding brass, or a tinkling cymbal. 2 And though I have

the gift of prophecy, and understand all mysteries, and all knowledge; and though I have all faith, so that I could remove mountains, and have not charity, I am nothing. 3 And though I bestow all my goods to feed the poor, and though I give my body to be burned, and have not charity, it profiteth me nothing. 4 Charity suffereth long, and is kind; charity envieth not; charity vaunteth not itself, is not puffed up, 5 Doth not behave itself unseemly, seeketh not her own, is not easily provoked, thinketh no evil; 6 Rejoiceth not in iniquity, but rejoiceth in the truth; 7 Beareth all things, believeth all things, hopeth all things, endureth all things. 8 Charity never faileth: but whether there be prophecies, they shall fail; whether there be tongues, they shall cease; whether there be knowledge, it shall vanish away. 9 For we know in part, and we prophesy in part. 10 But when that which is perfect is come, then that which is in part shall be done away. 11 When I was a child, I spake as a child, I understood as a child, I thought as a child: but when I became a man, I put away childish things. 12 For now we see through a glass, darkly; but then face to face: now I know in part; but then shall I know even as also I am known. 13 And now abideth faith, hope, charity, these three; but the greatest of these is charity.

II Corinthians 5:10 Be kindly affectioned one to another with brotherly love; in honour preferring one another;

II Corinthians 6: 6 By pureness, by knowledge, by longsuffering, by kindness, by the Holy Ghost, by love unfeigned,

II Corinthians 13: 11 Finally, brethren, farewell. Be perfect, be of good comfort, be of one mind, live in peace; and the God of love and peace shall be with you.

Galatians 5:13 For, brethren, ye have been called unto liberty; only use not liberty for an occasion to the flesh, but by love serve one another. 14 For all the law is fulfilled in one word, even in this; Thou shalt love thy neighbour as thyself.

Galatians 5:22 But the fruit of the Spirit is love, joy, peace, longsuffering, gentleness, goodness, faith,

Ephesians 2:4 But God, who is rich in mercy, for his great love wherewith he loved us,

Ephesians 3:17 That Christ may dwell in your hearts by faith; that ye, being rooted and grounded in love,

Ephesians 4:2 With all lowliness and meekness, with longsuffering, forbearing one another in love;

Ephesians 5:2 And walk in love, as Christ also hath loved us, and hath given himself for us an offering and a sacrifice to God for a sweetsmelling savour.

Philippians 1:9 And this I pray, that your love may abound yet more and more in knowledge and in all judgment;

Philippians 2:2 Fulfil ye my joy, that ye be likeminded, having the same love, being of one accord, of one mind.

Colossians 2: 2 That their hearts might be comforted, being knit together in love, and unto all riches of the full assurance of understanding, to the acknowledgement of the mystery of God, and of the Father, and of Christ;

I Thessalonians 3:12 And the Lord make you to increase and abound in love one toward another, and toward all men, even as we do toward you:

I Thessalonians 4:9 But as touching brotherly love ye need not that I write unto you: for ye yourselves are taught of God to love one another.

I Timothy 6:11 But thou, O man of God, flee these things; and follow after righteousness, godliness, faith, love, patience, meekness.

II Timothy 1:7 For God hath not given us the spirit of fear; but of power, and of love, and of a sound mind.

Hebrews 10:24 And let us consider one another to provoke unto love and to good works:

Hebrews 13:1 Let brotherly love continue.

James 1:12 Blessed is the man that endureth temptation: for when he is tried, he shall receive the crown of life, which the Lord hath promised to them that love him.

James 2:5 Hearken, my beloved brethren, Hath not God chosen the poor of this world rich in faith, and heirs of the kingdom which he hath promised to them that love him?

James 2:8 If ye fulfil the royal law according to the scripture, Thou shalt love thy neighbour as thyself, ye do well:

I Peter 1:22 Seeing ye have purified your souls in obeying the truth through the Spirit unto unfeigned love of the brethren, see that ye love one another with a pure heart fervently:

I Peter 2:17 Honour all men. Love the brotherhood. Fear God. Honour the king.

I Peter 3:8 Finally, be ye all of one mind, having compassion one of another, love as brethren, be pitiful, be courteous:

I John 2: 5 But whoso keepeth his word, in him verily is the love of God perfected: hereby know we that we are in him.

I John 2:15 Love not the world, neither the things that are in the world. If any man love the world, the love of the Father is not in him.

I John 3:1 Behold, what manner of love the Father hath bestowed upon us, that we should be called the sons of God: therefore the world knoweth us not, because it knew him not.

I John 3:11 For this is the message that ye heard from the beginning, that we should love one another.

I John 3:14 We know that we have passed from death unto life, because we love the brethren. He that loveth not his brother abideth in death.

I John 3:16 Hereby perceive we the love of God, because he laid down his life for us: and we ought to lay down our lives for the brethren.

I John 3:18 My little children, let us not love in word, neither in tongue; but in deed and in truth.

I John 3:23 And this is his commandment, That we should believe on the name of his Son Jesus Christ, and love one another, as he gave us commandment.

I John 4: 7 Beloved, let us love one another: for love is of God; and every one that loveth is born of God, and knoweth God.

8 He that loveth not knoweth not God; for God is love. 9 In this was manifested the love of God toward us, because that God sent his only begotten Son into the world, that we might live through him. 10 Herein is love, not that we loved God, but that he loved us, and sent his Son to be the propitiation for our sins. 11 Beloved, if God so loved us, we ought also to love one another. 12 No man hath seen God at any time. If we love one another, God dwelleth in us, and his love is perfected in us.

I John 4:16 And we have known and believed the love that God hath to us. God is love; and he that dwelleth in love dwelleth in God, and God in him. 17 Herein is our love made perfect, that we may have boldness in the day of judgment: because as he is, so are we in this world. 18 There is no fear in love; but perfect love casteth out fear: because fear hath torment. He that feareth is not made perfect in love. 19 We love him, because he first loved us. 20 If a man say, I love God, and hateth his brother, he is a liar: for he that loveth not his brother whom he hath seen, how can he love God whom he hath not seen? 21 And this commandment have we from him, That he who loveth God love his brother also.

I John 5:1 Whosoever believeth that Jesus is the Christ is born of God: and every one that loveth him that begat loveth him also that is begotten of him. 2 By this we know that we love the children of God, when we love God, and keep his commandments.

II John 1: 5 And now I beseech thee, lady, not as though I wrote a new commandment unto thee, but that which we had from the beginning, that we love one another. 6 And this is love, that we walk after his commandments. This is the commandment, That, as ye have heard from the beginning, ye should walk in it.

Jude 1: 21 Keep yourselves in the love of God, looking for the mercy of our Lord Jesus Christ unto eternal life.

Appendix L - Wisdom

Exodus 31:3 And I have filled him with the spirit of God, in wisdom, and in understanding, and in knowledge, and in all manner of workmanship,

Deuteronomy 34:9 And Joshua the son of Nun was full of the spirit of wisdom; for Moses had laid his hands upon him: and the children of Israel hearkened unto him, and did as the LORD commanded Moses.

I Kings 3:28 And all Israel heard of the judgment which the king had judged; and they feared the king: for they saw that the wisdom of God was in him, to do judgment.

I Kings 4:30 And Solomon's wisdom excelled the wisdom of all the children of the east country, and all the wisdom of Egypt.

I Kings 4:34 And there came of all people to hear the wisdom of Solomon, from all kings of the earth, which had heard of his wisdom.

I Kings 7:14 He was a widow's son of the tribe of Naphtali, and his father was a man of Tyre, a worker in brass: and he was filled with wisdom, and understanding, and cunning to work all works in brass. And he came to king Solomon, and wrought all his work.

I Kings 10:7 Howbeit I believed not the words, until I came, and mine eyes had seen it: and, behold, the half was not told me: thy wisdom and prosperity exceedeth the fame which I heard.

I Kings 10:23 So king Solomon exceeded all the kings of the earth for riches and for wisdom. 24 And all the earth sought to Solomon, to hear his wisdom, which God had put in his heart.

Ezra 7:25 And thou, Ezra, after the wisdom of thy God, that is in thine hand, set magistrates and judges, which may judge all the people that are beyond the river, all such as know the laws of thy God; and teach ye them that know them not.

Job 11:6 And that he would shew thee the secrets of wisdom, that they are double to that which is! Know therefore that God exacteth of thee less than thine iniquity deserveth.

Job 12:12 With the ancient is wisdom; and in length of days understanding. 13 With him is wisdom and strength, he hath counsel and understanding.

Job 28:12 But where shall wisdom be found? and where is the place of understanding?

Job 28:18 No mention shall be made of coral, or of pearls: for the price of wisdom is above rubies.

Job 28:20 Whence then cometh wisdom? and where is the place of understanding?

Job 28:28 And unto man he said, Behold, the fear of the LORD, that is wisdom; and to depart from evil is understanding.

Job 32:7 I said, Days should speak, and multitude of years should teach wisdom.

Job 34:35 Job hath spoken without knowledge, and his words were without wisdom.

Job 39:17 Because God hath deprived her of wisdom, neither hath he imparted to her understanding.

Psalms 37:30 The mouth of the righteous speaketh wisdom, and his tongue talketh of judgment.

Psalms 104:24 O LORD, how manifold are thy works! in wisdom hast thou made them all: the earth is full of thy riches.

Psalms 111:10 The fear of the LORD is the beginning of wisdom: a good understanding have all they that do his commandments: his praise endureth for ever. (fear - yare', pronounced yaw-ray'; fearing; morally, reverent.)

Proverbs 1:2 To know wisdom and instruction; to perceive the words of understanding; 3 To receive the instruction of wisdom, justice, and judgment, and equity; 4 To give subtilty to the simple, to the young man knowledge and discretion. 5 A wise man will hear, and will increase learning; and a man of understanding shall attain unto wise counsels: 6 To understand a proverb, and the interpretation; the words of the wise, and their dark sayings. 7 The fear of the LORD is the beginning of knowledge: but fools despise wisdom and instruction.

Proverbs 2:6 For the LORD giveth wisdom: out of his mouth cometh knowledge and understanding.

Proverbs 3:13 Happy is the man that findeth wisdom, and the man that getteth understanding.

Proverbs 4:7 Wisdom is the principal thing; therefore get wisdom: and with all thy getting get understanding.

Proverbs 4:11 I have taught thee in the way of wisdom; I have led thee in right paths.

Proverbs 5:1 My son, attend unto my wisdom, and bow thine ear to my understanding:

Proverbs 7:4 Say unto wisdom, Thou art my sister; and call understanding thy kinswoman:

Proverbs 8:11 For wisdom is better than rubies; and all the things that may be desired are not to be compared to it. 12 I wisdom dwell with prudence, and find out knowledge of witty inventions. 13 The fear of the LORD is to hate evil: pride, and arrogancy, and the evil way, and the froward mouth, do I hate. 14 Counsel is mine, and sound wisdom: I am understanding; I have strength.

Proverbs 9:10 The fear of the LORD is the beginning of wisdom: and the knowledge of the holy is understanding.

Proverbs 10:13 In the lips of him that hath understanding wisdom is found: but a rod is for the back of him that is void of understanding.

Proverbs 10:21 The lips of the righteous feed many: but fools die for want of wisdom.

Proverbs 10:23 It is as sport to a fool to do mischief: but a man of understanding hath wisdom.

Proverbs 11:2 When pride cometh, then cometh shame: but with the lowly is wisdom.

Proverbs 11:12 He that is void of wisdom despiseth his neighbour: but a man of understanding holdeth his peace.

Proverbs 12:8 A man shall be commended according to his wisdom: but he that is of a perverse heart shall be despised.

Proverbs 13:10 Only by pride cometh contention: but with the well advised is wisdom.

Proverbs 14: 6 A scorner seeketh wisdom, and findeth it not: but knowledge is easy unto him that understandeth.

Proverbs 14:8 The wisdom of the prudent is to understand his way: but the folly of fools is deceit.

Proverbs 14:33 Wisdom resteth in the heart of him that hath understanding: but that which is in the midst of fools is made known.

Proverbs 15:21 Folly is joy to him that is destitute of wisdom: but a man of understanding walketh uprightly.

Proverbs 15:33 The fear of the LORD is the instruction of wisdom; and before honour is humility.

Proverbs 16:16 How much better is it to get wisdom than gold! and to get understanding rather to be chosen than silver!

Proverbs 17:24 Wisdom is before him that hath understanding; but the eyes of a fool are in the ends of the earth.

Proverbs 18:1 Through desire a man, having separated himself, seeketh and intermeddleth with all wisdom.

Proverbs 18:4 The words of a man's mouth are as deep waters, and the wellspring of wisdom as a flowing brook.

Proverbs 19:8 He that getteth wisdom loveth his own soul: he that keepeth understanding shall find good.

Proverbs 21:30 There is no wisdom nor understanding nor counsel against the LORD.

Proverbs 23:9 Speak not in the ears of a fool: for he will despise the wisdom of thy words.

Proverbs 23:23 Buy the truth, and sell it not; also wisdom, and instruction, and understanding.

Proverbs 24:3 Through wisdom is an house builded; and by understanding it is established:

Proverbs 24:7 Wisdom is too high for a fool: he openeth not his mouth in the gate.

Proverbs 24:14 So shall the knowledge of wisdom be unto thy soul: when thou hast found it, then there shall be a reward, and thy expectation shall not be cut off.

Ecclesiates 1: 13 And I gave my heart to seek and search out by wisdom concerning all things that are done under heaven: this sore travail hath God given to the sons of man to be exercised therewith.

Ecclesiates 1:17 And I gave my heart to know wisdom, and to know madness and folly: I perceived that this also is vexation of spirit. 18 For in much wisdom is much grief: and he that increaseth knowledge increaseth sorrow.

Ecclesiates 2:3 I sought in mine heart to give myself unto wine, yet acquainting mine heart with wisdom; and to lay hold on folly, till I might see what was that good for the sons of men, which they should do under the heaven all the days of their life.

Ecclesiates 7:11 Wisdom is good with an inheritance: and by it there is profit to them that see the sun. 12 For wisdom is a defence, and money is a defence: but the excellency of knowledge is, that wisdom giveth life to them that have it. 13 Then I saw that wisdom excelleth folly, as far as light excelleth darkness.

Ecclesiates 7:19 Wisdom strengtheneth the wise more than ten mighty men which are in the city.

Ecclesiates 7:25 I applied mine heart to know, and to search, and to seek out wisdom, and the reason of things, and to know the wickedness of folly, even of foolishness and madness:

Ecclesiates 8:1 Who is as the wise man? and who knoweth the interpretation of a thing? a man's wisdom maketh his face to shine, and the boldness of his face shall be changed.

Ecclesiates 8:16 When I applied mine heart to know wisdom, and to see the business that is done upon the earth: (for also there is that neither day nor night seeth sleep with his eyes:)

Ecclesiates 9:10 Whatsoever thy hand findeth to do, do it with thy might; for there is no work, nor device, nor knowledge, nor wisdom, in the grave, whither thou goest.

Ecclesiates 9:13 This wisdom have I seen also under the sun, and it seemed great unto me:

Ecclesiates 9:15 Now there was found in it a poor wise man, and he by his wisdom delivered the city; yet no man remembered that same poor man. 16 Then said I, Wisdom is better than strength: nevertheless the poor man's wisdom is despised, and his words are not heard. 17 The words of wise men are heard in quiet more than the cry of him that ruleth among fools. 18 Wisdom is better than weapons of war: but one sinner destroyeth much good.

Ecclesiates 10:1 Dead flies cause the ointment of the apothecary to send forth a stinking savour: so doth a little folly him that is in reputation for wisdom and honour. 2 A wise man's heart is at his right hand; but a fool's heart at his left. 3 Yea also, when he that is a fool walketh by the way, his wisdom faileth him, and he saith to every one that he is a fool.

Ecclesiates 10:10 If the iron be blunt, and he do not whet the edge, then must he put to more strength: but wisdom is profitable to direct.

Isaiah 11:2 And the spirit of the LORD shall rest upon him, the spirit of wisdom and understanding, the spirit of counsel and might, the spirit of knowledge and of the fear of the LORD;

Isaiah 33:6 And wisdom and knowledge shall be the stability of thy times, and strength of salvation: the fear of the LORD is his treasure.

Jeremiah 9:23 Thus saith the LORD, Let not the wise man glory in his wisdom, neither let the mighty man glory in his might, let not the rich man glory in his riches:

Jeremiah 51:15 He hath made the earth by his power, he hath established the world by his wisdom, and hath stretched out the heaven by his understanding.

Daniel 5:14 I have even heard of thee, that the spirit of the gods is in thee, and that light and understanding and excellent wisdom is found in thee.

Matthew 12:42 The queen of the south shall rise up in the judgment with this generation, and shall condemn it: for she came from the uttermost parts of the earth to hear the wisdom of Solomon; and, behold, a greater than Solomon is here.

The Doctrines of Men

Matthew 13:54 And when he was come into his own country, he taught them in their synagogue, insomuch that they were astonished, and said, Whence hath this man this wisdom, and these mighty works?

Mark 6:2 And when the sabbath day was come, he began to teach in the synagogue: and many hearing him were astonished, saying, From whence hath this man these things? and what wisdom is this which is given unto him, that even such mighty works are wrought by his hands?

Luke 1:17 And he shall go before him in the spirit and power of Elias, to turn the hearts of the fathers to the children, and the disobedient to the wisdom of the just; to make ready a people prepared for the Lord.

Luke 2:40 And the child grew, and waxed strong in spirit, filled with wisdom: and the grace of God was upon him.

Luke 2:52 And Jesus increased in wisdom and stature, and in favour with God and man.

Luke 21:15 For I will give you a mouth and wisdom, which all your adversaries shall not be able to gainsay nor resist.

Acts 6:3 Wherefore, brethren, look ye out among you seven men of honest report, full of the Holy Ghost and wisdom, whom we may appoint over this business.

Acts 6:10 And they were not able to resist the wisdom and the spirit by which he spake.

Romans 11:33 O the depth of the riches both of the wisdom and knowledge of God! how unsearchable are his judgments, and his ways past finding out!

I Corinthians 2:6 Howbeit we speak wisdom among them that are perfect: yet not the wisdom of this world, nor of the princes of this world, that come to nought:

I Corinthians 2:7 But we speak the wisdom of God in a mystery, even the hidden wisdom, which God ordained before the world unto our glory:

Ephesians 1: 8 Wherein he hath abounded toward us in all wisdom and prudence;

Ephesians 1:17 That the God of our Lord Jesus Christ, the Father of glory, may give unto you the spirit of wisdom and revelation in the knowledge of him:

Ephesians 3:10 To the intent that now unto the principalities and powers in heavenly places might be known by the church the manifold wisdom of God,

Colossians 1:9 For this cause we also, since the day we heard it, do not cease to pray for you, and to desire that ye might be filled with the knowledge of his will in all wisdom and spiritual understanding;

Colossians 1:28 Whom we preach, warning every man, and teaching every man in all wisdom; that we may present every man perfect in Christ Jesus:

Colossians 2:2 That their hearts might be comforted, being knit together in love, and unto all riches of the full assurance of understanding, to the acknowledgement of the mystery of God, and of the Father, and of Christ; 3 In whom are hid all the treasures of wisdom and knowledge.

Colossians 3:16 Let the word of Christ dwell in you richly in all wisdom; teaching and admonishing one another in psalms and hymns and spiritual songs, singing with grace in your hearts to the Lord.

Colossians 4:5 Walk in wisdom toward them that are without, redeeming the time.

James 1:5 If any of you lack wisdom, let him ask of God, that giveth to all men liberally, and upbraideth not; and it shall be given him.

James 3:13 Who is a wise man and endued with knowledge among you? let him shew out of a good conversation his works with meekness of wisdom. 14 But if ye have bitter envying and strife in your hearts, glory not, and lie not against the truth. 15 This wisdom descendeth not from above, but is earthly, sensual, devilish. 16 For where envying and strife is, there is confusion and every evil work. 17 But the wisdom that is from above is first pure, then peaceable, gentle, and easy to be intreated, full of mercy and good fruits, without partiality, and without hypocrisy. 18 And the fruit of righteousness is sown in peace of them that make peace.

Revelation 5:12 Saying with a loud voice, Worthy is the Lamb that was slain to receive power, and riches, and wisdom, and strength, and honour, and glory, and blessing.

Revelation 7:12 Saying, Amen: Blessing, and glory, and wisdom, and thanksgiving, and honour, and power, and might, be unto our God for ever and ever. Amen.

Appendix M - Freedom and Liberty In the New Testament

* Freedom

John 8:32 And ye shall know the truth, and the truth shall make you free.

John 8:36 If the Son therefore shall make you free, ye shall be free indeed.

Romans 6:18 Being then made free from sin, ye became the servants of righteousness.

Romans 6:22 But now being made free from sin, and become servants to God, ye have your fruit unto holiness, and the end everlasting life.

Romans 8:2 For the law of the Spirit of life in Christ Jesus hath made me free from the law of sin and death.

I Corinthians 7:22 For he that is called in the Lord, being a servant, is the Lord's freeman: likewise also he that is called, being free, is Christ's servant.

Galatians 5:1 Stand fast therefore in the liberty wherewith Christ hath made us free, and be not entangled again with the yoke of bondage.

I. Peter 2:16 As free, and not using your liberty for a cloke of maliciousness, but as the servants of God.

* Liberty

Romans 8:21 Because the creature itself also shall be delivered from the bondage of corruption into the glorious liberty of the children of God.

I Corinthians 8:9 But take heed lest by any means this liberty of your's become a stumblingblock to them that are weak.

II Corinthians 3:17 Now the Lord is that Spirit: and where the Spirit of the Lord is, there is liberty.

Galatians 2:4 And that because of false brethren unawares brought in, who came in privily to spy out our liberty which we have in Christ Jesus, that they might bring us into bondage:

Galatians 5:1 Stand fast therefore in the liberty wherewith Christ hath made us free, and be not entangled again with the yoke of bondage.

Galatians 5:13 For, brethren, ye have been called unto liberty; only use not liberty for an occasion to the flesh, but by love serve one another.

James 1:25 But whoso looketh into the perfect law of liberty, and continueth therein, he being not a forgetful hearer, but a doer of the work, this man shall be blessed in his deed.

I Peter 2:16 As free, and not using your liberty for a cloke of maliciousness, but as the servants of God.

Appendix N - Faith

John 8:32 And ye shall know the truth, and the truth shall make you free.

Matthew 6:30 Wherefore, if God so clothe the grass of the field, which to day is, and to morrow is cast into the oven, shall he not much more clothe you, O ye of little faith?

Matthew 8:26 And he saith unto them, Why are ye fearful, O ye of little faith? Then he arose, and rebuked the winds and the sea; and there was a great calm.

Matthew 9:2 And, behold, they brought to him a man sick of the palsy, lying on a bed: and Jesus seeing their faith said unto the sick of the palsy; Son, be of good cheer; thy sins be forgiven thee.

Matthew 9:22 But Jesus turned him about, and when he saw her, he said, Daughter, be of good comfort; thy faith hath made thee whole. And the woman was made whole from that hour.

Matthew 9:29 Then touched he their eyes, saying, According to your faith be it unto you.

Matthew 14:31 And immediately Jesus stretched forth his hand, and caught him, and said unto him, O thou of little faith, wherefore didst thou doubt?

Matthew 15:28 Then Jesus answered and said unto her, O woman, great is thy faith: be it unto thee even as thou wilt. And her daughter was made whole from that very hour.

Matthew 17:20 And Jesus said unto them, Because of your unbelief: for verily I say unto you, If ye have faith as a grain of mustard seed, ye shall say unto this mountain, Remove hence to yonder place; and it shall remove; and nothing shall be impossible unto you.

Matthew 21:21 Jesus answered and said unto them, Verily I say unto you, If ye have faith, and doubt not, ye shall not only do this which is done to the fig tree, but also if ye shall say unto this mountain, Be thou removed, and be thou cast into the sea; it shall be done. 22 And all things, whatsoever ye shall ask in prayer, believing, ye shall receive.

Mark 5:34 And he said unto her, Daughter, thy faith hath made thee whole; go in peace, and be whole of thy plague.

Mark 11:22 And Jesus answering saith unto them, Have faith in God. 23 For verily I say unto you, That whosoever shall say unto this mountain, Be thou removed, and be thou cast into the sea; and shall not doubt in his heart, but shall believe that those things which he saith shall come to pass; he shall have whatsoever he saith. 24 Therefore I say unto you, What things soever ye desire, when ye pray, believe that ye receive them, and ye shall have them.

Luke 8:25 And he said unto them, Where is your faith? And they being afraid wondered, saying one to another, What manner of man is this! for he commandeth even the winds and water, and they obey him.

Luke 17:5 And the apostles said unto the Lord, Increase our faith. 6 And the Lord said, If ye had faith as a grain of mustard seed, ye might say unto this sycamine tree, Be thou plucked up by the root, and be thou planted in the sea; and it should obey you.

Luke 18:42 And Jesus said unto him, Receive thy sight: thy faith hath saved thee.

Acts 6:7 And the word of God increased; and the number of the disciples multiplied in

The Appendices

Jerusalem greatly; and a great company of the priests were obedient to the faith. 8 And Stephen, full of faith and power, did great wonders and miracles among the people.

Acts 13:9 The same heard Paul speak: who stedfastly beholding him, and perceiving that he had faith to be healed,

Romans 3:3 For what if some did not believe? shall their unbelief make the faith of God without effect?

Romans 3:28 Therefore we conclude that a man is justified by faith without the deeds of the law.

Romans 4:5 But to him that worketh not, but believeth on him that justifieth the ungodly, his faith is counted for righteousness.

Romans 4:20 He staggered not at the promise of God through unbelief; but was strong in faith, giving glory to God;

Romans 9:32 Wherefore? Because they sought it not by faith, but as it were by the works of the law. For they stumbled at that stumblingstone;

Romans 10:17 So then faith cometh by hearing, and hearing by the word of God.

Romans 4:13 For the promise, that he should be the heir of the world, was not to Abraham, or to his seed, through the law, but through the righteousness of faith. 14 For if they which are of the law be heirs, faith is made void, and the promise made of none effect:

Romans 14:23 And he that doubteth is damned if he eat, because he eateth not of faith: for whatsoever is not of faith is sin.

1 Corinthians 2:5 That your faith should not stand in the wisdom of men, but in the power of God.

1 Corinthians 15:14 And if Christ be not risen, then is our preaching vain, and your faith is also vain.

1 Corinthians 15:17 And if Christ be not raised, your faith is vain; ye are yet in your sins.

2 Corinthians 13:5 Examine yourselves, whether ye be in the faith; prove your own selves. Know ye not your own selves, how that Jesus Christ is in you, except ye be reprobates?

Galatians 2:16 Knowing that a man is not justified by the works of the law, but by the faith of Jesus Christ, even we have believed in Jesus Christ, that we might be justified by the faith of Christ, and not by the works of the law: for by the works of the law shall no flesh be justified.

Galatians 3:2 This only would I learn of you, Received ye the Spirit by the works of the law, or by the hearing of faith?

Galatians 3:5 He therefore that ministereth to you the Spirit, and worketh miracles among you, doeth he it by the works of the law, or by the hearing of faith?

Galatians 3:7 Know ye therefore that they which are of faith, the same are the children of Abraham.

Galatians 3:11 But that no man is justified by the law in the sight of God, it is evident: for, The just shall live by faith. 12 And the law is not of faith: but, The man that doeth them shall live in them.

Galatians 3:22 But the scripture hath concluded all under sin, that the promise by faith of Jesus Christ might be given to them that believe. 23 But before faith came, we were kept under the law, shut up unto the faith which should afterwards be revealed. 24

The Doctrines of Men

Wherefore the law was our schoolmaster to bring us unto Christ, that we might be justified by faith. 25 But after that faith is come, we are no longer under a schoolmaster.

Galatians 3:26 For ye are all the children of God by faith in Christ Jesus.

Galatians 5:5 For we through the Spirit wait for the hope of righteousness by faith. 6 For in Jesus Christ neither circumcision availeth any thing, nor uncircumcision; but faith which worketh by love.

Galatians 5:22 But the fruit of the Spirit is love, joy, peace, longsuffering, gentleness, goodness, faith,

Ephesians 2:8 For by grace are ye saved through faith; and that not of yourselves: it is the gift of God:

Ephesians 3:12 In whom we have boldness and access with confidence by the faith of him.

Ephesians 3:17 That Christ may dwell in your hearts by faith; that ye, being rooted and grounded in love,

Ephesians 6:23 Peace be to the brethren, and love with faith, from God the Father and the Lord Jesus Christ.

Philippians 3:9 And be found in him, not having mine own righteousness, which is of the law, but that which is through the faith of Christ, the righteousness which is of God by faith:

Colossians 1:4 Since we heard of your faith in Christ Jesus, and of the love which ye have to all the saints,

2 Thessalonians 1:11 Wherefore also we pray always for you, that our God would count you worthy of this calling, and fulfil all the good pleasure of his goodness, and the work of faith with power:

1 Timothy 1:14 And the grace of our Lord was exceeding abundant with faith and love which is in Christ Jesus.

1 Timothy 4:1 Now the Spirit speaketh expressly, that in the latter times some shall depart from the faith, giving heed to seducing spirits, and doctrines of devils;

Hebrews 11:1 Now faith is the substance of things hoped for, the evidence of things not seen.

Hebrews 11:3 Through faith we understand that the worlds were framed by the word of God, so that things which are seen were not made of things which do appear.

Hebrews 11:6 But without faith it is impossible to please him: for he that cometh to God must believe that he is, and that he is a rewarder of them that diligently seek him. 7 By faith Noah, being warned of God of things not seen as yet, moved with fear, prepared an ark to the saving of his house; by the which he condemned the world, and became heir of the righteousness which is by faith. 8 By faith Abraham, when he was called to go out into a place which he should after receive for an inheritance, obeyed; and he went out, not knowing whither he went. 9 By faith he sojourned in the land of promise, as in a strange country, dwelling in tabernacles with Isaac and Jacob, the heirs with him of the same promise:

Hebrews 11:13 These all died in faith, not having received the promises, but having seen them afar off, and were persuaded of them, and embraced them, and confessed that they were strangers and pilgrims on the earth.

Hebrews 11:33 Who through faith subdued kingdoms, wrought righteousness, obtained promises, stopped the mouths of lions.

James 5:15 And the prayer of faith shall save the sick, and the Lord shall raise him up; and if he have committed sins, they shall be forgiven him.

Appendix O - Power

Matthew 9:6 But that ye may know that the Son of man hath power on earth to forgive sins, (then saith he to the sick of the palsy,) Arise, take up thy bed, and go unto thine house.

Matthew 9:8 But when the multitudes saw it, they marvelled, and glorified God, which had given such power unto men.

Matthew 10:1 And when he had called unto him his twelve disciples, he gave them power against unclean spirits, to cast them out, and to heal all manner of sickness and all manner of disease.

Matthew 22:29 Jesus answered and said unto them, Ye do err, not knowing the scriptures, nor the power of God.

Matthew 28:18 And Jesus came and spake unto them, saying, All power is given unto me in heaven and in earth.

Mark 3:14 And he ordained twelve, that they should be with him, and that he might send them forth to preach, 15 And to have power to heal sicknesses, and to cast out devils:

Mark 6:7 And he called unto him the twelve, and began to send them forth by two and two; and gave them power over unclean spirits;

Luke 9:1 Then he called his twelve disciples together, and gave them power and authority over all devils, and to cure diseases.

Luke 9:43 And they were all amazed at the mighty power of God. But while they wondered every one at all things which Jesus did, he said unto his disciples,

Luke 24:49 And, behold, I send the promise of my Father upon you: but tarry ye in the city of Jerusalem, until ye be endued with power from on high.

John 1:12 But as many as received him, to them gave he power to become the sons of God, even to them that believe on his name:

Acts 1:8 But ye shall receive power, after that the Holy Ghost is come upon you: and ye shall be witnesses unto me both in Jerusalem, and in all Judaea, and in Samaria, and unto the uttermost part of the earth.

Acts 4:33 And with great power gave the apostles witness of the resurrection of the Lord Jesus: and great grace was upon them all.

Acts 6:8 And Stephen, full of faith and power, did great wonders and miracles among the people.

Romans 1:16 For I am not ashamed of the gospel of Christ: for it is the power of God unto salvation to every one that believeth; to the Jew first, and also to the Greek.

Romans 13:1 Let every soul be subject unto the higher powers. For there is no power but of God: the powers that be are ordained of God.

Romans 15:18 For I will not dare to speak of any of those things which Christ hath not wrought by me, to make the Gentiles obedient, by word and deed, 19 Through mighty signs and wonders, by the power of the Spirit of God; so that from Jerusalem, and round about unto Illyricum, I have fully preached the gospel of Christ.

I Corinthians 4:20 For the kingdom of God is not in word, but in power.

Ephesians 3:20 Now unto him that is able to do exceeding abundantly above all that we ask or think, according to the power that worketh in us,

Ephesians 6:10 Finally, my brethren, be strong in the Lord, and in the power of his might.

Colossians 1:11 Strengthened with all might, according to his glorious power, unto all patience and longsuffering with joyfulness;

Colossians 2:10 And ye are complete in him, which is the head of all principality and power:

I Thessalonians 1:5 For our gospel came not unto you in word only, but also in power, and in the Holy Ghost, and in much assurance; as ye know what manner of men we were among you for your sake.

II Timothy 1:7 For God hath not given us the spirit of fear; but of power, and of love, and of a sound mind.

I Peter 1:5 Who are kept by the power of God through faith unto salvation ready to be revealed in the last time.

Revelation 2:26 And he that overcometh, and keepeth my works unto the end, to him will I give power over the nations:

Revelation 11:3 And I will give power unto my two witnesses, and they shall prophesy a thousand two hundred and threescore days, clothed in sackcloth. 4 These are the two olive trees, and the two candlesticks standing before the God of the earth. 5 And if any man will hurt them, fire proceedeth out of their mouth, and devoureth their enemies: and if any man will hurt them, he must in this manner be killed. 6 These have power to shut heaven, that it rain not in the days of their prophecy: and have power over waters to turn them to blood, and to smite the earth with all plagues, as often as they will.

Appendix P - Women in the Bible

Abigail ("good") Abigail was the wife of Nabal. The following verses show that Abigail was an assertive, brave, and highly intelligent woman who was not afraid to take responsibility, no matter the consequences. Most importantly, Abagail had an unbreakable faith in God. 1 Sam 25:14 But one of the young men told Abigail, Nabal's wife, saying, Behold, David sent messengers out of the wilderness to salute our master; and he railed on them. 15 But the men were very good unto us, and we were not hurt, neither missed we any thing, as long as we were conversant with them, when we were in the fields: 16 They were a wall unto us both by night and day, all the while we were with them keeping the sheep. 17 Now therefore know and consider what thou wilt do; for evil is determined against our master, and against all his household: for he is such a son of Belial, that a man cannot speak to him. 18 Then Abigail made haste, and took two hundred loaves, and two bottles of wine, and five sheep ready dressed, and five measures of parched corn, and an hundred clusters of raisins, and two hundred cakes of figs, and laid them on asses. 19 And she said unto her servants, Go on before me; behold, I come after you. But she told not her husband Nabal. 20 And it was so, as she rode on the ass, that she came down by the covert on the hill, and, behold, David and his men came down against her; and she met them. 21 Now David had said, Surely in vain have I kept all that this fellow hath in the wilderness, so that nothing was missed of all that pertained unto him: and he hath requited me evil for good. 22 So and more also do God unto the enemies of David, if I leave of all that pertain to him by the morning light any that pisseth against the wall. 23 And when Abigail saw David, she hasted, and lighted off the ass, and fell before David on her face, and bowed herself to the ground, 24 And fell at his feet, and said, Upon me, my lord, upon me let this iniquity be: and let thine handmaid, I pray thee, speak in thine audience, and hear the words of thine handmaid. 25 Let not my lord, I pray thee, regard this man of Belial, even Nabal: for as his name is, so is he; Nabal is his name, and folly is with him: but I thine handmaid saw not the young men of my lord, whom thou didst send. 26 Now therefore, my lord, as the LORD liveth, and as thy soul liveth, seeing the LORD hath withholden thee from coming to shed blood, and from avenging thyself with thine own hand, now let thine enemies, and they that seek evil to my lord, be as Nabal. 27 And now this blessing which thine handmaid hath brought unto my lord, let it even be given unto the young men that follow my lord. 28 I pray thee, forgive the trespass of thine handmaid: for the LORD will certainly make my lord a sure house; because my lord fighteth the battles of the LORD, and evil hath not been found in thee all thy days.29 Yet a man is risen to pursue thee, and to seek thy soul: but the soul of my lord shall be bound in the bundle of life with the LORD thy God; and the souls of thine enemies, them shall he sling out, as out of the middle of a sling. 30 And it shall come to pass, when the LORD shall have done to my lord according to all the good that he hath spoken concerning thee, and shall have appointed thee ruler over Israel; 31 That this shall be no grief unto thee, nor offence of heart unto my lord, either that thou hast shed blood causeless, or that my lord hath avenged himself: but when the LORD shall have dealt well with my lord, then remember thine handmaid. 32 And David said to Abigail, Blessed be the LORD God of Israel, which sent thee this day to meet me: 33 And blessed be thy advice, and blessed be thou, which hast kept me this day from coming to shed blood, and from avenging myself with mine own hand.

Anna ("grace") Anna was the daughter of Phanuel of the tribe of Asher. She was the first to acclaim Christ as the Savior. She served in the Temple at Jerusalem and served God with fasting and prayer day and night. Anna is one of the thirteen prophetesses in the Bible. The following verses attest to Anna's character and her bravery. **Luke 2:36** And there was one Anna, a prophetess, the daughter of Phanuel, of the tribe of Aser: she was of a great age, and had lived with an husband seven years from her virginity; 37 And she was a widow of about fourscore and four years, which departed not from the temple, but served God with fastings and prayers night and day. 38 And she coming in that instant gave thanks likewise unto the Lord, and spake of him to all them that looked for redemption in Jerusalem.

Chloe ("a tender shoot") Chloe was a prominent woman of Corinth. She and her household told Paul of the divisions in the congregation of Corinth. 1 Corinthians 1:11 For it hath been declared unto me of you, my brethren, by them which are of the house of Chloe, that there are contentions among you

Claudia ("lame") Wife of the Roman knight, Pudens, Claudia was a disciple in the Christian Church in Rome. She was a close friend of Paul. She is thought to be the mother of Linus. 2 Timothy 4:21 Do thy diligence to come before winter. Eubulus greeteth thee, and Pudens, and Linus, and Claudia, and all the brethren.

Damarias ("heifer") Damarias was from Athens. Greek women lived in seclusion, so it is believed that she was a member of the Hetairai which was an intellectual class of women that were associates of philosophers and statesmen. They were the only free women in Athens. Acts 17:34 Howbeit certain men clave unto him, and believed: among the which was Dionysius the Areopagite, and a woman named Damaris, and others with them.

Deborah ("bee") Deborah was one of the thirteen prophetesses in the Bible. She was a judge of Israel, a poetess, and a military leader. She was the only woman judge in Israel in the Ephrim territory. She gave council and had more faith than most Israelite men. General Barak summoned the tribes to Mt. Tabor at her direction. He refused to go without her showing how much he valued her insight and bravery. Deborah was instrumental in delivering her people from Jabin and Sisera. This ended 20 years of Canaanite oppression. Judges 4:4 And Deborah, a prophetess, the wife of Lapidoth, she judged Israel at that time. 5 And she dwelt under the palm tree of Deborah between Ramah and Bethel in mount Ephraim: and the children of Israel came up to her for judgment. 6 And she sent and called Barak the son of Abinoam out of Kedeshnaphtali, and said unto him, Hath not the LORD God of Israel commanded, saying, Go and draw toward mount Tabor, and take with thee ten thousand men of the children of Naphtali and of the children of Zebulun? 7 And I will draw unto thee to the river Kishon Sisera, the captain of Jabin's army, with his chariots and his multitude; and I will deliver him into thine hand. 8 And Barak said unto her, If thou wilt go with me, then I will go: but if thou wilt not go with me, then I will not go.9 And she said, I will surely go with thee: notwithstanding the journey that thou takest shall not be for thine honour; for the LORD shall sell Sisera into the hand of a woman. And Deborah arose, and went with Barak to Kedesh. 10 And Barak called Zebulun and Naphtali to Kedesh; and he went up with ten thousand men at his feet: and Deborah went up with him. 11 Now Heber the Kenite, which was of the children of Hobab the father in law of Moses, had severed himself from the Kenites, and pitched his tent unto the plain of Zaanaim, which is by Kedesh. 12 And they shewed Sisera that Barak the son of Abinoam was gone up to mount Tabor.13 And Sisera gathered together all his chariots, even nine hundred chariots of iron, and all the people that were with him, from Harosheth of the Gentiles unto the river of Kishon. 14 And Deborah said unto Barak, Up; for this is the day in which the LORD hath delivered Sisera into thine hand: is not the LORD gone out before thee? So Barak went down from mount Tabor, and ten thousand men after him. 15 And the LORD discomfited Sisera, and all his chariots, and all his host, with the edge of the sword before Barak; so that Sisera lighted down off his chariot, and fled away on his feet.

Elisabeth/Elizabeth ("my God is my oath") Elisabeth was the wife of Zacharias and the mother of John the Baptist. She was descended from a family of priests. Elisabeth was barren until the angel Gabriel appeared to her husband Zacharias and told him that God was blessing them with a son. She was the first to greet Mary as "the Mother of our Lord". Luke 1:5 There was in the days of Herod, the king of Judaea, a certain priest named Zacharias, of the course of Abia: and his wife was of the daughters of Aaron, and her name was Elisabeth. 6 and they were both righteous before God, walking in all the commandments and ordinances of the Lord blameless. 7 And they had no child, because that Elisabeth was barren, and they both were now well stricken in years. 1:11 And there appeared unto him an angel of the Lord standing on the right side of the altar of incense.12 And when Zacharias saw him, he was troubled, and fear fell upon him.

13 But the angel said unto him, Fear not, Zacharias: for thy prayer is heard; and thy wife Elisabeth shall bear thee a son, and thou shalt call his name John. 14 And thou shalt have joy and gladness; and many shall rejoice at his birth. 15 For he shall be great in the sight of the Lord, and shall drink neither wine nor strong drink; and he shall be filled with the Holy Ghost, even from his mother's womb. 16 And many of the children of Israel shall he turn to the Lord their God. 1:36 And, behold, thy cousin Elisabeth, she hath also conceived a son in her old age: and this is the sixth month with her, who was called barren. 1:39 And Mary arose in those days, and went into the hill country with haste, into a city of Juda; 40 And entered into the house of Zacharias, and saluted Elisabeth. 41 And it came to pass, that, when Elisabeth heard the salutation of Mary, the babe leaped in her womb; and Elisabeth was filled with the Holy Ghost: 42 And she spake out with a loud voice, and said, Blessed art thou among women, and blessed is the fruit of thy womb. 43 And whence is this to me, that the mother of my Lord should come to me?

Esther ("star") Esther was the daughter of Abihail and wife of Ahasuerus. Esther is one of only two books in the Bible bearing a woman's name. Ester became queen of one of the most powerful world empires. She saved the Persian Jews from a massacre by Haman and had it written into law that Jews could defend themselves and slay their enemies. She was a courageous and brilliant woman. The verses below show her courage when she went in before the King to plead her people's case. Esther 4:5 Then called Esther for Hatach, one of the king's chamberlains, whom he had appointed to attend upon her, and gave him a commandment to Mordecai, to know what it was, and why it was. 6 So Hatach went forth to Mordecai unto the street of the city, which was before the king's gate. 7 And Mordecai told him of all that had happened unto him, and of the sum of the money that Haman had promised to pay to the king's treasuries for the Jews, to destroy them. 8 Also he gave him the copy of the writing of the decree that was given at Shushan to destroy them, to shew it unto Esther, and to declare it unto her, and to charge her that she should go in unto the king, to make supplication unto him, and to make request before him for her people. 9 And Hatach came and told Esther the words of Mordecai. 10 Again Esther spake unto Hatach, and gave him commandment unto Mordecai; 11 All the king's servants, and the people of the king's provinces, do know, that whosoever, whether man or women, shall come unto the king into the inner court, who is not called, there is one law of his to put him to death, except such to whom the king shall hold out the golden sceptre, that he may live: but I have not been called to come in unto the king these thirty days. 12 And they told to Mordecai Esther's words. 13 Then Mordecai commanded to answer Esther, Think not with thyself that thou shalt escape in the king's house, more than all the Jews. 14 For if thou altogether holdest thy peace at this time, then shall there enlargement and deliverance arise to the Jews from another place; but thou and thy father's house shall be destroyed: and who knoweth whether thou art come to the kingdom for such a time as this? 15 Then Esther bade them return Mordecai this answer, 16 Go, gather together all the Jews that are present in Shushan, and fast ye for me, and neither eat nor drink three days, night or day: I also and my maidens will fast likewise; and so will I go in unto the king, which is not according to the law: and if I perish, I perish. 17 So Mordecai went his way, and did according to all that Esther had commanded him.

Euodia ("fragrant") Euodia was a Christian at Philippi, where women first heard the

Gospel. She was possibly a deaconess or a prominent member of the congregation. Philippians 4:1 Therefore, my brethren dearly beloved and longed for, my joy and crown, so stand fast in the Lord, my dearly beloved. 2 I beseech Euodias, and beseech Syntyche, that they be of the same mind in the Lord. 3 And I intreat thee also, true yokefellow, help those women which laboured with me in the gospel, with Clement also, and with other my fellowlabourers, whose names are in the book of life.

Eunice ("victorious") Eunice was the mother of Timothy. She was praised for her faith by Paul in his second letter to Timothy. ♦ 2 Timothy 1:4 Greatly desiring to see thee, being mindful of thy tears, that I may be filled with joy; 5 When I call to remembrance the unfeigned faith that is in thee, which dwelt first in thy grandmother Lois, and thy mother Eunice; and I am persuaded that in thee also.

Eve ("life; life-giving") Eve is the first woman mentioned in Genesis. She was the first woman, wife, mother, and the first to be deceived, beguiled, and tempted. Genesis 3:13 And the LORD God said unto the woman, What is this that thou hast done? And the woman said, The serpent beguiled me, and I did eat. 3:20 And Adam called his wife's name Eve; because she was the mother of all living. 4:1 And Adam knew Eve his wife; and she conceived, and bare Cain, and said, I have gotten a man from the LORD

Hannah ("grace") Hannah was one of the thirteen prophetesses and one of the barren women in the Bible. Samuel, her son, was the earliest of the great prophets and the last judge of Israel. 1 Samuel 1:4 And he had two wives; the name of the one was Hannah, and the name of the other Peninnah: and Peninnah had children, but Hannah had no children. 5 But unto Hannah he gave a worthy portion; for he loved Hannah: but the LORD had shut up her womb. 1:19 And they rose up in the morning early, and worshipped before the LORD, and returned, and came to their house to Ramah: and Elkanah knew Hannah his wife; and the LORD remembered her. 20 Wherefore it came to pass, when the time was come about after Hannah had conceived, that she bare a son, and called his name Samuel, saying, Because I have asked him of the LORD.

Isaiah's Wife She was one of the thirteen prophetesses in the Bible and the mother of Mahershalalhashbaz. Isaiah 8:3 And I went unto the prophetess; and she conceived, and bare a son. Then said the LORD to me, Call his name Mahershalalhashbaz.

Jael ("a wild mountain goat") Jael was a brave but treacherous woman. In the war between the Canaanites and Israelites, she proved her bravery and loyalty to God's people by giving false comfort to Sisera, the Canaanite. Her hospitality towards Sisera gave him a false sense of security and he willingly went to her tent where she gave him milk to drink. He felt safe and fell asleep in her tent. While Sisera was sleeping, Jael took a large nail and drove it into his temple, killing him. Thus, Jael become a heroine of the Israelites. Judges 4:18 And Jael went out to meet Sisera, and said unto him, Turn in, my lord, turn in to me; fear not. And when he had turned in unto her into the tent, she covered him with a mantle. 19 And he said unto her, Give me, I pray thee, a little water to drink; for I am thirsty. And she opened a bottle of milk, and gave him drink, and covered him. 20 Again he said unto her, Stand in the door of the tent, and it shall be, when any man doth come and enquire of thee, and say, Is there any man here? that thou shalt say, No. 21 Then Jael Heber's wife took a nail of the tent, and took an hammer in her hand, and went softly unto him, and smote the nail into his temples, and fastened it into the ground: for he was fast asleep and weary. So he died. 22 And, behold, as Barak pursued Sisera, Jael came out to meet him, and said unto him, Come, and I will shew thee the man whom thou seekest. And when he came into her tent, behold, Sisera lay dead, and the nail was in his temples. 23 So God subdued on that day Jabin the king of Canaan before the children of Israel.

Jehoshabeath / Jehosheba ("Jehovah has sworn") Jehoshabeath was the daughter of Jehoram/Joram and the granddaughter of Jehoshaphat. She was a brave, resourceful, and courageous woman that helped conceal Joash from Athaliah for six years. 2 Kings 11:2 But Jehosheba, the daughter of king Joram, sister of Ahaziah, took Joash the son of Ahaziah, and stole him from among the king's sons which were slain; and they hid him, even him and his nurse, in the bedchamber from Athaliah, so that he was not slain. 2 Chronicles 22:11 But Jehoshabeath, the daughter of the king, took Joash the son of Ahaziah, and stole him from among the king's sons that were slain, and put him and his nurse in a bedchamber. So Jehoshabeath, the daughter of king Jehoram, the wife of Jehoiada the priest, (for she was the sister of Ahaziah,) hid him from Athaliah, so that she slew him not.

Joanna ("Jehovah has graciously given") Joanna was a women that was healed by and later ministered to Jesus and his disciples. She was among the women who went to the tomb to embalm Jesus' body and afterwards told the apostles that Christ had risen. Luke 8:1 And it came to pass afterward, that he went throughout every city and village, preaching and shewing the glad tidings of the kingdom of God: and the twelve were with him, 2 And certain women, which had been healed of evil spirits and infirmities, Mary called Magdalene, out of whom went seven devils, 3 And Joanna the wife of Chuza Herod's steward, and Susanna, and many others, which ministered unto him of their substance. Luke 24:9 And returned from the sepulchre, and told all these things unto the eleven, and to all the rest. 10 It was Mary Magdalene and Joanna, and Mary the mother of James, and other women that were with them, which told these things unto the apostles.

Jochebed ("whose glory is Jehovah") Jochebed had two sons, Aaron and Moses, and one daughter, Miriam. Jochebed's son Aaron, became the founder of the Hebrew priesthood. It was Jochebed who hid her son Moses from Pharaoh by placing him in a watertight cradle and placing it in the Nile River where Pharaoh's daughter found it. Pharaoh's daughter hired a Hebrew woman to nurse the infant and that woman was Jochebed, Moses own mother. Exodus 6:20 And Amram took him Jochebed his father's sister to wife; and she bare him Aaron and Moses: and the years of the life of Amram were an hundred and thirty and seven years. Numbers 26:59 And the name of Amram's wife was Jochebed, the daughter of Levi, whom her mother bare to Levi in Egypt: and she bare unto Amram Aaron and Moses, and Miriam their sister.

Julia ("soft-haired") Julia was a Christian woman at Rome. Paul saluted her in his Epistle. Romans 16:15 Salute Philologus, and Julia, Nereus, and his sister, and Olympas, and all the saints which are with them.

Lois ("pleasing, better") The pious women Lois was mother of Eunice and the grandmother of Timothy. Timothy 1:5 When I call to remembrance the unfeigned faith that is in thee, which dwelt first in thy grandmother Lois, and thy mother Eunice; and I am persuaded that in thee also.

Lydia ("which worshipped God") Lydia accepted Paul's teaching, was baptized and became the first Christian convert of Thyatira. She lived in Philippi and was a seller of purple dye. Acts 16:14 And a certain woman named Lydia, a seller of purple, of the city of Thyatira, which worshipped God, heard us: whose heart the Lord opened, that she attended unto the things which were spoken of Paul. 15 And when she was baptized, and her household, she besought us, saying, If ye have judged me to be faithful to the Lord, come into my house, and abide there. And she constrained us. Acts 16:40 And they went out of the prison, and entered into the house of Lydia: and when they had seen the brethren, they comforted them, and departed.

Martha ("lady") Martha was the sister of Mary and Lazarus. Jesus first declared "I am the resurrection, and the life." to the woman, Martha. Luke 10: 38 Now it came to pass, as they went, that he entered into a certain village: and a certain woman named Martha received him into her house. 39 And she had a sister called Mary, which also sat at Jesus' feet, and heard his word. John 11:5 Now Jesus loved Martha, and her sister, and Lazarus. 11:23 Jesus saith unto her, Thy brother shall rise again. 24 Martha saith unto him, I know that he shall rise again in the resurrection at the last day. 25 Jesus said unto her, I am the resurrection, and the life: he that believeth in me, though he were dead, yet shall he live: 26 And whosoever liveth and believeth in me shall never die. Believest thou this? 27 She saith unto him, Yea, Lord: I believe that thou art the Christ, the Son of God, which should come into the world.

Mary ("strong") Mary was the daughter of Joachim and Anna and the wife of Joseph. She was the mother of Jesus Christ, James, Joses, Juda, Simeon - and daughters who's names are not known. Her son James, was the author of the Epistle James and son Juda, of the Epistle Jude. Mary was present at the crucifixion of her son, Jesus Christ, and was with those that were gathered in prayer after his ascension to Heaven. Mary was humble, obedient, and devoted to God. Isaiah 7:14 Therefore the Lord himself shall give you a sign; Behold, a virgin shall conceive, and bear a son, and shall call his name Immanuel. Matthew 1:16 And Jacob begat Joseph the husband of Mary, of whom was born Jesus, who is called Christ Matthew 13: 55 Is not this the carpenter's son? is not his mother called Mary? and his brethren, James, and Joses, and Simon, and Judas? 56 And his sisters, are they not all with us? Whence then hath this man all these things? Mark 6:3 Is not this the carpenter, the son of Mary, the brother of James, and Joses, and of Juda, and Simon? and are not his sisters here with us? And they were offended at him. Luke 1:46 And Mary said, My soul doth magnify the Lord, 47 And my spirit hath rejoiced in God my Saviour. 48 For he hath regarded the low estate of his handmaiden: for, behold, from henceforth all generations shall call me blessed. 49 For he that is mighty hath done to me great things; and holy is his name.

Mary ("strong") Mary was the mother of John Mark/Marcus and the aunt of Barnabas. She was one of the earliest followers of Christ. Peter came to her home after his escape from prison. Acts 12:11 And when Peter was come to himself, he said, Now I know of a surety, that the LORD hath sent his angel, and hath delivered me out of the hand of Herod, and from all the expectation of the people of the Jews. 12 And when he had considered the thing, he came to the house of Mary the mother of John, whose surname was Mark; where many were gathered together praying.

Mary ("strong") Mary was a Roman Christian and a deaconess in the congregation. She was one of the twenty-four people to whom Paul sent special greetings. Romans 16:5 Likewise greet the church that is in their house. Salute my well-beloved Epaenetus, who is the firstfruits of Achaia unto Christ. 6 Greet Mary, who bestowed much labour on us.

Mary ("strong") Mary was the sister of Martha and Lazarus. Mary anointed Jesus with oil, wept with Jesus and rebuked him about Lazarus' death. She was praised by Jesus for choosing the best part. Matthew 26:7 There came unto him a woman having an alabaster box of very precious ointment, and poured it on his head, as he sat at meat. 8 But when his disciples saw it, they had indignation, saying, To what purpose is this waste? 9 For this ointment might have been sold for much, and given to the poor. 10 When Jesus understood it, he said unto them, Why trouble ye the woman? for she hath wrought a good work upon me. 11 For ye have the poor always with you; but me ye have not always. 12 For in that she hath poured this ointment on my body, she did it for my burial. 13 Verily I say unto you, Wheresoever this gospel shall be preached in the whole world, there shall also this, that this woman hath done, be told for a memorial of her. Luke 10:38 Now it came to pass, as they went, that he entered into a certain village: and a certain woman named Martha received him into her house. 39 And she had a sister called Mary, which also sat at Jesus' feet, and heard his word. 40 But Martha was cumbered about much serving, and came to him, and said, Lord, dost thou not care that my sister hath left me to serve alone? bid her therefore that she help me. 41 And Jesus answered and said unto her, Martha, Martha, thou art careful and troubled about many things: 42 But one thing is needful: and Mary hath chosen that good part, which shall not be taken away from her.

Mary Magdala / Magdalene Saved by Jesus from "seven devils", Mary Magdalene then became a faithful follower of Christ. She ministered to Jesus, was present at his crucifixion, was watching as he was entombed, and she was the first person to see Jesus after his resurrection. Matthew 27:55 And many women were there beholding afar off, which followed Jesus from Galilee, ministering unto him: 56 Among which was Mary Magdalene, and Mary the mother of James and Joses, and the mother of Zebedees children. 28:1 In the end of the sabbath, as it began to dawn toward the first day of the week, came Mary Magdalene and the other Mary to see the sepulchre. **Mark 16:1** And when the sabbath was past, Mary Magdalene, and Mary the mother of James, and Salome, had bought sweet spices, that they might come and anoint him. 2 And very early in the morning the first day of the week, they came unto the sepulchre at the rising of the sun. 3 And they said among themselves, Who shall roll us away the stone from the door of the sepulchre? 4 And when they looked, they saw that the stone was rolled away: for it was very great. 5 And entering into the sepulchre, they saw a young man sitting on the right side, clothed in a long white garment; and they were affrighted. 6 And he saith unto them, Be not affrighted: Ye seek Jesus of Nazareth, which was crucified: he is risen; he is not here: behold the place where they laid him. 7 But go your way, tell his disciples and Peter that he goeth before you into Galilee: there shall ye see him, as he said unto you. 8 And they went out quickly, and fled from the sepulchre; for they trembled and were amazed: neither said they any thing to any man; for they were afraid. 9 Now when Jesus was risen early the first day of the week, he appeared first to Mary Magdalene, out of whom he had cast seven devils. 10 And she went and told them that had been with him, as they mourned and wept. John 19:25 Now there stood by the cross of Jesus his mother, and his mother's sister, Mary the wife of Cleophas, and Mary Magdalene. 20:1 The first day of the week cometh Mary Magdalene early, when it was yet dark, unto the sepulchre, and seeth the stone taken away from the sepulchre. 2 Then she runneth, and cometh to Simon Peter, and to the other disciple, whom Jesus loved, and saith unto them, They have taken away the LORD out of the sepulchre, and we know not where they have laid him. 20:11 But Mary stood without at the sepulchre weeping: and as she wept, she stooped down, and looked into the sepulchre, 12 And seeth two angels in white sitting, the one at the head, and the other at the feet, where the body of Jesus had lain. 13 And they say unto her, Woman, why weepest thou? She saith unto them, Because they have taken away my LORD, and I know not where they have laid him. 14 And when she had thus said, she turned herself back, and saw Jesus standing, and knew not that it was Jesus. 15 Jesus saith unto her, Woman, why weepest thou? whom seekest thou? She, supposing him to be the gardener, saith unto him, Sir, if thou have borne him hence, tell me where thou hast laid him, and I will take him away. 16 Jesus saith unto her, Mary. She turned herself, and saith unto him, Rabboni; which is to say, Master. 17 Jesus saith unto her, Touch me not; for I am not yet ascended to my Father: but go to my brethren, and say unto them, I ascend unto my Father, and your Father; and to my God, and your God. 18 Mary Magdalene came and told the disciples that she had seen the LORD, and that he had spoken these things unto her.

Miriam ("strong") Miriam, the sister of Moses and Aaron, was one of the thirteen prophetesses. She was the first woman singer mentioned in the Bible.When Moses was put into the Nile, she guarded his cradle until Pharoah's daughter found the child. Miriam was struck with leprosy for rebuking Moses about his wife, Zipporah, but later was cured by Moses. She was a woman that proved that spiritual leadership was not reserved for men only. Exodus 2:4 And his sister stood afar off, to wit what would be done to him. **5** And the daughter of Pharaoh came down to wash herself at the river; and her maidens walked along by the river's side; and when she saw the ark among the flags, she sent her maid to fetch it. 2:20 And Miriam the prophetess, the sister of Aaron, took a timbrel in her hand; and all the women went out after her with timbrels and with dances. 21 And Miriam answered them, Sing ye to the LORD, for he hath triumphed gloriously; the horse and his rider hath he thrown into the sea.

Phebe/ Phoebe ("shining, bright") Phebe was a deaconess of the church at Cenchreae. Paul sent salutations to her. It is believed she is the women who carried Paul's letters to the Romans. **Romans 16:1** I commend unto you Phebe our sister, which is a servant of the church which is at Cenchrea: 2 That ye receive her in the Lord, as becometh saints, and that ye assist her in whatsoever business she hath need of you: for she hath been a succourer of many, and of myself also.

Prisca / Priscilla ("simplicity") Priscilla was the wife of Aquila. Together they ministered together as a team from their home showing that the ministry of women was readily accepted. Acts 18:2 And found a certain Jew named Aquila, born in Pontus, lately come from Italy, with his wife Priscilla; (because that Claudius had commanded all Jews to depart from Rome:) and came unto them. Acts 18:18 And Paul after this tarried there yet a good while, and then took his leave of the brethren, and sailed thence into Syria, and with him Priscilla and Aquila; having shorn his head in Cenchrea: for he had a vow. Acts 18:26 And he began to speak boldly in the synagogue: whom when Aquila and Priscilla had heard, they took him unto them, and expounded unto him the way of God more perfectly. Romans 16: 3 Greet Priscilla and Aquila my helpers in Christ Jesus: 4 Who have for my life laid down their own necks: unto whom not only I give thanks, but also all the churches of the Gentiles.

Puah Puah was a midwife, in Egypt, in the time of Moses. She disregarded the Pharaoh's order to kill all newborn Hebrew male infants. Exodus 1:15 And the king of Egypt spake to the Hebrew midwives, of which the name of the one was Shiphrah, and the name of the other Puah: 16 And he said, When ye do the office of a midwife to the Hebrew women, and see them upon the stools; if it be a son, then ye shall kill him: but if it be a daughter, then she shall live. 17 But the midwives feared God, and did not as the king of Egypt commanded them, but saved the men children alive.

Rachab/Rahab ("spacious, broad") Rahab was a harlot and an ancestress of Christ who helped the two Hebrew spies Joshua sent to Jericho. For her loyalty to God, she and her household were saved when the Israelites took the city of Jericho. She and Sarah are the two faithful women mentioned in Hebrews. Rahab manufactured linens, provided for her family, and was courageous and brave. She is remembered as one of the greatest heroines of Israel. By her kind and courageous acts, Rahab demonstrated her deep and abiding faith in God. Joshua 2:1 And Joshua the son of Nun sent out of Shittim two men to spy secretly, saying, Go view the land, even Jericho. And they went, and came into an harlot's house, named Rahab, and lodged there. 2 And it was told the king of Jericho, saying, Behold, there came men in hither to night of the children of Israel to search out the country. 3 And the king of Jericho sent unto Rahab, saying, Bring forth the men that are come to thee, which are entered into thine house: for they be come to search out all the country. 6:17 And the city shall be accursed, even it, and all that are therein, to the LORD: only Rahab the harlot shall live, she and all that are with her in the house, because she hid the messengers that we sent. 6:23 And the young men that were spies went in, and brought out Rahab, and her father, and her mother, and her brethren, and all that she had; and they brought out all her kindred, and left them without the camp of Israel. 24 And they burnt the city with fire, and all that was therein: only the silver, and the gold, and the vessels of brass and of iron, they put into the treasury of the house of the LORD. 25 And Joshua saved Rahab the harlot alive, and her father's household, and all that she had; and she dwelleth in Israel even unto this day; because she hid the messengers, which Joshua sent to spy out Jericho.

Rachel ("ewe, sheep, lamb") Rachel was the daughter of Laban, wife of Jacob and the mother of Joseph and Benjamin. She was one of the barren women of the Bible who was blessed by God with the gift of children. Rachel was the fourth matriarch of the Jewish peoples and is considered the mother of the five northern tribes. Her sepulchral pillar is the first memorial on record. Genesis 1:9 And while he yet spake with them, Rachel came with her father's sheep; for she kept them. 10 And it came to pass, when Jacob saw Rachel the daughter of Laban his mother's brother, and the sheep of Laban his mother's brother, that Jacob went near, and rolled the stone from the well's mouth, and watered the flock of Laban his mother's brother. 11 And Jacob kissed Rachel, and lifted up his voice, and wept. 12 And Jacob told Rachel that he was her father's brother, and that he was Rebekah's son: and she ran and told her father. 30:1 And when Rachel saw that she bare Jacob no children, Rachel envied her sister; and said unto Jacob, Give me children, or else I die. 2 And Jacob's anger was kindled against Rachel: and he said, Am I in God's stead, who hath withheld from thee the fruit of the womb? 30:22 And God remembered Rachel, and God hearkened to her, and opened her womb. 23 And she conceived, and bare a son; and said, God hath taken away my reproach: 24 And she called his name Joseph; and said, The LORD shall add to me another son. 48:7 And as for me, when I came from Padan, Rachel died by me in the land of Canaan in the way, when yet there was but a little way to come unto Ephrath: and I buried her there in the way of Ephrath; the same is Bethlehem. 1 Samuel 10:2 When thou art departed from me to day, then thou shalt find two men by Rachel's sepulchre in the border of Benjamin at Zelzah; and they will say unto thee, The asses which thou wentest to seek are found: and, lo, thy father hath left the care of the asses, and sorroweth for you, saying, What shall I do for my son? Jeremiah 31: 15 Thus saith the LORD; A voice was heard in Ramah, lamentation, and bitter weeping; Rahel weeping for her children refused to be comforted for her children, because they were not. 16 Thus saith the LORD; Refrain thy voice from weeping, and thine eyes from tears: for thy work shall be rewarded, saith the LORD; and they shall come again from the land of the enemy.

Rebecca/Rebekah ("tying, captivating") Rebecca was the daughter of Bethuel, wife of Isaac and mother of Esau and Jacob. She was the first women in the Bible to have twins. She saved Jacob from Esau's jealous fury. Rebecca was modest, beautiful, intelligent, and deceitful. She is the second matriarch of the Jewish people. Rebecca was buried at Machpelah in the family tomb along with Sarah and Abraham. Genesis 22:23 And Bethuel begat Rebekah: these eight Milcah did bear to Nahor, Abraham's brother. 24:42 And I came this day unto the well, and said, O LORD God of my master Abraham, if now thou do prosper my way which I go: 43 Behold, I stand by the well of water; and it shall come to pass, that when the virgin cometh forth to draw water, and I say to her, Give me, I pray thee, a little water of thy pitcher to drink; 44 And she say to me, Both drink thou, and I will also draw for thy camels: let the same be the woman whom the LORD hath appointed out for my master's son. 45 And before I had done speaking in mine heart, behold, Rebekah came forth with her pitcher on her shoulder; and she went down unto the well, and drew water: and I said unto her, Let me drink, I pray thee. 46 And she made haste, and let down her pitcher from her shoulder, and said, Drink, and I will give thy camels drink also: so I drank, and she made the camels drink also. 47 And I asked her, and said, Whose daughter art thou? And she said, the daughter of Bethuel, Nahor's son, whom Milcah bare unto him: and I put the earring upon her face, and the bracelets upon her hands. 48 And I bowed down my head, and worshipped the LORD, and blessed the LORD God of my master Abraham, which had led me in the right way to take my master's brother's daughter unto his son. 49: 30 In the cave that is in the field of Machpelah, which is before Mamre, in the land of Canaan, which Abraham bought with the field of Ephron the Hittite for a possession of a buryingplace. 31 There they buried Abraham and Sarah his wife; there they buried Isaac and Rebekah his wife; and there I buried Leah.

Ruth ("friendship, companion") Ruth was the ancestress of Christ. She was a Moabite and the wife of Mahlon and the daughter-in-law of Naomi. After Mahlon's death, she married Boaz. Ruth is one of the two women that have books named after them in the Bible. Ruth 1:4 And they took them wives of the women of Moab; the name of the one was Orpah, and the name of the other Ruth: and they dwelled there about ten years. 5 And Mahlon and Chilion died also both of them; and the woman was left of her two sons and her husband. 1:14 And they lifted up their voice, and wept again: and Orpah kissed her mother in law; but Ruth clave unto her. 15 And she said,

Behold, thy sister in law is gone back unto her people, and unto her gods: return thou after thy sister in law. 16 And Ruth said, Intreat me not to leave thee, or to return from following after thee: for whither thou goest, I will go; and where thou lodgest, I will lodge: thy people shall be my people, and thy God my God: 4:10 Moreover Ruth the Moabitess, the wife of Mahlon, have I purchased to be my wife, to raise up the name of the dead upon his inheritance, that the name of the dead be not cut off from among his brethren, and from the gate of his place: ye are witnesses this day.

Salome ("clothed, whole, perfect") Salome was a disciple of Jesus and witnessed the crucifixion. She was the wife of Zebedee and mother of the Apostles James and John. Matthew 20:20 Then came to him the mother of Zebedees children with her sons, worshipping him, and desiring a certain thing of him. 21 And he said unto her, What wilt thou? She saith unto him, Grant that these my two sons may sit, the one on thy right hand, and the other on the left, in thy kingdom. 22 But Jesus answered and said, Ye know not what ye ask. Are ye able to drink of the cup that I shall drink of, and to be baptized with the baptism that I am baptized with? They say unto him, We are able. 23 And he saith unto them, Ye shall drink indeed of my cup, and be baptized with the baptism that I am baptized with: but to sit on my right hand, and on my left, is not mine to give, but it shall be given to them for whom it is prepared of my Father. 27: 55 And many women were there beholding afar off, which followed Jesus from Galilee, ministering unto him: 56 Among which was Mary Magdalene, and Mary the mother of James and Joses, and the mother of Zebedees children.

Sarah ("my princess") Sarah was the wife of Abraham, the mother of Isaac, and one of the barren women in the Bible. She was the first Matriarch of the Jewish people. She is buried in the family cave at Machpelah. Genesis 16:1 Now Sarai Abram's wife bare him no children: and she had an handmaid, an Egyptian, whose name was Hagar. Isaiah 51:1 Hearken to me, ye that follow after righteousness, ye that seek the LORD: look unto the rock whence ye are hewn, and to the hole of the pit whence ye are digged. 2 Look unto Abraham your father, and unto Sarah that bare you: for I called him alone, and blessed him, and increased him. Isaiah 4:19 And being not weak in faith, he considered not his own body now dead, when he was about an hundred years old, neither yet the deadness of Sarah's womb: 20 He staggered not at the promise of God through unbelief; but was strong in faith, giving glory to God; Hebrews 11:11 Through faith also Sara herself received strength to conceive seed, and was delivered of a child when she was past age, because she judged him faithful who had promised.

Shiphrah Shiphrah was a midwife who disregarded the Pharaoh's orders to kill all the newborn male infants of the Jews. She showed great courage and faith by not obeying Pharaoh's decree. Exodus 1:15 And the king of Egypt spake to the Hebrew midwives, of which the name of the one was Shiphrah, and the name of the other Puah: 16 And he said, When ye do the office of a midwife to the Hebrew women, and see them upon the stools; if it be a son, then ye shall kill him: but if it be a daughter, then she shall live. 17 But the midwives feared God, and did not as the king of Egypt commanded them, but saved the men children alive.

Susanna ("lily") Susanna was one of the women who ministered to Jesus and the disciples. Luke 8:3 And Joanna the wife of Chuza Herod's steward, and Susanna, and many others, which ministered unto him of their substance.

Syntyche ("fortunate") Syntyche was a woman of the church of Philippi that was encouraged by Paul. Phillipians 4:2 I beseech Euodias, and beseech Syntyche, that they be of the same mind in the Lord.

Tabitha ("gazelle") Tabitha was a Christian woman of Joppa and a disciple of Christ. She was raised from the dead by Peter. Acts 9:36 Now there was at Joppa a certain disciple named Tabitha, which by interpretation is called Dorcas: this woman was full of good works and almsdeeds which she did. 37 And it came to pass in those days, that she was sick, and died: whom when they had washed, they laid her in an upper chamber. 38 And forasmuch as Lydda was nigh to Joppa, and the disciples had heard that Peter was there, they sent unto him two men, desiring him that he would not delay to come to them. 39 Then Peter arose and went with them. When he was come, they brought him into the upper chamber: and all the widows stood by him weeping, and shewing the coats and garments which Dorcas made, while she was with them. 40 But Peter put them all forth, and kneeled down, and prayed; and turning him to the body said, Tabitha, arise. And she opened her eyes: and when she saw Peter, she sat up. 41 And he gave her his hand, and lifted her up, and when he had called the saints and widows, presented her alive.

Tryphena and Tryphosa Tryphena and Tryphosa were two Christian women of Rome to which Paul sent greetings. Romans 16:12 Salute Tryphena and Tryphosa, who labour in the Lord. Salute the beloved Persis, which laboured much in the Lord.

The Other Women

Bernice ("victorious") Bernice, the eldest daughter of Herod Agrippa I and Cypros, is one of the most shameless and immoral women of the Bible. She had incestuous relationships with both her uncle Herod and her brother, Agrippa ll. She was also the mistress of Vespasian and Titus, but when Titus became emperor he cast her off. Acts 25:13 And after certain days king Agrippa and Bernice came unto Caesarea to salute Festus. 25:23 And on the morrow, when Agrippa was come, and Bernice, with great pomp, and was entered into the place of hearing, with the chief captains, and principal men of the city, at Festus' commandment Paul was brought forth. 26:30 And when he had thus spoken, the king rose up, and the governor, and Bernice, and they that sat with them:

Cozbi ("deceitful") Cozbi was the daughter of Zur, Chief of the Midianites. She was one of the sinners put to death at the Israelite camp at Shittim. Moses gave orders to execute the chiefs and all those guilty of whoredoms in Baal-Peor. Cozbi had a javelin thrust through her stomach for her blatant disregard of the injunction against intimacies between the men of Israel and the Midianite and Moabite women. Numbers 25:15 And the name of the Midianitish woman that was slain was Cozbi, the daughter of Zur; he was head over a people, and of a chief house in Midian. 16 And the LORD spake unto Moses, saying, 17 Vex the Midianites, and smite them: 18 For they vex you with their wiles, wherewith they have beguiled you in the matter of Peor, and in the matter of Cozbi, the daughter of a prince of Midian, their sister, which was slain in the day of the plague for Peor's sake.

Delilah Delilah, a Philistine, was paid 1100 pieces of sliver to find out the secret of Samson's strength. Samson, dedicated as a Nazarite, was never to have his hair cut. His weakness for women was his undoing. Delilah discovered Samson's secret and while he was sleeping she cut his hair and delivered him into the hands of the Philistines. Judges 16: 4 And it came to pass afterward, that he loved a woman in the valley of

Sorek, whose name was Delilah. 5 And the lords of the Philistines came up unto her, and said unto her, Entice him, and see wherein his great strength lieth, and by what means we may prevail against him, that we may bind him to afflict him; and we will give thee every one of us eleven hundred pieces of silver. 16: 17 That he told her all his heart, and said unto her, There hath not come a razor upon mine head; for I have been a Nazarite unto God from my mother's womb: if I be shaven, then my strength will go from me, and I shall become weak, and be like any other man. 18 And when Delilah saw that he had told her all his heart, she sent and called for the lords of the Philistines, saying, Come up this once, for he hath shewed me all his heart. Then the lords of the Philistines came up unto her, and brought money in their hand. 19 And she made him sleep upon her knees; and she called for a man, and she caused him to shave off the seven locks of his head; and she began to afflict him, and his strength went from him. 20 And she said, The Philistines be upon thee, Samson. And he awoke out of his sleep, and said, I will go out as at other times before, and shake myself. And he wist not that the LORD was departed from him. 21 But the Philistines took him, and put out his eyes, and brought him down to Gaza, and bound him with fetters of brass; and he did grind in the prison house.

Gomer ("completeness; ripeness") Gomer, the harlot, was the daughter of Diblaim and the wife of Hosea. Gomer is considered a symbol of Israel's unfaithfulness to God. Hosea 1: 2 The beginning of the word of the LORD by Hosea. And the LORD said to Hosea, Go, take unto thee a wife of whoredoms and children of whoredoms: for the land hath committed great whoredom, departing from the LORD. 3 So he went and took Gomer the daughter of Diblaim; which conceived, and bare him a son. 4 And the LORD said unto him, Call his name Jezreel; for yet a little while, and I will avenge the blood of Jezreel upon the house of Jehu, and will cause to cease the kingdom of the house of Israel. 5 And it shall come to pass at that day, that I will break the bow of Israel, in the valley of Jezreel. 6 And she conceived again, and bare a daughter. And God said unto him, Call her name Loruhamah: for I will no more have mercy upon the house of Israel; but I will utterly take them away. 7 But I will have mercy upon the house of Judah, and will save them by the LORD their God, and will not save them by bow, nor by sword, nor by battle, by horses, nor by horsemen. 8 Now when she had weaned Loruhamah, she conceived, and bare a son. 3:1 Then said the LORD unto me, Go yet, love a woman beloved of her friend, yet an adulteress, according to the love of the LORD toward the children of Israel, who look to other gods, and love flagons of wine. 2 So I bought her to me for fifteen pieces of silver, and for an homer of barley, and an half homer of barley: 3 And I said unto her, Thou shalt abide for me many days; thou shalt not play the harlot, and thou shalt not be for another man: so will I also be for thee. 4 For the children of Israel shall abide many days without a king, and without a prince, and without a sacrifice, and without an image, and without an ephod, and without teraphim:

Herodias ("heroic") Herodias was the wife of Herod Philip and Herod Antipas. She was the mother of Salome. Both of her marriages were incestuous; Philip and Antipas were both her uncles. John The Baptist denounced her marriage to Herod Antipas and lost his life for his criticism. Herodias was a wicked, sinful influence on both her husband and her daughter. Matthew 14:3 For Herod had laid hold on John, and bound him, and put him in prison for Herodias' sake, his brother Philip's wife. 4 For John said unto him, It is not lawful for thee to have her. 5 And when he would have put him to death, he feared the multitude, because they counted him as a prophet. 6 But when Herod's birthday was kept, the daughter of Herodias danced before them, and pleased Herod. 7 Whereupon he promised with an oath to give her whatsoever she would ask. 8 And she, being before instructed of her mother, said, Give me here John Baptist's head in a charger. 9 And the king was sorry: nevertheless for the oath's sake, and them which sat with him at meat, he commanded it to be given her. Luke 3:19 But Herod the tetrarch, being reproved by him for Herodias his brother Philip's wife, and for all the evils which Herod had done,

Jezebel ("chaste") Jezebel was the wife of Ahab, the eighth King of Israel. She was a faithful Baal worshiper and an immoral, idolatrous, heartless, and wicked queen of Israel. She had Naboth stoned and Elijah fled from her wrath. Jezebel was thrown from the palace window and was eaten by dogs, fulfilling the prophecy of Elijah. Jezebel was the first female religious persecutor in recorded history. Kings 21:23 "And of Jezebel also spake the Lord, saying, The dogs shall eat Jezebel by the wall of Jezreel." Kings 9: 32 And he lifted up his face to the window, and said, Who is on my side? who? And there looked out to him two or three eunuchs. 33 And he said, Throw her down. So they threw her down: and some of her blood was sprinkled on the wall, and on the horses: and he trode her under foot. 34 And when he was come in, he did eat and drink, and said, Go, see now this cursed woman, and bury her: for she is a king's daughter. 35 And they went to bury her: but they found no more of her than the skull, and the feet, and the palms of her hands. 36 Wherefore they came again, and told him. And he said, This is the word of the LORD, which he spake by his servant Elijah the Tishbite, saying, In the portion of Jezreel shall dogs eat the flesh of Jezebel: 37 And the carcase of Jezebel shall be as dung upon the face of the field in the portion of Jezreel; so that they shall not say, This is Jezebel.

Jezebel Jezebel was an adulteress and a false prophet in the city of Thyatira. She misled the church. Revelation 2:20 Notwithstanding I have a few things against thee, because thou sufferest that woman Jezebel, which calleth herself a prophetess, to teach and to seduce my servants to commit fornication, and to eat things sacrificed unto idols.

Lot's Wife Lot's wife showed willful disobedience to God's word. Genesis 19:24 Then the LORD rained upon Sodom and upon Gomorrah brimstone and fire from the LORD out of heaven; 25 And he overthrew those cities, and all the plain, and all the inhabitants of the cities, and that which grew upon the ground. 26 But his wife looked back from behind him, and she became a pillar of salt.

Noadiah ("the Lord has arranged an encounter") Noadiah was a prophetess. She tried to prevent Nehemiah from rebuilding the walls of Jerusalem. Nehemiah 6:14 My God, think thou upon Tobiah and Sanballat according to these their works, and on the prophetess Noadiah, and the rest of the prophets, that would have put me in fear

Salome ("clothed, whole, perfect") Salome was the daughter of Herod Philip and Herodias. She, at the instigation of her mother, Herodias, danced before Herod Antipas and requested the head of John The Baptist. Mark 6:21 And when a convenient day was come, that Herod on his birthday made a supper to his lords, high captains, and chief estates of Galilee; 22 And when the daughter of the said Herodias came in, and danced, and pleased Herod and them that sat with him, the king said unto the damsel,

Ask of me whatsoever thou wilt, and I will give it thee. 23 And he sware unto her, Whatsoever thou shalt ask of me, I will give it thee, unto the half of my kingdom. 24 And she went forth, and said unto her mother, What shall I ask? And she said, The head of John the Baptist. 25 And she came in straightway with haste unto the king, and asked, saying, I will that thou give me by and by in a charger the head of John the Baptist. 26 And the king was exceeding sorry; yet for his oath's sake, and for their sakes which sat with him, he would not reject her. 27 And immediately the king sent an executioner, and commanded his head to be brought: and he went and beheaded him in the prison, 28 And brought his head in a charger, and gave it to the damsel: and the damsel gave it to her mother.

Sapphira ("beautiful, sapphire") Sapphira was the wife of Ananias. They were both members of the early Christian congregation at Jerusalem. Their deception and cunning brought about their deaths. Acts 5:1 But a certain man named Ananias, with Sapphira his wife, sold a possession, 2 And kept back part of the price, his wife also being privy to it, and brought a certain part, and laid it at the apostles' feet. 3 But Peter said, Ananias, why hath Satan filled thine heart to lie to the Holy Ghost, and to keep back part of the price of the land? 4 Whiles it remained, was it not thine own? and after it was sold, was it not in thine own power? why hast thou conceived this thing in thine heart? thou hast not lied unto men, but unto God. 5 And Ananias hearing these words fell down, and gave up the ghost: and great fear came on all them that heard these things. 6 And the young men arose, wound him up, and carried him out, and buried him. 7 And it was about the space of three hours after, when his wife, not knowing what was done, came in. 8 And Peter answered unto her, Tell me whether ye sold the land for so much? And she said, Yea, for so much. 9 Then Peter said unto her, How is it that ye have agreed together to tempt the Spirit of the Lord? behold, the feet of them which have buried thy husband are at the door, and shall carry thee out. 10 Then fell she down straightway at his feet, and yielded up the ghost: and the young men came in, and found her dead, and, carrying her forth, buried her by her husband. 11 And great fear came upon all the church, and upon as many as heard these things.

Appendix Q - Devils, and Unclean, Evil, or Familiar Spirits

Leviticus 17:7 And they shall no more offer their sacrifices unto devils, after whom they have gone a whoring. This shall be a statute for ever unto them throughout their generations.

Leviticus 19:31 Regard not them that have familiar spirits, neither seek after wizards, to be defiled by them: I am the LORD your God.

Leviticus 20:6 And the soul that turneth after such as have familiar spirits, and after wizards, to go a whoring after them, I will even set my face against that soul, and will cut him off from among his people.

Leviticus 20:27 A man also or woman that hath a familiar spirit, or that is a wizard, shall surely be put to death: they shall stone them with stones: their blood shall be upon them.

Deuteronomy 32:17 They sacrificed unto devils, not to God; to gods whom they knew not, to new gods that came newly up, whom your fathers feared not.

Deuteronomy 18:11 Or a charmer, or a consulter with familiar spirits, or a wizard, or a necromancer.

Judges 9:23 Then God sent an evil spirit between Abimelech and the men of Shechem; and the men of Shechem dealt treacherously with Abimelech: It is not clear in this context whether the Elohiym sent an "evil spirit" or "in spirit sent evil".

1 Samuel 16:14 But the Spirit of the LORD departed from Saul, and an evil spirit from the LORD troubled him. 15 And Saul's servants said unto him, Behold now, an evil spirit from God troubleth thee. 16 Let our lord now command thy servants, which are before thee, to seek out a man, who is a cunning player on an harp: and it shall come to pass, when the evil spirit from God is upon thee, that he shall play with his hand, and thou shalt be well.

1 Samuel 16:23 And it came to pass, when the evil spirit from God was upon Saul, that David took an harp, and played with his hand: so Saul was refreshed, and was well, and the evil spirit departed from him.

1 Samuel 18:10 And it came to pass on the morrow, that the evil spirit from God came upon Saul, and he prophesied in the midst of the house: and David played with his hand, as at other times: and there was a javelin in Saul's hand.

1 Samuel 19:19 And the evil spirit from the LORD was upon Saul, as he sat in his house with his javelin in his hand: and David played with his hand.

1 Samuel 28:3 Now Samuel was dead, and all Israel had lamented him, and buried him in Ramah, even in his own city. And Saul had put away those that had familiar spirits, and the wizards, out of the land.

1 Samuel 28:7 Then said Saul unto his servants, Seek me a woman that hath a familiar spirit, that I may go to her, and enquire of her. And his servants said to him, Behold, there is a woman that hath a familiar spirit at Endor. 8 And Saul disguised himself, and put on other raiment, and he went, and two men with him, and they came to the woman by night: and he said, I pray thee, divine unto me by the familiar spirit, and bring me him up, whom I shall name unto thee.9 And the woman said unto him, Behold, thou knowest what Saul hath done, how he hath cut off those that have familiar spirits, and the wizards, out of the land: wherefore then layest thou a snare for my life, to cause me to die?

2 Kings 21:6 And he made his son pass through the fire, and observed times, and used enchantments, and dealt with familiar spirits and wizards: he wrought much wickedness in the sight of the LORD, to provoke him to anger.

2 Kings 23:24 Moreover the workers with familiar spirits, and the wizards, and the images, and the idols, and all the abominations that were spied in the land of Judah and in Jerusalem, did Josiah put away, that he might perform the words of the law which were written in the book that Hilkiah the priest found in the house of the LORD.

1 Chronicles 10:13 So Saul died for his transgression which he committed against the LORD, even against the word of the LORD, which he kept not, and also for asking counsel of one that had a familiar spirit, to enquire of it;

2 Chronicles 11:15 And he ordained him priests for the high places, and for the devils, and for the calves which he had made.

2 Chronicles 33:6 And he caused his children to pass through the fire in the valley of the son of Hinnom: also he observed times, and used enchantments, and used witchcraft, and dealt with a familiar spirit, and with wizards: he wrought much evil in the sight of the LORD, to provoke him to anger.

The Appendices

Psalms 106:37 Yea, they sacrificed their sons and their daughters unto devils,

Isaiah 8:19 And when they shall say unto you, Seek unto them that have familiar spirits, and unto wizards that peep, and that mutter: should not a people seek unto their God? for the living to the dead?

Isaiah 19:3 And the spirit of Egypt shall fail in the midst thereof; and I will destroy the counsel thereof: and they shall seek to the idols, and to the charmers, and to them that have familiar spirits, and to the wizards.

Isaiah 29:4 And thou shalt be brought down, and shalt speak out of the ground, and thy speech shall be low out of the dust, and thy voice shall be, as of one that hath a familiar spirit, out of the ground, and thy speech shall whisper out of the dust.

Zechariah 13:2 And it shall come to pass in that day, saith the LORD of hosts, that I will cut off the names of the idols out of the land, and they shall no more be remembered: and also I will cause the prophets and the unclean spirit to pass out of the land.

Matthew 4:24 And his fame went throughout all Syria: and they brought unto him all sick people that were taken with divers diseases and torments, and those which were possessed with devils, and those which were lunatick, and those that had the palsy; and he healed them.

Matthew 7:22 Many will say to me in that day, Lord, Lord, have we not prophesied in thy name? and in thy name have cast out devils? and in thy name done many wonderful works?

Matthew 8:16 When the even was come, they brought unto him many that were possessed with devils: and he cast out the spirits with his word, and healed all that were sick:

Matthew 8:28 And when he was come to the other side into the country of the Gergesenes, there met him two possessed with devils, coming out of the tombs, exceeding fierce, so that no man might pass by that way.

Matthew 8:31 So the devils besought him, saying, If thou cast us out, suffer us to go away into the herd of swine.

Matthew 8:33 And they that kept them fled, and went their ways into the city, and told every thing, and what was befallen to the possessed of the devils.

Matthew 9:32 As they went out, behold, they brought to him a dumb man possessed with a devil 33 And when the devil was cast out, the dumb spake: and the multitudes marvelled, saying, It was never so seen in Israel.

Matthew 9:34 But the Pharisees said, He casteth out devils through the prince of the devils.

Matthew 10:1 And when he had called unto him his twelve disciples, he gave them power against unclean spirits, to cast them out, and to heal all manner of sickness and all manner of disease.

Matthew 10:8 Heal the sick, cleanse the lepers, raise the dead, cast out devils: freely ye have received, freely give.

Matthew 12:22 Then was brought unto him one possessed with a devil, blind, and dumb: and he healed him, insomuch that the blind and dumb both spake and saw.

Matthew 12:24 But when the Pharisees heard it, they said, This fellow doth not cast out devils, but by Beelzebub the prince of the devils.

Matthew 12:27 And if I by Beelzebub cast out devils, by whom do your children cast them out? therefore they shall be your judges.28 But if I cast out devils by the Spirit of God, then the kingdom of God is come unto you

Matthew 12:43 When the unclean spirit is gone out of a man, he walketh through dry places, seeking rest, and findeth none.

Matthew 15:22 And, behold, a woman of Canaan came out of the same coasts, and cried unto him, saying, Have mercy on me, O Lord, thou son of David; my daughter is grievously vexed with a devil.

Matthew 17:18 And Jesus rebuked the devil; and he departed out of him: and the child was cured from that very hour.

Mark 1:23 And there was in their synagogue a man with an unclean spirit; and he cried out,

Mark 1:26 And when the unclean spirit had torn him, and cried with a loud voice, he came out of him. 27 And they were all amazed, insomuch that they questioned among themselves, saying, What thing is this? what new doctrine is this? for with authority commandeth he even the unclean spirits, and they do obey him.

Mark 1:32 And at even, when the sun did set, they brought unto him all that were diseased, and them that were possessed with devils.

Mark 1:34 And he healed many that were sick of divers diseases, and cast out many devils; and suffered not the devils to speak, because they knew him.

Mark 1:39 And he preached in their synagogues throughout all Galilee, and cast out devils.

Mark 3:11 And unclean spirits, when they saw him, fell down before him, and cried, saying, Thou art the Son of God.

Mark 3:15 And to have power to heal sicknesses, and to cast out devils:

Mark 3:22 And the scribes which came down from Jerusalem said, He hath Beelzebub, and by the prince of the devils casteth he out devils.

Mark 3:30 Because they said, He hath an unclean spirit.

Mark 5:2 And when he was come out of the ship, immediately there met him out of the tombs a man with an unclean spirit,

Mark 5:8 For he said unto him, Come out of the man, thou unclean spirit.

Mark 5:12 And all the devils besought him, saying, Send us into the swine, that we may enter into them. 13 And forthwith Jesus gave them leave. And the unclean spirits went out, and entered into the swine: and the herd ran violently down a steep place into the sea, (they were about two thousand;) and were choked in the sea.

Mark 5:15   And they come to Jesus, and see him that was possessed with the devil, and had the legion, sitting, and clothed, and in his right mind: and they were afraid. 16 And they that saw it told them how it befell to him that was possessed with the devil, and also concerning the swine.

Mark 5:18 And when he was come into the ship, he that had been possessed with the devil prayed him that he might be with him.

Mark 6:7 And he called unto him the twelve, and began to send them forth by two and two; and gave them power over unclean spirits;

Mark 6:13 And they cast out many devils, and anointed with oil many that were sick, and healed them.

Mark 7:25 For a certain woman, whose young daughter had an unclean spirit, heard of him, and came and fell at his feet: 26 The woman was a Greek, a Syrophenician by

nation; and she besought him that he would cast forth the devil out of her daughter
Mark 7:29 And he said unto her, For this saying go thy way; the devil is gone out of
thy daughter. 30 And when she was come to her house, she found the devil gone out,
and her daughter laid upon the bed.
Mark 9:38 And John answered him, saying, Master, we saw one casting out devils in
thy name, and he followeth not us: and we forbad him, because he followeth not us.
Mark 16:9 Now when Jesus was risen early the first day of the week, he appeared first
to Mary Magdalene, out of whom he had cast seven devils.
Mark 16:17 And these signs shall follow them that believe; In my name shall they cast
out devils; they shall speak with new tongues;
Luke 4:33 And in the synagogue there was a man, which had a spirit of an unclean
devil, and cried out with a loud voice,
Luke 4:35 And Jesus rebuked him, saying, Hold thy peace, and come out of him. And
when the devil had thrown him in the midst, he came out of him, and hurt him not. 36
And they were all amazed, and spake among themselves, saying, What a word is this!
for with authority and power he commandeth the unclean spirits, and they come out.
Luke 4:41 And devils also came out of many, crying out, and saying, Thou art Christ
the Son of God. And he rebuking them suffered them not to speak: for they knew that
he was Christ.
Luke 6:18 And they that were vexed with unclean spirits: and they were healed.
Luke 7:21 And in that same hour he cured many of their infirmities and plagues, and
of evil spirits; and unto many that were blind he gave sight.
Luke 8:2 And certain women, which had been healed of evil spirits and infirmities,
Mary called Magdalene, out of whom went seven devils,
Luke 8:27 And when he went forth to land, there met him out of the city a certain man,
which had devils long time, and ware no clothes, neither abode in any house, but in the
tombs.
Luke 8:29 (For he had commanded the unclean spirit to come out of the man. For
oftentimes it had caught him: and he was kept bound with chains and in fetters; and he
brake the bands, and was driven of the devil into the wilderness.) 30 And Jesus asked
him, saying, What is thy name? And he said, Legion: because many devils were
entered into him.
Luke 8:33 Then went the devils out of the man, and entered into the swine: and the
herd ran violently down a steep place into the lake, and were choked.
Luke 8:35 Then they went out to see what was done; and came to Jesus, and found the
man, out of whom the devils were departed, sitting at the feet of Jesus, clothed, and in
his right mind: and they were afraid. 36 They also which saw it told them by what
means he that was possessed of the devils was healed.
Luke 8:38 Now the man out of whom the devils were departed besought him that he
might be with him: but Jesus sent him away, saying,
Luke 9:1 Then he called his twelve disciples together, and gave them power and
authority over all devils, and to cure diseases.
Luke 9:42 And as he was yet a coming, the devil threw him down, and tare him. And
Jesus rebuked the unclean spirit, and healed the child, and delivered him again to his
father
Luke 9:49 And John answered and said, Master, we saw one casting out devils in thy

name; and we forbad him, because he followeth not with us.

Luke 10:17 And the seventy returned again with joy, saying, Lord, even the devils are subject unto us through thy name.

Luke 11:14 And he was casting out a devil, and it was dumb. And it came to pass, when the devil was gone out, the dumb spake; and the people wondered. 15 But some of them said, He casteth out devils through Beelzebub the chief of the devils.

Luke 11:18 If Satan also be divided against himself, how shall his kingdom stand? because ye say that I cast out devils through Beelzebub. 19 And if I by Beelzebub cast out devils, by whom do your sons cast them out? therefore shall they be your judges. 20 But if I with the finger of God cast out devils, no doubt the kingdom of God is come upon you.

Luke 11:24 When the unclean spirit is gone out of a man, he walketh through dry places, seeking rest; and finding none, he saith, I will return unto my house whence I came out.

Luke 13:32 And he said unto them, Go ye, and tell that fox, Behold, I cast out devils, and I do cures to day and to morrow, and the third day I shall be perfected.

John 6:70 Jesus answered them, Have not I chosen you twelve, and one of you is a devil?

John 7:20 The people answered and said, Thou hast a devil: who goeth about to kill thee?

John 8:44 Ye are of your father the devil, and the lusts of your father ye will do. He was a murderer from the beginning, and abode not in the truth, because there is no truth in him. When he speaketh a lie, he speaketh of his own: for he is a liar, and the father of it.

John 8:48 Then answered the Jews, and said unto him, Say we not well that thou art a Samaritan, and hast a devil? 49 Jesus answered, I have not a devil; but I honour my Father, and ye do dishonour me.

John 8:52 Then said the Jews unto him, Now we know that thou hast a devil. Abraham is dead, and the prophets; and thou sayest, If a man keep my saying, he shall never taste of death.

John 10:20 And many of them said, He hath a devil, and is mad; why hear ye him? 21 Others said, These are not the words of him that hath a devil. Can a devil open the eyes of the blind?

Acts 5:16 There came also a multitude out of the cities round about unto Jerusalem, bringing sick folks, and them which were vexed with unclean spirits: and they were healed every one.

Acts 8:7 For unclean spirits, crying with loud voice, came out of many that were possessed with them: and many taken with palsies, and that were lame, were healed.

Acts 10:38 How God anointed Jesus of Nazareth with the Holy Ghost and with power: who went about doing good, and healing all that were oppressed of the devil; for God was with him.

Acts 16:13 And I saw three unclean spirits like frogs come out of the mouth of the dragon, and out of the mouth of the beast, and out of the mouth of the false prophet.

Acts 19:9 And the evil spirit from the LORD was upon Saul, as he sat in his house with his javelin in his hand: and David played with his hand.

Acts 19:12 So that from his body were brought unto the sick handkerchiefs or aprons, and the diseases departed from them, and the evil spirits went out of them. 13 Then certain of the vagabond Jews, exorcists, took upon them to call over them which had evil spirits the name of the LORD Jesus, saying, We adjure you by Jesus whom Paul preacheth.

Acts 19:15 And the evil spirit answered and said, Jesus I know, and Paul I know; but who are ye? 16 And the man in whom the evil spirit was leaped on them, and overcame them, and prevailed against them, so that they fled out of that house naked and wounded.

2 Corinthians 10:20 But I say, that the things which the Gentiles sacrifice, they sacrifice to devils, and not to God: and I would not that ye should have fellowship with devils. 21 Ye cannot drink the cup of the Lord, and the cup of devils: ye cannot be partakers of the Lord's table, and of the table of devils.

1 Timothy 4:1 Now the Spirit speaketh expressly, that in the latter times some shall depart from the faith, giving heed to seducing spirits, and doctrines of devils;

James 2:19 Thou believest that there is one God; thou doest well: the devils also believe, and tremble.

Revelation 9:20 And the rest of the men which were not killed by these plagues yet repented not of the works of their hands, that they should not worship devils, and idols of gold, and silver, and brass, and stone, and of wood: which neither can see, nor hear, nor walk:

Revelation 16:14 For they are the spirits of devils, working miracles, which go forth unto the kings of the earth and of the whole world, to gather them to the battle of that great day of God Almighty.

Revelation 18:2 And he cried mightily with a strong voice, saying, Babylon the great is fallen, is fallen, and is become the habitation of devils, and the hold of every foul spirit, and a cage of every unclean and hateful bird.

Appendix R - The Lost Books of the Bible

A
Abdias
Abercius, Inscription of
Abgarus, King of Edessa and the
Epistle of Jesus Christ
Abraham, Book of
Abraham, Testament of
Acts of A King
Adam, The Book of
Adam, The Apocalypse of, (Revelation of)
Adam and Eve, The Books of, The Latin Translation
Adam and Eve, Life of, The Slavonic Translation
Adam and Eve, Life of, the Greek Translation
Adam and Eve, The First Book of
Adam and Eve, The Second Book of
Adam and Eve, An Electronic Edition
Addeus the Apostle, The Teachings of
Against the Heresies
Ages of The World, The
Aggeus
Ahikar, Grand Vizier of Assyria, The Story of
Allogenes
Andrew, Acts and Martyrdom of the Holy Apostle
Andrew, Gospel of
Andrew and Matthew, The Acts of
Andrew and Matthias, Acts of
Andrew, Other Books
Anointing, On the

The Doctrines of Men

Irenaeus of Lyons
Isaiah, Ascension of
Isaiah, The Martyrdom of
Isidore
Israel And The Holy Land
J
Jacob, Ladder of
Jacob, Prayer of
Jacob, The Vision of
James, Secret Book of
Jannes and Jambres
Jasher
James, The First Apocalypse of
James, The Second Apocalypse of
James, The Apocryphon of
James, Book of, The Gospel of, Protevangelion
James, The Gospel of
Jesus Christ, The Sophia of
Jesus, Epistle to Peter and Paul Available
Jesus, The New Sayings of
Jeremiah, Letter of
Jeu, Books of
Job, Testament of
Job, Targum of
Jonathan, Prayer for King
John, The Acts of
John, The Acts of, Excerpt from the Mystery of Cross
John, The Apocryphon of
John, The Book of, Concerning the Death of Mary
John the Evangelist
John the Theologian, The Revelation of
Joseph of Arimathaea and Aseneth
Joseph of Arimathaea, The Narrative of
Joseph the Carpenter, The History of
Jubilees, Book of
Judas Iscariot, Gospel of
Jude, Gospel of
Julius Cassianus
Justin Martyr
Justin Martyr, First Apology

Justin Martyr, Second Apology
Justin Martyr, Dialogue with Trypho
Justin Martyr, Fragments from the Lost Writings of Justin
Justin Martyr, Hortatory Address to the Greeks
Justin Martyr, On the Sole Government of God
Justin Martyr, On the Resurrection
Justin Martyr, Discourse to the Greeks
K
Kerygmata Petrou
Kings, The Third Book of
Kings, The Fourth Book of
Knowledge, The Interpretation of
L
Laodiceans, The Epistle to
Last Days: A Commentary on Selected Verses
Letter of the Law : Ordinances, The
Lentitus, Acts of the Apostle
Leontius, Acts of the Apostle
Leucius, Acts of the Apostle
Leuthon, Acts of the Apostle
Leviticus
Litany Of The Angels
Liturgical Calendar, A
Liturgy, A
Lord, Gospel of the
Lucian of Samosata
Lucian of Samosata, Alexander the False Prophet
Lucian of Samosata, The Passing of Peregrinus
Lucianus, The False Gospels
M
Maccabees, Third Book of
Maccabees, Fourth Book of
Magnesians
Manasseh, The Prayer of
Maniclees, Acts of the Apostles used by
Marcion, Gospel of the Lord *and HERE*
Mara Bar Serapion
Marcionite, Anti-Prologues

The Appendices

The Doctrines of Men

Peter and Paul, Preachings of
Peter to Philip, Letter of
Peter, The Apocalypse of (Fragment)
Peter, The Last Gospel
Peter, The Lost Gospel According to

Peter, Coptic Apocalypse of
Peter, Preaching of
Peter, The Revelation of
Peter and the Twelve Apostles, The
Acts of
Philadelphians
Philip, The Acts of
Phillip, Additions to the Acts of
Philip, T he Gospel of
Philip, Journeyings of the Apostle
Philippians 2
Philostratus
Phylactery (Tefillin) Scroll
Pilate, Acts of
Pilate, Letters of
Herod to Pilate
Pilate to Herod
Pilate to Tiberius 1
Pilate to Tiberius 2
Pilate to Augustus Caesar
Pilate, The Trail and Condemnation of
The Death of Pilate
Pontius Pilate, The Giving Up of
Philadelphians
Pistis Sophia
Pistis Sophia, Excerpts from
Pistis Sophia, First Book
Pistis Sophia, Second Book
Plea for Deliverance
Plea For Grace
Pliny the Younger
Polycrates of Ephesus
Polycarp, Martyrdom of
Polycarp to the Philippians
Power, The Concept of Our Great
Prayer for Intercession
Prayer of Praise
Priestly Service
Prophets, The Lives of the
Protevangelion 2nd Century, The

Proverbs, A Collection of
Psalms, Commentary on
Psalms:Dead Sea Scroll
Ptolemy
Ptolemy, Commentary on The Gospel
Of John Prologue
Ptolemy's Letter to Flora
Q
Q, Gospel referred to by the letter
R
Rechabites, The History of the
Redemption and Resurrection
Resurrection, Treatise on the
Reworked Pentateuch
Rheginos, The Epistle to
Rhodon
Ritual Purity Laws
S
Saviour, The Avenging of the
Savior, Dialogue of the
Savior, Gospel of the
Scillitan Martyrs, Passion of the
Scythianus, Gospel of
Secret of The Way Things Are, The
Secrets, The Book of
Sedrach, Apocalypse of
Seleucus, The Acts of the Apostles
Serapion of Antioch
Seth, Revelation of Adam`s Origin
Seth, The Second Treatise of the
Great
Seth, The Three Steles of
Sextus, The Sentences of
Shem, The Paraphrase of
Shemaiah the Prophet
Shepherd of Hermas
Signs Gospel
Silvanus, The Teachings of
Simon Cephas, The Teaching of
Smyrnaeans
Solomon, Odes of
Solomon, Psalms of
Solomon, Testament of
Solomon, The Wisdom of
Songs of the Sabbath Sacrifice
Sophia of Jesus Christ

The Doctrines of Men

Bibliography

The Achaemenids and Israel, Zarathustra, Philo, Lawrence Mills, Leipzig 1903

Ante Pacem: Archaeological Evidence of Church Life Before Constantine, Graydon F. Snyder, Mercer University Press 1985

The Apocryphal Literature: A Brief Introduction, Charles Cutler Torrey, Yale University Press, 1975

The Apostolic Fathers: An Introduction, Robert M. Grant, Thomas Nelson & Sons, 1964

Babylon Mystery Religion - Ancient and Modern, Woodrow

The Bible in Art: Miniatures, Paintings, Drawings and Sculptures Inspired by the Old Testament, Heidi Heimann, Paidon Press, 1956

Bible English, Lewis Davies, London: George Bell & Sons 1875

The Bible Through Dutch Eyes: From Genesis Through the Apocrypha, Alfred Bader, Milwaukee Art Center, 1976

Bible Words That Have Changed in Meaning, Luther Weigle, Thomas Nelson and Sons 1955

Biblical Revelation, Clark Pinnock, Baker Book House, 1973

Cambridge Ancient History, Cambridge University Press 1956

The Catholic Catechism, John A. Hardon S.J., Doubleday

Conflict in Rome: Social Order and Hierarchy in Early Christianity, J.S. Jeffers, Fortress 1991

Constantine the Great, Holsapple, Lloyd. Sheed and Ward

The Conversion of Constantine, Eadie, John, Holt, Rinehart and Winston

Dictionary of Jesus and the Gospels, Green, Joel, Intervarsity Press. 1992

Discovering the Gospels, Ralph, Margeret Nutting. Paulist Press 1990

The Encyclopedia of Ancient Civilizations, Cotterell, Arthur, Rainbird Publishing Group Limited 1980

Encyclopedia of Early Christianity, Ferguson, Everett, Garland Publishing 1997

Encyclopaedia Judaica Jerusalem, Keter Publishing House, 1971

Encyclopedia of Religion, Eliade, Mircea, McMillan Publishing Company.

Encyclopedia of the Roman Empire, Bunson, Matthew, Facts on File 1994

A General Introduction to the Bible, Norman Geisler and William Nix, Moody Press 1986.

The Genesis of Israel and Egypt, Sweeney, E.J.

Gnosticism and Early Christianity, Robert M. Grant, 1959

The Histories, Herodotus, Penguin Books

History of Christianity, Introduction to the, Dowley, Tim, First Fortress Press.

Idols of Perversity: Fantasies of Feminine Evil in Fin-de-Siecle Culture, Bram Dijkstra Oxford University Press, 1986

An Introduction to the Apocrypha, Bruce M. Metzger, Oxford University Press, 1957

An Illustrated Encyclopedia of Traditional Symbols, J.C. Cooper.

Jesus and Christian Origins Outside the New Testament, F. F. Bruce, Eerdmans, 1974

Jewish Literature Between the Bible and the Mishnah: A Historical and Literary Introduction, George W.E. Nickelsburg, Fortress Press, 1981

The Doctrines of Men

Josephus, Complete Works, Kregel, 1960

Josephus, The Works of, Translated by W Whiston. Hendrickson

Judaism Outside the Hebrew Canon: An Introduction to the Documents, Leonhard Rost, Abingdon Press, 1976

The King James Bible Word Book: Ronald Bridges and Luther Weigle, Thomas Nelson 1994

The Language of the King James Bible: A Glossary Explaining its Words and Expressions, Melvin E. Elliott, Doubleday 1967

The Last Days of Greco-Roman Paganism, Johannes Geffcken

Legends of the Jews, Ginsberg A. Philadelphia.

The Life of the Blessed Emperor Constantine, Eusebius Pamphilius.

The Lost Books of the Bible, Bell Publishing Co. 1979

The Lost Books of the Bible and the Forgotten Books of Eden, L.B. Press

Martyrdom and Persecution in the Early Church, W.H.C. Frend, Oxford Blackwell 1965

The Martyrs: A Study in Social Control, D.W. Riddle, University of Chicago Press 1931

The New Testament Apocrypha, Schneemelcher

The Other Bible, Barnstone

The Oxford Dictionary of the Christian Church Cross, Oxford University Press 1974

Pagans and Christians, Fox, Robin Lane, . Alfred A. Knopf Inc.

Peake's Commentary on the Bible, Matthew Black and H.H. Rowley, Revised edition, Nelson 1982

The Sword and the Cross, Robert M. Grant, Macmillan 1955